www.wadsworth.com

wadsworth.com is the World Wide Web site for Wadsworth and is your direct source to dozens of online resources.

At *wadsworth.com* you can find out about supplements, demonstration software, and student resources. You can also send email to many of our authors and preview new publications and exciting new technologies.

wadsworth.com
Changing the way the world learns®

Stone and thatch house, 1977

Katun

A Twenty-Year Journey with the Maya

Cindy L. Hull
Grand Valley State University

 Case Studies in Cultural Anthropology: George Spindler, Series Editor

THOMSON
™
WADSWORTH

Australia • Canada • Mexico • Singapore • Spain
United Kingdom • United States

THOMSON

WADSWORTH

Anthropology Editor: *Lin Marshall*

Assistant Editor: *Analie Barnett*

Editorial Assistant: *Amanda Santana*

Marketing Manager: *Diane Wenckebach*

Project Manager, Editorial Production: *Emily Smith*

Print/Media Buyer: *Rebecca Cross*

Permissions Editor: *Sarah Harkrader*

Production Service: *Sara Dovre Wudali, Buuji, Inc.*

Copy Editor: *Cheryl Hauser*

Illustrator: *Valerie Hover/Eunah Chang, Buuji, Inc.*

Cover Designer: *Rob Hugel*

Cover Image: *Cindy L. Hull*

Compositor: *Buuji, Inc.*

Text and Cover Printer: *Webcom*

The logo for the Cultural Anthropology series is based on an ancient symbol representing the family: man, woman, and children.

For more information about our products, contact us at:
Thomson Learning Academic Resource Center
1-800-423-0563

For permission to use material from this text, contact us by:
Phone: 1-800-730-2214   **Fax:** 1-800-730-2215
Web: http://www.thomsonrights.com

Library of Congress Control Number: 2002115047

ISBN 0-534-61290-3

Wadsworth/Thomson Learning
10 Davis Drive
Belmont, CA 94002-3098
USA

Asia
Thomson Learning
5 Shenton Way #01-01
UIC Building
Singapore 068808

Australia/New Zealand
Thomson Learning
102 Dodds Street
Southbank, Victoria 3006
Australia

Canada
Nelson
1120 Birchmount Road
Toronto, Ontario M1K 5G4
Canada

Europe/Middle East/Africa
Thomson Learning
High Holborn House
50/51 Bedford Row
London WC1R 4LR
United Kingdom

Latin America
Thomson Learning
Seneca, 53
Colonia Polanco
11560 Mexico D.F.
Mexico

Spain/Portugal
Paraninfo
Calle/Magallanes, 25
28015 Madrid, Spain

This book is dedicated to the people of Yaxbe who have shared their lives with me and my family for many years, have given generously of their time, and who have shaped my life in ways that words cannot express.

A mis amigos en Yaxbe, muchísimas gracias por su amistad.
Que Díos les bendiga.

— Politics & Village Values & Ideals
— Religion
    — Traditional / Folk Religion
    — Catholicism
    — Seventh-Day Adventists / Pentacostals

Contents

Figures and Illustrations   ix

Foreword   xi

Preface   xiv

PART I   THE MAYA OF NORTHWEST YUCATÁN: HISTORICAL AND ECONOMIC CONTEXT

Chapter 1   A *Katun* with the Yucatec Maya   1

The Mayan Landscape   1
Entering the Village, 1976   2
Returning to Yaxbe, 1998   5
The Objective and Subjective in Anthropology   7
Method: Longitudinal Research   8
Ethnographic Essay: Doña Isabel: A Woman of Substance   10

Chapter 2   The Historical Context   13

Anthropology, History, and Economic Theory   13
The Maya World   14
Pre-Conquest Maya   15
Conquest to Independence   16
Henequen and the Post-Independence Era   16
The Decline and Fall of the Henequen Era   19
Conclusion   21

Chapter 3   The Economy of Yaxbe, 1976–1989   22

World Systems Theory and Agency in Yucatán   22
The Economic Structure   23
Ethnographic Essay: The CIA and Other Conspiracies, 1976   34
Conclusion   36

PART II   YAXBE: THE SOCIAL CONTEXT

Chapter 4   Village Life: Resilience and Change, 1976–1998   37

The Village   37
The People   41
Culture and the Individual: The Life Cycle   45
Village Cohesion   52
Ethnographic Essay: The Funeral   54

Ethnographic Essay: The Fire   56
Education   56
Health and Medicine   59
Ethnographic Essay: On Becoming a *Compadre*   62
Conclusion   66

Chapter 5   The Political Structure of Yaxbe, 1976–1998   67
National and Local Politics   67
Crime and Punishment in Yaxbe   80
Ethnographic Essay: Of Cameras and Turkey Thieves   82
Conclusion   85

Chapter 6   Mayan and Catholic Roots in Yaxbe   87
Mayan and Catholic Syncretism   87
The Place of Ancient Spirits in a Modern World   91
Ethnographic Essay: *Huay Pop*   92
A Tale of Two Rituals   95
Ethnographic Essay: The Last *H-men*, 1998   96
Conclusion   106

**Chapter 7   A Religion for Business and One for Sunday:
                The Seventh Day Adventists   108**
Protestantism in Yaxbe   109
The Impact of Protestantism on the Lives of Men and Women in Yaxbe   115
Ethnographic Essay: Becoming a Seventh Day Adventist   116
The Pentecostals   118
The Impact of Protestantism on Village Life   119
Field Journal: Dorcas   120
Conclusion   124

**PART III   HENEQUEN'S LAST GASP:
                THE DEATH OF THE KING OF HENEQUEN**

Chapter 8   In the Ashes of the Henequen *Ejido*   125
Peasants and the World System Revisited   125
Journal Entry: The King Is Dead, Long Live the King   126
Economic Diversification in the Village   129
Commuting as Economic Strategy   136
Migration as Economic Strategy   139
The New Social Class System, 1977–1998   142
Conclusion: The New Yucatecan Family   146

Chapter 9   Mayan Women: Beyond the Stereotypes   147
The Anthropology of Gender Roles and Statuses   147
From the Woodwork to the Double Day   151
Case Studies   152
Women and Economic Production   157

Ethnographic Essay: *Sí, Podemos Mandar* (Yes, We Can Lead)   162
Women in Yaxbe   164
Conclusion   166

Chapter 10   From Tortillas to Bread   168
From Tortillas to Bread:
    The Tortilla as Metaphor for Economic and Social Change   168

Epilogue   Return to Yaxbe, 2001   174

Appendix   178

Glossary   180

References   183

Credits   186

Index   187

Figures and Illustrations

FIGURES

Stone and thatch house, 1977   Frontispiece

1.1   Yucatán Peninsula, Mexico   3
1.2   LaVail with the Yaxbe soccer team, 1977   6
1.3   Reymundo with wife and children, 1992   8
1.4   Doña Isabel: A woman of substance   11
2.1   Freshly cut henequen leaves and fibers hanging to dry, Cordemex   18
2.2   A bicycle repair shop and store in the government-subsidized market   20
3.1   The henequen political structure as it pertained to *ejidatarios* and *parcelarios*, 1976   26
3.2   Man carrying corn from his *milpa* to Yaxbe, using a tumpline, 1977   29
3.3   Woman carrying corn to Yaxbe for grinding, 1977   30
3.4   Don Justo in his store, 1977   31
3.5   Doña Leticia keeping track of credit in her bakery, 1977   32
4.1   Map of Yaxbe illustrating major landmarks and population growth, 1976–2001   39
4.2   This large extended family includes four brothers, their wives and children, 1992   44
4.3   Carlos, the son of Pedro and Dora, at Dzibichaltún, 1998   47
4.4   Marta, with two of her children, 1992   50
4.5   Cemetery, Yaxbe   53
4.6   Don Juan, 1977   63
5.1   *Ayuntamiento,* 1995   71
5.2   Don Armando, police chief, 1976–1977   81
6.1   LaVail with his entourage, 1977   92
6.2   The *h-men,* 1998   97
6.3   Man preparing ritual food at the *comistraje,* 1977   99
6.4   A young Yaxbeña represents the village for the *jarana, fiesta,* 1998   104
7.1   Don Max, 1977   114
7.2   Don Pablo, 1977   117
7.3   Dora, 1989   121
7.4   The Dorcas group, 1998   123
8.1   Don Justo, 1998   130
8.2   Pedro at his ranch, 1998   135
8.3   Author with Carla and her children, 1998   142
8.4   A modern house in Yaxbe   144
9.1   Group I of the *horchata* cooperative in front of the *camioneta,* 1998   155
9.2   Group II of the *horchata* cooperative in front of the new factory, 1998   155
9.3   Doña Paula, president of the *horchata* cooperative, 1998   156
9.4   Doña Ana and María work at the *tortillería* cooperative in 1995   157

9.5   The original UAIM group at their chicken ranch, 1995   163
10.1   Doña Fidelia making tortillas, 1977   170
E.1   Five generations in a matrifocal family, 2002   176

ILLUSTRATIONS

1.   Mayan temple   xiv
2.   Henequen plant   1
3.   *Hacienda*   13
4.   Donkey and cart   22
5.   Thatch house with electrical wires   37
6.   Political poster   67
7.   Virgin of Guadalupe   87
8.   Seventh Day Adventist church and school: *Iglesia/Escuela*   108
9.   Bus and people   125
10.   *Ix Chel*   147
11.   Tortilla making and bread truck   168
12.   Street scene in Yaxbe   174

Foreword

ABOUT THE SERIES

These case studies in cultural anthropology are designed for students in beginning and intermediate courses in the social sciences, to bring them insights into the richness and complexity of human life as it is lived in different ways, in different places. The authors are men and women who have lived in the societies they write about and who are professionally trained as observers and interpreters of human behavior. Also, the authors are teachers; in their writing, the needs of the student reader remain foremost. It is our belief that when an understanding of ways of life very different from one's own is gained, abstractions and generalizations about the human condition become meaningful.

The scope and character of the series has changed constantly since we published the first case studies in 1960, in keeping with our intention to represent anthropology as it is. We are concerned with the ways in which human groups and communities are coping with the massive changes wrought in their physical and sociopolitical environments in recent decades. We are also concerned with the ways in which established cultures have solved life's problems. And we want to include representation of the various modes of communication and emphasis that are being formed and reformed as anthropology itself changes.

We think of this series as an instructional series, intended for use in the classroom. We, the editors, have always used case studies in our teaching, whether for beginning students or advanced graduate students. We start with case studies, whether from our own series or from elsewhere, and weave our way into theory, and then turn again to cases. For us, they are the grounding of our discipline.

ABOUT THE AUTHOR

Cindy Vandenbergh Hull was born in Grand Rapids, Michigan, in 1950. She studied sociology and anthropology at Grand Valley State College earning her B.A. in sociology in 1972. She earned her M.A. (1975) and Ph.D. (1980) degrees in anthropology from Wayne State University. After a study abroad experience in Yucatán, she and her husband, LaVail returned there to conduct dissertation research during 1976 and 1977. Since that time, she has returned to the same village six times, often with LaVail and their three children.

Hull's initial research centered on the impact of the collapse of the mono-crop henequen system on families in one village. Longitudinal research has allowed her to follow the same families for over 20 years, using the method of participant-observation to both analyze their adaptation to intense economic transformation and to share in their daily lives and rituals.

The Hulls have also lived and worked on the Micronesian Island of Pohnpei. Today, Professor Hull is an associate professor at Grand Valley State University. She and her family live in their own small village of Chippewa Lake, Michigan.

ABOUT THIS CASE STUDY

Cindy Hull, the author, has studied the village of Yaxbe, in northwest Yucatán, over a 20-year period. She started out in 1976 studying the effects of the collapse of the henequen (sisal) industry on village life. In 2002, she continues to study change in Yaxbe. Currently, she examines the adaptation of Mayan women and their growing power to the economic and social changes consequent to world events and the collapse of the henequen mono-crop. In between, she studied animal husbandry; kinship and residence as they adapted to change; daily life as it was affected by economic and social change; village cohesion; education, health, and medicine; politics and business; crime and punishment; religion and the growth of Protestantism; the survival of traditional rituals; the fate of the *h-men* (a Mayan priest); economic diversity, including occupations, henequen, women and income production, and jobs and commuting; migration as economic strategy; the social class system; and numerous subcategories of these major headings for significant social, economic, political, and cultural processes. This case study could only have been written by someone who had studied one place in its area for a sustained period of time, and studied it from the point of view of a resident as well as an anthropologist.

This study provides the reader with insight into the most significant processes of adaptation taking place in our time. Everywhere on this earth in greater or lesser degree the same processes have been set in motion by globalization, shifts in technology, economic and political realignments, population growth, and revolutions in communication. The ways of making a living have undergone radical change, and the distribution of wealth as well.

I am reminded of the sweeping changes that have taken place in a small rural area of northeast central Wisconsin with which I have been familiar since 1948, when Louise Spindler and I started doing field work with the Menominee Indians. This was and is a dairying area, with small farms with their red outbuildings and silos dominating the landscape. A farmer and his wife and family, usually about five children, including some sons who would take over, occupied and operated the farm, usually consisting of about 200 acres of pasture, woodland, and scrub, and 30 to 75 head of milking cows. The only difference between 1948 and 2002 is that the barns and silos are still there but four out of five are empty, out of business. Small farms began to fail shortly after World War II, but their failure did not become epidemic until the mid-1980s. Most of the acreage went to a few big farmers, who milked at least 250–300 head and drew from a thousand to fifteen hundred acres.

Individual farmers try various strategies to maintain their farms—raising buffalo, llama, ostriches, deer, or emu for meat and soy beans or flax for food. It is not that people are drinking less milk. It is a variety of factors—increasing machinery costs, costs for automation to take the place of farm labor that is no longer available, increased costs for distribution and collection, the relatively low price for milk, general decline in the interests of young people in farming—all of which make only the truly big operator capable of making any money.

The social, cultural, and political effects in the area are much like those we have seen in Yaxbe. In the 1950s a network of relations joined everyone in the area. Social events unified everyone except a few hermits by choice. There was the Catholic church, and the Lutheran church, and one was a member of one or the other, and they had their separate but socially overlapping membership. Everyone knew everyone, and they all knew what their lives would be like when they were very young, even where they would be married, and buried. That is pretty much gone today or at least badly eroded. The first subdivision, an extension of the town in the area, went in just three years ago, The farms that are still intact will be divided into small acreages for exurbanites. Out-migration is claiming the young people. This is the pattern for rural areas everywhere in America. There is no direct connection between rural Wisconsin and Yaxbe, but they are both responding to the same forces.

This case study is therefore not just a study of Yaxbe and its environs. It is a study that strikes to the heart of what is happening worldwide.

George Spindler
Series Editor

Preface

Not only did the Indians have a count for the year and months, as has been before set out, but they also had a certain method of counting time and their matters by ages, which they counted by 20-year periods, counting thirteen 20s, with one of the 20 signs in their months, which they call *Ahau,* not in order, but going backwards. . . . In their language they call these periods *katuns.* . . . thus it was easy for the old man of whom I spoke in the first chapter to recall events which he said had taken place 300 years before. Had I not known of this calculation I should not have believed it possible to recall after such a period.

(Friar Landa, 1978 [1566]: 81)

INTRODUCTION TO THE YUCATÁN, MEXICO

I was introduced to Yucatán and its people in 1971, when, as undergraduate students, my future husband, LaVail, and I studied for three months at the Colégio Peninsular in Mérida as part of a study abroad program sponsored by Grand Valley State College in Michigan and Central College in Iowa. At first, my attention was focused on Mérida, the capital of Yucatán, with its European charm and colorful markets. My first glimpses of the ruins at Dzibichaltún, Chichén Itzá, Mayapán, and Tulúm changed my life and my academic goals forever. As I surveyed the landscape of Chichén Itzá from atop El Castillo, and stood mesmerized as the waves beat upon the cliff that was the pedestal of the walled city of Tulúm, my future career began to take shape before my eyes. I realized that I had to be an anthropologist and that my focus was destined to be the descendants of the people who constructed these monuments.

As we crisscrossed the peninsula in second-class buses, I gazed out the window, hypnotized by endless stretches of *henequen* (called sisal elsewhere), the cactus-like plant growing, it appeared, from limestone crevices in a cracked, parched earth. Along the dusty highway, men, dressed in white trousers and open front shirts, rested on 50-pound sacks of corn. Their gnarled feet are adorned by home-woven sandals cut from automobile tires and tied to their feet and ankles by straps made of henequen fibers. Their heads are protected from the sun by well-worn woven panama hats. Women, wearing white smock-like *huipiles,* lean against limestone fences, their long shawls are pulled up over their heads, their plastic or woven henequen bags resting at their feet. They seem to be in the middle of nowhere, awaiting buses that periodically appeared out of the dust and disappeared back into it en route to the next bus stop, and ultimately to Mérida, the hub.

I wondered how these individuals and families struggled to make a living within the confines of this demanding environment. I wondered how they managed to persevere in the intersection of two economic systems, one ancient and based on subsistence corn production and one, imposed from the outside and based on mono-crop production and wage labor. Despite my naiveté, I already understood that the Maya, like all people, exist within a social system that simultaneously encompasses their everyday lives and connects them with the wider social order, far beyond their village. As such, Yucatán must be appreciated, not only as the home of the Maya, but as a state within a developing nation, characterized by the uncertainties of a mono-crop economy and political neglect by the central government located 2,600 miles away, beyond formidable geographic and cultural barriers. How did these factors mold the Yucatecan culture? How is their existence different from that of other Maya cultures elsewhere? These impressions and questions induced me to return to Yucatán five years after my initial visit, as a Ph.D. candidate in anthropology.

From September of 1976 to August of 1977, LaVail and I lived in Yucatán. My purpose was to investigate the phenomenon of migration as a response to economic insecurity due to the decline in the henequen market. On our arrival in Mérida, our first concern was finding a village that would meet several criteria. First, the village must be dependent mainly on henequen, the dominant export crop of Yucatán. Second, the village must be large enough to have economic and social heterogeneity; that is, a rural class or status system, religious and political diversity, and traditional and modern distinctions of dress, language, and custom. Third, and conversely, it must be small enough to allow for a comprehensive investigation of migration. Fourth and foremost, the villagers and political leaders must be willing to accept into their fold two outsiders. After several weeks of research and travel around the Yucatecan countryside, we found our niche, thanks to Dr. Alfredo Barrera Vásquez of INAH (National Institute of Anthropology and History). Dr. Barrera Vásquez and Dr. Edward Kurjack, an archaeologist, had received assistance from the villagers and president of Yaxbe while Dr. Kurjack was conducting preliminary excavations at a nearby site. Dr. Barrera Vásquez felt that Yaxbe fit the criteria that I had formulated. He accompanied LaVail and me to the village, and introduced us to the president. Several days later we were living in the scorpion-infested abandoned medical clinic.

Yaxbe did, in fact, meet my specifications. The village, located approximately 20 miles east of Mérida, supported a population of nearly 1,800. These residents represented a wide range of economic and social circumstances including individuals who wore both Mayan and Spanish dress, spoke both the Mayan and Spanish anguages and, although predominantly Catholic, practiced three distinct religions. The villagers represented various occupational groups ranging from the traditional agriculturist, now a mono-crop henequen producer, to self-employed contractors and artisans, to storekeepers and factory workers.

THE PURPOSE OF THIS STUDY

It has been more than 20 years since that first research period in Yaxbe. Since 1977, I have returned six times to update my data and visit the people who have now become *compadres* (co-parents) and friends. My research has spanned a remarkable period of transition and adaptation. In 1976, 80 percent of village men were employed in the henequen industry, compared to less than 20 percent today. In my initial research, I was seeking to understand how families in the henequen zone would adapt to the decline in the mono-crop market. Over the years, families have been struggling to find new sources of income as the henequen market slowed and then collapsed altogether. I could not have anticipated the changes that occurred in 1992 when President Salinas abolished the communal land system altogether, totally disrupting the economic and social basis for village life.

While my original research concentrated on the incidence of migration and return migration, the scope of this ethnography is broader, encompassing many aspects of life in the henequen zone and the dramatic transformations in the land tenure system that are now threatening to undermine the fabric of village life. My purpose in writing this ethnography is grounded in these events. Over the years, I have had the opportunity to observe an economic system, entrenched in Mexican history, as it floundered and died. I have listened as people discuss among themselves what will happen to their village when their lands are privatized. I have watched as families I have known for many years struggle with the new realities that face them, and I have reveled in their ability to overcome tremendous hurdles and economic burdens in order to feed their families and to maintain meaningful social networks within their village. I have been honored to be accepted into this village, and to be able to share, from time to time, in their struggles and in their accomplishments.

In this ethnography, I hope to describe and analyze the new integration of Yucatec Maya culture with the dominant Yucatecan and Mexican society. My focus is the village of Yaxbe. I am particularly interested in the shift in economic strategies adopted by villagers as the henequen market has collapsed. I will further explore the transformations of social relations within Yaxbe as women become integrated into the wage economy and expand their involvement in the economic and political life of the village. The current history of Yucatán is being written now in hundreds of villages like Yaxbe. This is an account of one village as its meets this challenge.

In the following chapters I will examine both the integration of Yaxbe with the larger society and also the capability of the Yucatec Maya to maintain those aspects of their traditional society that are important to them.

Part One sets the stage for a study of Yaxbe. Chapter 1 outlines the historic and geographic setting of Yaxbe as well as an introduction to the village. Here I outline the ethnographic method and the value of longitudinal research.

Chapter 2 outlines the theoretical and historical context of the ethnography. I will place the rural Yucatecan within the milieu of the wider world system and develop a model by which we can understand the rural peasant within the international arena.

I will then briefly examine the history of the Yucatec Maya as it relates to the ethnography.

The third chapter outlines the economic structure of Yaxbe, focusing on the henequen cycle and delineating the diverse economic strategies pursued by the men and women of Yaxbe. While current economic structures are foreshadowed in this chapter, the emphasis will be placed on the economic situation and strategies as they existed at the time of the initial research up to the critical events of the early 1990s.

Part Two investigates the social context of village life. Chapter 4 describes the daily life in the village, including the life cycle and agencies of socialization. This chapter also investigates kin and fictive kin networks and a discussion of gender roles. Chapter 5 examines the local level political and economic structure of the village, including both village and state level organization.

Chapter 6 documents briefly the traditional Mayan religion and how it still functions in the village today. The Maya religion acts as a backdrop to Catholicism, which is still the dominant religion throughout Mexico. Chapter 7 introduces the Seventh Day Adventists as a major force in the religious and social life of the village.

Part Three describes and examines the economic and social changes that have occurred in the nation, state of Yucatán, and the village since 1990. Chapter 8 describes the collapse of the henequen market and how villagers have adapted to the current economic crisis. Chapter 9 highlights the transformation of women's participation—economic, social and political—in the village, and Chapter 10 employs a final ethnographic essay to illustrate how events at the national level affect even the most intimate of social and economic rituals. The Epilogue provides a brief summary and observations based on a research visit to Yaxbe in the summer of 2001.

A Note on Names and Places in the Village

I have used pseudonyms for Yaxbe and all of the haciendas surrounding it. I have also changed the names of individuals to protect their privacy.

A Note on the Pronunciation of Spanish and Maya Words

In Spanish, the "j" is pronounced as an "h" and the "h" is almost silent so *hijo* is pronounced "ee-ho." The Spanish use masculine and feminine forms of nouns; thus the "o" at the end of a word denotes both the masculine and generic form, and the "a" at the end of a word denotes the feminine form.

In Maya, the letter "x" is pronounced as "sh" so Yaxbe is pronounced "Yash-bay"; the plural in Maya is "ob." In Mayan, the "h" is pronounced as in *h-men* (*heh-mén*).

ACKNOWLEDGMENTS

This ethnography was more than 30 years in the making. My adventure started in undergraduate school when I first visited the Yucatán through a Grand Valley State College program sponsored by Central College in Pella, Iowa. I am indebted to Dr. George Ann Huck and the other faculty who introduced me to the Maya. The anthropology graduate department at Wayne State University supported my graduate studies, and Dr. Bunny Kaplan mentored me in many ways. In Yucatán, I would not have found Yaxbe without the assistance and support of Dr. Alberto Barrera Vazquez of INAH. LaVail and I have especially fond memories of Dr. Asael Hanson with whom we spent many wonderful hours.

Since 1989, my research in Yaxbe has been supported by research and development grants from Grand Valley State University. In 1992, Grand Valley supported my student research assistant, Cathy Looby, whose mapmaking skills and observations were greatly appreciated that summer.

Thanks also to colleagues who have critiqued my writing from time to time or who have given me advice and encouragement over the years: Bunny Kaplan at Wayne State University, James Hopgood at Northern Kentucky University, Alan and Pamela Sandstrom at IUPU—Fort Wayne, and James Dow at Oakland University.

I want to thank Valerie Hover for accompanying me to Yaxbe in 2002. Her perspective "from the outside" allowed me to see Yaxbe again, as I saw it the first time . . . with wonder, awe, and some intimidation. Her illustrations depict Yaxbe with an artist's eye that I could never duplicate with photographs. I will never see the village dogs in the same way again.

In Yaxbe, I can never repay the friendship and patience offered me freely by many villagers. I owe a great debt to those in Yaxbe who taught and mentored me in Yaxbeño culture, who took me into their homes and shared their lives with us. Here, I would like to give a special thank you to Hernán Lozada and Silvia Uc, and Pedro Chan and Deisy Pech, and their extended families. These families are forever engraved into my heart.

My special appreciation goes out to my family who has persevered through many years of research and endless writing. I am grateful for my husband, LaVail, who sacrificed a year of his career to follow me to the Yucatán and to be my unpaid research assistant and companion. Without his support, this research would have been impossible. I also owe unending gratitude to our children, Sarah, Nathan, and David, for their patience with me as I have worked many years on this project. Thank you all for accompanying me into the field, enduring my obsession with fieldwork, encouraging me when I needed it, and for sharing your lives with my friends in Yaxbe.

I would also like to acknowledge and thank my mother, Lorraine Vandenbergh, who has waited patiently many years for her daughter to finally finish her book. Thank you for inspiring me over the years, for your confidence in me, and for your inner strength and character, which I hope I have inherited.

This book is completed in the memory of three men who were very special to me during my life, who have shaped me in very diverse, yet critical ways. Without these three men, our world is a lesser place.

In memory of:
My father, Arthur Vandenbergh (1927-1994)
My father-in-law, James Gravelyn (1930-2000)
My *compadre,* Don Juan Aguilar Luna, Yaxbe, Yucatán

September 2002, Chippewa Lake, Michigan

1/A *Katun*
with the Yucatec Maya

When Francisco Hernández de Córdoba came to this country and landed at the point he called Cape Cotoch, he met certain Indian fisherfolk whom he asked what country this was, and who answered *Cotoch*, which means "our houses, our homeland," for which reason he gave that name to the cape. When he then by signs asked them how the land was theirs, they replied *Ci uthan*, meaning "they say it," and from that the Spaniards gave the name Yucatán. This was learned from one of the early conquerors, Blas Hernández, who came here with the admiral on the first occasion (Landa 1978 [1566]: 2).

THE MAYAN LANDSCAPE

Anyone who has traversed the Yucatán peninsula, venturing from the sunny beaches of Cancún to the awe inspiring archaeological sites of Chichén Itzá, or who has followed one of the two-lane highways that lead, like spokes of a wheel, from Mérida, has a sense of what a Yucatec Maya village looks like. On such a journey, one passes endless miles of *monte* (semitropical brush) interspersed with *milpa* (corn fields) or henequen plants. Villages have unpronounceable names such as Dzitas, Tzimin, or Tekax. Entrances to towns are marked by a series of speed bumps that jar the bones, but allow for measured glimpses of village life. Shifting incessantly from first to second gear and back again, one's vehicle lurches through town, dodging running children and dogs lazing in the middle of the road. Oval-shaped houses, constructed of wattle and daub (vertical wooden tree branches tied together and patched with mud or clay), and covered with tall thatch roofs are the dominant feature of any Yucatecan village. From the road, one can glance into these houses and discern faded hammocks suspended over dirt or cement floors. The romantic visitor laments at the tangle of electrical wires and the crooked television antennae protruding from the thatch roofs and the blare of music from competing radios. The observant visitor notices that houses are arranged in clusters within enclosed homesteads, called *soláres*. The fences that separate individual *soláres* are constructed of large limestone boulders that often tumble in disarray onto the roadway. (See Figure 1.1.)

The road invariably leads to the center of the town that wears the mark of its colonial past: a central park flanked by a Catholic church and government buildings. The past significance of any town is evident in the size of the church and whether it has a market along the fringes of the park. Since the conquerors built their churches from the rubble of Mayan temples, it is evident that populations of Maya had once lived here, but the structure of the town has taken on a European pattern to conform to the colonial functions of the conquerors: religious and administrative. From the center of town, the Spanish conquerors designed these towns in their own image, in a neat grid, with straight streets that dissolve into rocky footpaths as one moves away from the town center.

The villagers observed from the tourist bus or rental car seem quaint, from another time. Women, short and stocky with dark complexions and round distinctive faces, wear *huipiles*, striking white dresses with embroidered trim and, despite the heat, shawls wrapped artistically around their shoulders and under their arms. There is something monotonous, yet striking, about the sea of white *huipiles*, magenta shawls, and long dark hair tied back in tight buns. These are minuscule women carrying burdensome loads, large porcelain bowls perched mysteriously on upright heads, a child's hand gripped tightly on her dress. The boys wear shin length pants and tattered shirts; girls wear faded, worn skirts and dresses—clothes that have been handed down from child to child to child. Older children, barefoot or adorned in plastic sandals, carry infants on their hips as they rush to keep up with the brisk pace of their mother or grandmother who hurries toward the store or bus stop so that she can relieve herself of her load.

The men who loiter in the village during the day are older, with dark weatherbeaten faces. They wear Mayan *traje*, white slacks and shirt with the optional white apron, and sandals made of henequen fibers and automobile tires. They might be carrying a heavy load of corn using the ancient tumpline or lounging in front of the government building. If one were to pause to buy a Coke or wander through a market, one would hear several languages spoken, one European and familiar, the other strange, yet musical to the ear, halting and tonal. One cannot help but sense the tranquil pace of life here that contrasts sharply with the noise of city streets and the bustle of the urban tourist markets.

ENTERING THE VILLAGE, 1976

October 29, 1976

Dear Family,

We are alive and well in Yaxbe, a lovely town of 1,800 people deep in the henequen zone. We are being crushed with kindness.

Our "house" is actually the old medical clinic. We have a wonderful location, being situated along the south side of the central park. We have a verandah in front of our house,

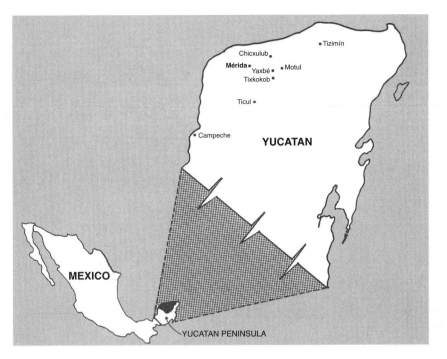

Figure 1.1 Map of the Yucatán Peninsula, Mexico. From The Naked Anthropologist, *ed. Philip DeVita, Wadsworth, 1992, p. 131.*

with cement benches where villagers wait for the bus and visit. It gives us a great view of the park and the activities in the center of town.

For reasons unknown, the clinic was abandoned and is now the abode for several colonies of scorpions. We have access to five rooms, three toilets, and two showers, but there is only one room that is really livable. It is a tiny enclosed room about 9 × 12, with two doors and a window to the outside. We do have a sink and electricity, but as yet no stove. An unnecessarily large maintenance crew has been hired by the president to make the clinic comfortable for us, cleaning out one of the shower and toilet rooms, and enclosing some of the open spaces for privacy and security. Besides the maintenance crew, there are a variety of other men who seem to have been assigned to protect us, as they come to visit several times a day to make sure that we are happy. We have only learned a few of their names so far.

Children comprise the most conspicuous group of visitors. There are hundreds of them and they are all at our house—in the morning on their way to school, between noon and 2:00 and after school. In the evenings, the adult and teenage men arrive. The first day here we didn't eat because there was always someone in the house. We haven't seen many girls, and today was the first day that married women came to visit. Doña Isabel arrived at 7:00 this morning to show me where they butcher and sell chicken. Remind me to tell you about purchasing fresh meat sometime. Love, Cindy

When Dr. Alfredo Barrera Vazquez suggested that LaVail and I visit Yaxbe, we were skeptical. We had driven through many villages and were frustrated, fearing that we would never find a place to live. However, as we bounced over the first set of speed bumps, Yaxbe somehow seemed different. The park was particularly inviting, with large Flamboyan trees protruding from nicely cultivated cement planters that served as benches for evening strollers. S-shaped lovers' seats, a characteristic of the various parks in Mérida, also adorned the plaza and surrounded a small circular stage area. Although Yaxbe didn't have a market, there was a bustle of people, and stores lined both sides of the main road that passed through town.

One of the features that most appealed to us was the relative isolation of the village. It was not located on the main road to Mérida and only two other villages lay beyond it on the bus route. As a result, it was not on the tourist path, nor did many people pass through accidentally. Yet, it was close enough to Mérida to provide convenient access to the urban markets. This proximity would later prove to be one of the major factors in Yaxbe's survival as a village, but I wasn't thinking of that at the time.

Although we were totally enamored by the village itself, I could not deny a certain disappointment in the villagers. They did not conform to my romanticized recollections of the Maya, still imprinted in my memories of my earlier visit to the peninsula as a college student. Here, in the henequen zone, fewer women wore the *huipil*, and even fewer men wore the *traje*. There was more diversity in clothing and hairstyles than I had remembered. I was later to find that fewer villagers spoke Maya as a first language; in fact, the Maya language was rapidly becoming a language for old people.

Nevertheless, my disappointment waned, and our excitement grew as we settled into the abandoned medical clinic located at the edge of the park. During those first days, as we chased away scorpions, cleared away huge spiderwebs, washed floors and walls, and finally unpacked our suitcases, we experienced conflicting emotions, vacillating erratically from total elation to abject fear. On the one hand, we were ecstatic because we had finally found "our village" and somehow, it felt "right." On the other hand, we wondered if the villagers would accept us, and I had terrible misgivings about my ability to conduct fieldwork. Would I ever learn Spanish well enough to conduct interviews, or be understood by people? Would they answer my questions? Or would they merely ignore me? The first week in the village was a blur. My early entries in my field notes and journal display my fears and misgivings. The first pages of notes are filled with confused descriptions of people, embarrassing misunderstandings, and frantic attempts to start my fieldwork.

Our first visitors were children, their timidity overcome by an overwhelming curiosity about the strangers in their midst, not to mention our possessions: a car, a typewriter, camera, and tape recorder . . . and books in a different language. The children often entered the house eating some unfamiliar fruit, spitting the seeds on our cement floor, and throwing the peelings out the window. Some would come and just stand in the doorway or peer in from the window. Others, braver, would come in, make themselves at home in a hammock and peruse our books, poke through our belongings, and ask unintelligible questions.

The teenage boys arrived next, and then the adult men. After the first week, the women arrived, bearing gifts of tamales, chicken, and exotic fruits. They usually came with small children and sat quietly, nursing a baby, quieting young ones who cried or fussed, comfortable in silence. As a victim of my own culture that devalues silence, I tried to fill the gaps with questions, but more often than not, what conversation ensued in those early days concerned the weather (it's either good or bad) and the amount of rain (too much or not enough).

Despite our attempts to explain why we were living in their village, most people assumed we were there to learn Maya. Many of our early conversations, awkward and uncertain, consisted of attempts by older women to teach us Maya vocabulary. As I sat with women in their outdoor kitchens, I learned the Mayan words for household items and domesticated animals, fruits and vegetables, construction materials, and many miscellaneous greetings, questions, and answers. It was during these informal language lessons that I learned the extent to which Maya was being lost to the young people. Teenagers in the home during these visits were often embarrassed by their mothers' and grandmothers' attempts to teach the obviously feebleminded foreigner their language. I learned that the young children in these same households could understand their grandmother's orders, but could not speak Maya themselves. Yet, I was mildly encouraged as I began to hear Mayan being spoken still by older villagers. As I sat in the park or rode the bus, I listened to conversations, and learned to appreciate the sound of the ancient language, in a losing battle with the language of conquest and nation building.

As the weeks passed, our knowledge of Spanish improved and the many blurred faces began to take shape before us. We learned people's names, learned to associate the many children to their parents, and began to discern personalities. In these early days, relationships were formed that bonded us to the village for more than 20 years. One of the first to bond with us was a young man named Reymundo (see Figures 1.2 and 1.3), the younger brother of the village president, who attached himself to us and has, since then, acted as my major informant and interpreter of events. He has the ability—imperative in an informant—to interpret his own culture in ways that are meaningful to the outsider. Now, when I return to Yaxbe, I often stay at his house with his wife and two children.

Don Juan[1] was the second villager who shaped our lives in the village, acting as mentor and surrogate grandfather. Don Juan was a non-Mayan brought to Yaxbe as a child during the Revolution who lived the life of a *henequeñero*. Wizened in his 60-plus years, he was retired from agriculture and was employed as the caretaker of the medical clinic. As such, he became our housemate, sleeping several nights a week in another room of the clinic. He watched over us, a responsibility we did not seek, but which he took on nevertheless, as his "*cargo*" (burden). In turn, my husband guided him to his hammock when he came "home" inebriated, and we bandaged him up when he fell out of his hammock in the middle of the night. It was a fair exchange, as we became *compadres* to his daughter, and we now have a permanent link to him, even after his death. (See On Becoming a *Compadre* in Chapter 4.)

RETURNING TO YAXBE, 1998

Journal: Thursday, January 22, 1998

The rain has stopped. The days are warm and the nights chilly. Sonia, Reymundo, and I walk the three blocks to the park. The kids are already there, having left before us. Now that the clouds have cleared, I can marvel once again on the unending blanket of stars above. As I stroll in the cool of the evening, sharing greetings with neighbors, I am overcome by a feeling of contentment and a sense of belonging. In the park, I sit on one of the

---

[1]Don (male) and Doña (female) are terms of respect used generally for middle-aged or elderly villagers. The term precedes the first name. Villagers do not refer to each other with the more formal Señor or Señora followed by a surname.

Figure 1.2 LaVail with the Yaxbe soccer team, 1977. Reymundo is second from the left.

new, yet uncomfortable, metal benches that have replaced the love seats I remember from the past. I reminisce as I watch the familiar scene around me. Young barefoot boys are playing soccer, wildly kicking the nearly deflated ball from one end of the plaza to the other. Girls are playing tag, chasing each other among the boys in a teasing and taunting game of "notice me." [My thirteen year-old son] David comes hobbling toward me, another skinned knee from the soccer game. The importance of being accepted.

The faces of the children are somehow familiar, but it is their parents' faces I am remembering, when they were young. I see Carla, who was a beautiful teenager 20 years ago, lost to the village early, moving to Mexico City to work as a domestic. Tonight, she is sitting near me, with her 16-year-old son who reminds me of [my other son] Nathan, of the same age whom I haven't seen for six months. Carla is here to see her sister who is stricken with an undiagnosed illness. Enérica, another sister, has also arrived from northern Mexico with her four children. In my memory, Enérica was a vivacious and mischievous 12 year old. Now her own small children are clambering around me as she and her younger sisters did many years ago. Both women have borne a great expense to be here, both expecting to see their sister for the last time.

I have returned to Yaxbe seven times since my initial research, once for a short visit and six times to update my data and document changes that have occurred over the years. Each time, I have brought one of our three children to stay with me, to learn Spanish, and to share in my experiences. It is gratifying to have a 20-year connection with villagers who have watched my children grow up as I have watched theirs. I can share in their triumphs and in their sorrow as they can share mine. I learn of the deaths of old people, and some young people as well. I learn that my ***ahijado*** (godchild) is married and has two children, and during my last visit in 2002, the entire family, including my *comadre* came from Cancún to visit me in Yaxbe.

In the winter of 1998, I returned to the village with our youngest son, David, whom I enrolled in the Seventh Day Adventist primary school. At the end of our two-month stay, LaVail joined us and we took a family vacation, visiting some of the archaeological sites we visited long ago. One night, back in the village, we visited Reymundo and Sonia. During this conversation, filled with reminiscing, we learned about the legends that have grown up around the gringos of Yaxbe, "our gringos." We laugh about the time LaVail went to the store and asked for four kilos of cheese instead of a quarter kilo; and when we set off fireworks in the plaza on July 4. We replayed the events that led up to our camera being stolen during the *Fiesta* that year and speculated, as we did so long ago, on who might have stolen it. Which of the turkey thieves was at the party? How did he take the camera without being seen? Where did he sell it? Our children have also become part of the local legends, especially the summer when Nathan, my student assistant, Cathy, and I got caught in the crush of a major protest in Mérida and found ourselves surrounded by well-armed police and the Mexican military. That same summer, Nathan and Cathy found themselves on an unplanned excursion with several policemen that resulted in a major search party being sent out from the village and several terrifying hours for me as I awaited their fate.

When we visit people, they tell us stories, remembering things that happened many years ago, some of which we had forgotten. At one house, we are reminded that LaVail took the woman of the house to the hospital when her son was born. The son is now 20 years old. We remembered being frustrated and angry because of the many requests for rides to the market, the doctor, and even to visit friends. Somehow, seeing the young man before us, our frustration didn't seem important any more.

Another woman stops me in the street and tells me she still has the sweater and clothes I gave her 20 years ago when her house caught fire and everything was lost. I remembered the fire and the columns of men hauling buckets from a nearby well, but I had forgotten about the clothes. She had not. Nevertheless, for every small favor we performed during that first year and in later years, there were hundreds of small courtesies bestowed on us that we can never repay, countless meals and celebrations shared, friendships offered, interviews freely and patiently given, and myriad memories, both happy and bittersweet.

THE OBJECTIVE AND SUBJECTIVE IN ANTHROPOLOGY

The history of anthropology is one of conflicting theory and method. Beginning with Franz Boas, the "Father of Anthropology," anthropologists have defined the discipline as scientific, consisting of testable hypotheses, rigorous research, and published results. The burden of the anthropologist is, as much as possible, to remove personal biases from the research, to practice **cultural relativism** (not judging the culture by Western standards), and to use the scientific method. The anthropological text, or ethnography, is academic and written in the third person, with the anthropologist removed from the action, present, but unobtrusive, and having minimal impact on the culture being described. Yet, anthropologists do have an impact on the culture they study. They bring ideas of technology, and technology itself, they give gifts, and they

Figure 1.3 Reymundo in 1992 with wife, Sonia, and children, Carmen and Hector, at Hector's kindergarten graduation

are consumers. Anthropologists may also give advice about projects, or teach English to the children.

Current ethnographies reflect shifts in anthropological theory and practice. The anthropologist as invisible recorder of events is being replaced by the anthropologist as guide into the lives of people from diverse worlds. In these new ethnographies, both the subject and the anthropologist are visible. People are brought to life through such methods as testimonies, interviews, indigenous journals or writings, and deeper insights into their everyday lives.

In 25 years, I have collected a tremendous amount of objective and quantitative data that includes occupations, family histories and kinship charts, information on religious participation, politics, and education. I have also collected life histories, interviews, and stories. The material presented in this ethnography originates from various sources: my field notes and quantitative data collection; observations recorded in my journal and in letters; personal interviews; stories I have collected from villagers; and academic sources. My goal in this ethnography is to provide an academic framework with which to understand this particular village and its place in a larger world system, and, within this framework, to allow the people to come alive and speak to you about their lives.

METHOD: LONGITUDINAL RESEARCH

The most valuable research is that which can be validated or tested. There are several ways in which this validation process can occur. The first occurs when several anthropologists conduct research in the same location. All anthropologists bring into fieldwork personal histories and cultural filters through which they view their own world and that of others. This method provides a means in which data can be tested and reviewed. A second method is longitudinal research in which one or more researchers return to the same location over a period of time. Frequent research visits facilitate the correction of errors, updating data, and most importantly, the ability to observe and measure changes over time.

This study is of the latter type. My initial research in 1976 focused on the study of out-migration as a consequence of the decline in the henequen industry. During that research year, I collected economic data on almost 200 families, including data on those who had migrated to other areas. In 1989, my goal was to update my migration data, recording new migrants and following up on those who migrated earlier. When I returned in 1992, I found that the tide of out-migration had slowed and that villagers had begun to shift strategies in fascinating ways. Among my findings in 1992 were the following: first, fewer people were leaving the village; second, instead of migrating, men were adopting mixed economic strategies that allowed them to stay in the village; and, third, women were participating in the workforce in growing numbers. Consequently, I began to shift my focus from migration to local economic strategies and to view migration as one of these strategies. Since 1995, my overall research goal is to document the strategies employed by villagers to compensate for their loss of agricultural employment. In this ethnography, I will begin with a description of the village as it appeared in 1976, enmeshed in mono-crop henequen production. I will then explore how the collapse of the henequen market has shaped the current economic and social structure of Yaxbe today. My purpose is not to show Yaxbeños as victims of progress, but as active agents reacting to new circumstances beyond their control while simultaneously demonstrating considerable resistance and resilience in maintaining elements of their culture that are important to them.

Longitudinal research is not only a valuable method of field study, but it is personally satisfying as well. I am privileged to have been a part of the lives of Yaxbeños for more than 20 years. I have watched their children grow up as they have watched mine. Whenever I visit Yaxbe, I am already anticipating my next visit, and I always leave them with feelings of sadness and loss.

ETHNOGRAPHIC ESSAY
DOÑA ISABEL: A WOMAN OF SUBSTANCE

In 1948, Doña Isabel's husband went to prison for murder. Her husband, Don Jose, was the son of the former foreman of *Hacienda* Santiago just north of the village. When his parents left the *hacienda*, Jose continued to work there. The details of the murder are muddled, the story having several versions. Sources agree that Jose, in an alcohol-related incident, fought with a *hacienda* worker and killed him. He was convicted and served 11 years of a 16-year sentence in the state prison in Mérida.

During those years, Isabel raised and supported her family that included Ernesto, who was very young when his father went to prison, and three more children (two daughters and a son) who were born while he was in prison, due to the Mexican penal policy which allows conjugal visits. According to Ernesto, the whole family went to Mérida twice a week to visit their father and deliver food and clothes. Isabel worked at the *hacienda* and sewed clothing to support her young family.

When I met Isabel, she had eight children ranging in age from 29 to 2 years old, six of whom were living with her in the *solár*. Ernesto, the oldest, was the current village president. He was in the process of building a new home in a nearby *solár* for his family, his wife, and four children. While his **Cordemex** (factory that processes the henequen leaves) wages and presidential income supported his own family, he also helped his mother. The second oldest child Carolina, whose husband died during our visit, also lived in the *solár* with her five children. Two other daughters lived with their husbands elsewhere. The second son Reymundo, at 21, was a bachelor who lived in the *solár* and provided a large portion of his income from Cordemex to his mother's support. The three youngest daughters completed the crowded landscape. These sixteen people, with Isabel and Jose, now released from prison, shared two houses in the family *solár*.

Don Jose was an alcoholic. He was a constant embarrassment to his children who ushered him out of public buildings and away from villagers and the local gringos. When sober, he worked at the *hacienda*, but his meager income did not support his family. However, despite his behavior and neglect of his family, I never heard Doña Isabel utter an ill word about him. Instead, she continued to work at the *hacienda*, sew clothing, and weave hammocks. Her widowed daughter and daughter-in-law did the same, but primarily they were responsible for the multitude of children and household chores. The household was largely dependent on the two factory salaries: Ernesto's and Reymundo's.

Doña Isabel is the heart and soul of the family. When she speaks, her dark eyes are intense, yet smiling. One would never guess she had lived the life she did, or given birth to as many children as she has. Her surname, which is Spanish, belies a history blended of various racial and ethnic roots. In fact, her facial features do not conform to those that typify the Maya. Her complexion is light and her features small. She wears her hair bobbed and held out of her face with combs, not long and knotted like other women her age. She is petite and fragile looking, and does not fit the description given to her by the elderly police chief who described her as a *luchadora*, a fighter. Her fighting spirit is well hidden within her diminutive form, and behind a face that expresses only serenity and happiness. She revels in her children and grandchildren. She sees humor in mis-adventure and always makes me feel as if I am one of the family.

It was to her home that I returned in 1989 with my own children, and she welcomed us with open arms and a glad heart. Don Jose had died not long after we left in 1977, the result of an accident. Isabel lived in the older of the two houses with her sister and three youngest daughters. Ernesto and his family now lived in their new house across the street. Carolina lived on Cancún with her new husband, but several of her children lived in the *solár* with Isabel. Reymundo, the second son, was the head of the household now, living in the newer cement house with his wife, Sonia, and two children. As before, the *solár* was filled with children, and the mood was the same as I remembered it 12 years earlier. And Don Jose's death? Reymundo said, "It was the best thing that could have happened for our mama." (Written in 1990) (See Figure 1.4.)

* * *

It is the winter of 1998, and I am staying in the newer of the two houses where the above story took place. I am the guest of Reymundo and his family. The house is much quieter now, as all the remaining family members have found new roots and have moved elsewhere. The house now contains a **nuclear** family, and it seems somehow empty. Doña Isabel still lives in the older, traditional house within the *solár* with her youngest and unmarried daughter, Margarita, who is 22 years old and works at a nearby factory.

One day I visited Doña Isabel and talked to her as she worked on a hammock she was weaving for me. With the exception of the small television and the

Figure 1.4 Doña Isabel: A woman of substance

refrigerator from which she sold soft drinks, the house looked the same as it did 20 years ago, now one of the few that still has a thatch roof. In the back is a small cooking shed with a hearth that she still uses to cook, though she no longer makes homemade tortillas, much to my dismay. She has no bathroom of her own, though she and Margarita use the new attached bathroom that Reymundo built behind his own house. The *solár* has several wash tubs, one for her and one for Sonia. Clotheslines crisscross the yard, tied to a variety of fruit trees: orange, lime, tamarind, and grapefruit. Doña Isabel loves flowers, and her house is surrounded by roses, hibiscus, and tree-high *flor de navidad* (poinsettia). Clustered among the trees and flower

(*continued*)

ETHNOGRAPHIC ESSAY
DOÑA ISABEL: A WOMAN OF SUBSTANCE (*continued*)

bushes are various vegetable plants including aloe. The *solár* is further cluttered with a noisy and rude batch of chickens, several turkeys, and pigs that belong to both her and Sonia, and the dog, Bingo, who slouches humbly from house to house looking for handouts.

I am invited to enter her home from the back entrance. I maneuver my height around various pots, ropes, and gourds that hang from the beams that support the thatch roof. She motions me to sit on wobbly wooden chair at her wooden kitchen table, and she joins me there. I have asked her if she will talk to me about the old days when her husband was in prison and she was raising the children alone.

I was born at the Finca [*Hacienda*] San Martín. I think it exists today, but I'm not sure. My parents were from Tixcuncheil. There was no work there so they went to San Martín where I was born. My father died, and my brothers were married and living in Yaxbe. My mother and I came here; I married Jose who was a farmer at [*Hacienda*] Santiago, and I moved there with him. We lived there for six years. Then Jose had a fight with another farmer and killed him. They took him and gave him a sentence of 16 years; but he didn't serve 16; he only served 11. I came back to Yaxbe and lived with my mother who still lived. My children grew and I worked. I had four children during that time. I worked by sewing and I'm still here [laughter]. I earned my *centavos* (pennies).

[Today] I feel happy because nothing can bother me. There is no one who fights with me . . . because I weave [make hammocks] and go to Mass. For me God is everything. I'm very content because God accompanies me in all things . . . in all moments."

I asked her what she would want for her children and grandchildren. "I want that they are happy and have work . . . especially to have work. They all took the good road. I want that they have tranquility in their families. I don't care if they are rich, but that they have established work . . . I don't want them to be poor. I told my kids I don't want them to be in *cantinas* (bars). Be in your homes, in the church. I don't want a house of fighting and drinking. I want a tranquil house. I told my children they must respect themselves if they want people to respect them. If you do not have self-respect, if you drink and fight, people won't respect you.

Doña Isabel tells me that she is 67 years old. This means that she was between 18 and 20 years old when she was left alone with a growing family, earning *centavos.* She has earned her tranquil life, filled with grandchildren and the Catholic church that has given her strength. This story, this one life, opens a window to the understanding the roles of women in rural Yucatecan society. Although Isabel is descended from the **Creole** (people of Spanish descent born in Mexico) administrators sent to the Yucatán, she has lived the life of the Yucatecan **peasant.** She was the emotional and economic core of a large extended family, seeking respect and *centavos* wherever they might be found.

2/The Historical Context

ANTHROPOLOGY, HISTORY, AND ECONOMIC THEORY

This chapter will examine the historical context of the present study. No nation, regardless of its wealth and power, exists in an economic or political vacuum. Because of this, we will be viewing Mexico within the context of three complex political matrices: (1) the relationship between Mexico and Spain; (2) the relationship between Mexico and the United States; and (3) the relationship between the Mexican government and its diverse regions. It is within the context of these complex relationships of colonialism, nationalism, and the formation of modern social institutions that we can best comprehend diversity, sources of inequality, and identity within the current social and political arena.

Historically, anthropologists focus on communities and culture and have been primarily interested in events at the local level. Research typically emphasizes the behavior of individuals within groups and how communities adapt to changes within their local physical and cultural environment. Many early anthropologists were criticized for their reluctance to look beyond the community in their research, and for harboring a myopic view of "their" village as an isolated system, fully self-reliant and in a state of equilibrium.

As indigenous cultures become absorbed into the dominant society or eradicated altogether, and as the global economy begins to capture more and more of the world markets, anthropologists can no longer envision indigenous people as members of closed communities. Rather, it is imperative to examine local communities within a larger context, expanding outward from village to region to nation and to the international sphere. Ironically, the first step in this journey involves an understanding of the past political and economic relationships between colonial power and peripheral or emerging nations. This paradigm, known as **World Systems Theory** (see Wallerstein 1974), focuses on how colonialism, or international, national, and state policies direct transformations in local forms of production and social organization. This ethnography will demonstrate how the economy and culture of Yaxbe are embedded in a national and international world system.

THE MAYA WORLD

The Maya world extends from the modern Mexican states of Campeche and Chiapas south and eastward, including the states of Yucatán and Quintana Roo in Mexico, Guatemala, Belize (formerly British Honduras), Honduras, and part of El Salvador. Although the Maya regions share basic cultural similarities, there is no single Maya culture, nor has there ever been. The diversity of geography—encompassing the flat, dry Yucatán peninsula, the wet tropical lowlands, and the Mexican and Guatemala highlands—is reflected in a patchwork quilt of cultural adaptations, each section unique in shape, color, and texture, yet all conforming to the pattern that one can readily define as "Maya." However, unlike a quilt that one day will be completed, the Maya culture has been continually reworked to conform to new patterns, imposed from the outside. Yet despite these new designs, the individual squares, colors, and stitching are defined by the Maya themselves, drawn from their history, values, and traditions that have persisted over many millennia.

The ability of the Maya to design their own cultural quilt is indicative of their resilience. They are not, nor have they ever been, passive people. They have fought persistent enemies: Toltec, Spanish, and Mexican; and when the battles were ultimately lost, they continued to resist the destruction of their culture. The result has been the evolution of creative and innovative responses and adaptations to external powers.

Yaxbe is located in the northern lowland zone of the Yucatán Peninsula. The peninsula encompasses all of the state of Yucatán, the northern—and major portion of the state of Campeche, and all of Quintana Roo. With the exception of the Puuc Hills in southwest Yucatán and northeast Campeche, the peninsula is flat and dominated by scrub forest that is replaced by rain forest as one moves south and east across the peninsula. This northern region boasts some of the major classic and postclassic Maya civic centers: Uxmal, Chichén Itzá, Cobá, Tulúm, and Mayapán.

The environment of the state of Yucatán has shaped its history and influenced its place in the Mexican economic system. First, the region suffers from a lack of rainfall. Yucatán has a rainy season that is limited to four months, June through September, during which time 80% to 90% of the annual rainfall occurs (Roys 1972[1943]:10). Unfortunately, this concentration of precipitation does not guarantee ample moisture for all **swidden** (slash and burn) farmers, for the amount of rainfall varies markedly from region to region, increasing as one moves to the south and east.

The lack of rainfall is exacerbated by the unique topography of the peninsula, notable for what it lacks rather than what it has. As a resident of Michigan, a state that abounds in lakes and rivers, the lack of surface rivers and streams in Yucatán is a most obvious misfortune. Instead of feeding natural bodies of water, the sparse rain that does fall is absorbed like a sponge into limestone crust (**karst**) that covers the peninsula. Consequently, the only source of potable water for the ancient Maya were *cenotes* (*dzonot* in Maya), which formed when the limestone karst collapsed along fault lines, permitting water to rise from the water table below. Most Maya ceremonial centers were built near these *cenotes*. Today, while some villages still rely on water from *cenotes*, most villages have either community wells or individual wells within each *solár*.

This uninviting topography is further hindered by a lack of soil cover—less than two inches in most areas. The challenge for the Mayan cultivator, then, is enormous. It is virtually impossible to grow many crops, including those, such as wheat, that require rich soils and those whose fruit grows under ground. What is truly remarkable is the diversity of crops that are grown in this terrain: such major food crops as corn, beans, and squash (the trilogy) as well as a vast array of vegetable and fruit crops including tomatoes, chili peppers, cabbage, green peppers, oranges, grapefruit, bananas, and papaya.

PRE-CONQUEST MAYA[1]

Given the topography of the Yucatán Peninsula, it is not unreasonable to ask why or how a civilization as complex as that of the Maya could have developed in such a formidable place. Yet, the Maya did thrive here, supported by swidden agriculture and by irrigation and terracing systems in some regions. Agriculture was supplemented by hunting everywhere and fishing along the peninsular shores. In fact, the Yucatán Peninsula has been continuously occupied since the Formative Period (1000 B.C.) when the Olmecs introduced their calendar and architectural style to the region.

There was no central seat of power among the Maya as there was at Teotihuacán or at Tenochtitlán in the central valley of Mexico. Rather, Maya regions were ruled by politically autonomous yet economically and politically linked ceremonial centers. Uxmal, Chichén Itzá, and Cobá were major centers during the Classic Period (A.D. 600–900). Toltec trade expeditions, followed by military invasions from Tula in the Late Classic Period, disrupted the traditional power structure, shifting control from within the peninsula to the valley of Mexico.

By A.D. 1200, the Mexica empire, centered at Tenochtitlán, present day Mexico City, had permeated Maya-Toltec culture, ruling ineffectively from the great distances that separated them. Meanwhile, in the Yucatán, local power centers shifted from Chichén Itzá to Mayapán to Tulúm as fading clans feuded among themselves.

Although the Yucatecan coast was traversed several times by the Spanish, the inhospitable Indians and the dearth of natural resources discouraged the earliest conquerors from pausing here. Hernán Cortés, in 1519, landed on the Caribbean island of Cozumél where he met the famous Doña Marina. But he did not dawdle there; instead, he set sail for Veracruz where he set up his base of operations. It was not until 1527, after the defeat of Moctezuma at Tenochtitlán, that the Spanish, under the command of Francisco de Montejo, returned to Yucatán. By this time, the power vacuum left by the feuding clans had resulted in the abandonment of many of the ceremonial centers. Yet the Maya, even without a centralized military, did not surrender easily. The Spanish had to defeat each center separately, until they were finally able

[1]Much literature exists on the ancient Maya. See J. E. Thompson 1970, 1975 [1966]; J. Henderson, 1981; R. Roys 1957, 1972 [1943]; J. Helms 1975; G. R. Willey, 1966.

to establish a stronghold at the minor ceremonial center, T'ho, which was renamed Mérida.

CONQUEST TO INDEPENDENCE

The history of colonial rule in Mexico is complex and outside the scope of this book (see Roys 1972 [1943]; Helms 1975). Yet certain aspects of that history pertain to the present study and should be summarized.

The Spanish Crown, in order to reward the **conquistadores,** granted them large tracts of land, called **encomiendas,** that provided desired products for the mother country. Yucatán, lacking both exploitable natural resources and viable agriculture, was slow to be divided up in this way. Eventually, however, the potential of this area for cattle became apparent, and by Independence (1821), nearly 90% of Yucatecan land was held in *encomienda,* and beef was traded to Spain's other colony, Cuba, in exchange for sugar (Chamberlain 1948: 330-331).

The *encomienda* lands carved up huge tracts of land that included existing indigenous communities. These communities and the families who lived in them were the property of the **encomendero,** who not only exploited indigenous labor, but also extracted tribute from them in the form of food and services. The *encomendero* himself did not live on the land, but rather oversaw his holdings from his mansion in Mérida.

The Indian villages maintained a certain amount of autonomy in that the inhabitants were not forced to live on the *encomienda* (Chamberlain 1948:240). However, in order to maintain certain aspects of the traditional social organization and minimize the possibility of Indian revolt, the Spanish appointed the Maya **halach uinic** (hereditary regional ruler) and the **batabob** (town leaders) to positions of leadership. These leaders, called **caciques** became the political bridge between the Indian community and the Spanish Crown. The loyalty of the *caciques* toward their Indian communities was constantly compromised as the Spanish co-opted them and their families into Spanish administrative positions within the *haciendas* and the villages (Roys 1957: 6-7).

The *encomienda* system was eventually abolished and replaced by another land tenure system, the *hacienda* (Helms 1975: 190). While the *encomienda* was oriented toward the production of one commodity for export and elite consumption, each *hacienda* was a self-sustaining enterprise, producing food for export and to support the **hacendado** and his family who often lived on the estate. In northern Yucatán, subsistence was supplemented by the production of an export crop, first cattle, and later, henequen. The *hacienda* system relied on resident laborers who were tied to the *hacienda* by **debt peonage** (Strickon 1968: 44-45).

HENEQUEN AND THE POST-INDEPENDENCE ERA

Life was easier in the early years because things were cheaper. But we had to work very hard [at *Hacienda* San Martín].[2] We worked from 3:00 in the morning to 7:00 at night every day, but there was always work and we could afford food. The owner of [the *hacienda*] was "*mala gente*" (bad person), but there was not slavery. We were paid $30

---

[2]The haciendas and their owners are pseudonyms.

[pesos] a week and were paid in paper to be redeemed at his store. You might have a debt of as much as $25 [pesos], which you couldn't repay. He was very wealthy. He had three corrals and 300–400 head of cattle. He also had henequen but no *disfibradora* (processing factory). [The *hacienda*] was abandoned because "*Díos le castigó*"(God punished him). His sons robbed him and there was a cattle epidemic that killed most of his cattle. He sold the rest and abandoned the *hacienda*. (Don Juan [age 67], 1976)

[The] Perez family owned *Hacienda* San Martín, *Hacienda* Balám, and two other *haciendas*. They were very rich. His sons had many henequen fields. When the changes came in the 1930s, and all the *haciendas* were divided into small parcels, the Perez family went to Mérida and did other things with their money. They abandoned the fields and opened pharmacies. They are still rich. (Don Max [mid-60s], 1977)

My father worked at *Hacienda* Santiago in the days of slavery [1920s–1930s—before the Cárdenas reforms]. I was very young, but my father talked about those days. The foreman was Ricardo Vargas who was a very bad man. He beat the men if they didn't work hard enough. The workers were paid 75 *centavos* a day. They also had to carry a large stone back to the village after they worked all day. The stones were used to build the large house on the corner. Those were terrible times. (Don Ernesto [age 88], 1998)

Yucatán represents a microcosm of post-conquest economies that permeate Mexico. Throughout its colonized history, Yucatán has been dependent on **cash crops** that enriched the coffers of the rulers, both Spanish and Mexican, at the expense of the indigenous population. When Mexico gained its independence from Spain in 1821, it lost its source of sugar. To provide this commodity for the elite, the government transformed the southern areas of Yucatán, heretofore isolated and sparsely populated, into sugar plantations. Ironically and tragically, it was to this region that thousands of indigenous families had fled from the brutal *hacienda* system in the north. Here, in the rain forest, they had settled into an existence as subsistence farmers. Now, they were pursued again and forced to transform themselves from subsistence farmers to peons, tied to the sugar plantation by debt peonage. The Caste War, waged by the Maya Indians against the Mexican government (1847–1848), marked the end of the plantation system in the sugar zone and left a temporary void in the export economy of Yucatán and Mexico (see Reed 1964).

This void was filled by henequen, and the *hacienda* system that accompanied it became the core of economic and political power in Yucatán. The Maya cultivated henequen (*agave fourcroydes*) in pre-conquest times, using the fibers for clothing, rope, and hammocks (Chardon 1961: 14–15) and its thorns for needles (Brockway 1979: 170–171). Because it is an agave, it is well-adapted to the conditions of Northwest Yucatán, thriving in conditions of dry heat and poor soils. The transformation of henequen from a small-scale family crop to international mono-crop occurred as a result of several related events.

The first event was the Yucatecan invention, in the mid-1800s, of a mechanized decorticator that strips the fibers from the thorny leaves (Brannon and Baklanoff 1987: 26). A second event was the invention in the United States of the McCormick reaper that utilized the binder twine produced from the Yucatecan fibers (see Figure 2.1). What resulted was a henequen boom that lasted until the end of the Mexican Revolution in the early 1900s (Brannon and Baklanoff 1987: 26).

As with the cattle *encomiendas* and sugar plantations, the wealth produced by henequen production did not go to the producers. Henequen production, like cattle and sugar that preceded it, was part of an international system of exchange that used

Figure 2.1 Freshly cut henequen leaves (foreground) and fibers hanging to dry (background), Cordemex

indigenous labor to fill government and private coffers. Indigenous laborers and the communities in which they live are part of a periphery far distant from the economic centers of Mérida, Mexico City, and even the United States. Because the local elite had the capital to purchase the henequen fibers and the decorticating machines, the Mexican government allowed them to maintain their *haciendas* and their access to local labor. As the primary destination for Yucatecan twine and rope, the United States was able to control the prices of fibers imported from Mexico. Naturally, these prices remained low for the United States and International Harvester Corporation, the manufacturer of the McCormick reaper. The Mexican elite, who also owned the Yucatecan export houses, became wealthy and ultimately developed close cultural ties to the United States, often sending their children to school there (Brannon and Baklanoff 1987: 38–41).

The history of Mexico, from Independence in 1821, to the presidency of Porfirio Díaz (1876–1880, 1884–1911), was one of economic and political domination by the wealthy, both within and outside of the country. The Mexican political leaders and the wealthy elite alienated Mexico's land by selling it to foreign powers, particularly the United States. By 1910, the United States owned 100 million acres of Mexican land, or 22% of its land surface. Much of this land was valuable mining and agricultural land. Consequently, approximately 90% of the peasants were landless by that year (Fuentes 1996: 38). This situation was replicated in all regions of the country, including Yucatán (see Shuman 1974, Simpson 1937, Strickon 1968). This era in Mexico's history culminated in its revolution (1910–1914).

One of the major consequences of the revolution was the expropriation of these lands from the wealthy elite and foreign interests and their redistribution to the peasants. Article 27 of the 1917 Mexican Constitution provided the mechanism for this redistribution in the form of *ejidos,* lands that would be controlled by rural villages and held in usufruct, that is, parcels could be used by individuals within a community, passed on to children, but could not be sold. Unused lands would be reassigned to other individuals within the community. This redistribution is one of the cornerstones of the Mexican revolutionary reforms. Another important reform, important in this discussion, is the abolition of debt peonage.

The goals of the Mexican Revolution were slow in coming to Yucatán. The strength of the wealthy oligarchy exceeded that of the reformers and in Yucatán the *hacienda* still reigned in 1927 with 600 haciendas still owning or controlling more than 410,000 acres of henequen land (Simpson 1937: 5–6). Real land reform did not come to Yucatán until the presidency of Lázaro Cárdenas (1934–1940). Bringing the spirit of the revolution to the henequen zone, Cárdenas began expropriating *hacienda* lands and privately owned decorticating plants from the owners and placing them in *ejidos.* By 1937, Cárdenas expropriated 80% of the land in the henequen zone, including the decorticating plants (Raymond 1968: 464).

Between 1937 and 1955, many modifications were made to the henequen *ejido* to resolve certain problems inherent in henequen production, the long maturation of henequen leaves, the rural mechanization process, and the difficulties of transportation from the periphery to the urban market. By the 1960s, there were two parallel systems of producing henequen:

1. A modern *hacienda* system in which private individuals owned *haciendas* and hired villagers and resident laborers to plant the crop and work in the privately owned decorticating plant.
2. The henequen ejido in which men worked on village owned land but whose labor was managed and reimbursed by the state.

Regardless of the system, henequen production was tightly controlled by the state, which determined the amount of henequen planted and harvested, as well as wages paid to the workers. While peasant unions have been able to shape policies and direct wages somewhat, the dependence of laborers on mono-crop production places them in a vulnerable bargaining position.

THE DECLINE AND FALL OF THE HENEQUEN ERA

When I arrived in Yaxbe in 1976, the henequen era was already in decline. According to Joseph (1982 in Yoder 1993: 328), in 1910, Yucatán was producing 98% of the world's production of henequen; by 1950, the state was producing nearly the same amount of henequen but this only represented 14% of the world's total. This decline was due to a number of factors including increased worldwide competition in sisal production, the rise of the petrochemical industry, and the production of less expensive synthetic substitutes for binder twine and sisal rope. The precipitous drop in demand for Yucatecan henequen has drastically transformed the economic landscape of the state that depended on mono-crop production for approximately 100 years.

These factors have been exacerbated by events at the national level that have changed the face of rural Mexico forever. Economic decline, precipitated by the oil and debt crisis in the 1980s, resulted in closer economic ties to the United States, which loaned money and credit to Mexico. The year 1992 was a watershed year for Mexico as the major defining section of the post-revolutionary Mexican Constitution

Figure 2.2 A bicycle repair shop and store in the government subsidized market, dubbed "la mall"

was amended to help pave the way for **NAFTA.** President Salinas de Gortari, in justifying the "reforms" to Article 27, claimed that in order for Mexico to modernize, the peasantry must be transformed and absorbed into a more progressive agricultural system. To Salinas, part of this modernization included the privatization and commercialization of peasant held land (Collier 1994b: 85). As they were finally implemented, the reforms allow *ejidatarios,* through local agreement, to sell, buy, or rent land and legally hire laborers; further, *ejidatarios* can hold contracts or establish joint ventures with domestic and foreign private investors (Stephen 1994a: 2). **PROCEDE,** the official process through which these reforms will be implemented, has been slow in arriving in Yucatán. In fact, during my 1998 visit, Yaxbe had its first introductory meeting of the *Procuria Agraria,* the government department responsible for educating peasants on the system of privatization.

The current history of Yucatán, that which is being written now in hundreds of villages like Yaxbe, is one of adaptation, survival, and a revival of old traditions. The henequen *ejido* is dead; it no longer exists. Its death knell sounded in June 1992. But even before that time, as already seen, the henequen era was waning. The question then is what can replace henequen as the livelihood of Yucatecan peasants? What is the next boom? So far, the answer is that there is none. (See Figure 2.2.) The future of Yucatán and all the states of the Yucatán peninsula will depend on two sources of foreign capital: tourism and the ***maquila*** (foreign-owned factories) industry. Both tourism and transnational investment have drawn villagers into the urban sphere.

CONCLUSION

This ethnography is written in the context of these dramatic economic shifts and uncertainties. It is an attempt to document how individuals and families endure, and in some cases, flourish, within this milieu. I will explore shifts in the daily flow of life as men who once boarded pre-dawn horse drawn carts that took them to the henequen fields now board buses and taxis to jobs in factories, or trucks from town to town selling vegetables, clothing, and furniture. I will explore these new strategies within the context of cultural values that are holding firm as the eye of a hurricane as the world is thrashing and whirling around them. What are they doing now? And what lies ahead in their future?

3/The Economy of Yaxbe, 1976–1989

History is not simply something that happens to people, but something they make—within, of course, the very powerful constraints of the system within which they are operating. A practice approach attempts to see this making whether in the past or in the present, whether in the creation of novelty, or in the reproduction of the same old thing (Ortner 1984: 159).

WORLD SYSTEMS THEORY AND AGENCY IN YUCATÁN

As we begin to examine the strategies and the transformations in rural Yucatán, it is important to keep in mind certain principles of cultural change:

1. *Current economic and social conditions and patterns of culture change are enmeshed in history and must be understood within a larger context of shifting political policies and decisions related to the allocation of land and the exploitation of natural resources.* In Chapter 2, we reviewed the economic history of Yucatán using a world systems perspective as our organizing principle. This perspective allows anthropologists, political scientists, economists, and others to envision the impact of global economics on peripheral areas and rural people. In this and future chapters, we will be turning our attention to the evolving strategies that are being developed locally in response to the collapse in the henequen market.

2. *That, within this larger context, individuals and groups are agents of change, shaping their own futures and adapting to events beyond their control.* While anthropologists explore both macro- and micro-level events, their strength lies in their ability to comprehend the intricacies of social life in a way that macro-theories like world systems cannot. Anthropologists attempt to locate and assess the local within the global; to understand how people perceive of themselves and their place in the larger social and economic system; and to examine how they act within the constraints of that larger system. In Yaxbe we will explore how villagers patterned their lives around henequen production and, now that the system has begun to unravel, how they are now restructuring economic and social relations to adapt to these changes. Rather than portraying villagers as victims, this ethnography will emphasize the flexibility and the resourcefulness of villagers in this endeavor, and how shifts in economic opportunities have altered social relationships within the village and within the home.

3. *Human responses to these events and conditions are not identical or predictable in all places.* Human agency is based on many factors both within the family and within the social structure of the community. Poor families do not have the same options as wealthier families; women's options differ from those of men; those of the uneducated differ from those of educated individuals. All social action is also performed within the context of ethnicity, social class, wealth, religion, age, and gender. In addition, all individuals and families perceive their own potential and options in diverse ways.

In Yaxbe, we will explore how individuals and families are agents of both change and resistance while simultaneously acting within the context of events that are beyond them, geographically and politically.

THE ECONOMIC STRUCTURE

Making a Living in Yaxbe

In 1977, Yaxbe had a population of 1,750[1] comprised of 334 families. Over the course of my fieldwork year, I obtained detailed information on 286 families whose members (1,473 individuals) represented approximately 84% of the total population. Table 1 (Appendix) outlines the occupations for adult men and women in 1977 and 1998. Table 2 (Appendix) illustrates the extent to which henequen-related occupations dominate the economy of Yaxbe during the time of my initial research and in 1998.

In 1977, 65% of the adult men designated agriculture as their primary occupation (Table 1). However, Table 2 indicates that most of these men were employed in henequen production. Women, in contrast, had very little involvement with henequen or *milpa* production. While women may have assisted their husbands in the *milpa* from time to time, henequen production is very arduous and requires many hours of labor far from home. The women's realm was the home and the village. Within these confines, however, women had considerable influence and made countless economic contributions to the family.

---

[1]Population figures are mine, obtained as part of the research questionnaire. Cook and Borah (1974:101) give municipal figures of 1974. The figure given above includes Yaxbe, one *hacienda,* and one population center just outside the village, all Yaxbeños.

Although few women earned wages in 1977, most of the families I interviewed reported that at least one resident female provided income to the family. These sources of income included hammock weaving, sewing, or selling fresh produce or prepared foods, as well as pensions received as a result of their husbands' work in the *ejido*. The number of women making these informal and undocumented contributions was certainly higher than reported since many women or their husbands did not consider such contributions "economic."

Economic contributions of younger household members are also crucial to the economic success of the family unit. In 1977, at least 100 young men, ranging from age 10 to their early 20s, worked with their fathers in the *ejido*. Several adult dependents worked at the Cordemex factory and others earned money sewing clothing for their friends, selling fruits and vegetables, driving trucks for the **sindicato** (trucking union or syndicate), or working in local stores. Even boys and young men who attended school regularly were expected to assist the family in some way, through agriculture or through wage-earning jobs.

Young women were also economically productive, not only earning money in home-centered activities, such as sewing and hammock weaving, but also outside the home, as sales clerks or baby-sitters. Increasingly, young women, like their male counterparts, have chosen to migrate and send remittances home to the family (Chapter 8).

It is important to recognize that the key for economic survival was, and still is, diversification. Most, if not all, *henequeneros* supplement their incomes in a variety of ways: *milpa* and private henequen parcels, selling produce, construction, or in family stores. Every child over age 10 contributes in some way to the family labor pool. Few families can survive on what the husband earns in the henequen *ejido*; and no households in the village depend on a single income. We will now turn to a discussion of the various occupations found in Yaxbe with an emphasis on those related to henequen production (see Tables 1 and 2 in the appendix for the data that accompany this discussion).

Henequen Production

THE HENEQUEN CYCLE   Yaxbeños live within the constraints of two diverse agricultural cycles. The first, and most demanding, is the henequen cycle. As stated earlier, henequen (*ki* in Maya) is an agave used for making twine and rope. *Henequeneros* extract the fiber by cutting and stripping the leaves from the large cactus-like plants, which grow to six feet in height at maturity.

The life cycle of henequen is unlike most other subsistence crops in that the plants require seven years of care before they produce their first viable leaves. This requires a long-term commitment, and ideally, the ability to produce multiple fields at various stages of maturity. Once the plant matures, it produces leaves for 10 to 12 years. However, again unlike subsistence crops that do not require constant care, the Yucatecan "Green Gold" is a harsh taskmaster, requiring patience and skill for its exploitation. Plants must be continuously weeded and cut at the proper time to assure their quality. Overcutting results in the early death of the plant, and neglect results in inferior fibers.

As the plant ages, a thick stem grows from the plant, and when the plant dies, a flower blooms from this stem. When this occurs, the stem must be cut, since the flower produces a poisonous sap which, if it falls on the other plants in the row, kills them by poisoning their core (Chardon, 1961:49-50; Shuman 1974:150). When the plant is completely dead, the left over stump, or *bob,* is used as kindling for the kitchen fire.[2] Because of poor soils, fields with dead henequen or corn are allowed to remain fallow, or unused. The ideal fallow period is from 7 to 10 years, but limited land holdings will often necessitate shorter fallow periods.

HENEQUEN PRODUCTION   Until 1992, village land was exploited through two mechanisms, the *ejido* (the workers on which are called ***ejidatarios***) and ***parcelas*** (private parcels—the owners are called ***parcelarios***).

THE HENEQUEN *EJIDO*   As we have learned, the majority of men in Yaxbe were *ejidatarios* in 1976, working for wages in the village *ejido.* We have also learned that the *ejido* system was carved out of the expropriated *haciendas* after the revolution. The history and structure of the various types of *ejido* work groups is complex, and beyond the scope of this ethnography. However, a brief description of the system will illustrate the hierarchical nature of the henequen *ejido* and how it defined the local class system (see Figure 3.1). In the following discussion I use the present tense even though the *ejido* has officially been abolished. Because of the delay in implementing the reforms of 1992, the system described below is still in effect unofficially and in a less structured form.

The henequen *ejido* system is controlled by the state and national governments that subsidize the production of henequen and reimburse all of the *ejidatarios* with funds funneled through various state banks. The banks establish guidelines regarding the length and the quantity of leaves harvested and set quotas and the prices paid for various lengths of leaves. The bank officials dictate this information to the local representative of the state apparatus, the ***socio delegado*** who is the foreman of all of the work groups within a village.

The *socio delegado* (usually called the "*socio*") is the second most powerful person in the village, next to the village president. As foreman of the *ejido* lands, the *socio* decides who works in the fields on any given day, whether that individual weeds or cuts the leaves, and in which field he works. If a worker complains too much or angers the *socio,* he might be assigned to new fields with few mature leaves or might be overlooked entirely and omitted temporarily from the work list.

The *socio* follows the dictates of the various credit banks by providing work lists and harvesting information to the ***checador,*** a political appointee of the *socio* who sets the daily quotas, assigns the work groups, and oversees the workers. The *checador* is also a powerful man because of his position of trust with the *socio.* He can blacklist a worker whom he does not like or give special favors to relatives and others who have helped him in the past.

The third officer in the *ejido* is the ***consejo viligancia*** or the vigilance officer whose responsibility it is to inspect the fields to make sure the work was completed and to check on the condition of the henequen plants. This position is second in

[2]In 2001, the stumps were being sold for use in the production of tequila (Chapter 8).

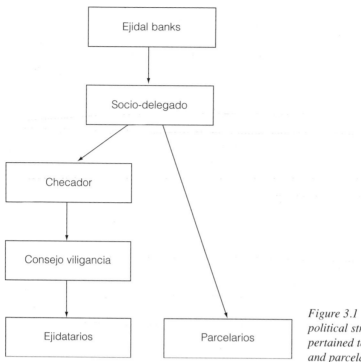

Figure 3.1 The henequen political structure as it pertained to the ejidatarios and parcelarios in 1976

command to that of *socio delegado,* but it is not a patronage position. The *consejo* is the man with the second-highest number of votes in the tri-annual elections for socio *delegado.*

PARCELARIOS   *Parcelarios* are private landowners. They petition the *socio-delegado* for uncultivated or abandoned land belonging to the *ejido.* This land cannot be sold by the *parcelario.* Rather, it is passed on to his children or abandoned. In the case of abandonment, the land reverts back to the *ejido* after two years and is reassigned or resold. The cost per *mecate* (about 24 square yards) depends on whether it is planted with henequen and maturity of the plants. Abandoned plots can be obtained free of charge, but substantial costs are incurred as the *parcelarios* must purchase their own **hijos** (young henequen plants) and whatever supplies they require. They must also enlist the help of relatives to assist them in weeding and harvesting the leaves. Once this is accomplished, the *parcelarios* must then pay to transport their leaves from the field to Cordemex.

Although *parcelarios* have the potential of becoming wealthy, the small land-holder seldom is. The initial outlay for land, labor, and money is great and the delay in financial return can be disastrous to the small farmer. Clearly, not every family is capable of purchasing a *parcela.* Rather, private ownership allows families with capital earned from other enterprises to reinvest their capital and to amass even more wealth. The average *ejidatario,* earning between US$5–$8 a week, could not afford the capital outlay necessary to obtain a parcel, even an abandoned one.

DECORTICATING FACTORIES   In 1976–1977, there were two decorticating factories in Yaxbe, the *Hacienda* Santiago just north of the village and Cordemex, to the south. Because of the labor-intensive nature of henequen production and the necessity of expensive rasping machinery, henequen production was allowed to remain in private hands until long after the 1917 post-revolutionary reforms. Even after President Cárdenas finally expropriated the large Yucatecan henequen *haciendas* in 1937, 20% of the henequen *hacienda* land was still held by the descendants of the original *hacendados* (Raymond 1968: 464). In 1976, the owner of *Hacienda* Santiago, an absentee landlord living in Mérida, employed 25 workers, all of whom lived either on the *hacienda* or in Yaxbe. The *hacienda* had an *encargador,* or foreman, a towns-man who acted as *checador* and *socio delegado,* organizing and overseeing the henequen production on the *hacienda,* and paying the producers and the factory workers with funds provided by the owner.

Cordemex is a national corporation that owns all of the decorticating plants in the state of Yucatán (except those at the *haciendas*). These factories are located through-out the henequen zone. The local Cordemex factory served the *parcelarios* of Yaxbe and surrounding villages. In 1977, Cordemex employed two shifts, each with 40 workers, most of whom resided in Yaxbe. The supervisory personnel, however, were from Mérida. The factory had one union with a Yaxbeño steward. The wages and benefits far exceeded that of any other local occupation; workers earned between US$60–$75 a week and received seniority and benefits such as vacations. The lucra-tive nature of this job resulted in a long waiting list for employment. Here, as in other occupations, patronage thrived as employees could and would urge the management to hire their relatives or friends. In seven cases, there were two Cordemex employ-ees within the same household *solár,* greatly increasing the standard of living for that family unit.

SINDICATO (SYNDICATE)   The *sindicato* was a trucking operation, contracted by Cordemex, to transport the henequen leaves or fibers from the village to the main Cordemex plant in Mérida. One elderly villager owned the only two local trucks used by the syndicate in 1977, and he hired drivers to make the trips. Some of these drivers worked for the syndicate full-time; others also worked as *ejidatarios* or *parcelarios.*

The Milpa Cycle

The second agricultural cycle is tied to the rhythm of the seasons. In Mexico, *milpa* refers to the traditional agricultural system and the dominant crops of Mesoamerica—the trilogy of corn, beans, and squash. Farmers grow a variety of crops in addition to the trilogy: chiles, tomatoes, and yams. Compared to the North American corn crop that is planted in long neat rows on large tracts of land, in Yucatán, *milpa* is rather uninspiring. Corn is planted in small clumps of land or in between rows of young henequen; yams, squash, and beans are planted among lime-stone outcroppings and buried under new undergrowth.

Farmers obtain their *milpa* in the same way that villagers obtain their parcels. They solicit the *socio* for a parcel of land, for which they pay nothing or a designated amount depending on the quality of the plot (where it is in the fallow cycle) or what has already been planted. *Milpa* land is also held in usufruct, being passed down to children, but without the right to sell it.

It is not an easy environment in which to produce food crops. In the dry season, November to May, men clear a small patch of land for their *milpas*. Because of the poor soils, *milpas* must be moved yearly so that the soil can rejuvenate itself. Clearing the underbrush and trees (called *monte*) is difficult work. The vegetation grows rapidly and is dominated by thorny brush, tangled vines, and old henequen. The *milpero* works around huge limestone outcroppings and a rich variety of fruit trees.

Once a small area is cleared, the brush is left to dry. At the end of the dry season, in May, the fields are burned, and for a month, the acrid smell of burning fields permeates the village. Once this is done, the *milpero*, using his digging stick, punches holes in the charred earth. As he does this, one hole at a time, he drops three corn kernels within each opening, and then pats dirt over the hole, and moves on down the jagged rows, following the contours of rocks and trees. He then waits for the rain, which should begin in June. The Mayan **Chachac** ceremony (called the comistraje by villagers) takes place in early June, supplicating the rain god, **Chac,** to provide the rains necessary for their crops to grow. Because of the demands of henequen, only 3% of the household heads consider the *milpa* as their primary occupation. The products of the *milpa* are largely for household consumption (see Figures 3.2 and 3.3).

Animal Husbandry

Many families supplement their income through the herding of cattle, the sale of domesticated animals and their byproducts, and by beekeeping. With a few exceptions, these enterprises are usually secondary, performed in conjunction with henequen production. In fact, domesticated animals such as chickens, turkeys, and pigs usually belong to the woman of the house, and the income generated from the by-products and sale of domesticated animals, and household vegetable and fruit gardens is spent by the women for household expenses and for the needs of the children.

Miscellaneous Nonagricultural Occupations

Various other occupations are of importance in Yaxbe. This diversity reflects the evolution of Yaxbe from a small village to an economic center of some significance. Besides the natural growth rate of the village, there has been a constant influx of new residents from smaller villages and *haciendas* since Yaxbe became a **municipio** (a county). In addition, the Cordemex factory introduced a new affluence that enriched not only the worker and his immediate family, but which also trickled down to his extended family. This combination of growth and affluence produced an increased demand for more service-orientated occupations.

CONSTRUCTION   The growing demand for construction workers reflects the changing values of the community. Historically, families built their own stick and thatch houses. Today, as the traditional stick and thatch homes fall into disrepair, villagers build multiroom homes of bright pastel stucco and laminated roofs. Often, families will add stucco rooms to the rear of their existing traditional houses so that one walks first through the old house and enters directly into the new one.

Figure 3.2 Man carrying corn from his milpa to Yaxbe, using a tumpline, 1977

Most of the older masons learned their trade during the building boom on Cancún and Cozumél in the 1970s. There, they learned not only construction, but also the rudiments of plumbing and electrical skills, and they brought this knowledge back to the village with them. They, in turn, taught their male relatives who served as assistants and apprentices, often working part-time to supplement agricultural labor. By 1998, home construction was a thriving full-time occupation, requiring knowledge of sophisticated construction techniques, arches, windows, and cement fences. To accommodate the building boom, many men are learning plumbing and electrical trades and other new skills such as laying tile and installing glass.

TAILORING In 1976–1977, tailoring was a major occupation for men and women. Most village tailors and seamstresses specialized in everyday clothing—shirts and pants. Others specialized in *guayaberas,* the Yucatecan dress shirt (considered casual wear by the tourist), *huipiles,* or "*fina,*" special dresses for weddings, **quinceñeras** (15th birthday parties), and first communions. Today, there are few full-time tailors and seamstresses who work from their homes. Women with marketable skills now

Figure 3.3 Woman carrying corn to Yaxbe for grinding, 1977

seek employment in one of the several clothing factories blossoming on the edges of Mérida.

STORES, RESTAURANTS, AND BARS   Stores, *loncherías* (restaurants or, more accurately, snack bars), and bars are family enterprises that depend on the cooperation of large extended families and, especially, the ability of women and children to contribute to the long hours and hard work. There are several large stores (*tiendas*) in the village that carry a wide variety of food and nonfood items. Each of these stores has a **molino** (mill) that grinds corn into **masa,** the dough from which tortillas are made. The newest addition to each of the stores in 1976 was a *tortillería* where tortillas are prepared and baked by machine. While nearly every village woman took advantage of the *molino,* few women used the *tortillería* at first. It was utilized primarily by women for the evening meals, and by the inept anthropologist. The store-bought product was inferior by far to the hand-pressed variety, cooked over an open

Figure 3.4 Don Justo in his store, 1977

fire. By 1998, unfortunately, all villagers bought prepared tortillas and the art of handmade tortillas was being lost by the younger generation of women (Chapter 10).

In 1976, Don Berto, the president of the trucking syndicate, owned one of the two largest stores in Yaxbe. His wife and two eldest sons ran the store while Don Berto tended to his trucking business and multiple private parcels of both henequen and corn. Because of his diverse enterprises, Don Berto was one of wealthiest men in Yaxbe, but by 1998, Don Berto was deaf and unable to work. His wife and several daughters-in-law continue as the primary storekeepers. A smaller store specializing in fresh meat has been built in the same *solár* and is tended by two of Don Berto's daughters.

Don Justo, a former *Meridano* who married a local woman, owns the other large store in the village, located on the main intersection of the village at the major bus stop (see Figure 3.4). Both of these stores sell a wide variety of canned goods as well as bulk items such as flour and sugar. Many varieties of crackers and cookies are sold in small quantities, wrapped expertly in scraps of brown paper. Eggs are bought individually and also wrapped. While Don Berto had a large family in 1977 and could always rely on family labor, Don Justo had four small children and had to rely on paid employees to assist his wife in the store. When we returned to Yaxbe in 1989, Don Justo's now grown children all worked in the store, which is now expanded in both size and inventory. In 1998, his oldest son, Adam, had built his own store, attached to the *molino,* where he sold fresh produce and fruit.

In addition to these enterprises, several smaller establishments have proliferated in recent years. These smaller house-front stores have limited inventories and specialize in certain items, such as baked goods or fresh meat. In addition, several families cook and sell tacos, *salbutes,*or *panuchos* from their homes on certain evenings,

Figure 3.5 Doña Leticia keeping track of credit in her bakery, 1977

providing the village equivalent of fast food. When refrigeration arrived in the village, those women fortunate enough to own refrigerators began to sell soft drinks, popcicles, and ice from their homes.

Most Yaxbe women are very astute shoppers, and they know which stores have the best prices for all products. When sending their children out to purchase food, women tell them which stores to visit for each item, making shopping a very complicated and time-consuming endeavor. These lessons in shopping were also taught to the clueless anthropologist. My strategy for shopping in the village is to patronize all the stores, so that I don't show favoritism. This also allows me to talk to more villagers on an informal basis. One day, I purchased some fresh bread and pastries from one of the bakeries to take home as a special treat for the family with whom I was staying. Instead of expressing joy at seeing the variety of luscious turnovers, my hostess asked me where I had purchased them. When I told her, she scoffed and said that I had paid too much. I should have purchased them from Doña Leticia who sold really fresh pastries at a much lower price (see Figure 3.5).

In the village, three *cantinas* or bars are licensed to sell beer. Licenses are obtained from the president of the village for a fee, but only a limited number are issued. Those that do not have beer licenses sell one of the locally brewed beverages—***aguardiente*** made from henequen, or mezcal. These small *aguardiente* bars are open only in the evenings and weekends. Women do not enter the *cantinas*. They are the domain of men.

In 1976, the closest thing to a family bar was located near the park. Here Doña María ran a store and *lonchería* or restaurant. The lonchería was only open in the late afternoons and served whatever Doña María prepared that day, tamales wrapped in banana leaves, tacos, *panuchos,* or *salbutes.* She also sold soft drinks and assorted snacks. In the back of the store, Doña María's husband, Don Ignacio was the proprietor of one of the largest *cantinas* in the village. They also had something else that no one else owned in the village—a black and white television. Twice a week, in the evenings, Don Ignacio and Doña María opened their large living area to the public, and for a small fee, villagers could watch Capuchín, the famous Mexican comedian. On these nights, their house would be filled with children and adults. This was obviously a lucrative enterprise since the television room was strategically located between the *cantina* and the *lonchería/tienda.*

Today, many homes have television sets and Doña María no longer sells prepared foods. Her children, however, have followed her in business. One of her sons has a fruit stand attached to her store. Another son has a store of his own on the other side of the plaza, and a third son has built a "super" (supermarket) on the south end of the plaza and right next door to Don Justo.

HAMMOCK WEAVING Hammock weaving for the tourist market was one of the major sources of secondary income for women in the village in 1977. Although weaving was never a primary economic activity, it had a major impact on the village economy because of the volume of production. Hammock weaving is conducive to the daily routine of women whose "free" time is fragmented into short segments in between household and childcare duties. Consequently, it is work that a busy woman can perform in her spare time and in spurts, leaving it momentarily and easily picking up where she left off. In 1977, women worked their looms indoors during the day, but in the late afternoon or early evening, they brought them outdoors so they could visit with their neighbors and other villagers who passed by.

Young girls learned this trade early, first on small looms where they wove hammocks for their dolls or baby siblings and eventually graduated to the large frame. Mothers were very patient as their daughters learned. I remember one day visiting with a woman who was carefully taking apart a large portion of a hammock her daughter had been working on. As she unraveled the tangled threads, she was explaining to her daughter what she had done wrong. She turned to me and said, "This is very difficult for little girls because their fingers are so small."

The exploitative nature of this enterprise cannot be ignored. Alice Littlefield has written extensively (1978, 1979, and 1990) on the nature of such cottage industries and how they exploit not only women's labor but that of children as well. The women in Yaxbe and hundreds of other villages were (and some still are) subcontractors in the hammock enterprise, and thus are an integral part of this "putting-out" system. They obtained the skeins of fiber from women who represent the major distributors in Tixkokob, a town in a nearby *municipio.* In 1977, weavers were paid piecemeal for each hammock completed, earning between US$2–$3 per hammock depending on size. Most women claimed that it took them approximately two weeks to complete one hammock These figures were rough estimates, however, for the speed with which one completes a hammock depends on many factors, including number of small children underfoot, daily responsibilities, and motivation. Meanwhile, young men from Tixkokob carry their brightly colored bundles daily to the capitol or distant port towns and sell them for an amazing range of prices (US$20–$50), depending on hammock size and on the gullibility and language skills of the buyer. The same hammocks cost even more in the English-speaking tourist stores.

ETHNOGRAPHIC ESSAY
THE CIA AND OTHER CONSPIRACIES, 1976

On our arrival in Yaxbe, I was very concerned about my legitimacy in the village. I was armed with my letter of introduction from INAH, and I made the rounds of the village, showing it to the president and anyone else who was willing to look at it. One of the officials I was anxious about was the *socio delegado.* Because I was researching the decline of the henequen industry, it was important to me to understand how the *ejido* system was organized and how it functioned at the local level. To this end, I enlisted my husband as companion and we headed to the edge of the village where the *socio delegado* lived.

We followed the main road for several blocks and then cut down a narrow side street, stumbling over limestone outcroppings. We passed a row of wattle and daub houses, most of which were dilapidated, with sparsely thatched roofs, and disturbing gaps between the thin vertical branches that comprise the house walls. Following the directions of numerous curious children, we finally arrived at Don Julio's house. Although modest like those around it, the *socio's* house was freshly plastered, with a full clean thatch roof. We stood outside the crumbling limestone wall, waiting for someone to notice our presence.

After a few moments, a middle-aged woman, alerted by a young child, appeared from behind the house and motioned us in. After ascertaining that she was Don Julio's wife, we introduced ourselves to her while she nervously sent her children off in several directions. She urged us to sit in hammocks, which she quickly detached from S-hooks embedded in the plaster wall and stretched to complementary hooks on the opposite wall. Within a few minutes, one of the children arrived with two 16-ounce bottles of soda, which they offered us with a ceremonious air.

We sat awkwardly in the hammocks nursing our Cokes, while Doña Candelaria pulled up a wooden chair and sat between us, pulling her clean white *huipil* down over her knees. Her graying hair was tied back severely into a bun, but her dark face was timeless. After a few moments of awkward silence, she commenced with the line of questioning that we were now accustomed to—about our families, our jobs, and why we didn't have children. After several minutes, I asked if Don Julio were around, and, as if on cue, he entered from the rear of the house, led by one of the children sent out earlier. It was obvious that Don Julio had just returned from the henequen fields. He leaned his machete against the wall and when he noticed us, he brushed the dust from his shirt and baggy pants.

His discomfort was apparent immediately. I suddenly felt like an intruder and, handing my soft drink to my husband, I edged clumsily out of the hammock to present him with the letter of introduction I had clutched in my hand. He opened it quickly and, without reading it, folded it up again and handed it back. I asked if we could meet some day so that he could explain to me how the *ejido* system worked. He cautiously agreed to this request and offered to come to our house the following week.

My field notes for the next three months lament the numerous appointments made with Don Julio, none of which materialized. Either he did not come as planned or he arrived at our door intoxicated. My frustration led to resignation that I would never get that interview, more coveted in its elusiveness than it truly deserved.

It wasn't until the following summer, six months later, that I found out the reason for his avoidance. On that day, Reymundo and I were discussing the election for a new *socio* that had just taken place. I mentioned my past attempts to talk with Don Julio, and Reymundo disclosed a critical piece of information. He told me that the *socio* had avoided me because he thought I was from the government, presumably the CIA, and that I was sent to investigate him. Further, poor Don Julio had been afraid that I would report his *ejido* activities to certain authorities—which authorities, or even which activities, I could not comprehend. Shortly after this election, Don Julio enthusiastically met with me, spoke freely about the *ejido* and the problems of being a *socio*.

This event illustrates a basic misunderstanding that occurs at the intersection of two realities: that of the anthropologist and that (or those) of "the Other." In this case, my reality involved my desire to "get the facts" about an aspect of Yucatecan culture and my naïveté in misinterpreting Don Julio's reticence. Don Julio's reality consisted of his and others' perceptions of us (their "Other"), and of my motives for coming to live in their village.

There is no way that villagers could understand the academic world and why someone from the powerful United States would want to come and live in their town. Likewise, there is no way that I can ever understand what it is like to be a Yucatecan, coping with the daily realities of their lives. Political intrigue and corruption are facts of everyday life in the village, whether in the *ejido* groups or in the government. Everybody recognizes it, but nothing is done about it, because it is a system that people understand. Everyone knows that the *socio delegado* is padding the work list to receive more wages, or perhaps, as occurred in the declining years, deleting disloyal men from the official work list. Every *socio delegado* left office wealthier than when he entered. Some, though not the one in this case, built large and decorative houses, purchased cars, and obtained other symbols of wealth. But still, people rally behind these same men in the hope that they might be beneficiaries of the *socio's* largesse. These practices coalesce into a pattern of behavior that encourages suspicion of one's motives and actions, yet encourages personal loyalty (Chapter 5). Because men partake of these small conspiracies, they assume others are also involved. My curiosity could not be explained in any other way.

This incident taught me an important lesson. While the villagers cannot be expected to understand my motives, it is imperative that the anthropologist be aware of the complexity of village life and how his or her presence further complicates it. My inability to appreciate his reality caused him unnecessary anxiety and fear. The fact that I interpreted his discomfort as noncompliance and translated his lack of cooperation in terms of my own selfish ends reveals and highlights some of the more critical ethical issues in anthropology.

CONCLUSION

The above section has delineated the major occupations of Yaxbeños. Yet few families depend on only one source of income. It is instructive to those who describe a culture as agricultural, or homogeneous, to delineate the many and diverse ways in which people make a living. The preceding discussion of major economic activities is not exhaustive, for it does not include many activities that are sporadic or seasonal, such as selling wood, fruit, healing herbs, or lottery tickets. Nor does it include such services as barbering, baby-sitting, midwifery, curing, or officiating as the *h-men* at the annual ceremony for the rain god, *Chac;* or remuneration for certain part-time political offices such as village secretary or deputy sheriff. These hundreds of part-time occupations fill a vast mosaic of activities, social as well as economic that, taken as a whole, yield a society of remarkable complexity camouflaged by a superficial veneer of homogeneity and simplicity.

4/Village Life
Resilience and Change, 1976–1998

THE VILLAGE

In this chapter, I will provide an ethnographic summary of Yaxbe, with an emphasis on cultural patterns within their historic and modern contexts. The theme of this chapter is resilience and change. I have included various ethnographic essays that illustrate the village during my first visit and consequent visits.

Yaxbe at Conquest

At the time of the conquest, Yaxbe was a minor Maya settlement. According to one local historian, the current village center, where the Spanish replaced a ceremonial temple with a Catholic church, is not the true center of the ancient settlement. Rather, Don Max argues that the remnants of a temple located west of the current village center, is the true Mayan ceremonial center. Villagers refer to this temple, now a pile of rubble overrun by brush and the home to iguanas and snakes, simply as *"los cerros"* (the hills).

According to the *Crónica de Yaxbe*[1], the Spanish plotted out the Yaxbe *encomienda* in 1542. Conforming to the strategies outlined in Chapter 2, one of the members of the local ruling Maya family, Ah Macan Pech, was appointed *cacique* or local administrator, thus allowing his family to reinforce it's own power, both as indigenous leaders and as power brokers between the Maya and their conquerors.

[1]The *Crónica de Yaxbe* (a pseudonym) relates the story of Yaxbe as compiled and reported by Ah Macan Pech, the first *cacique* of the municipality. It was written in segments between 1542 and 1555.

Yaxbe Today

Today, Yaxbe is the political center of the *municipio* of the same name. It consists of the village and seven henequen *haciendas,* only one of which was in operation and had a permanent resident population in 1976. The remaining *haciendas* were either abandoned or incorporated into the Yaxbe *ejido.* Most of the population of the *municipio* (estimated at 3,500 in 1995) resides in the village.

Yaxbe is laid out in a grid pattern characteristic of Spanish cities throughout Mexico. The highway divides the village in half, entering from the south and then making a right turn at the main intersection of the village, continuing northeast toward the adjoining *municipio* (see Figure 4.1). The road that extends from the highway to the north ends at the *Hacienda* Santiago. The westward extension of the highway extends past *los cerros* and the cemetery, continuing to other villages and towns. This intersection divides the village into four quadrants that are further divided into blocks. Many of the village streets, which are no more than two tracks, follow the ancient **sacbeob,** the raised stone roads built by the Maya to link ceremonial centers.

A tall stone building with stucco façade and a tile roof dominates the southwest corner of the main intersection and extends one entire block. This building was originally the residence of Spain's representative in Yaxbe. On the northeast corner of the main intersection is the section known as the plaza. Here a jagged limestone field accommodates the local soccer and baseball teams. Adjacent to the plaza is the Catholic church, built for defense as much as worship. In 1976, piles of limestone rubble were all that remained of the Maya temple that once stood on this location. By 1995, the rubble had been used to build a stone wall around the church.

The central park is located across from the church, in the northwest quadrant. North of the park is a courtyard with basketball hoops at either end, which is used as an open auditorium for graduations, national holiday "marches," and special performances, including the dances during *fiesta.* Just beyond the courtyard is the government building (**palacio**), which houses the president's office, administrative offices, police, and jail. A covered verandah and tiled dance floor flank the *palacio.* Here the traditional dances of the *fiesta* are held. A small covered stage at one end is used for special events, speeches, and performances. Behind the *palacio* is a huge open area used for weddings and which serves as the government-sponsored bar during *fiesta.* On the south edge of the park is a small playground and next to it is the abandoned medical clinic that became our home.

The Solár

As we have already learned, households in a Maya community are easily distinguished by the limestone fences that enclose the area where related families reside (*soláres*). The characteristic *solár* contains several houses that are generally located toward the front, near the road. Within the *solár,* new homes are built as families grow and as traditional houses fall into disrepair. Small bathing shanties, raised wash tubs, clotheslines, and pigpens complete the structural landscape. Each *solár* has its own well, and today, most *soláres* also have potable water piped from the deep well in the village center. This valued water is used only for cooking and drinking.

All families grow small amounts of vegetables, herbs, and fruit within the *solár.* Because of the rugged terrain, vegetables such as peppers and tomatoes grow in small patches of dirt, and herbs are planted in old paint cans. Assorted fruit trees such

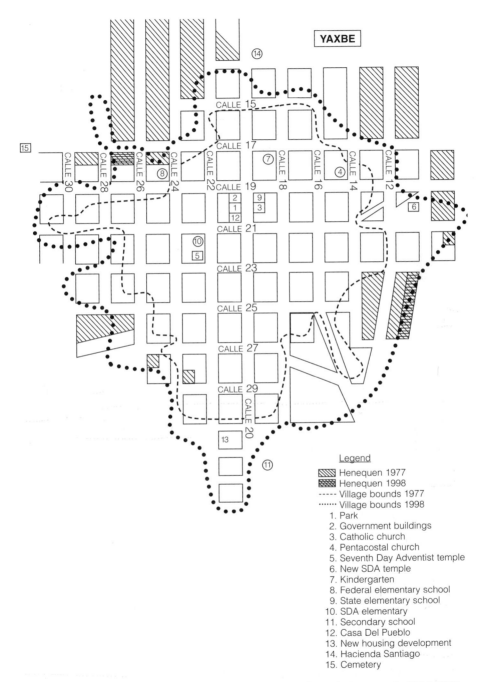

Figure 4.1 Map of Yaxbe illustrating major landmarks and population growth, 1976–2001. Adaptation by Valerie Hover from original map by Juan Cervantes. Adapted with permission.

as orange, grapefruit, banana, papaya, and guava adorn the *soláres* and provide a wide variety of supplemental foods. Most *soláres* also contain a variety of domesticated animals that serve as sources of supplemental food as well as sources of family income. The most common animals are chickens and turkeys, although some families will have pigs or goats. The farthest area from the house is used for garbage disposal and for sanitary purposes. In 1976, few families had outhouses and only one had indoor plumbing. By the 1990s most new houses had indoor plumbing.

In 1976, most of the houses in the village were oval-shaped, windowless, and constructed of wattle and daub and thatch, as already described. Others were rectangular and constructed of stone with cardboard or laminated tin roofs. Regardless of the shape, most traditional houses had shared features: they had only one room, used for living and sleeping, and two doors aligned front and back to allow for maximum air and light flow.

Most traditional houses were sparsely furnished. Hammocks were, and still are, the dominant feature in any house. Used for sleeping and resting, hammocks are expertly knotted when not in use and hung on hooks that line both of the long walls. One or two wooden wardrobes hold all of the family's clothes and possessions. Religious paraphernalia, rosaries, and colorful pictures of Jesus and the Virgin of Guadelupe adorn the walls and the wardrobe mirrors of Catholic households. More affluent families have several chairs for company, a radio, and, more currently, a television set.

Since traditionally women cooked over a fire, the kitchen was located outside the house under a lean-to or a larger wood and thatch structure that was open on at least one side for ventilation, and was usually attached to the oldest house in the *solár.*These outdoor kitchens are fascinating structures. Cooking pots, water gourds, wire egg baskets, and liquor bottles filled with oil and other cooking liquids hang by binder twine from the stick walls or corner posts. Various herb pots lay helter-skelter around the kitchen area or protrude from the thatch of the kitchen roof, and chickens peck for scraps around the cooking pit. The only furnishings in these kitchens include a small low wooden work table and one or two three-legged stools (*kanche*) on which women sit while patting and heating tortillas over the low flames of the cooking fire.

Gradually, the traditional houses have been replaced with modern structures of cement block coated with crushed stone or stucco, as we have already seen. Initially, these modern houses were the second home in a *solár,* built directly behind the traditional house. Most of these early cement-block houses were simple in design and function following the pattern of the traditional. However, as villagers acquired more modern tastes and as the skills of the local craftsmen improved, the houses also evolved into multiroom structures with a bedroom for the parents, indoor kitchens, and bathrooms.

This transformation of the Yucatecan house was accelerated by several factors. The first was Hurricane Gilbert, which raged across the peninsula in 1988. Not only did the horrendous winds and rain destroy many of the traditional homes, villagers withstood many long-term consequences: contaminated wells, loss of electricity, and lack of food and water. These conditions lasted for months with little assistance from the state or federal government. The second factor that resulted in the escalation of new house construction was the liquidation or severance pay received by factory workers as a result of the economic downturn. Many men used their severance pay to build new houses for their families, recommitting themselves to the village. As men and their families found new jobs these houses were filled with desired consumer goods: upholstered furniture, stoves and refrigerators, televisions, and VCRs. Today several families have microwaves, computers, and hot water heaters.

Modern house exteriors reflect a changing value system as well: louvered windows, decorative trim, and even tiled patios. In more affluent homes, the short limestone fences have been replaced by tall cement walls with steel gates that allow the entrance of the most extravagant symbol of wealth—the automobile. Now, a visitor can no longer peer over the fence to see the woman of the house working in her yard. The new fences instill a sense of isolation, privacy, and exclusion.

What has not changed, however, is the commitment to extended families within the *solár*. Families still prefer to build new houses within a *solár* if space permits. However, as families expand and grow it is increasingly difficult to accommodate all family members, and some children are forced to purchase a plot at the outskirts of the village, initiating a new core family. I am encouraged by this continued commitment to the village, as it symbolizes the persistence of a vibrant community where families will continue to thrive for many years.

THE PEOPLE

Ethnic and Social Distinctions in Yaxbe

Although Yaxbeños consider themselves a unified village with shared values, observation indicates various factors that mark differences among villagers. This section examines several ethnic and cultural markers that distinguish Yaxbeños.

RACE AND ETHNICITY   Studies in Latin America normally include a section depicting the racial differences between the indigenous "Indian" and the descendants of the Spanish conquerors. Anthropologists are generally very uncomfortable with the distinction of "races," as these categories are largely arbitrary and in many cases associated with social and political implications. Five hundred years of intermarriage in the Yucatán has produced a population very diverse in its physical characteristics. This blended population is commonly referred to in the literature as ***mestizo.***

That race is primarily a cultural concept is evident in Mexico generally and in Yucatán in particular, where the term *mestizo* is used differently, describing men and women who wear the indigenous clothing, regardless of their physical characteristics. Those who wear Western dress are ***catrín,*** even if they have strong Mayan physical features. Children in Yaxbe are socialized to be *catrín,* not *mestizo.* Only infant girls are ever dressed in a *huipil,* and this is often only for the *hetzmek* ceremony (this chapter). Today, only elderly villagers wear the *traje* or *huipil.* The stylized version of this clothing is reserved for the ***jarana*** where it has been appropriated as a symbol of the traditional Mayan culture.

LANGUAGE   A second cultural marker is language. In Yaxbe, those who speak Maya as their primary language are designated *mestizo,* especially if they also wear traditional clothing. In 1976, a few elderly villagers spoke only Maya. Most of the elderly could also speak Spanish, though many of these were not fluent. I found that most people over age 30, in 1976, were bilingual Spanish and Maya speakers. Young adults could speak rudimentary Maya, and those in their teens and younger could understand Maya spoken between their parents and grandparents, but could not speak it well themselves. In fact, some of the teen boys told me they were ashamed because in my short stay in the village I could speak and understand Maya better than they could. Today, elderly villagers and their middle-aged children are still bilingual speakers. Unfortunately, however, few children speak Maya. Even parents who speak Maya do not teach it to their children. That Maya is nearly lost is clear in several conversations that I had with villagers in 2002, where people identified other villages as towns "where they speak Maya."

SURNAME   A third marker of ethnicity is surname. Because of Yaxbe's role as a colonial political center, there were various Spanish or Creole government administrators and *hacienda* owners living in the village and thus today, there are both Spanish and Mayan surnames in the village. However, there is no nonlocal ruling or merchant class. As a result, the Spanish surnames have dissipated among the population giving no clues as to wealth, power, or even physical characteristics.

RELIGIOUS DIVERSITY   The complex relationship between traditional Mayan religion, Catholicism, and Protestantism will be discussed at length in Chapters 6 and 7. Here, it is important to distinguish briefly between these religions as they relate to the current discussion of village life and social organization. Religion being an integral part of every society, the intrusion of new beliefs will have an impact on traditional values and everyday ritual and social interaction.

Because Catholicism has been the dominant religion in Mexico since the 16th century, it has become entrenched in the daily lives of all Mexicans. Even though Maya rituals are still practiced in many villages, Catholicism permeates all aspects of life throughout Mexico. The cathedral dominates the central area of every village and daily activities are dictated by the Catholic calendar, from saint days to the annual *fiesta* when every Mexican village celebrates its patron saint.

Since the Seventh Day Adventists arrived in Yaxbe in the 1950s, their beliefs have pervaded the lives of many villagers and have affected all social institutions, as will be seen in Chapter 7. The Adventists (also abbreviated as SDA in this book) demand individual reform with the promise of salvation. They deny the Catholic liturgy and scorn those social events that revolve around the Catholic calendar. These strictures force Adventists to alter forever their relationship with the traditions that have evolved in Mexico for 500 years.

SOCIAL CLASS   Social class is discussed in Chapters 3 and 8. For this chapter, I will outline briefly the historic roots of local social distinctions. In the colonial period, social class could be described in broad terms as a two-tiered system with the Spanish aristocracy located firmly at the top echelons of the social and economic system. After independence, the elite consisted primarily of the descendants of the Spanish aristocracy with the *mestizos* (traditional usage) finding their place among the newly forming working and middle classes. Since the Revolution, the focus of wealth has shifted from the foreign-born aristocracy to local families who were well-situated to acquire land under the new land-tenure systems or fill niches in the local economy as merchants, transporters, or government officials. In all of these constructs, the indigenous populations continued to be securely entrenched in the lower class of landless laborers. While this institutionalized system still persists, there is more diversity in villages such as Yaxbe. We have already seen that today Spanish surnames and Spanish roots are no longer markers of ethnicity. Nor are they markers of social class. In 1976, the wealthiest families had names such as Tun, Chan, Uc, and Pech, not Morales, Gonzales, or Gomez.

Despite the fact that wealthy families could be identified by certain possessions, there still existed an ideology of egalitarianism. Affluent families and individuals were expected to share with others, participate in *compadrazgo* (this chapter), and contribute generously to village celebrations and religious events. Today, wealthier families are those who have diversified into new economic strategies or who have gained marketable skills or professions. While the expectation of generosity is still important, values have shifted gradually toward personal accumulation of goods within the family and more evidence of conspicuous consumption. Nevertheless, the family is still the most important concern of all villagers. Those who neglect family members—who fail to share with or care for parents, siblings, or children—are ostracized and are the target of intense village gossip. Following is a discussion of village kinship and family.

Kinship and Residence

The kinship system of the pre-conquest Maya was a ranked, corporate, **patrilineal, patrilocal** system that was strictly **exogamous**. Any two individuals of the same surname, regardless of the distance of their relationship, were forbidden to marry. Land and most property passed from father to son. The Maya system, however, had elements of **double descent** in that women were able to hold land and property and passed these possessions on to their daughters. Both men and women gained status from the rank of their mother's and father's lineage group and each person carried the name of their father and their mother (Roys 1972 [1943]: 36; Henderson 1981: 62–63).

The Spanish conquerors imposed their own system on the Maya, enforcing **bilateral** kinship, early marriages, and the nuclear family. These imposed marriage patterns allowed the Spanish to extract more tribute from the Indians who paid their head tax based on the household head (Kintz 1990: 51). Ultimately, bilateral kinship did not conflict markedly with the Mayan double-descent structure, and the dual surname persists today with each person carrying both her father's and mother's patronymic, with the father's name first, reinforcing the importance of the father's line in both cultures. For example, the daughter of Juan Chan Pech and Marta Tun Ake would be Clara Chan Tun, carrying forward her father's paternal name and her mother's paternal line. Women do not take the name of their husbands on marriage.

According to Henderson (1981: 63), a newly married couple in pre-conquest Yucatán moved into the home of the wife's family where the new husband performed an extended period of **bride service** for his in-laws. After approximately six years, the couple moved to the husband's extended family household. Today, the ideal residence pattern is for newlywed couples to live in nuclear family units within the husband's household in a modified patrilocal pattern. Post-marital residence is flexible, however. Couples base their decisions on pragmatic factors: the size of each *solár,* the relative wealth of the families, the need within each household for male labor, the number of nuclear families already living in each *solár,* and such personal factors as the acceptance of the new spouse and the personalities of the older members of the household (see Figure 4.2).

Figure 4.2 This large extended family includes four brothers, their wives, and children, 1992

Compadrazgo: Fictive Kinship and Social Bonds

Compadrazgo (co-parenthood), or god-parenthood, came to the New World as part of the Catholic religious complex that links families to the Church. As practiced, parents chose another person or couple to sponsor their child for baptism. That person or couple accepted a certain responsibility toward the future well-being and religious training of the child. The Maya, however, molded the Catholic concept of god-parenthood to meet their own needs and to reinforce their cultural values. Today *compadrazgo* links villagers to one another through a complex network of mutual assistance and social support. It also represents a system of sponsorship for children as they progress through the various life stages, from baptism to marriage (see Kintz 1990: 53–54 and re Cruz 1996: 183–184 for discussions on *compadrazgo* in the Yucatán).

Compadrazgo functions as a form of fictive kinship that crosscuts family ties. While the Spanish institution of god-parenthood emphasized the relationship between the godparent and the godchild, Mexican *compadrazgo* emphasizes the relationship between the two sets of parents. Initially, the obligation of the *compadre*[2] is financial in nature, purchasing baptismal clothing or sponsoring a First Communion. The initial ritual establishes an enduring relationship between the **padrino** or **madrina** (godfather or godmother) and the **ahijado/a** (godchild) as well

---

[2]*Compadre* refers to the "co-father." *Comadre* is the "co-mother." *Compadre* is also the generic form of the word, meaning co-parent.

as between the two new sets of *compadres*. The parents of the child and the god-parents continue to call each other "*compadre*" and their association lasts forever. *Compadres* can ask each other for favors or financial assistance, and the relationship is reinforced by future rituals and ceremonies. The above networks are horizontal in nature, linking families and villagers of similar economic and social standing.

Villagers also seek sponsors who have higher economic or social status. Anthropologists refer to this relationship as "vertical *compadrazgo*." While most vil-lagers still refer to these unequal sponsors as "*compadres*," wealthier or more pres-tigious *compadres* (for example, doctors or employers) are referred to as "*patrón(a)*." When it occurs within a village, vertical *compadrazgo* serves as a **lev-eling mechanism,** a means by which those who are affluent contribute more to the community, expending their wealth, and gaining prestige in return. Successful rela-tives or wealthy villagers, visiting doctors or teachers are more often asked to be *compadres* for more expensive ceremonies such as *quinceñeras* and weddings. Villagers who repeatedly turn down such requests risk criticism and a loss of respect in the community.

As more villagers work outside the village and hope to gain some leverage for their own children in higher education or the job market, they initiate asymmetrical relationships with nonvillagers. In 1977, one woman had five *compadres,* all of whom were professionals in Mérida. Although she is active in the village, her sights were set, at least for her children, to the outside world and what it could offer, not only them, but herself as well. Thus, the practice that cements the community in multistranded relationships, increasingly forms new networks and connections that extend beyond the village and may ultimately act as a lifeline out of the village for future generations.

The economic importance of sponsors has grown in recent years as ceremonies have become more extravagant and more expensive. In 1976–1977, we attended sev-eral weddings. They were informal affairs in which the bride wore a church dress and the groom wore his best clothes and purchased perhaps his first pair of leather shoes. The reception was held in the *solár* of the groom and consisted of beer, sandwiches, and perhaps a phonograph player for dance music. Thus, I was very surprised when I attended two weddings in 1992 in which the bride wore a full-length white dress and the groom a suit. The events included bridesmaids and groomsmen, magnificent receptions with many guests, live music, extravagant food, a wedding cake, and drinks (nonalcoholic at the Adventist wedding). Conspicuous displays of wedding gifts, wrapped in clear plastic wrap reveal a new level of materialism. Since the cost of these weddings was obviously beyond the capabilities of all but the wealthiest families, I was not surprised to discover that these extravagant affairs were subsi-dized by numerous relatives, *compadres,* and *patróns* of the groom who contributed such items as the cake, band, clothing, or alcohol. The cost of the wedding was thus widely dispersed, reducing the economic burden for the groom's family, but conse-quently, incurring future obligations.

CULTURE AND THE INDIVIDUAL: THE LIFE CYCLE

In this section, we will follow the life stages a typical Yaxbeño or Yaxbeña experi-ences from birth to death, investigating child-rearing practices, socialization, and important rituals that mark one's passage through life. We will also see how both change and resilience are evidenced in the daily lives of villagers.

Birth

In 1976–1977, 87 babies were born to Yaxbeñas. Most of these were delivered by Doña Justa, the village midwife for 25 years. Doña Justa's services, for which she charged 80 pesos (US$5), included prenatal care, massage, and the actual delivery.[3] Although she was trained as a midwife and administered injections, Doña Justa always insisted that "Yo no soy médica" (I am not a doctor). She made it clear to me that she did not want to compete with the hospital located in a nearby village, and whenever she anticipated a difficult delivery or medical complications, she advised her patient to go there. By 2002, Doña Justa had passed away, and all women delivered their babies in one of the local hospitals.

A child's life is marked by a series of transitions that are celebrated by religious rituals. These rites of passage give significance to these crucial stages and are celebrated within a close-knit group of kin and *compadres.* When a child is old enough to be carried on the hip, at 3 or 4 months of age, a Mayan ceremony, the *hetzmek* is performed. Here, in the presence of special *compadres,* the child is introduced to those gender specific items with which they will be identified for the rest of their lives, the boys to henequen fiber and a machete, the girls to a *mano* and *metate* (corn grinding implements). The *hetzmek* is performed primarily by more traditional families, and is an excellent example of **syncretism** as described in Chapter 6.

The formal baptism for an infant may take place before or after the *hetzmek.* Baptism requires a *compadre* who is responsible for the child's clothing and for a family celebration held after the event. The Adventists believe that infants do not understand religion and that children should not be baptized until they are older, at age 11 or 12. Instead, because Adventist parents fear that their infants might not live until their "true" baptism, the temple has devised a ceremony in which the infant is "introduced" into the religion. This is an informal ceremony, but it is done with water in much the same way as a traditional baptism and is seen as a protection for the infant until his or her true baptism into the Adventist temple.

Early Childhood

The childhood years are carefree for the majority of young Yaxbeños (see Figure 4.3). Children are free to roam the village, visiting relatives and running errands. Parents are indulgent with their children, not in material ways, for there are few toys or sources of entertainment in the village, but in their activities and pranks. Children bubble with enthusiasm and have no inhibitions. The girls are as mischievous as the boys, participating with boys in all games, including "street soccer."

As they get older, young children are given more responsibilities, particularly the girls who are expected to help their mothers care for smaller children and run errands. Young girls also learn early how to weave hammocks on the loom, hand wash clothes, and (until recently) make tortillas. Boys, at around 9 years old, will begin to accompany their fathers to the henequen fields or *milpa* in the summer when they are not attending school. Because henequen labor is dangerous, young boys do not cut or weed, but they may help by counting or tying bundles. In the *milpa,* they may be of more assistance, helping to plant or harvest corn and other vegetables.

---

[3]For an excellent description of a Yucatecan midwife, see Brigitte Jordan (1993).

Figure 4.3 Carlos,
the son of Pedro and Dora,
at Dzibichaltún, 1998

Adolescence

When girls and boys reach age 10, the gap between male and female role expectations begins to widen. Adolescence signals their passage into adult responsibilities. Gradually, young people learn new rules of behavior, and their actions are more carefully monitored by adults. While this is true primarily for teenage girls, teen boys are also expected to be more responsible and to contribute more to the family labor pool. Today, as more young adults attend secondary, and even high school together, this stage of gender separation is disappearing. Girls are less shy around boys, and it is increasingly more difficult for parents to supervise their children, as we will see later.

In Mexico, several important rituals mark the passage from childhood to adulthood. For Catholics, the first ritual is First Communion. For the Adventists, it is baptism. The second ritual, performed by Catholic and Protestant alike is the *quinceñera*, which marks the passage of young girls into womanhood. In the past, this was a simple ceremony, consisting of a special Mass in the Catholic church or a special service in the temple, followed by a party at the family home. Today, however, the *quinceñera,* like the weddings described in the earlier section, has become a major ceremony with expensive dresses and extravagant parties. Our friends, in planning their daughter's *quinceñera,* realized that her birthday was on the day before a national election when no alcohol can be sold or consumed. Rather than forego the alcohol, they changed the date of the party.

Traditionally, the *quinceñera* marked a young woman's eligibility for marriage. While women are marrying later today, the ceremony still celebrates her entry into adulthood. This is a very delicate stage for young women, not yet married, but interested in finding a husband. The path to marriage contains numerous land mines, and a young woman's reputation can be endangered very easily. While young men have more freedom of movement and are expected to be more aggressive in their pursuit of women, the women themselves have to protect themselves from the appearance of unacceptable behavior. Perhaps the most effective way of illustrating the expected behavior of young women is to look at several stories that defined deviance in 1976.

CARLA   In 1976, Carla was a beautiful 18 year old who had left the village a year or so before our arrival. She was living in Mexico City where she worked as a nanny, a position she obtained through a *comadre.* I was anxious to meet Carla because we were close to her family—her sisters being part of our entourage of children and her mother being one of our frequent visitors. One day, Carla's sisters ran to our house screaming in excitement that Carla had returned home. Indeed she had. She found a job at the corner store and settled back into village life. In one of our many conversations, she told me that she was unhappy in Mexico City and planned to stay in the village.

I asked Carla about the differences in courtship between the village and the city. She told me that a girl's life is difficult in the village because girls cannot talk freely to boys, yet the boys try to engage them in forbidden conversation. In the village, when a girl and boy start to *pasear* (walk together) in the park and the boy starts to visit her at her home, the relationship is considered serious. Once a couple becomes labeled as ***novios*** (girlfriend/boyfriend), there is an expectation of marriage. Girls, depending on how they respond to the advances of the boys, can gain a reputation of either being unfriendly if they rebuke the advances, or bad (*mala*), if they encourage them. In Mexico City, Carla argued, a girl can be friends with boys without the whole village talking or caring about it.

Carla's reputation in Yaxbe was ambiguous. The young men with whom I spoke, including one whom Carla's mother identified as her *novio,* indicated that she had an "*asi asi*" (not bad, but not real good either) reputation before she left the village. They told me that she had "walked with" several boys and that she would talk to boys while she was "walking with" another. In fact, Carla continued this behavior on her return. During her stay, she was seen with several of the young men and at one point, there were obvious conflicts among those who wished to court her.

Although Carla told me that she had returned to the village to stay, she did not. She left again after three months, returning to her previous employer. Before leaving she confided in me that the boys in the village were too immature . . . that she preferred boys in the city who were sophisticated and smart. Carla represents women caught between two cultures, in this case the urban and the rural culture. She realized that she would not be able to return to the village life. She was correct. Her values and her expectations had been transformed and had become incompatible with those of Yaxbe. People had begun to gossip about her behavior, and she became increasingly distressed by the attentions given her by the young men and the villagers. Her return to Mexico City provided her with an escape from the marginalization she would have suffered in the village. Today, Carla lives in Mexico City with her husband and three children (see Returning to Yaxbe, Chapter 1).

MARTA   In 1976, Marta was the only child of a staunch Catholic family who was so protected by her mother that she was not allowed to attend the evening English classes that LaVail and I conducted in the *palacio*. My most vivid memory of Marta, however, is not of a submissive village girl, but as a budding feminist publicly challenging the status quo. The scene was a small village festival sponsored by one of the parents' groups to raise money for a school project. Small metal tables and chairs were scattered around the park and in front of our house. From my vantage point, I watched in awe and disbelief as Marta and a girlfriend sat at a table, nonchalantly drinking beer. As I watched with a small group of village women, the scene became even more bizarre. Two young men joined them at the table and the four young people chatted and laughed. It was a scene that would not have raised an eyebrow in my hometown, but I had never seen this type of intimate, male-female interaction since my arrival. My attention, however, was not totally focused on the young people; I was also observing the growing congregation of older women who were watching this scene in disbelief and horror. The women whispered among themselves in agitation for several minutes and finally one of them, Doña Juana, approached the table and said some words to the group at which point, the boys and Marta's girlfriend quickly departed.

To my surprise, Marta stood and spoke angrily to Doña Juana. I could not hear her words, but the look on her face was one of defiance, not shame or embarrassment. When Marta left the scene, the women stared after her in stunned silence. After a few moments, they all began speaking at once, berating her behavior, and announcing how Marta had no shame and how she had brought dishonor to her poor mother (see Figure 4.4).

The circumstance that most marginalizes a young woman, however, is unplanned pregnancy. Although girls are supervised, young couples manage to sneak away and the result (lacking knowledge about birth control) is often pregnancy. The burden of illegitimacy is placed firmly on the shoulders of the woman. The most common outcome is immediate marriage, and both families pressure the young couple to marry. A young pregnant woman has few options if the man refuses to marry her. She can choose to remain with her family and have the child or leave the village temporarily. In either case, her future prospects for marriage are threatened (see On Becoming a *Compadre,* this chapter).

Today, a number of women in the village are raising children without husbands. One of the local teachers was unmarried and pregnant at the time of my 1998 research. Having no plans to marry, I asked her if she would be allowed to continue teaching when her baby is born. She answered sharply that the school did not discriminate against her because she was single and that the principal was not concerned with her predicament. "He is only interested that I do a good job."

Figure 4.4 Marta, with two
of her children, 1992

Marriage

The preferred sequence, of course, is marriage after courtship, although there is much variation in how this occurs. One option is common law marriage. This option is not recognized legally and is discouraged by both the Catholic and Protestant churches. A second option, inexpensive but legally recognized, is a civil ceremony, performed by the civil justice. Those entering second or third unions employ one of these options. Most young couples, however, opt for a more formal, church wedding with a reception afterwards.

Carla's story outlines the courtship patterns that were accepted in 1976. These patterns still exist in the ideal, though the gradual breakdown of gender-based segregation among young people opens up many more opportunities for teens to interact informally. Despite this, a young couple today will still attempt to be very circumspect in their mutual affection. When their feelings deepen, the young man will begin to visit her house in the evening and they will start to "walk together." These seemingly innocent behaviors mark an important stage in their relationship and people will begin to see them as *novios*. At some point, the young man will talk to the girl's father and the marriage plans will commence.

The responsibility for the wedding costs lies with the groom's family. It is his family that arranges for the many *compadres* and sponsors who help to defray the many costs of the wedding. A short story illustrates, not only the differences in American and Mexican customs, but how American customs can be viewed by others. When I was asking an acquaintance about how the groom's father chooses sponsors and *compadres,* he looked confused and asked me quizzically, "How do you pay for weddings in the United States?" When I told him that it was our custom that the bride's family pays for the wedding and reception, he looked at me in disbelief. "Do you mean that a woman has to pay for her own wedding?" As an anthropologist, I regularly ask others to explain their rituals and their feelings, but, in this instance, I was at a loss to explain my own culture to my friend. The shock exhibited in his answer forced me to analyze a custom that I had not questioned before. To this day, whenever I return to the village, my friend asks me again, as if he heard it wrong or I didn't understand the question: "Are you sure that the bride's family pays? Nobody can believe that it is true!"

Most young people marry someone from the village. In 1977, nearly 70% of the marriages united two Yaxbeños. Village **endogamy,** marrying someone from the same village, is one of the characteristics of peasant communities. Even though many villagers have left to work and live elsewhere, the pattern still exists. Of 73 marriages that occurred between 1992 and 1998 (of which I have data), 44, or 60%, were between two villagers. Those villagers who married outsiders were usually migrants living temporarily in other areas, and it is likely that these people will be lost to the village.

Because postmarital residence is usually patrilocal, the new wife comes under the influence of her husband and his parents. The birth of her first child establishes her within the household, and when she and her husband move into their own house, her confidence grows. Over time, she gains considerable influence over her children and she often becomes an important asset to her aging in-laws.

The husband is expected to treat his wife well. Wife abuse is not condoned, but it does occur. When it does, it is often rationalized as the result of drinking, which makes a man "crazy" and unable to control himself. Men who continually beat their wives are often sanctioned by the president and may be divorced or abandoned by the wife. Drinking is associated with numerous problems within the community and family, such as fighting and crime. However, the most serious consequence of drinking is economic. Women complain that their husbands spend their wages at the bar. Because of this, many women do the budgeting for the family and give their husbands spending money. Otherwise, they say, "How are we to eat?" Surprisingly, most men do not complain about this practice, admitting that women are more rational and sensible about money.

Divorce is more common today than it was in the past, but it is still an unusual occurrence in the village. Since divorce is technically prohibited by the Catholic Church and discouraged by the Protestants, it usually is a rather informal procedure, with one partner simply leaving. The reasons for separation or divorce differ for men and women. Men will leave (or send their wife away) primarily so that they can move in with another woman or because of domestic disagreements that cannot be resolved. While irreconcilable differences are also a major cause of divorce for women, the latter most often leave their husbands because of drinking or abuse. The existence of strong family ties and the proximity of families within the village allow women the opportunity to leave an abusive or alcoholic husband and have a safe haven to which she can return. In the rarer cases where the husband moves in with the wife's family, the woman has even a stronger leverage, both to influence her husband's behavior and to evict him should his behavior become unacceptable.

The ideal in Yaxbe is for all villagers to marry. There is strong mutual dependence between males and females following a strict gender-based division of labor. Men and women gain respectability through marriage and parenthood, not through careers. Childlessness is pitied. Men who do not marry are often believed to be homosexual. There are homosexual men in the village, though I am aware of only one woman who is rumored to be a lesbian. Homosexual men (and otherwise unmarried men) remain within their natal home, contributing to the family income. No bachelors live alone, nor do homosexuals cohabit in the village.

Old Age

Yaxbeños enjoy a long and healthy life. There are many people in their 70s and 80s. Even today, there are several men and women who were alive during the Cárdenas reforms in the Yucatán who remember the days of "slavery." The most common cause of death for the elderly is heart failure, though some have died of tuberculosis. There are no nursing homes, and no self-respecting family would confine their elderly to a home. When an elderly person is debilitated by senility or illness, he or she is cared for within the family unit. Villagers grow old and die in their own homes with their family around them.

Death

Generally Yaxbeños are very stoic about death. They do not readily show emotion, instead attempting to show a strong defiant façade, at funerals and in discussing the dead. When someone dies, there is no formal church service. Rather, the body is displayed in the home of the deceased. All burials take place in the tiny village cemetery, regardless of religion. Dirt mounds edged with limestone pebbles mark each new grave. At the head is a wooden cross, etched with the person's name and the date of his birth and death. Sometimes the family will plant a stalk of corn or place a votive candle at the gravesite. There are also crypts along the tall walls surrounding the cemetery. These small structures are purchased and used by extended families. In small windowed enclosures, families place small trinkets and mementos of deceased family members as well as candles and religious paraphernalia if the deceased was Catholic (see Figure 4.5).

VILLAGE COHESION

Volunteer Associations

Village cohesion is maintained in many ways: kinship, *compadrazgo,* shared values, and ritual. These mechanisms, however, are often obligatory and strictly regulated. A civil society also requires networks that crosscut kinship ties. Voluntary associations are one example of how these social and economic networks are formed. In this section, I will outline several types of voluntary associations that link villagers across familial and social boundaries.

SCHOOL ASSOCIATIONS   Each of the three elementary schools and the secondary school has a parents committee, called the *Sociedad de Padres de Familias.* The committees act as the fundraising arm of each local school and, to a lesser extent, as a PTA. While men are usually the officers of each group, the women are very active in the fundraising activities. The most popular fundraising event is the **kermesse,** a village-wide bazaar featuring food, children's games, and local music. The *kermesse*

Figure 4.5 Cemetery, Yaxbe

is organized and run largely by the women and it always coincides with another social event that will bring outsiders to Yaxbe, such as an inter-village baseball game or a dance. A Commission of the Three Schools oversees and coordinates the activities of the three elementary schools, coordinating events and thus eliminating the possibility of competing fundraising activities or activities that conflict with other religious or civil events.

COMMUNITY SERVICE   During my first visit, several state-sponsored programs sent representatives to Yaxbe to promote and organize state-sponsored programs. Such programs as the **PACR** and **DIF** (Chapters 5 and 9) were initiated over the years with varying success. The most successful groups, however, are those that are formed informally, for short-term projects such as cleaning the park or the plaza, and painting the Catholic church for *fiesta*. The same type of community effort resulted in the building of the Adventist temple and school.

Mutual Assistance

Another way in which village ties remain strong is through mutual assistance and the idea of "civil society." The history of the Maya is one in which people had to provide for themselves and their families within a context of economic and political oppression. While the *hacendados* and factory owners may provide loans and other forms of patronage, people have learned to be self-reliant in their individual and family needs, but mutually dependent in their societal needs. People need to be able to rely on others in times of special need. My husband and I learned of two examples of mutual assistance that we would not have discovered if two events had not occurred—one humorous, one tragic.

ETHNOGRAPHIC ESSAY
THE FUNERAL

Journal March 3, 1998

Don Sevino Aguilar Luna died at 4:00 this morning. I had missed the funeral of his brother, our *compadre* Don Juan (see Becoming a *Compadre*), and I wanted to attend this wake to say good-bye to both men who had been a part of our earlier years in the village. Mourners visited his house all day, but I did not arrive until this afternoon. Doña Cristina and I walked the four blocks to his house. Children played in the road in front of the house, and neighbors worked in their *soláres*. The normal noises of daily life were muted today as neighbors greeted us, and family members hastened out of the house to lead us in. Wooden folding chairs were set up along three walls of the rectangular house. Along the fourth wall sat a wooden table covered with a white cloth. The handmade wooden coffin rested on the table, its lid leaning against the wall. Don Sevino was covered with a white cloth. Small votive candles lined the table in front of his casket, and flowers, some in vases and others in mayonnaise jars, had been placed on the floor in front of the table.

Doña Cristina and I were led to chairs along the wall. We were greeted by Don Jorge and Doña Gloria, Don Sevino's son and sister. Jorge had shed his everyday peasant slacks and shirt and wore dark slacks and a white *guayabera*. He still wore his traditional sandals, but he had polished them carefully. Doña Gloria wore a colorful full-waisted dress and black plastic shoes. She alternately sat and stood, weeping and receiving solace from those around her. I recognized some of the visitors, others I did not. Those who came from other villages were identifiable by the quality of their clothing, their leather shoes, and for the women, their coiffed hair and excessive make-up. The visitors gazed at me uncertainly, wondering who I was and why I was there.

One of the women was in the process of telling a humorous story about Don Sevino and snakes. I missed the point of the story and suddenly felt very much the outsider. However, as I sat listening and taking mental notes on my surroundings, I learned that Don Sevino was 98 years old and one of the first members of the Seventh Day Adventist Church. I remembered that Don Juan, a Catholic, had referred to Don Sevino and his wife as "those poor *Adventistas*." And how religion had split that family many years ago.

On the 4th of July, LaVail and I were feeling a little homesick and wanted to celebrate what to us was a national holiday. We had enjoyed the fireworks that accompanied the village *fiesta* and bullfights and decided, without asking anyone, to have our own fireworks.

We bought some fireworks from the local store. The store owner joked mildly about the gringos having a revolution and we smiled back enthusiastically. We waited until dark and lit our fireworks in the plaza, totally unprepared for the effect it had on the villagers. Men converged on us from all directions, in varying stages of undress, tucking in shirts, and zipping pants. Most of them carried machetes and some carried hunting rifles. When they saw us, they all stopped and stared at our bewildered faces. After we explained our motives, we learned that it is illegal to use fireworks without a permit; that setting them off means that there is an emergency

A lay pastor from the Adventist temple led prayers and hymns. Finally, Don Jorge placed the lid on the coffin, and several men helped him place nails into the wood, tapping them down only part way. Members of the immediate family carried the coffin and some of the flowers outdoors and placed them on the back of a pick-up truck. Young men assisted Sevino's closest relatives into the cab of the truck and the rest of us, some carrying flowers, others carrying water jugs and wreaths, either preceded the truck or followed behind. Our procession followed the westbound highway, through the village, past the new soccer field and into the cemetery. People we passed along the way stopped to gaze at the truck, made small conversations with he mourners, and continued on their way.

On entering the cemetery, six men carried the coffin to a small covered chapel along the back wall. An odd thing happened then. While a core of relatives and Adventist mourners followed the coffin to the chapel, the majority of the mourners took their flowers and water jugs to other graves and crypts along the wall of the cemetery. It was as if they had thought in unison, "Well, I'm going to the cemetery; I'll just take care of Uncle Jose while I'm there." One woman had a two-liter pop bottle and watered plants that had been placed recently on a grave. Another man started cleaning out the small enclosure of his family crypt and replaced the candle and flowers. Rosa, representing the temple, tried, in vain, to coax people back into the chapel, but the mourners continued to work quietly. As the service progressed, the hymns sung and the prayers repeated, people slowly worked their way back to the chapel, joining in the final prayers.

After the prayers, the top was taken off the casket and the sheet taken away from the face. Don Sevino looked much smaller than I remembered him, but he was still a tall man by village standards, with thick gray hair and large ears which reminded me of my own grandfather who had just recently died. As mourners approached the coffin, they broke off small petals from the flower arrangements and placed them in the casket. Once again the cover was placed on top; this time it was nailed tight. The casket was carried to the prepared gravesite and placed in position using two ropes. When the casket had been lowered, the non-family mourners retreated and left the cemetery, leaving the family to mourn alone.

(insurrection level emergency); and that everyone is obligated to respond. The punishment for breaking this law is jail.

When everyone realized that it was only the hapless gringos and not a revolt, the crowd, numbering nearly 50 men, laughed and joked about us having to spend the rest of our time in Yaxbe in the *cárcel* (jail). Needless to say, we were humbled and humiliated. We did not have to go to jail, but there were times when we felt that would have been the easier punishment, for our misadventure was the topic of conversation in the village for some time, under the category of "Would you believe what the gringos did this time . . .?"

One additional poignant example illustrates the willingness of villagers to help one another in times of crisis.

ETHNOGRAPHIC ESSAY
THE FIRE

Contrary to many romantic stereotypes of anthropological fieldwork, life in most rural villages is very monotonous. Like our own lives, village life is not a continuous round of parties, ceremony, and excitement. Few conversations divulge ancient secrets or juicy gossip. Rather, one engages in hundreds of conversations about the weather: When will it rain? When will it stop raining? It's very hot/cold/windy. Likewise, my husband and I became accustomed to the daily routine. We were able to tell the time of day by the arrival in town of the various buses that stopped at the corner across from our house. "Is that the 11:00 bus already?" We learned that it is useless to shop between 1:00 and 5:00 because all the stores were closed for *siesta*.

We also learned how to decipher the series of bells that were rung on Sunday morning to call villagers to Mass. We had learned to distinguish and count the bells, so that we knew how late we could sleep and still get to Mass on time.

Early one Sunday morning in July 1977, the first bell rang. LaVail and I moaned in a tired harmony and rolled over in our hammocks. We could hear activity in the street outside our home.

We were the only late risers in the village—late being defined as anything after 5:00. It was far past 5:00, however, as the sun was shining around the crack where the tarp hung over our paneless window. When the bell rang again, it seemed too soon, somehow. A half-hour could not have passed. The pealing of the bell was different, more urgent, and rapid, as if several men were pulling ropes simultaneously. Shaking myself out of my slumber, my foggy brain began to register other nonroutine noises . . . excited voices calling to each other in a cacophony of Maya and Spanish. As we hastily rolled out of our hammocks, throwing on clothing, masses of running feet passed our house toward the west. LaVail pushed the tarp aside and stuck his head out the window to ask what was happening. "*¡Fuego!*" "Fire!" They were yelling as they ran past. Everyone had some type of container, a bucket, a plastic wash bin, a liter-sized soft drink container

We followed the crowd, which was, by now, most of the village. We could see bright flames shooting above thatch roofs a few blocks away. Large puffs of gray smoke indicated that the fire fight-

EDUCATION

I wanted my children to have opportunity, because I grew up in the *campo (ejido)*. I don't know how to read or write, but my wife and I want them to learn and finish school.—Don Maximiliano (age 60), 1998

Our father had cattle, henequen, bees, trucks, and many things, but now he has nothing. He spent everything sending his children to school (SDA primary schools and universities). My parents had economic problems just like everyone else, but our father wanted to send us and our mother agreed with this. That is why our mother always said, "if you want to buy a soft drink, you have to pay for it." We began to work, earning what money we could. (Rosa [age 40], 1998)

One of the major agencies of socialization in any society is education. Indigenous cultures pass information down through the generations by means of stories and oral

ing was already underway. The crowd and flames led us down a dirt road several blocks from the center of the village. The house was an oval stone structure with a thatch roof through which spikes of fire were shooting, threatening other adjacent houses. As we approached the house, engulfed in flames, our passage was impeded by several bucket brigades, spidering in all directions from the burning structure to wells located behind neighboring houses. Men, women, and children formed each line, passing containers of all sizes from the wells to a core of middle-aged men who tossed the water on the structure. The villagers seemed to know what to do. There was little talking as the villagers passed the containers on. The faces of the men were streaked with dirt and sweat. The women, dressed in their stained *huipiles*, worked at a slower pace, at the edge of the group, passing smaller containers and yelling orders at the children. One man stood on the frame of an adjacent thatch house, dousing it with water passed up to him from family members below.

My husband joined a bucket brigade while I wove through the crowd to get a closer look. Family and friends were comforting Doña Sedi who was weeping silently as everything she owned dissolved in flames in front of her eyes. I didn't know Doña Sedi well, but I recognized her for the beautiful *huipils* she tailored for sale in the village. Many of the decorative *huipiles* worn at the *jarana* were made by her skilled hands on the trundle sewing machine that was now melting in the intense heat of the fire.

The following day, I collected a plastic bag of clothes and a blanket, and wandered back to Doña Sedi's house to survey the damage and visit Doña Sedi who was staying with a family member several doors down from her house. After she graciously accepted our meager gifts, she walked with me back to her destroyed house, now just a charred stone shell. The burned remnants of dressers, household items, and the mass of fused metal that was once her sewing machine were all that remained. Yet, she had accepted her loss with a stoicism that I have found characteristic of the Maya. It was all right, she said. No one had died, *gracias a Diós,* and they had a place to live.

traditions. Children learn about their origins, religion, and values by listening to their elders. They learn future roles by daily example and practice. They gain status and prestige by performing their roles in exemplary ways, as warriors, healers, or craftsmen.

When indigenous cultures are conquered or otherwise absorbed into another, more dominant culture, these traditional methods of education are undermined. Colonial administrations and religious missions replace one value system with another, validate a new worldview while simultaneously devaluing that which has been the source of cultural identity for many years. As we have seen, religious and cultural indoctrination was facilitated by the destruction of the tangible symbols of Maya culture, the religious temples that formed the geographic and symbolic core of each community. The missionaries then set about to destroy the books and codices that exhibited the intellect and sophistication of the Maya, opening the way for conversion to Catholicism.

Likewise, an important component of nation building is constructing and repro-
ducing shared knowledge and experiences among all citizens. Thus, throughout
Mexico, children are taught Mexican (post-conquest European-based) history in the
Spanish language. I was dismayed in 1976 at how little the children, and villagers
generally, knew about Maya history. One villager asked me if it was true what he had
heard from a Mormon—that the Maya were the lost tribes of Israel.

Primary education (to 6th grade) is mandatory in Mexico today, but it is difficult
to enforce attendance, especially in the rural areas where children's labor is often
essential for the survival of the family. Many children only attend four years, as poor
families often consider that sufficient for a child to learn how to read and do basic
math. In 1976–1977, more than 80% of children in Yaxbe were enrolled in primary
school, whereas, in their parents' generation, only 25% had completed 6th grade.
This sharp increase in education within one generation attests to the importance that
modern parents place on the success of their children, male and female.

There are three primary schools in Yaxbe: a federal school, state school, and a
private school run by the Seventh Day Adventists. The state and federal schools were
linked to the state and national establishment as well as to the Catholic liturgical calendar. In 1977, all of the teachers were from Mérida and commuted daily to the village. Today, there are several teachers from the village.

The third primary school is a private school built by the Seventh Day Adventists
in 1975. In 1977, the school boasted 77 students and 3 teachers. In 1998, the school
had 90 students and 5 teachers. Enrollment in the SDA school requires tuition, the
purchase of a uniform, and active participation of the parents in the parents' committee. Although scholarships are available, parents sacrifice greatly to enroll their
children. In return for their tuition, the school offers various advantages for its students: a small student-teacher ratio and highly motivated teachers, most of whom
live in the village and all of whom attend temple regularly. Even though only one of
the three teachers was actually certified in 1977, the perception of many in the village was that children received a superior education.

In 1977, it was becoming increasingly common for young people to attend secondary school (comparable to junior high school), even though they had to commute
to another village to do so. Although the schools themselves do not charge tuition,
students are often hindered by the cost of books and transportation. In 1990, a new
secondary school was built in Yaxbe, and this has had a tremendous impact on the
advancement of education among villagers. Today, nearly all village children attend
secondary school and many continue to high school (called *prepa*). In Mexico, there
are two educational tracks for those who attend school beyond secondary. The first
option is to attend vocational schools, often called *colégios,* that prepare students for
specific careers such as office/clerical, tourism, cosmetology, and, in the rural areas,
various agricultural specialties. Most Yucatecan parents recognize the importance of
vocational training for better jobs, and encourage their children to attend these
schools. Graduation from a vocational school or *colégio* is a prestigious achievement
for a rural student.

The second track is the professional career route. Students who wish to pursue a
professional career first complete high school and then proceed to a university or special college. These students earn degrees in teaching, nursing, medicine, law, min-
istry, accounting, or business administration. The University of Yucatán in Mérida is
the only liberal arts university in the state.

The proliferation of secondary schools, high schools, and vocational colleges is indicative of a changing perception of the importance of education among urban and rural families. When the henequen *ejido* reigned as the only source of income for villagers, many parents did not understand how education benefited their lives. They believed that their sons would work in the *ejido* as they themselves did, and as did their own fathers and grandfathers. Education curtailed the wage labor supplied by sons in agriculture or other endeavors. Likewise, parents often felt that girls did not need education since they would be married early, and education prevented them from assisting their mothers and learning the skills they would need as housewives.

As the realities of rural Yucatán have shifted away from agriculture, perceptions of education have also transformed. Today, most villagers acknowledge the importance of education for their sons and daughters. They recognize that their sons will not be working in the *ejido* and that all of their children will have to make their way in a very different world. Consequently, parents are more insistent that their children attend secondary school and are more supportive of young people who are looking ahead to new opportunities.

In 1977, there were nine villagers, five men and four women who had completed preparatory or vocational school. Today the village boasts a vast array of occupations: fifteen teachers, some of whom teach in the local schools; nine nurses; two doctors (one of these a woman); a veterinarian; ten accountants and managers; secretaries; lab technicians; two engineers; four pastors; eight administrators, including the director of the secondary school; a social worker; and a professional violinist with the Yucatán Symphony Orchestra.

HEALTH AND MEDICINE

Yaxbe has always been a healthy village. Death rates and infant mortality rates are low and children, for the most part, are well-nourished. Babies are born healthy, and they are nurtured and loved. They can expect to live a long life with few of the health concerns that plague those of us who live in the modern world: cancer, stroke, heart attack, and diabetes. Only eight villagers died in 1997, two of these from car accidents, the major cause of death for younger villagers. Only one death was reported as cancer, a disease still rare in the village. Most deaths were of elderly people, with only one infant death of the eight. The primary causes of death in Yaxbe are respiratory and cardiovascular diseases, bronchitis, and heart failure.

To cure common ailments, Yaxbeños have a vast body of knowledge from which to draw. In this section we will examine both traditional and Western healing; we will also address the benefits and detriments of Western conveniences.

Traditional Health and Healing

The Bible story says: all sacrifices will be a measure of the *sacerdote* (priest). But [we are] lower . . . we make offerings of food. Yes, people come to be cured . . . if they have a fever, diarrhea, or if they are dispirited. If someone comes, we burn copal and make offerings: money, a small chicken, or a small meal. Those who don't look to doctors still believe in *yerba* (herbs). (Don Teofanis, *h-men* [age 70s], 1998)

Yaxbeños syncretize two philosophies on health and illness: traditional beliefs in the spirit world and Western medicine. Ancestral conceptions of disease focus on natural forces and the ill will of other humans. The winds are considered a strong force of nature, and bad winds (***mal viento***) or the innocuous warm air of the midday sun can cause ailments such as headache and malaise. Illness in children may be caused by ***mal ojo*** (evil eye), suspected when someone gazes too long at an infant or child. While modern Yaxbeños downplay these traditional causes of illness, it is still very common for people to blame colds and flu on *mal viento,* much like Americans might blame these ailments on "change of weather."

Likewise the cures or redresses are in the hands of those who are able to communicate with or manipulate the spirit world. The Mayan religious leader is called a *h-men*. *H-menob* (plural) have various functions or responsibilities. The primary role of the *h-men* is to diagnose illness and heal (see Redfield and Villa Rojas 1990 (1934): 160–180 for a detailed discussion of Maya healing practices in Chan Kom). A second responsibility, discussed in Chapter 6, is to direct the *Chachac* or annual rain ceremony.

H-menob have knowledge of a vast cornucopia of herbs and plants that can cure a wide variety of daily physical and emotional ailments, including cuts, diarrhea, and general malaise. This knowledge, along with the chants used to communicate with the spirits, is not innate, but is learned through apprenticeships with other *h-menob,* often one's father or grandfather. However, if the ailment is more serious and is diagnosed as caused by the evil winds, *mal ojo,* or more malevolent forces of sorcery, the cure is also more complicated. The *h-men* and his client, and sometimes members of the client's family, will gather together and burn copal (incense made from Protium—the copal tree) to find the cause of the illness. Then, they might sacrifice a chicken or turkey, consume ***balché*** (ceremonial fermented wine), and pray to the spirits for a cure.

While beliefs of sorcery are less common today, fear of the unknown is still a part of life for more traditional villagers. Sorcerers can send illness via the winds or secretly add poisons to food. I was told that some elderly villagers still would not eat food that is offered to them if they did not participate in its preparation or watch it being prepared. *H-menob* can also be sorcerers or witches although, according to Redfield and Villa Rojas (1990 [1934]: 75–76), their primary responsibility is to find the cause of illness and cure their clients. In general, *h-menob* who get a reputation of sorcery will lose credibility as a healer.

While only men fill all of the responsibilities of the *h-men,* women have often filled the role of healer or ***yerbatera.*** Like the *h-men,* women often follow in the footsteps of their mothers, learning the cures for many daily ailments. Female curers grow a variety of plants and herbs in their *soláres,* specializing in ailments that are linked to women's health—menstruation, fertility, pregnancy, childbirth, and menopause. One area of healing in which women traditionally dominate is that of midwifery. While no woman can conduct a *Chachac* ceremony (Chapter 6), no man would enter this specialty profession.

Today, many Yaxbeños still rely on traditional methods of curing everyday ailments, such as diarrhea, stomach problems, headache, using herbs and plants that are believed to be effective against these conditions. Many people have a general knowledge of the curative power of various plants and cultivate them in their *soláres* or know of their location in the *monte.* Various villagers have shown me the two plants whose sap stops bleeding immediately on application and that also heal cuts. In recent years, the choice of curers has diminished greatly as the elders die and the younger men and women have less faith in the ancient cures. There are only two acknowledged *yerbateros* in the village today, the *h-men* himself and an elderly woman who lives at the edge of town.

According to the *h-men*, there is no one to replace him when he is no longer able to perform rituals. He studied for more than six years, watching his father and then taking on the responsibility himself. His own sons are not interested in carrying on the tradition. "People today want to be free," he complains. "They aren't locked into work, attached to their work. They don't want to be inconvenienced."

Western Medicine

It was last Christmas when I got so sick. At first I had pains in my stomach, but then it spread to my whole body. I couldn't work in the house or take care of the children the pain was too intense. Reymundo took me to the hospital. They did a test on my kidneys and other tests too. They gave me a lot of medicine. It cost a lost of money, and I didn't get better. My mother kept trying to get me to go to a *yerbatero* because she believes in them, but Reymundo doesn't believe and he didn't want me to go. Finally, I got so sick that I went to Tixkokob with my mother and visited a famous *yerbatero*. He gave me some herbs and medicines and I got better right away. I haven't been sick since.(Sonia [age 25], 1995)

I think it [traditional herbology] is a good tradition. There are some famous *yerbateros* in Yucatán. Many medicines are based on natural ingredients and there are many uses for traditional plants. If people believe in traditional medicine, it works for them. Most people use both. (Dr. R. Pino, Yaxbe, 1998)

Recently, a new medical clinic was built in Yaxbe. Two doctors, one director, and another young doctor fulfilling his health care service, work at the government clinic that is open every day and is free to villagers. The clinic promotes public health by providing free immunizations against such childhood diseases as whooping cough, measles, and polio.

According to one doctor whom I interviewed in 1998, the most common ailments are gastrointestinal infections, viral and bacterial, and respiratory problems such as bronchitis. Although few villagers smoke cigarettes, much dust and dirt is blown around by the winds and ingested or breathed in by villagers, reinforcing the traditional beliefs in the *mal viento* as a major cause of illness. There are no factories in the immediate vicinity that produce toxins, but there is a tremendous increase in the number of cars, trucks, and motorcycles in the village, none of which has sufficient exhaust controls.

The doctor attributes several factors to the overall good health of villagers. The first is the persistence in the practice of breastfeeding. The doctor was pleased that the women in Yaxbe continue to breastfeed because of the benefits it provides for infants, especially the natural immunities that pass from mother's milk to her children.

The second factor in good health among villagers is family planning. In the 1970s it was not at all uncommon for couples to have eight to ten children and some of the older families had up to 12 children. Large families were adaptive historically because of the importance of the agricultural cycle, and the desire to have adult children to care for elderly parents. Cultural factors also influence family size. One of these is the assumption that men desire large families as proof of their virility and

ETHNOGRAPHIC ESSAY
ON BECOMING A *COMPADRE*

It was the second week of February, a sluggish time of the year because of the oppressive heat and dryness. The fields had been slashed and cleared and would be burned and planted just before the rainy season. Work in the henequen fields continued as always, but the mood of the entire village was lethargic. There was more activity in the park at night as the men took advantage of the less demanding work schedule, and drinking was more apparent. The annual *fiesta* for the Virgin of Candelaria ended the week before, and it seemed like everyone was worn down from the endless rounds of bullfights, *gremios,* and dances. It was time to return to the routine of daily life. This was as true for my husband and myself as it was for the other villagers.

On this particular Friday evening, we were especially tired. We had just returned from Mérida where we had spent several days recuperating from the excitement of the *fiesta*. Nevertheless, as much as we enjoyed the anonymity of the city, being able to speak English, and indulge in little pleasures such as movies and restaurants, it was always nice to return to the village, to our 9×12 room in the medical clinic. LaVail was reading in his hammock, and I sat bleary eyed at my desk, a small wooden table that miraculously appeared in our room during the first week of our stay. I was plucking slowly at my portable typewriter, recording those events and occurrences that I had previously scribbled in the small notebook I always carried in my purse. As I typed, Don Berto was serenading us from outside our house, a mournful ballad of unrequited love.

"*Bueno . . .*" The salutation from outside our door startled us.

"*Pase usted.*"

It was Don Juan, the caretaker of the medical clinic and a treasured friend.

"*Buenas tardes,* Don Bo (LaVail's nickname) . . . señora." Because of my childlessness, I had not earned the title of "Doña."

Don Juan cradled three Cokes in his arms and placed them carefully on our counter. Juan Aguilar was not Mayan, but had come to Yucatán as a child when his father, a soldier, was stationed in this backwater territory during the Mexican Revolution. His family remained, and Juan eventually married a local woman (a common law marriage since he always insisted, "She is my woman, but we have six children") and settled into the Yucatecan way of life, raising corn and working in the henequen fields.

Don Juan is a distinguished looking man, nearly 60 years old with gray hair and a crooked nose, the victim of past fights or perhaps inebriated misadventures. He is pencil thin. His baggy pants are held up by long strand of henequen fiber, his shirt is buttoned askew. But still there is something dignified about Don Juan. He is modest and soft-spoken. We look forward to his visits.

And his visits were frequent, for he was the caretaker of the medical clinic. Before our arrival, Juan slept in our room several nights a week. I'm not sure what he was protecting, since the clinic was empty except for the healthy population of scorpions. But it was his job, earned because of his support of the village president in his election campaign. Since we were now living in the clinic, there was no need for him to sleep away from his family, but he insisted on sleeping in one of the open rooms, burdened by inclement weather and attacked by all kinds of semitropical insects, including the dreaded flying cockroaches. We always felt guilty about this, but it was his responsibility, taken on himself now, not only to protect the building, but to

Figure 4.6 Don Juan, 1977

take care of the poor gringos who inhabited it (see Figure 4.6).

Tonight it was obvious that Don Juan had been drinking, not excessively, but enough to build the courage to discuss something with us. While I opened the Cokes, Juan, normally a shy man with few words, began expounding on our *"confianza"* and how we are good people (*buena gente*) and very nice (*simpatico*). His hands were in a now familiar pose, nearly praying, fingers together pressed against his chest.

He then began to talk of his daughter, Manuela, and her young child. We had heard rumors about Manuela and her baby born out of wedlock, but we had not yet met her. We knew who the father was, though Juan referred to him only as a bandit. As his monologue progressed, it soon became clear that he was asking us to be *compadres,* yet he never actually said so. I was trying desperately to find

meaning in his story that jumped from compliments about us and comments about the poor abandoned child and the bandit who was his father. LaVail and I kept glancing at each other, trying to ascertain if we were both receiving the same message and what we should do about it.

Finally, our heads throbbing from concentration, we asked if he wished us to be *compadres*. His face did not alter its serious countenance, but he responded, *"Si . . . si . . ."*

The pressure relieved, we began earnestly to ask him what we should do. He suddenly became quiet and reflective. "You should meet Manuela. She will visit and talk about those things."

Not knowing the proper way to respond to such a request as this, we thanked him for the honor of being a *compadre.*

"¿Porque?" (why?) was his response.

The baptism took place in March, but it did not occur in the village church. For reasons never explained, but nonetheless understood, they preferred to have the ceremony performed in Mérida. On this day, Manuela, her son Carlos, and her mother Doña Fidelia accompanied LaVail and me to the main cathedral in Mérida. Don Juan did not attend.

We approached the large central park with its trees squared off, crossed the busy boulevard, and entered the spectacular cathedral, bypassing a cluster of elderly women selling fetishes and begging. Nearly every pew was occupied, for the priest was conducting Mass. We were directed to a small room adjoining the sanctuary, where we filled out a form and paid our 21 pesos. We stood uncomfortably with ten other babies and their

(continued)

ETHNOGRAPHIC ESSAY
ON BECOMING A *COMPADRE* (*continued*)

entourages in the small hot room, waiting for the priest.

Manuela and her mother chatted
together in low voices. The daughter
resembled her mother more than she did
Don Juan. They shared small dark eyes
and large hook shaped noses. Neither
could be called pretty, by Mayan or
Western standards. Yet Manuela
possessed a maturity uncommon among
19 year olds. She was poised and, in this
strange place, her mother looked to her
for guidance.

Carlos was dressed in the white
gown and shoes I had bought for him.
Now, as we waited in the sticky, dark
anteroom, the outfit was becoming wrinkled with sweat. As he fussed, we passed
him around among us. The other babies
in the room, similarly attired were likewise being passed among loving, yet
uncomfortable relatives and future
padrinos.

Finally the Mass ended and the
priest entered the room in a perfunctory
fashion. He did not smile. This was his
job. The crowd collected around the baptismal font in the center of the room and
listened while the priest performed the
short ceremony. The babies fussed and
cried in their *padrinos'* arms as he
anointed each of them in turn. LaVail
held our *ahijado* who had joined the cho-
rus. In five minutes it was over.
Somehow it seemed a relief to walk out
into the intense Yucatecan sun.

In the summer of 1989, many things
had changed. On our arrival in the village, LaVail and I, with our three culture-
shocked children in tow, walked
expectantly to Juan's house, which in the
months after the baptism had become
familiar to us. It had become our routine
to visit this house, lounge in the hammock, and rock the fast-growing Carlos.

Their house had a dirt floor, was
dark, and in ill repair, serving as a passage way to the rear of the house where
Doña Fidelia worked. In this space, pigs
and chickens roamed, clothes were
washed and hung to dry, and food was
prepared. Since Doña Fidelia was a *yerbatera,* many plants grew helter-skelter
in the yard. It was here where the elder
woman would always be found, squat-
ting on the low three-legged stool, her

---

social status; and desired by women as a means of asserting their adulthood. Religion
is another important factor, especially in Catholic countries where the Church
opposes the use of birth control.

Despite these factors, young families today seldom have more than three children
and many families have stopped at two. One day, a friend asked me why I had three
children. While I stumbled for a response, she stated that she and her husband
stopped at two because of the high cost of raising children. She insisted that they
wanted to give their children every advantage. I asked how she limited her family,
a reasonable question since she and most villagers are Catholic. She said simply
"control."

The presumption of the ***machismo*** complex (see Chapter 9) as a detriment to
family planning has also proved to be overstated. Although there are still some very
large families, and men may see children as a form of status, the doctor has found
that men often accompany the women when they come to talk to him about family
planning. For men today, the ability to support one's family is more important than

plain cotton *huipil* stuffed between her legs, delicately flipping tortillas onto the metal griddle over the fire.

On this sweltering July day, however, it was clear that no one graced the house. Tall weeds broke through the cracks of the cement blocks of the front house and behind, the stick and daub house had long since collapsed, its thatch rotted and lying along the ground. We learned that Don Juan now lived elsewhere; he had sold his house to his son who had since moved to Cancún. In fact, most of Juan's family had migrated to Cancún, including Manuela and Carlos, and Doña Fidelia was visiting her daughter and grandson there at the time of our visit.

Don Juan was living in a small thatch house adjacent to that of another of his sons. There was nothing in the room except a table, on which a fly-infested food dish sat, and the hammock in which our friend rested. He was emaciated and so weak that he could hardly lift himself out of his hammock. His skin felt like tissue, so fragile it might tear.

But he recognized us immediately and we introduced him to our children. We rejoiced at the whispered salutation, "Don Bo" and I was now "Doña Cindy." As we were leaving, one of Juan's grandsons arrived with a pot of food and explained to us that Don Juan was "sick in the head" and not expected to live long.

Despite the distance of Cancún from the village, word of our return spread rapidly and within one week, Manuela and Carlos visited us in the village. Manuela had done well for herself, better than an unwed mother would have done in the village. She worked as a supervisor for maids at a tourist hotel on the resort strip. Carlos was a very tall young man, shy, and not sure what to think of the strangers who called him "*ahijado*." I will always remember Don Juan's family. But I know that I will never see Don Juan again.[4] (1989)

[4]Both Don Juan and his wife have since died. Manuela lives in Cancún, as does Carlos, who is now married with children of his own.

---

how many children one has. As providing for one's family becomes more problematic and stressful, and as women are increasingly expected to contribute to the household income, both men and women recognize that they cannot have as many children and that the children they do have should be spaced.

The one area of increased concern for the young village doctor is nutrition, not the quantity of food consumed, but the quality. Northern Yucatán basks in an abundance of fresh fruits, vegetables, and grains, as already seen. All village stores stock a wide variety of local and regional foods and most people still grow fresh fruits in their *soláres*. Yet, today, the children prefer to eat the food they see advertised on the television: soft drinks, potato chips, candy, and chocolate. White bread is replacing the nutritious tortilla (Chapter 10), and canned foods often replace fresh. For example, the favorite foods of Reymundo and Sonia's children are hotdogs and white bread with processed cheese spread.

According to Dr. Pino, "nutrition is a problem here, but it is not really a problem of poverty, but of education." Children are eating empty calories. They buy junk food at school and their parents don't have the time to monitor their diets. As a result, he predicts an increase in the Western diseases and ailments such as obesity, diabetes, high blood pressure, and cardiovascular problems. The doctor placed part of the blame of these unhealthy dietary shifts on the power of the United States to both influence the social fabric of Mexican society and to impose its capitalistic world-view on a poor country.

CONCLUSION

People do not live in a vacuum, not even people in developing countries or people who are labeled as traditional. They are adaptable and flexible and must make choices daily about how to live their lives. Unlike our stereotypes of traditional people, they are not inflexible in their thinking or actions. The Maya have many choices and they do not feel compelled to choose one path over another. They make their decisions based on what they perceive is best for their families. So far, despite their poverty and their lack of Western technology and science, they are healthy. Babies are robust; they are nurtured and loved. Villagers expect to live a long life, free of serious illness. There are no day care centers or nursing homes. Those who are vulnerable are cared for by family and neighbors. In the village, people are safe and insulated, at least for now, from the violence and oppression pervasive in other, not so distant, regions of the country.

5/The Political Structure of Yaxbe, 1976–1998

NATIONAL AND LOCAL POLITICS

PRI, PAN, and National Politics

From 1946 to 2000, Mexico was ruled by one political party, the **PRI** (Institutional Revolutionary Party). The ongoing success of the party, as it evolved under the rule of President Lázaro Cárdenas, was due to the ability of PRI to bring competing interest groups into its fold. By incorporating business, industry, government agencies, and peasant and workers' unions under the umbrella of the larger political party, PRI was able to pursue its programs while appeasing these numerous and often conflicting groups (La Botz 1995: 56–57). Utilizing this process of "co-optation" and political patronage, PRI has also been able to neutralize potential opposition parties.

PRI maintained its power through its political largesse, providing a myriad of social and economic programs such as the DIF (*Desarrollo Integral de la Familia*) and PACR (*Programa del Alimentacíon Complementaria Rural*). PRI further entrenched its power by providing improvements in rural infrastructure, such as free medical clinics and hospitals, schools, and roads. That these programs often came at the expense of real development was not widely recognized at the local level until recent years.

Despite the party's dominance, recent dissatisfaction with national leaders and the insipid corruption and election fraud resulted in the growth of various opposition parties that threatened the hegemony of PRI. Two of these parties emerged from within the tightly woven web of the PRI. One of these is **PAN,** a conservative party, popular with merchants and owners of small businesses. PAN (National Action Party and Spanish for "bread") gained much strength in various regions of Mexico, including Yucatán that has managed, despite PRI's history of corrupt elections, to elect *PANista* (members of PAN) governors and mayors. In recent years, the PRD has also emerged as a legitimate opposition party. Many political observers believe that the PRD (Party of the Democratic Revolution), a liberal party led by Cuahtemoc Cárdenas, the son of former President Lázaro Cárdenas, won the presidential election of 1988. Extensive election fraud has been documented for the election in which Carlos Salinas de Gortari became president. In 2000, the yoke of PRI was finally broken when Vicente Fox, the PAN candidate, defeated the PRI and the PRD. Time will tell if his presidency opens up the political process, allowing for a more democratic system of government for the Mexican people.

In this chapter, we will be exploring further the intersection between national government and its policies and local agencies. We will continue to examine the theme of resilience and change as it applies to local-level politics.

PRI, PAN, and Local-Level Politics: Becoming a President in Yaxbe

In 1976, there was only one admitted *PANista* in Yaxbe, as PAN sympathizers were largely reluctant to openly declare their allegiance to the opposition party. Since the victory of Vicente Fox, PAN supporters in the village have become emboldened and in my 2001 visit, many posters and a new PAN headquarters were in evidence. In Yaxbe, however, a candidate's party affiliation is not the most important consideration for political success. Rather, voters are concerned primarily with the personality of the candidate and the perceived benefits they can gain by supporting one candidate over another, as we shall see.

Over the years different factions have dominated local politics in Yaxbe. Prior to the 1970s, most of the presidents were merchants who, because of their relative wealth and networks, were able to amass the support and funds needed to win an election. In the late 1970s, Cordemex bred a new class of workers, unified and affluent. Don Ernesto, president during my initial research, was the second factory worker to be elected president, thus shifting the local political pendulum from the wealthy merchant class to the incipient middle class. Don Ernesto told me that, although the merchants did not support him, he drew support from the families of factory workers and many others who did not trust the merchants to act in the best interest of the village.

Several presidents were elected from among the ranks of Cordemex in the 1970s and 1980s, but when the factory jobs disappeared, merchants regained their political influence. The presidents in office during my 1989 and 1992 visits were both businessmen. Since that time, occupation has become a less important variable as candidates and presidents have emerged from a variety of backgrounds, reflecting the same diversity of occupation and lifestyle that was developing in the rest of the village.

RECRUITING SUPPORTERS   In general, a person considering a candidacy must be well-situated economically and socially in the village. He[1] must have both a broad base of support and access to money: his own or that of his relatives. A tentative can-

---

[1]I am using the terminology he and his in a generic sense. However, historically, all political candidates have been male except for one special case that will be discussed in Chapter 9.

didate will first casually express his interest to relatives, *compadres,* and friends. Sometimes, the process is reversed, as friends and relatives may urge a reticent villager to run for office.

As gossip moves quickly through a small village, the word will soon be out he is interested, and people will start talking about him as a candidate. He will use his familial contacts as a gauge of villagers' interest in him. Eventually, people will wish to test his resolve by approaching him for advice, small loans, or money gifts, always requested as a favor for a sick mother or to pay a debt. The candidate's response to these requests is crucial to his success. He must graciously give money, thus becoming a *patrón.*

The candidate must be prepared to spend a tremendous amount of money. This is a precarious system at best, as expending money and giving gifts does not guarantee a vote. Unlike in the United States, where campaign contributors have a stake in their candidate and will usually promote him or her to their friends, Yaxbeños are very fickle. They will approach several or all candidates with financial requests and then vote for the one who is most magnanimous or who can promise the most patronage if elected.

While the candidate is expected to be generous in his actions and to become a local *patrón,* he must also raise money for his campaign. In addition to a 1,200 peso registration fee, the candidate must be prepared to spend up to 50,000 pesos (around US$7,000) for food, gifts, and loans. The costs incurred are all expended in the village, in gifts and purchasing alcohol and food for supporters and potential supporters. This is a tremendous amount of money for a small village, especially when the average farmer earns around US$1,700–$2,000, and a schoolteacher earns on average US$5,000 per year.

Because of these costs, the candidate must rely on his family connections to raise money. He solicits his family members and *compadres* for loans or favors that he can then turn over to his potential supporters. In return, those who contribute to the campaign war chest will often earn favors in the form of jobs or contracts if the candidate wins. Even if the candidate loses, these contributions also serve to reinforce economic and social networks that might benefit the donors in their own future endeavors.

One component of local politics that might be the most uncomfortable to the American consciousness is the "buying of the vote." This practice is discouraged by the state, but it continues today and is found in all elections (the *socio delegado* candidates, for example, also do this). Candidates announce in advance what their supporters will receive for their vote, usually 1–2 pounds of beef. This practice compromises the secret ballot in that the individual, having voted, reports to a representative of the candidate for whom he or she voted and receives a ticket that entitles the voter to the promised portion of meat or other compensation. This ticket also allows the voter to visit the home of the candidate on the evening of the election for food and beverages. The food and cash offerings are short-term incentives, however. Individuals also follow a candidate who can promise future rewards. The election of a family member can translate into economic and political advantage for relatives and supporters.

During the campaign season, enthusiasm for one's candidate runs high. Candidates are supported for a variety of reasons: family and *compadragzo* relationships; honesty and integrity; and what the candidate can do for the village and for the voter. It is clear to me that villagers agonize over their choice, weighing numerous factors. The fact that one's vote is not private increases the anguish as a vote against a relative and a vengeful candidate can have future repercussions. Consequently, the period following the election is a time for mending fences. Once elected, the new president should aid in this process of healing by carefully choosing his appointees and by opening avenues of communication with his opponents. Slowly the flow of village life returns, political wounds heal, and the elections fade into the background.

THE RESPONSIBILITIES OF THE VILLAGE PRESIDENT   Given the political and economic costs of the election process, what are the benefits of victory? The job of president is not lucrative in and of itself. The salary is nominal and the president continues to work in his previous occupation, sometimes in a lessened capacity. The benefits gained by a president are largely intangible: respect, authority, and prestige. The responsibilities of a president, however, are many and very important, as he is expected to fulfill a number of roles: public safety director and mediator between interest groups and individuals, as well as village administrator. As administrator, he is responsible for maintaining the parks and streets; obtaining grants for improving infrastructure, such as new roads or public services; supervising government programs; and assisting villagers in obtaining employment and applying for grants.

The core of government offices is called the *Ayuntamiento.* It consists primarily of four formal officers: the president, the treasurer, secretary, and the police chief (see Figure 5.1). The police chief, with the advice and consent of the president, appoints two deputies who serve under him. The president also appoints caretakers for two village parks, the *casa del pueblo* (where we lived our first year), and the *palacio,* a librarian, and other minor officials. The lesser offices are patronage positions, awarded to family members, *compadres,* and others who have supported the candidate.

The president also makes a recommendation to the governor, who appoints an important village officer, the *judicio civil,* or the civil judge. The judge, in 2002 a local woman with a legal degree, has many responsibilities including the registering of all births, marriages, and deaths. She also presides over civil marriages and divorces, if there are no disputes over property or children. Any contested divorces (there have been none that I know of) would be heard in a formal court in Mérida.

One of the president's most important unofficial functions is the planning of the annual *fiesta* for the patron saint, Candelaria (see Chapter 6). While he is not involved in the religious aspects of the *fiesta,* he is responsible for its occurrence, contracts with the carnival people, vendors, musicians for the popular dances, and the organization of the *jarana* and the *corrida* (bullfights). It is for this reason, among others, that an Adventist has never been elected president, even though one very qualified man runs nearly every election. The Catholic majority fears that an Adventist president would not sponsor a *fiesta* on religious grounds.

The presidency also holds an important role for the president's wife who becomes president of the local DIF program. The wife of the president organizes and coordinates these programs that provide food distributions, nutritional programs, and sewing classes. She, in turn, can appoint her relatives and friends to positions within this program.

Figure 5.1 Ayuntamiento, 1995. From left: secretary, president, police chief, and treasurer

EVALUATION OF VILLAGE PRESIDENTS   Local officials, like those at the national level, can serve only one term. The village president serves one 3-year term, with no reelection. At the local level, the 3-year no reelection rule has advantages, in that it allows for the dispersal of local power within a village and discourages the formation of strong factions. That village presidents have emerged from various economic groups and families speaks to this advantage.

Although the single-term system diminishes the opportunity for one leader to entrench his power, there are drawbacks to the system. Primary among these difficulties is the lack of accountability toward constituents. Once elected, many politicians lose their zeal for the goals they so enthusiastically espoused during the campaign. While this occurs with all politicians everywhere, it has special implications when one does not have to face the voters for a second chance.

For the anthropologist, local elections provide a fascinating study of village values and how these are reflected in both the expectations villagers have for their public leaders and in the ultimate failure of these leaders to fulfill these goals. In the following discussion, I will examine some of these values, how candidates emulate them during the campaign, but how these same individuals, once elected, often lose sight of them, thus forfeiting that hard-earned trust. It is important to remember, however, that the candidate/official is in a precarious position because, like the American public, opinions are diverse, and are often based on personal experience and expectations. The following list of values is particularly interesting in two respects. First, the list indicates how the expectations of villagers toward their leaders shift once the leaders take office. Second, the values listed are often contradictory in practice, an irony not unknown in American politics where a candidate is expected to refrain from favoring all special interests except one's own.

1. *One is loyal to family and compadres.* A president is expected to support relatives over nonrelatives in social conflict, elections, and in political factions. This is not always possible, nor is it always heeded. There are cases when special issues or personality can supersede kinship, and more commonly, situations in which several candidates are related to the voter in some way. Likewise, once elected, the officer is expected to give preference to his or her family for jobs and other favors. Disregarding one's relatives once in office is a serious offense, which everyone in the village notices, criticizes and remembers for many years.

2. *Egalitarianism is favored.* While all peasant villages have a stratified system of wealth and prestige, villagers maintain an egalitarian ideal, in which the affluent do not flaunt their wealth. Villagers who display wealth instill jealousy or even suspicion in others (see **Huay Pop** in Chapter 6). Instead, prosperous families are expected to invest their wealth in the village through the sponsorship and support of social events and religious ceremonies. While, in reality, this value has declined in recent years as the middle class has expanded and the proliferation of consumer goods has increased, the ideal remains deeply embedded in the village psyche and worldview.

3. *Prestige is earned, not through the accumulation of wealth, but in the sharing of one's wealth with others.* Those who are willing and able to give generously will garner political and social support. An important consideration in choosing a candidate is "What can he do for me?"

4. *Honesty, integrity, and fairness.* These are always important qualifications. People discuss quite openly how honest someone might be, whether he has *vergüenza* (shame). Yet, this value can be stretched or overshadowed by Value #3.

5. *Patronage and nepotism are expected and valued.* Unlike the United States, where we value, and often demand, hiring by merit and credential, Mexico and other "familial" cultures favor the principle of patronage, however unfair it might be to those who do not have the connections necessary for such advantage. This is a precarious value, however; for it can backfire if villagers perceive that one's patronage hurts the village or is overtly unfair to particular groups or individuals.

6. *To the victor go the spoils.* This expectation appears to contradict several of the above-mentioned values, and indeed does so. Yet, the history of Mexican politics since the Revolution is one of collusion and patronage. It is a truism repeated often in the village that every political official, whether village president or *socio delegado,* leaves office wealthier than when he entered. After leaving office, a recent *socio delegado* built a beautiful house with tiled portico and the village's only satellite dish. Other officials have built homes, purchased cars, made additions to their homes, expanded their economic operations, and have generally prospered. While this is expected, villagers do not really approve and will often grumble about unearned privilege. This is especially true if village consensus is that the official abused his power, neglected his constituents, or overtly violated the above virtues and community values.

It is ironic and interesting that the values that placed a man in office are often contradictory to those by which he is judged during his term in office and after he leaves office. Outgoing presidents are measured on a number of issues:

1. *What did he do to benefit the village?* A president is evaluated on how well he promoted the village through the sponsorship of important events: *fiestas,* government programs, and improvements in infrastructure.
2. *How did he benefit individuals in the village?* Despite the value of patronage, there are sometimes complaints concerning unfairness of the president toward certain individuals or groups. For example, merchant presidents have the potential to harm other local businesses by building personal monopolies. In their turn, Adventists often perceive themselves as persecuted by Catholic presidents who do not support loans or grant proposals for individuals in the minority religion. Women are becoming a major voice in the village as they openly criticize presidents who condescend to them and hinder their entrepreneurial enterprises. In contrast, women become active supporters of presidents or candidates who promote their projects.

These criteria indicate the development of factions in the village that crosscut kinship ties. Some of these special interest groups are informal and often temporary, focused on specific projects or concerns. Others, such as the Adventists, are more entrenched as discrimination—even inadvertent—is institutionalized in local practice and religious ideology. The emergence of special interest groups and factions is a function of the increased heterogeneity of society, as I have observed in Yaxbe.

That villagers in Yaxbe, and indeed in Western culture, interact within these contradictory and shifting values, contributes to understanding society as complex and dynamic. It also reflects diverse values and special interests among competing groups within a community—religious, economic, social, as well as demographic groups based on age and gender. The following case studies will exemplify these evolving and often conflicting values.

Case Study 1: Eduardo: Confusing Politics with Business

In 1976, Eduardo was the 20-year-old son of the wealthiest merchant family in the village. In addition to the family store, *molino,* and *tortillería,* Eduardo's father had many **hectares** (one hectare equals 2.49 acres) of henequen land, cornfields, and some cattle. He also owned three cargo trucks and enjoyed a near monopoly on the transport of henequen to the decorticating plants. The entire family was involved in the family businesses. Eduardo's mother, sisters, and aunts worked in the store; his uncles and brothers worked in various aspects of the agricultural or merchant enterprises.

Eduardo was a hardworking young man. While his friends were attending English classes sporadically in Mérida, playing soccer after their factory shifts, and doing the "*fiesta* circuit" on weekends, Eduardo worked long days for his father, in the fields, driving a truck, or assisting in the management of the store. He was a handsome young man, taller than the average villager, with dark complexion, thick black curly hair, and an infectious smile. Yet, despite his easy smile, he was aloof, more serious than his years should demand. In fact, his entire family was reticent and unapproachable, and my various attempts to befriend them were met with suspicion and polite indifference.

In 1992, Eduardo, age 36, was president of the village. He seemed to be on top of the world. His family's corner *solár* had been enlarged to accommodate a new family enterprise in the wholesale and retail sale of construction materials. Eduardo and his wife had built a beautiful home with tiled verandah, pillars, and louvered windows. His father still ran the agricultural businesses, although the henequen industry by this time was on the wane. Their transport trucks now carried more building materials than henequen. The store and *molino* thrived under the charge of Eduardo's mother and sisters, and his wife was, by custom, the president of the DIF program. He owned two Jeeps, a conspicuous sign of affluence. He drove one himself and loaned the other to family members. He was bedecked in gold jewelry and had a car phone, the only telephone in the village. I saw him daily, driving through the village, phone to his ear, conducting business. Since his was the only phone in the village, it was a mystery to many people as to whom he could be speaking.

I was quite surprised in 1998 to observe that Eduardo's empire had collapsed, or at least, declined markedly. The construction business seemed to have disappeared altogether as the now empty area behind the store attested. There were no large flatbed trucks parked in front of the store. The store itself had reduced its inventory, though it was still one of the largest in the village, and the *molino* and *tortillería* still commanded an impressive business as women were shifting from homemade tortillas to processed ones. Eduardo only owned one of the Jeeps, now badly dented and worn; the car phone and gold jewelry had disappeared. Instead of cruising in his Jeep, Eduardo was more often seen driving a battered pick-up truck around the village delivering **bagazo** (the green remnant of the henequen plant used for fertilizer and cattle feed) from the factory to the various ranches in the village. I was told that he still owned a pig farm, but that he sold few pigs. At his house, his wife and children sold prepared foods and rented videos.

According to his cousin, Eduardo's sin was that he confused politics with business, and this sin, combined with greed and disregard for the people, diminished his reputation in the village. Villagers attested that Eduardo was very generous when he ran for president. He gave people sheets of laminated roofing and other building materials in order to build his support group. He also began to participate more in the village affairs, assisting families with economic problems and concerns, as was expected of the serious political candidate. However, this was not natural for him, and once he was elected, he once again distanced himself from the villagers and neglected the patronage expected of him. He was no longer generous and, in fact, began to act in ways that were interpreted as greedy and self-serving.

For example, while he was president, several women in the village solicited his assistance in applying for a government grant for a cooperative *molino* and *tortillería*. At that time, there were only two *tortillerías* in the village, his and Don Justo's. There was an increasing demand for processed tortillas and besides, as the women argued, there was little competition as both stores charged the same prices for *masa* and tortillas. Eduardo refused to assist the women in their project, because, in their opinion, it would compete with his own family business. The women were not able to get the grant until the next president came into office.

Another incident was even more blatant and affected the entire village. During his presidency, Eduardo received a 140 million peso grant to improve the four village schools. However, he did not initiate any projects and the villagers began to suspect that he was diverting the government funds to his business or to his family members. The *Padres de Familia* of the four schools formed a committee, led by two women, to meet with him. When the meeting failed, the women organized a demonstration in front of his office, after which Eduardo complied with their demands and the various projects went forward. However, Eduardo still benefited because he purchased all the supplies and materials through his own construction business, being both seller and purchaser.

Consequently, Eduardo has earned a reputation contrary to the values still esteemed by the village. His critics argue that he has so many enemies now that he is afraid to enter the bar because men shun him. Perhaps the most feared social position a villager can have is a pariah, where he or she has lost the trust and confidence of fellow villagers. This, it seems, has happened to Eduardo who paid dearly for his actions.

Case Study 2: The Making of a Village President, 1998

On a sunny day in February, Yaxbeños participated in a ritual that is replicated in all American towns and cities, the primary elections for local officials. As this was only a PRI primary, it was generally conceded that the victor of this election would be the next village president, defeating whomever might dare to run on the PAN ticket.[2] The truism that "all politics are local" applies in both Mexico and in the United States. Even though many villagers are skeptical of the national government, they do not hold their local leaders responsible for the policies of national leaders. Mexicans in general and villagers in particular are more concerned with local-level issues, as we have seen already. A summary of one such primary election in Yaxbe in February 1998 will provide some insight into the personalities and issues that prevail in one local community, as well as how factions form and how individuals decide which candidates to support.

There were three contenders for the PRI candidacy in 1998. In such cases, the state PRI officials will request that the pool be limited to two candidates. To this end, a committee of villagers met with the local PRI representative and the candidates. The purpose of this meeting was to decide which two candidates were stronger and to urge the weaker candidate to withdraw from the race for the good of the party. Unfortunately, the man considered the weakest candidate refused to step down, so voters were faced with a field of three PRI candidates: Don Lorenzo, Don Martín, and Don Ricardo.

Don Lorenzo, the younger brother of the current president, Don Alberto, was the favored candidate. Don Alberto was a controversial president, considered effective by some and ineffectual by others. Those who benefited from his largesse and wealth as an entrepreneur, were supportive of him. His prestige was further augmented because several valuable government projects came to the village during his presidency, including the medical clinic and resident doctor, a new library, and market. Others were not so impressed by his capabilities, asserting that those projects were initiated during the term of the previous president and that Don Alberto was

---

[2]This election took place before the 2000 election when the PAN candidate Vicente Fox defeated the PRI candidate for the first time since the birth of the modern political system in Mexico.

dishonest in accepting credit. In fact, there was convincing evidence that Don Alberto actually hindered development. For example, several women's groups had approached him during his term requesting assistance for their cooperatives (Chapter 9). His disregard and even hostility toward their programs earned him the reputation as unsympathetic toward women. The undisputed fact that Don Alberto supported two households, that of his wife and children, and that of his mistress, reinforced women's distrust of his personal and civic morality.

In contrast, Lorenzo was considered a dedicated family man who earned the reputation as a "good man" who, unlike his brother, did not neglect his family obligations. In his own campaign for president, Lorenzo benefited from his brother's position. He was part of Alberto's entourage, and was given the opportunity to do favors for villagers, building his own reputation as a generous and capable leader. Since the brothers worked together in the various family enterprises; beekeeping, agriculture, trucking, and store-keeping, they shared the reputation of hard workers and men of earned wealth.

Detractors (and supporters) of Lorenzo noted that he was the most generous in his campaign promises, offering nearly one pound of beef, tacos, and beer for those who voted for him. More cynical villagers complained that Lorenzo was blatantly buying votes, offering a rumored 50 pesos for each vote.

The second candidate was a very quiet and unassuming man, Don Martín, who worked at the government-subsidized grocery store. His was a subdued campaign, and I mistakenly assumed that the lack of discussion about him was evidence of a weak candidacy. Villagers all held strong opinions about Don Lorenzo (either for or against him) and also about Don Ricardo, discussed below, yet when I tried to elicit comments and opinions about Martín, people all said simply, "he is '*buena gente*'." I was thus very surprised as I watched the long line of supporters form outside his house on election day to collect his modest offerings of tacos and soft drinks. While Martín did not win,[3] he accumulated the second largest number of votes, including the vote of my friend who was related to the third candidate, Don Ricardo.

Don Ricardo's candidacy was widely debated for several reasons. First, it was he who had been encouraged to drop from the race at that initial meeting and who had refused to do so, claiming that he had considerable support in the village. Second, his candidacy was controversial because he was the first candidate to associate himself with, and seek support from, the "professional" class of Yaxbe.

Don Ricardo is a teacher and the director of the village secondary school. He is one of a growing class of village professionals, yet his social standing in the village did not elicit the enthusiasm that he expected from his educated peers nor did he gain any support from the vast majority of individuals who had not attained his level of education. He made several fatal errors in his candidacy. First, he called for a "party of the professionals" and assumed that other educated people in the village would endorse him based on shared social status. While he may have received votes from other professionals in the village, it was presumptuous to believe that people would support him for that reason. In fact, the village value of humility is still strong, and most villagers, professional and otherwise, were offended by his haughty demeanor and elitism.

---

[3]When I returned to the village in 2001, I discovered that Don Martín had just recently won election as the new president, replacing Don Lorenzo.

Second, Don Ricardo had a reputation for condescending to villagers, and for lacking tolerance for those, including his own brother, who suffered from the economic and social afflictions stemming from the abuse of alcohol. Last, villagers considered Ricardo stingy. He did not follow the tradition of charity and gift giving, eschewing the *patrón* role expected of a candidate. Further, he did not even promise any food offerings for his supporters after the election. Although his family did prepare food on election day, no lines formed outside his house at any time.

Don Ricardo's most serious error was articulated well by Reymundo, his cousin. In his view, Don Ricardo confused politics with professional approval. Approximately a year earlier, there had been numerous complaints from students and parents about teachers at the secondary school who didn't come to classes or who arrived late. There was particular concern over one teacher who regularly came to school intoxicated. The *Padres de Familia* made a formal complaint to Don Ricardo, and he acted swiftly, enforcing promptness and firing the teacher accused of drunkenness. In response, the teacher's union attempted to discredit Don Ricardo and petitioned the state to fire him. The *Padres de Familia* defended Don Ricardo, and he retained his position at the school. Unfortunately, Don Ricardo believed that the support he received from the parents would carry over into his political campaign. He was surprised when this did not happen. The reluctance of villagers to transfer their approval from the professional to the political realms was based primarily on his personal characteristics. Instead of being humbled and appreciative of the community endorsement, he had become more arrogant and self-righteous about his position at the school and his social status.

The excitement of the elections built up over the weeks. Candidates and their followers visited homes, trying to win over undecided villagers or convince others to switch sides. Stories and gossip hung in the air as election day approached. Everyone had an opinion; everyone had heard a story in support of a candidate's outstanding character or had heard evidence of his deceit. Genealogies were compared: who came from a trustworthy family, whose father did a good deed or despicable act. Without television or radio media to shape opinions, success or failure rides on a multitude of factors, many of which are beyond the candidate's control. Reputation is constructed of layers of fact and fiction, shaped in part by the lives of those who lived before, such as the candidate's grandparents and parents. A candidate's life is an open book, but it is a book open to interpretation; character is exposed for debate and criticism; and in the end, each villager votes according to a complex decision-making process where kinship, status, selfish calculation, personality, and character intersect.

On the evening before the election, I was washing dishes in Dora's kitchen when I heard a low rumbling that increased in intensity to a raucous cacophony of voices, primarily female. Looking out the window above the sink, I watched as a crowd, dominated by women, advanced along the road that bypasses the house. As they approached, our neighbors came to their windows or out into the street, exchanging greetings and joking with those passing by. Several women joined the group as it moved on, laughing and singing.

This lighthearted episode taught me about an important component of village elections—women. Because the president's wife becomes the president of the DIF program, she and her relatives and friends have a stake in the outcome of the election. As stated earlier, women can appoint others to fill important DIF positions, allotting them a substantial amount of prestige in the community. Beyond the promises that she can make to her supporters, a candidate's wife can make an important contribution to her husband's campaign. A woman who is generous, outgoing, and who belongs to a variety of local groups will be able to generate enthusiasm and support for her husband and aid him greatly in his candidacy. This group of women that passed by comprised one of these groups.

Later, when I wandered to the park, I found that the three wives' groups had converged in the plaza. Women and children in each group were throwing jovial barbs back and forth, and taunting those who were walking along the streets or loitering outside stores and houses. Passers-by and villagers lounging in the park watched with interest as the boisterous, jumbled bands of recruiters strolled by, waving and calling them to follow. Men, gathered in small clusters in front of the government building, looked on with bemusement, waving and joking with the passing groups.

According to Mexican law, it is illegal to sell, purchase, and consume alcohol on the day preceding and the day of an election. Thus, villagers approach the election sober and thoughtful. The somber mood permeated the village the following morning as villagers lined up along the *palacio* to vote. After casting their ballots, they lined up again at a smaller table to receive their stamped receipt that allowed them to collect their meat portion. Men then returned to work, and women proceeded to their candidate's house to obtain their meat portion.

Election day is always spent in idle speculation, as the villagers slowly return to their normal routines. But their eyes and ears are acutely tuned to what is happening at the homes of the candidates. A candidate's success or failure is measured by the lines outside his house. Villagers comment on who is standing in whose line as each villager's vote is made public and open to excited gossip and further speculation. Neighbors evaluate and analyze why certain individuals might have voted for certain candidates, especially if they were expected to support someone else. Rumors of possible political patronage or individual benefit are repeated and expanded on as the day wears on.

Later in the evening when the alcohol ban is lifted, husbands and wives will attend the party at the home of their candidate. This can be an awkward situation as husbands and wives do not always vote for the same candidate. Reymundo and Sonia laugh about how they often cancel out each other's vote. A certain amount of finesse is needed to balance these social occasions, for rumor and miscommunication can result in harmful gossip. Some villagers have the reputation of being dishonest about their vote in order to celebrate with the winning candidate, and others are accused of obtaining tickets from more than one candidate in order to collect food from several sources. Although it is considered bad manners, some people are known to crash several parties, taking advantage of the generosity of the candidates. Once the parties begin, it becomes clear who the winner is, though the results aren't final until the next day.

In this election, to no one's surprise, Lorenzo defeated Martín and Ricardo. Also to no one's surprise but my own, Ricardo came in last place. One villager noted that Ricardo's own brother, an unemployed alcoholic, did not vote for him, and had attended the party of one of the other candidates.

I asked our friend Reymundo who would run against Lorenzo in the general election. He noted that men are reluctant to commit themselves to a PAN candidacy. There was a fear, encouraged by the PRI, that the election of a PAN candidate would mean a loss of government-sponsored programs for their community. Now that PAN has proven its legitimacy as a political party, this view may change. But at that time, Reymundo's response was that "PRI always wins."

Conclusion

It is impossible to experience a local Mexican election without making comparisons to the election process in the United States. We may be critical of the "food for votes" campaign strategy, but we must place it into a perspective of village life. Villagers themselves outwardly disapprove of the practice, at least in conversations with me. Yet, the willingness to provide a food gift, to have a party, is part of the value system embedded in village life. Candidates are judged, not by their accumulation of wealth, but by their generosity. A candidate indicates his future beneficence by promising a gift now, or by giving a loan, or paying for someone's medicine. These are examples of his commitment to community, his willingness to share.

Villagers' complaints about the candidate's gifts followed two divergent philosophies. Don Lorenzo was criticized because his gifts were outrageous by local standards. Payment of 50 pesos per vote is crass. It is demeaning and evidence of arrogance and wealth that exceeds the expectation of generosity tempered by humility. By giving lavish gifts, he was bragging about his wealth, putting it out for display, thus violating an important traditional value in village life.

On the other hand, Don Ricardo was criticized for not offering food gifts or patronage. In this case, he was violating the custom of generosity. He garnered votes based on his personal achievements, not on community values. Placing himself outside of the traditional prestige system, Ricardo did not feel that he needed to participate in the established mechanisms of political largesse. In this election, tradition proved triumphant, and Lorenzo won the election. Generosity, however extravagant it might have been, defeated the incipient values of accumulation, individual success over community benefit, and social pretense over humility.

In the United States, even the most local elections are dependent on the promotion and "selling" of a candidate whom few people actually know personally. The more local an election is, the more likely that candidates are known and their views are common knowledge. People gossip about a candidate's family history, and the skeletons are dragged from closets. Candidates are also chosen according to their personal characteristics and what they might be able to offer voters as individuals, or how the candidate could promote the local interests or needs of his or her community. It is a truism where I live in rural Michigan that the road to the township supervisor's house is always paved. This may seem a trite or provincial consideration to one who lives in a city, but to a dairy farmer or simply any resident who tires of bumping down pot-holed gravel roads, this can be a strong voting incentive.

Before questioning the integrity of Mexican elections, we need to consider one important fact. In the United States, only 40–60% of registered voters vote in the general elections; the percentage is even lower in primaries, where party candidates are chosen. In the village election of 1998, 90% of the eligible voters went to the polls. Even though they may be cynical about the political process, they are optimistic enough about their leaders and concerned enough about their village that they choose to participate in the process. Voting is a highly valued civic responsibility and one that is taken seriously.

CRIME AND PUNISHMENT IN YAXBE

In 1976, my first indication that Yaxbe was generally peaceful community emerged when I met Don Armando, the 75-year-old police chief. A diminutive man, so thin and frail it seemed a child could easily topple him, Don Armando commanded respect in the village (see Figure 5.2). In his wisdom, he had appointed two sober middle-aged men as his deputies and he, taking his position seriously, made daily rounds in the village. Being almost a foot taller than the elderly man, I always felt huge and ungainly when I stood next to him, but since he rarely sat in an office, I had to talk to him as he walked in his clipped pace around the village. In one of these walking interviews, I asked him if Yaxbe had many murders. I had read about many villages in which family and political factions resulted in bloodshed and death, and I wondered if this was common in rural areas. In response to my question, Don Armando paused, lifted his panama hat, scratched his head, and told me that there had not been a murder in the village since 1948 when Don Jose had killed the *hacienda* worker. Ironically, it was Don Jose's son, Don Ernesto, the current village president (1976–1977), who had appointed Don Armando to his position as Police Chief. The irony was not lost on the aging man, as he noted earnestly that Don Jose's children were all good people and that his wife was well-respected and *una luchadora* (a fighter). Since the 1948 murder, I have only heard of one additional murder in the village, one that occurred several years before my 1998 visit. This recent murder appears to have been the result of a fight between two intoxicated men. While the victim's family insists that it was murder, the family of the perpetrator insists it was an accident. In 2002, the convicted man was still in prison, serving a 10-year sentence. His wife is also a victim in this tragedy as she is struggling to support herself during his absence.

The major offenses in Yaxbe, even today, are theft and drunkenness. Robberies usually involve turkeys and pigs that can be quickly sold. Several local men have spent time in the state prison because of repeat offenses of this nature. During our first stay in the village there was an unsolved robbery of unique quality, one that even the victims could not fault for its creativity. The *Padres de Familia* of one of the public schools had planted a small field of henequen for the purpose of raising money. The fathers had donated the *hijos* and volunteered their time to plant and weed the henequen. One day, when a group of men set out to cut some leaves, they discovered that someone (or several men) had harvested all the leaves, leaving only the center stalk. There were no leaves left to harvest! While everyone was understandably frustrated and distraught by the theft, there was an undercurrent of awe and curiosity. Who had the nerve to cut the leaves and how were they able to sell them without arousing any suspicion? The culprit or culprits were never discovered, at least during our stay in the village.

Drunkenness is a major cause of local concern, especially on weekends and during *fiestas.* While men work very hard in the fields during the week, there is a pattern of heavy drinking on the weekend. Some men do not work regularly and have the reputation for drinking away their family's income. Police deputies will place men who are drunk and disorderly in the local jail until they sober up, or take them home to their irate wives or mothers. The police seldom arrest men who are fighting, unless someone is injured. The president resolves most minor offenses, whether alcohol- or theft-related. He decides whether the men will spend any time in jail, for how

Figure 5.2 Don Armando, Police Chief, 1976–1977. The Catholic church is in the background.

long, and whether restitution should be paid. He also resolves domestic assaults, many of which are alcohol-related. Most of these complaints and crimes are settled without formal sanction.

Women, despite the stereotype of demure passivity, can be very assertive when it comes to the conduct of their sons and husbands. On several occasions, I watched the human circle around two drunken brawlers open as a mother or wife approached. In one case, an elderly mother, dressed in a *huipil* and shawl, forced her way between two fighters and hauled her son from the circle. Dragging him by the arm, she bombarded him with a barrage of angry Mayan expletives. Several men from the circle then assisted the remaining man to his feet while the crowd dispersed. In the past, women often had to tolerate the drinking of their husbands, saying little. Today, because many wives are less dependent on the income of their husbands, they are more likely than before to leave them and return home to their families. In cases where the families live **neolocally** (separate from both parents) or **matrilocally** (with or near the wife's family), the wife has more influence over her husband.

Contending with drunken men was the most perplexing problem for me in Yaxbe. While my husband was able to defuse and divert drunks by putting his arm around them in a friendly fashion and then leading them away from our house or from me, that was not a culturally acceptable technique for me. While I never felt threatened by intoxicated men, it was difficult to avoid their attentions when they decided that

ETHNOGRAPHIC ESSAY
OF CAMERAS AND TURKEY THIEVES

For many months in late 1976, LaVail and I waited with intense anticipation for the annual *fiesta* for Yaxbe's patron saint, the Virgin of Candelaria, which would take place in February of 1977. I had read extensively about these important celebrations, and I had nagged everyone to tell me every detail about the preparations and the daily festivities. As the long anticipated event approached, we had been invited to several parties, and we were in the mood for the *fiesta* proper to begin. Yet, the day before the *jarana,* something happened which, from that point onward, transformed our relationship with the villagers.

We were invited to what I thought was a **gremio,** a religious procession sponsored by volunteer organizations (Chapter 6). In my excitement, I invited my mentor, a retired anthropologist who was living in Mérida, and he all too graciously accepted our invitation. It was a beautiful warm day and normally we would have walked to the *hacienda* where the "*gremio*" was being held, but because of the frail health of Professor Hanson, we rode with him in his car. That there was no procession did not immediately draw my attention, nor did the fact that the Virgin was not present at the hosting house. Rather, as it turned out, this was a mere pre-*fiesta* event, a nice party with beer and tacos. I had been taking pictures of those in attendance and carelessly placed my camera under my chair. Later, in the crush of good-bye hugs and well wishes, I left my camera behind. Halfway back to the village, I remembered it and we returned to find that it was gone.

The family that sponsored the party was very upset about the disappearance, for they had seen the camera, placed it up on their dresser for safekeeping, and did not see anyone take it. The host and hostess misunderstood my distress as accusation, and the encounter took on an unpleasant air. As I asked questions as to who might have stolen it, and who was there when they placed it on the wardrobe, the couple became more and more defensive and upset. Inadvertently, we had made them responsible for the loss of our camera, and they did not know us well enough to know how we would resolve the predicament. Later, I learned from friends that they feared that we would demand that they replace the camera, although that had never entered our minds. Nor did we suspect them as the thieves.

We never officially reported the theft to the president. That was hardly necessary since the story had spread through the village almost instantaneously. Although villagers outwardly sympathized with us and noted the lack of shame of those who would steal, no one expressed much hope of ever finding the camera. The local police never came to talk to us about it. In fact people were, to our thinking, exploiting our plight as a source of entertainment and mirth. "Well, I wonder where your camera is now," one man mused. "Is it worth a lot of money?" Another man chuckled, "Well, with the money from the camera, the thief is probably in the United States by now—maybe he bought a house." When we complained to Reymundo about the general disregard for our feelings, he insisted that they were concerned, but that there is nothing that could be done. The camera was gone. Then, in the sage way he had of putting the most complex ideas into perspective, he noted that, after all, "*La oportunidad hace el ladrón.*" (Opportunity makes the thief.)

The fieldwork experience is filled with small occurrences that teach us more than the larger events we had so enthusiastically anticipated. Such it was that this event, so distressing at the time, fostered one of those serendipitous lessons. As part of my fieldwork, I was interested in the incidence of certain crimes in the village. Although Yaxbe seemed a very quiet community, with the obvious exception of the weekend drinking behaviors, I was sure that there had to be crimes and criminals. Yet, villagers were very reluctant to discuss the topic beyond the generic "Yaxbe is a peaceful village." When pressed, villagers would make brief mention of turkey thieves, but informants seemed almost embarrassed to mention such a lowly group of miscreants. I was encouraged by this information, which fit nicely into my romanticized vision of rural life.

Yet, there were some disturbing clues fluttering at the back of my mind, which at the time caused only minimal discomfort. First, was the inordinate amount of debate and concern expressed on our arrival about the security of our medical clinic house. There was much discussion, most of which we didn't understand at the time, that resulted in closing up the airy cement lattice work along the outside of the building. Then there was the day when a Mérida police car raced into the village in a cloud of limestone dust and stopped at the president's office. As I and many others watched, a man unknown to me was hustled out of the jail and into the police car that then disappeared as quickly as it had appeared, leaving another cloud of choking dust in its wake. My questions about the identity and the crime of the individual were answered with a shrug and "it's one of the turkey thieves."

The theft of our camera, much later, was the event that cracked the veneer of the "ideal" culture. It was then that I

learned that, despite everyone's earlier assertions that there were no serious criminals in the village, there were. Suddenly villagers wanted to tell me about the bad people ("*mala gente*") in the village. I then began to compile a list of all the village thieves. Most of these criminals were still designated as turkey thieves, but I became aware of the seriousness of this crime. Turkeys (and pigs) are a type of savings account. Women purchase turkeys as chicks and raise them, investing much time and some money into their food and care. Female turkeys are raised for their eggs or for their chicks that are sold; adult toms are sold or used by the family for important celebration feasts: *gremios, quinceñeras,* or weddings. The theft of a turkey can be a major loss of income for a family and especially for elderly women who may depend on their fowl for their livelihood. In relative economic term, the loss of a turkey over the long term may more accurately compare to the loss of a car than to a camera.

As the list of turkey thieves grew, several villagers noted that one of these men was, unbeknownst to me, at the party in question. Conventional wisdom soon prevailed that he was the thief. In fact, I was told, he was the man who had been taken by the Mérida police on that day earlier in our research year. But alas, he had returned in time for *fiesta.* Consequently, after so much anticipation, I had no photographs of the *fiesta* of 1977, the *jarana,* or the bullfight.

It was for this reason that I was even more anxious about attending the *fiesta* of 1998. I had both camera and video camcorder at the ready. Each time I passed the man who is the alleged thief, I held my camera more closely to my side and averted my gaze. I suspected he

(*continued*)

ETHNOGRAPHIC ESSAY
OF CAMERAS AND TURKEY THIEVES (*continued*)

was still living off the money he received for my new Canon and telephoto lens. I wasn't particularly enthusiastic about subsidizing the rest of his life with my new equipment. Besides, I told myself, he was never proven to be the culprit and might be perfectly innocent. Although I feel certain that many people know the truth, I will never know for sure. Nor should I. It is another of those local conspiracies, and now a local legend in which the Yaxbe gringos are forever part of their village history.

they wanted to talk to me in the street. Often men who were otherwise very courteous and soft-spoken when sober (when I truly wanted to speak with them), became overly friendly and verbose once intoxicated. They wanted to shake my hand, put their arm around me and tell me the history of their family, why their wives left them, or what I always wanted to know about the corruption in the village. Unfortunately, they were not coherent in this state nor could I trust the validity of their statements. At first, spectators nearby would intercede on my behalf if I were accosted, for which I was simultaneously thankful and embarrassed. Later, when my Spanish improved, and people were accustomed to my presence, they often just watched in amusement as I tried to deflect the attentions of these men or extricate myself from their uninvited hugs.

I have inserted this discussion on alcohol abuse, not to reinforce the stereotypes many Americans hold of Mexican men, but to elaborate on a social problem which is not limited to Mexico, but one which often accompanies poverty and social powerlessness. In ancient tradition and ceremonies, native alcoholic beverages such as *balché* were consumed for religious purposes, as part of ritual. The use of alcohol as an escape from the harshness of life is a recent phenomenon, arriving with colonialism and early slavery and peonage. Alcoholism or alcohol abuse is not endemic in the village. Many men do not drink at all or drink only socially. It is a few men who abuse alcohol, just as there are in the United States and everywhere else where alcohol is consumed. It is this minority, however, who are visible, reclining in doorways or staggering down the road. These men cause many difficulties to their families, deplete already limited resources, and sometimes abuse their family members. However, the strength of the familial networks diffuses the problem somewhat by providing support for women and their children. As will be seen in Chapter 7, the Seventh Day Adventists have also increased their numbers by promoting abstinence. It is often the wives and mothers of alcoholics who come to the temple for solace and support, eventually convincing or shaming their menfolk to attend services with them and mend their ways.

Social Control

I have shown that Yaxbe is a peaceful town, for the most part, untroubled by violent factionalism and capital offenses. This relative calm is a result of several important social and economic factors:

EXTERNAL SOURCES OF FACTIONALISM AND TENSION   Unlike many areas of Mexico, Yaxbe lacks a nonlocal class system, as we have already seen. Any urban representatives, *hacendados,* government officials, or priests are no longer resident in the village, and the descendants of the Spanish aristocracy do not constitute a privileged class. In addition, the *ejidal* system imposed in the henequen zone is not conducive to the evolution of a landed gentry class as found elsewhere. While some merchants and *parcelarios* represent an affluent class, wealth distinctions are not always obvious and income is not necessarily translated into political power. Thus the political factionalism, violence related to land issues, and internal conflict found elsewhere in Mexico are minimized here.

INTERNAL SOURCES OF COHESION   As we have already seen, village endogamy and *compadrazgo* function to establish and reinforce village networks. These patterns further reduce the possibility of village tension. Even in such potentially volatile situations as village elections, people are civil, and emotions are restrained by the complexity of ties that bind people to one another. Where mutual respect and civility may fail, other mechanisms of social control, such as gossip and ostracism, become important. In small communities, the pressure to conform is strong, and individuals are unlikely to intentionally violate social norms. While some individuals continuously operate at the margins of society (such as the thieves and to some extent the alcoholics), these are in the minority. These individuals are known in the village, and although they are generally tolerated, villagers are aware of their vices and distance themselves and their children from them. In other words, villagers do not condone the behavior but they accept the deviant, because he or she is tied to the community in a web of kinship and social ties that must be honored in order for the society to function.

CONCLUSION

Far from being isolated peasants, mired in local conservatism, Yucatecan villagers are embroiled daily in local, state, and national events and issues. And they are not passive disinterested people, concerned only with events within the limits of their village. They participate in political discourse and vote regularly. Doña Rosa, the president of the PACR in 1976, was later a local delegate to PRI who traveled to Mexico City to meet with President Zedillo. Villagers and Mexicans in general are avid newspaper readers, and I am always impressed by their level of knowledge of state and national events. Mérida has three newspapers and I can tell a villager's political leanings by the paper he or she reads on a daily basis. I would even suggest that Yaxbeños are better informed about Yucatecan state politics than many Americans are about their own local and state issues. In other words, they are active agents, interested and opinionated.

Yaxbeños live in a complicated world, yet they have found the means to construct a stable local government, based on strong values of family and reciprocity. They are adept at taking what comes their way from the government and accepting or rejecting it in ways that reflect resilience and a subtle pattern of resistance and manipulation. They have a civil society that is not burdened by crime or widespread corruption or abuse of power. They have a healthy cynicism about their government and about their future. In short, they have learned how to maintain a stable society that has accepted diversity of class, religion, ethnicity, and is in the process of absorbing new ideas of women's economic and social roles, as well as widespread changes in their economic realities. Their history of resilience and tolerance will serve them well in these new challenges.

6/Mayan and Catholic Roots in Yaxbe

[A]ll primitive religions are grotesque and to some extent unintelligible. . . .

—Lewis Henry Morgan, 1964 [1877]: 13

These people also used certain characters or letters, with which they wrote in their books about the antiquities and their sciences; with these, and with figures, and certain signs in the figures, they understood their matters, made them known, and taught them. We found a great number of books in these letters, and since they contained nothing but superstition and falsehoods of the devil we burned them all, which they took most grievously, and which gave them great pain.

Friar Diego de Landa, 1566, translated by Gates 1978: 48–49

MAYAN AND CATHOLIC SYNCRETISM

Introduction

In this chapter, we will explore the impact of Catholicism on the indigenous Mayan religion. First, I will provide a brief summary of the Mayan religion as it pertains to our discussion, then the impact of Catholicism on colonial Mexico. Next, I will turn to the factors that facilitated the conversion of an entire country to Catholicism and how Mexicans have managed to maintain many of their traditional beliefs. Throughout this discussion, I will emphasize the resilience of traditional religion and customs and the ability of the Maya of Yaxbe to syncretize two religious beliefs into an integrated system of belief. Before examining Maya and Catholic religious beliefs specifically, let's take a brief look at the anthropological perspective on religion.

Religion in an Anthropological Context

Anthropologists have always been keenly interested in the religious lives of non-Western peoples. The earliest British anthropologists and social philosophers, such as Sir James Frazer (*The Golden Bough 1911–1915*) and E. B. Tylor (*Primitive Culture* 1958 [1871]) earned their reputations by reporting and examining the religious life of exotic peoples "discovered" by 19th century missionaries and explorers. In 12 volumes, Sir James Frazer catalogued the many beliefs of native peoples—such as beliefs in ghosts or ancestors—as well as their religious rituals. Using the unilineal evolutionary model dominant at that time, these early philosophers believed that human religious beliefs and culture evolve from "primitive" to civilized with Western and Christian beliefs being the ultimate forms.

This belief system reflected very neatly the social philosophy of 19th century Europe whose colonial tentacles permeated the non-Western world—Africa, India, and Asia. It served as a rationale for colonialism, forming the basis for the moral mandate of colonial Europe to bring "primitive" people out of their savage state so that they could benefit from the fruits of civilization, live like Europeans, and participate in European lifestyle. For missionaries, colonialism was a vehicle to convert the indigenous people to their religious beliefs—thus be saved in the afterlife as well.

Since Frazer, anthropologists have come to understand that religion and supernatural beliefs frame one's worldview and present an explanation for things beyond one's comprehension. Anthropologists recognize that religions are valid symbolic systems that reflect the cultures and shape the value systems in the societies where they are found. Origin myths form the basis of a cultural worldview, explaining the origins of the universe, and how the animals and humans came to live here. In band and tribal societies, the supernatural consists of animistic spirits and demons that reside in nature, lurk in forests, and reside in plants. But these spirits are not omnipotent. Rather they, like humans themselves, are part of nature.

When societies become more complex and develop characteristics of state-level societies (social hierarchies, complex division of labor and economic systems, and written language, for example), religion also evolves to reflect the new social realities. Omnipotent gods and goddesses replace the temperamental and unpredictable spirits. These new deities form supernatural hierarchies and control natural and social domains: the rains, fertility, and wildlife, as well as war and peace. Nevertheless, within these new hierarchies, earlier religious beliefs and spirits persevere and still influence the daily lives of humans.

This type of state-level religion is **polytheistic**; that is, it consists of a **pantheon** of gods who share power over the natural and social environment and who have a hierarchy among themselves of lesser and more powerful deities. When the Maya social organization developed into a state-level society, a pantheon of dangerous and powerful gods that ruled the heavens and the underworld superceded local spirits. Most Westerners are more familiar with another type of state-level religion, **monotheism,** in which a single all-powerful deity demands love and respect. The conquest of the New World was not a conquest of state society over band-level animists, but of one state-level society over another.

Mayan Roots

The Maya developed a complex stratified society in which specialists filled political, economic, and religious positions. The *halach uinic* was the hereditary ruler, or governor, of a ceremonial center. While his major functions were military and political, he was also the dominant religious leader for the region, comparable to a bishop. Men of noble families not in line for the *halach uinic* were prominent in politics, their sons prominent in commerce or the priesthood. The priesthood was also open to young men of lesser birth who were believed to have special abilities. As in the celestial sphere where hierarchy and specialization divided the world and the roles of the gods, so too were the responsibilities of the priests. Young men learned their specialties through strenuous training and years of apprenticeship. Some of these specialties were ritualistic in nature requiring the ability to perform certain generalized ceremonies, such as healing. The most exalted and skilled priests are those who were specialists in the various sacrificial rites and the **chilamob** who were skilled at interpreting the prophecies (Henderson 1981: 62–63).

The Mayan priesthood interpreted a complex cosmological system consisting of 13 tiers comprising earth, sky, and the underworld. Each tier was represented by a vast collection of gods and goddesses who acted ultimately under the rule of the creator god, **Itzamná.** The earth gods command the daily lives of the Maya. Among these deities are the god of maize and **Ix Chel,** the goddess of weaving and childbirth. Occupation and social class are also replicated within the terrestrial plane in the presence of gods of merchants, cacao producers, and **Kukulkan,** the feathered serpent and the god of the aristocracy (Henderson 1981: 85). For the Maya, the most prominent god within this realm is *Chac,* the god of rain and thunder to whom the lowland Maya offered human sacrifices in the past and to whom they still pay homage today. Humans, in order to assure the continuation both of the life cycle and the agricultural cycle, made sacrifices to these various gods. Many of these sacrifices were minimal, small animals or pilgrimages to sacred caves. However, some deities such as *Chac,* because of his power in delivering the rain necessary for their survival, demanded extraordinary sacrifices of human blood.

Catholicism

The roots to both Spanish and Catholic imperialism in the New World lay in the history of Spain itself (Carmack, et al. 1996: 123). Starting in the 1300s, after Spain regained its lands from the Moors and reestablished Catholicism as the religion of Europe, an era of nationalism and Catholic fervor defined the Spanish worldview. When King Ferdinand and Queen Isabella sent Columbus to discover the westward route to Asia, their goals were threefold: (1) to claim Spanish sovereignty over all those regions "discovered" along the way; (2) to discover trade routes; and (3) to spread the Catholic religion throughout the world (ibid.1996: 125).

After Cortés conquered the Aztecs (1520s) and Montejo pacified the Maya (1540s), it was the work of the priests and friars to convert the indigenous populations to Catholicism. In order to pacify and to rule the Indians, the early colonialists faced several challenges. First, many of the Indians had escaped into the mountains and rain forests to avoid conquest. Further, the process of conquest had reduced indigenous populations dramatically; in some areas populations declined 90–95% in the first 75 years of contact (Carmack, et al. 1996: 128). In order to resolve the dilemma of controlling and converting small and dispersed groups of hostile Indians, the Spanish colonists set aside certain villages, placing them under the jurisdiction of local Spanish administrators and a parish priest or friar. These *reducciones* often brought together Indians of divergent traditions and languages, forming new social congregations without shared cultures.

The diversity of cultures and languages facilitated the pacification of these various groups and gave the religious leaders a compliant group of potential converts. To promote a sense of unity within these newly formed communities, each was assigned a patron saint that became the focus for religious events within the village. Villagers were expected to support and promote the various saint days of the Catholic calendar, with special attention given to their own patron saint who was celebrated yearly with special Masses, processions, and secular activities.

The Catholic Church in Yaxbe

In all Mexican villages, the church is a microcosm of the urban cathedral, built as both a fortress and place of worship. The church in Yaxbe is no exception. The Catholic Church itself is monolithic. The priest is the head of the parish and controls all activities. In most villages, he visits only weekly for Mass, performing a circuit between various towns and *haciendas* in a particular parish. The priest is often assisted by a *padre,* or non-ordained clergyman, who performs many of the more secular services of the church: organizing events and leading youth groups and catechism classes. The priest, *padre,* and two nuns who served Yaxbe, three other villages, and five *haciendas,* lived in a nearby village. A new priest arrived during our stay, a young Yucatecan who spoke several languages, including Maya, and who had actually been to Rome.

Most villagers consider themselves Catholic and identify with the precepts of the Church. The Church permeates the daily life of the villagers in various ways. First it is the location for most important rites of passage, baptism, First Communion, *quinceñeras,* and weddings. Second, school and village holidays and events revolve around the liturgical calendar that dictates saint days and the annual *fiesta.*

Women are the core of the Catholic Church, comprising the majority of the Sunday congregation. With the exception of the men who serve as lay leaders and caretakers of the priest's religious paraphernalia, women perform many of the day-to-day functions of the church, taking care of the Virgin of Candelaria, and scheduling rosary readings. As we will see, women are also very active in the *gremios,* or voluntary groups that care for and sponsor the Virgin of Candelaria during the annual *fiesta*. They are marvelous organizers and well-disciplined when it comes to finances and shared responsibilities. As in Catholicism everywhere, women have an ambiguous position in the church. They are valuable members, but are unable to hold any positions of authority. This reluctance of the Catholic Church to give legitimacy to the dedicated faith of Catholic women is one of various reasons why many women turned to the Seventh Day Adventists, as we will see in the next chapter.

The Social Construction of Religion: Syncretized Religious Meanings

When the Catholic friars imposed their God on the Maya and Aztec pantheons, a process of syncretism began. Syncretism is a process through which deities, beliefs, and practices from distinct religions "become reinterpreted and transformed in situations of cultural encounter" (Carmack, et al. 1996: 303). In this way, the Catholicism that is practiced today in Mexico is one quite distinct from the mother religion. For example, Mexicans idolize the Virgin of Guadelupe, an indigenous version of Mary, who showed herself to an Indian man in 1531 and for whom an exquisite cathedral has been built near Mexico City. Catholic rituals and customs, such as *compadrazgo* and the various processions and *fiestas* for village saints, have a decidedly indigenous component. Likewise, traditional local ceremonies, such as the *comistraje,* have incorporated Catholic elements, with saints being supplicated along with the Mayan gods.

In some cases, the Maya accepted Christian symbols and rituals because they were already embedded in their traditional beliefs. First, a coincidence of symbols gave the Catholics an important inroad to the Mayan religion. The cross, a vital symbol for Christians, was also important to the Maya who placed them at the openings of caves and other sacred places where the gods lived. Second, both Maya and Catholics created engraved images of their gods or saints, so the practice of worshipping these images was familiar to the Maya, even though the new gods were not. Third, both religions are militaristic, many deities representing important symbols for warfare and conquest, as well as peace. Finally, the Maya also shared various rituals with the Christians. Prayer, sacrifice, and procession were all-important elements of both Maya and Catholic religions. Thus the saint-day processions, the procession to the cemetery for the **Day of the Dead,** and the Christmas *posadas*[1] coalesced well with their traditional practices of visiting the sacred caves and *cenotes* to worship their gods and spirits (Carrasco 1990: 137–145).

In the following sections, we will examine three areas of syncretism. In the first section, we will look at the role of ancient spirits in reinforcing local values. In the second section, we will examine two rituals. The first is the *comistraje,* an ancient rain ceremony, conducted by the *h-men,* that has absorbed Catholic elements over 400 years of practice. The second ritual is the annual *fiesta,* embedded in Catholic symbolism, yet enmeshed in rural culture and tradition.

THE PLACE OF ANCIENT SPIRITS IN A MODERN WORLD

Social Control and the Aluxes

As a model of social integration, indigenous religions promote a sense of solidarity, and, negatively, act as a means of social control. Religion is usually a conservative force, encouraging, through sanction, conformity to community beliefs and values, and discouraging behavior that violates these norms. In societies where the rule of law is weak or the central authority is distant geographically, social control and social boundaries are often maintained through supernatural means, through beliefs in sorcery, witchcraft, ghosts, or ancestors. These beliefs, often reinforced by gossip, are powerful mechanisms for maintaining cultural conformity.

---

[1]Saint-day processions involve a slow march of adherents from the church in which the saint is carried on a litter. The group walks around the block that encompasses the church in a quiet procession. The Day of the Dead occurs on October 31 to November 2 and involves visiting the graves of the ancestors and leaving food, drink, and candles. This is an excellent example of syncretization of indigenous and Catholic ritual. The Christmas *posada* occurs in the days prior to Christmas and reenacts the plight of Mary and Joseph who are seeking a place for the baby Jesus to be born. A large procession, with people and children in costume, visits two houses where they are refused entry and finally approaches a home where a party celebrates the birthplace of Jesus.

ETHNOGRAPHIC ESSAY
HUAY POP

One of my favorite photographs from our first stay in Yaxbe is one of LaVail standing outside the *lonchería* holding a young boy over the front stoop. A small group of other children are crowding around him and smiling as he pretended to drop Roberto off the stoop. Beside them is Roberto's older brother, Mundo (nickname for Edmundo). (See Figure 6.1.) Mundo and Roberto were the sons of Doña Maria and Don Ignacio, the owners of the store, *lonchería-cantina,* and television house discussed in Chapter 3. When we returned to the village in 1989, Mundo was married to the granddaughter of Don Berto, the wealthiest merchant in town, and the young married couple ran a small store near Don Berto's large enterprise. In 1992, Mundo was divorced from his first wife and had remarried. He had a newborn baby by his second wife and a new store, *"Tienda Gonzales,"* located near the main square. Mundo and his new family lived above the store in one of the villages first second-story buildings. The store was unique in that it had a soda fountain and the village's first video rental and video game arcade. Needless to say, his store was the favorite hang out for many young boys, including my sons.

In 1998, Mundo had renamed his store *"Huay Pop."* The soda fountain and video rentals were no longer there, but in

Figure 6.1 LaVail with his entourage, 1977

their place, he now sold cosmetics and pharmaceuticals. The video games were located in an enlarged area at the back of the store. Although his is no longer the only store with video games, he has the largest collection in the village. Mundo also has the reputation of being generous

Yaxbeños still believe in two types of apparitions that are part of the Maya supernatural realm: ***aluxob*** and ***Xtabai****. Aluxob* are small spirits that reside in nature, in the brush or *milpa*. They are mischievous, causing misfortune to those who find themselves outside the village at night. I realized that Yaxbeños believed in *aluxob* late one evening when I was sitting with Reymundo's family on their back patio after a party. It was nearly 2:00 in the morning, and I was nodding from fatigue. Everyone had been drinking and discussing the upcoming village election when gradually the conversation drifted and one man, Reymundo's brother-in-law, told a story about sleeping in the *monte* and feeling something crawl up his leg. When he had flashed his flashlight

with tokens and fair with the children when the machines malfunction.

At first, I thought that *Huay Pop* was a cute name for a store, and was surprised when, one day, I noticed that he had painted it over, leaving the store nameless. I began to ask villagers what *huay pop* meant, and I received coy smiles in response. My interest in the store and its unconventional owner peaked when I interviewed the *h-men* who, it turned out, was Mundo's uncle. As I spoke to the *h-men* about *aluxes* and sorcerers, he mentioned *huay pop* and laughed. He began to speak in hushed tones about spirits who sleep on mats like poor people, and winds that can transform themselves and move around at night; it was very mysterious but not very enlightening.

Later, other people shared *huay pop* stories with me. One story described a storekeeper in a nearby town who had a vast inventory, yet a supply truck never stopped in front. Every day the store was full of goods and the man became very wealthy. Another villager related another story that directly related to Mundo. This story, told by a man who lives in a house across from *Huay Pop* highlighted the suspicions that people had of him and his success. According to the story, the neighbor could not sleep one night and as he lay in his hammock he heard a knocking sound coming from the store.

After a few minutes, he climbed out of his hammock and went to his window and looked out. He saw an apparition at the door of *Huay Pop,* trying to enter the store. The narrator was certain that it wasn't Mundo because it resembled an animal. This story has circulated around the village. When I left the village, the store was still nameless and a smirking Mundo would not comment on the unfortunate choice of name.

When I returned to the United States and began to research *huay pop*, I found an interesting collection of references and stories that paralleled those I heard in the village. I have since found various references to this spirit, alternately referred to as *uay pop* or *uay cot* (Redfield and Villa Rojas 1990 [1934]: 179–180) and *uay kot* (re Cruz 1996). In a recent study of Chan Kom, Alicia re Cruz (1996:70) refers to a witch named "*uay-kot*" (Eagle witch) who is associated with storeowners and businessmen. She relates an *uay kot* story that is very close to the one that villagers told me. In Chan Kom, according to re Cruz, there is a storekeeper and moneylender who has a reputation of miserliness who has earned the reputation of "*uay kot*." He seldom leaves his store, yet has a large inventory which, though very disorganized, has earned him success (1996: 69–70).

on his leg, however, nothing was there. I jolted to consciousness as the conversation suddenly became animated. Excitedly the others related similar stories, all of which involved an overnight stay in one's *milpa* or *monte*. The stories ranged from instances of rustling in the bushes to experiences of a wind or breeze-like feeling on one's body while sleeping. No apparition was ever seen, however. When I asked about these sensations, wishing I had my tape recorder handy, they said that there are *aluxob* in the *monte* and they would hurt you if you didn't wake up and scare them away.

Now, shaken out of my sleepiness, I asked if *Xtabai* also lived in the *monte*, and the refrain from everyone in the group was "yes, she exists!". According to folklore,

Xtabai is a spirit who appears to men who wander in the *monte* in the evening. The spirit appears as a beautiful woman dressed in a *huipil*. She lures men who have been drinking or who just wandered too close to certain trees (particularly the *ceiba*), and the man will go with her into the *monte,* never to be seen again (Redfield and Villa Rojas 1990 [1934]: 122). Several of the men shared stories they had heard of how *Xtabai* had been seen in the brush surrounding Yaxbe, but none in the group claimed to have seen her.

These stories or folklore beliefs function to uphold certain moral values in the village, particularly against drinking and being away from the village after dark. They serve as a warning to those who do not stay at home. The story on *Huay Pop,* illustrates the important role of traditional beliefs in maintaining social control and in defining the marginal individuals in society.

The folklore stories illustrate the power of gossip and supernatural belief in maintaining social boundaries and in labeling those who do not conform in some way to the expectations of villagers. The *Huay Pop* story also raises the issue discussed often in Mesoamerican ethnography about the importance of egalitarianism in village life. George Foster's (1965) concept of the "limited good" is often held up as a model for egalitarianism. Briefly, in peasant societies, people believe that everything in life, good and bad, has a limited quantity. In other words, there is a limited amount of good health, wealth, and luck, and one's gain in any of these areas is another's loss. Thus, the man who is a successful merchant and whose daughters all marry well and have healthy children is often suspected of using sorcery or supernatural means of obtaining this advantage. His happiness is believed to subtract from everyone else's. The stories of *uay pop* (*kot, cot,* etc.) serve as both morality lessons and as means of explaining the wealth of others, that somehow these wealthy merchants have struck a deal with the devil.

In anthropology it is recognized that witchcraft and sorcery accusations are a strong means of social control in tribes and villages. Such accusations or fear of accusation can serve as a deterrent for those who might accumulate wealth or power or at least serve as an incentive to share one's wealth or participate in expected social activities. Witchcraft accusations can also be a means of labeling those who are deviant. Mundo may be considered deviant in two respects. First, he is one of the villagers who is openly *PANista*. The PAN mural on the wall of his store was the only one in the village until Vicente Fox was elected in 2000. He is also marginalized because he married and then divorced a woman from the most prominent family in the village. Several publicly observed and widely discussed confrontations in his store between Mundo and his ex-wife indicate that the wounds have not healed with the breakup of the marriage. This animosity and interfamily competition was further intensified when his ex-wife opened a new store, funded by her father and grandfather, on the same street as Mundo's. In divorcing his well-connected wife and marrying a woman from a poor family, Mundo lost a substantial source of capital. Instead, he is now responsible not only for maintaining his inventory, but for the livelihood of his own family and for his father-in-law who works for him. The fact that Mundo has been successful, that he is a young man with his own business, that he is able to pay employees, and that he is successfully in competition with his wealthy former in-laws are all possible reasons for accusations based on jealousy.

A TALE OF TWO RITUALS

Syncretism in religion can be seen in several aspects of village life. We have already seen how traditional healing contrasts to and has merged with modern concepts of health and healing. Now we will look at two ritual events, paying attention to how each has incorporated elements of both traditional and modern customs in order to maintain relevance and symbolic meaning. The first ritual is one in which Mayan elements dominate, the annual *comistraje,* or rain ceremony. In this ceremony, Catholic saints and Christian personages have found a home in ancient ritual.

Second, we will look at a ritual that defines the Catholic presence in Mexico, the *fiesta* for the village patron saint. This ritual, predominantly Catholic, illustrates the similarities in Maya and Catholic ritual: procession, feasting, and sacrifice. The annual *fiesta* has incorporated various elements of traditional Maya belief and is also an example of the syncretism between the sacred (religious) and the secular (non-religious). For example, while Christmas is a religious holiday for Christians, it has many secular elements—Santa Claus, Christmas trees, gifts, and parties. The secular elements of Christmas have recreated a celebration very far removed from the historical event, in meaning and form.

The Comistraje, 1977

In addition to his role as a traditional healer, the *h-men* is also responsible for communicating with the spirit world for the benefit of the entire community. He is called on to perform the annual *comistraje* (called *chachac* in the literature) in which the rain gods are propitiated to bring rain.

> I asked Don Teodoro about the Maya gods, the *Chacs,* and the winds that cause illness. He told me about the gods who live in the caves and how one must enter caves with respect so as not to offend them. "Anyone can enter and take water, if they enter with honor. The gods of the *cenotes* respect the farmer and he can always enter for water without asking permission. But if he brings in the bad air (*mal aire*), it is dangerous." The *cenotes* where the *Chacs* (rain gods) live are particularly dangerous and require the work of the *h-men.* "*Chac* likes to be coaxed; when it is very hot, [the *h-men*] organizes a *comistraje* to cry out to god to bring rain. When we signal to god that we want water and he goes to look for it in the *cenote.* As a sign, we go to look for water for *chachac* (at the four cardinal points)." (Field notes, 1998)

Although at the time of conquest, smaller city-states were all that remained of the earlier powerful theocratic society, those localized leaders and the gods that legitimized them still commanded respect and obedience. Many of the gods and goddesses remained paramount, *Itzamá, Ix Chel,* and the *Chacob.* In this dry region rain was of paramount concern, and human sacrifice to assure its timely arrival became another of the Maya preoccupations. To placate *Chac,* the most common technique was the wrenching of the beating heart from a victim, usually a prisoner or slave. Ritual specialists and four assistants performed the ceremony. It was followed by ritualized cannibalism to assure the well-being of the god, *Chac* (Henderson 1981: 67). This ceremony is still performed in many Maya villages, although turkeys and chickens have replaced humans as the sacrificial victims.

ETHNOGRAPHIC ESSAY
THE LAST *H-MEN*, 1998

I was nervous and tired as I stood once again outside the *h-men's* house. This was my third trip in several days. Somehow, it was fitting that the last Mayan shaman should live in the last house in the village, beyond the electrical poles, beyond the pavement. Yet, it was a long walk and on my two previous trips, he had not been home. I decided to return in the afternoon, when only the anthropologist ventures out into the sun. His house was not what I had expected. I anticipated a traditional house with thatch roof, but I found a simple rectangular house constructed with cement block and a crushed stone façade, a flat tin roof, and a wooden door that probably was removed from the original structure.

I called out in the expected manner from outside the limestone fence. "*¿Bueno?*" Several repetitions were rewarded with the faint creaking of hammock ropes rubbing against the hooks that connected it to the wall. "*Momentito.*" I listened to the faltering rhythm of sandals shuffling along a cement floor. When he pulled open the large door, his eyes flashed in recognition and he flashed me an almost toothless grin.

Don Teodoro is a gnarled old man, in his 70s now, not the imposing figure I remember from 20 years ago. His face is leathery and wrinkled, his eyes squinted from many years of working in the Yucatecan sun. His hair is gray, sparse, and disheveled. He is wearing a shirt that is torn and ragged. His buttons, almost a waste of time, are askew and his pants, held up with a length of rope, bag around his thin torso. He is also wearing handmade sandals, with henequen fiber straps and soles cut from old automobile tire remnants (see Figure 6.2).

He invited me into his house, dark except for the sunlight that passed through two windows on the front of the house and the open door that led out the back to his *solár.* Two faded hammocks, frayed and torn, hung from hooks on either side of the entrance doors, one of nylon and the other of henequen fibers. His meager possessions were piled in stacks along the walls; boxes overflowed with clothing, plastic containers, and agricultural tools. An old calendar fluttered in the hot breeze that blows in from the back entrance. He has no kitchen lean-to, but there is a cooking fire and a wash tub for his laundry. A widower of 35 years has few needs.

He is pleased that I have visited him. I have always shown an interest in his craft. Twenty years ago, after I spoke to him about the upcoming *comistraje,* he came to our house with a notebook, pages ripped and dirty and asked me if I

Because women are prohibited from attending the ritual, the *h-men* invited my husband to attend and allowed him to tape record and photograph the ceremony. Preparations for the *comistraje* began weeks before the event. One man was appointed the boss, and it was his job to collect the food and other supplies needed for the ceremony. Forty-one men contributed chickens, honey, chiles, and money. The total cost of the *comistraje*, including the 200 peso fee to the *h-men*, was 1,672 pesos (approximately US$45 in 1977). Several days before the ceremony, the men cleared and burned a section of land at the outskirts of the village, and collected water from sacred wells at each of the four cardinal points. They then constructed an

Figure 6.2 The h-men, 1998

freely about his life and his beliefs. I was fortunate that I was able to tape the interview as his Spanish is hard to follow. His stories are sprinkled with Mayan words and ideas that describe his universe— words that have no equivalence in a European tongue or worldview.

"I am a *sacerdote* (priest)," he begins. But he immediately makes a clarification. "We (*h-menob*) are *sacerdotes*, but "*Indio*" (Indian) *sacerdotes* not of the (Catholic) Church. . . . The Bible story says that all sacrifices will be a measure of the priest. But (we are) lower . . . we make offerings of food. . . ." He also makes a careful distinction between "his" gods and the Christian God: "God is one in the world, but he has his workers. Thus, like God has his angels and archangels, we have others to help us to see, like a wind."

Here, Don Teodoro is expressing the ambiguity between the Maya gods who are within his domain and the dominant Christian God. He is trying to make a place for both of them in the present day, articulating an uneasy coexistence of the two religions. The *h-men* has become, then, not only the Mayan shaman, but the arbiter between two belief systems, two ways of curing, and two ways of fashioning the world.

would make a copy for him on my typewriter. The notebook contained the prayers and ritual for the *comistraje*. I asked if I could make a copy for myself as well and he said "*¿porque no?*" Today, he tells me that he remembers that I made the new copy for him and that he still has it.

For the interview, he offered me a *kanche,* a low stool used by women when they sit by the fire and make tortillas. Situating himself in his worn henequen hammock, he asked if I wanted him to sing, and of course I did. He has no fear of the tape recorder, and talked

altar from sticks and rope, on which the ceremonial items and sacred water would be displayed.

On the night preceding the ceremony, several men slept in the field. Traditionally, all participants would remain away from home since sexual relations with one's wife during these days would destroy the ritual (Thompson 1975: 275). Before dawn on the day of the ceremony, men began to gather in the clearing. A sizeable collection of live chickens and turkeys, tied at the legs, flopped around near the center. A large pot of water was cooking over a fire as preparations were made. The sacred water, from special *cenotes* at each of the cardinal points, was poured into four gourds and placed on the altar. The rest of the sacred water was strained through a large handkerchief and used for the food preparation throughout the morning. Ordinary water, collected from the cemetery well, was not used except to wash hands and utensils.

At dawn, more men began to arrive. There were approximately 25 men in all, most between the ages of 35 and 60. Young boys attended with their fathers or grand-fathers, but they did not participate. The participants were dressed in a mixture of *mestizo* and *catrín* clothing. All were Catholic and they did not express any conflict between their Catholic faith and the ancient ritual they celebrated today. When asked, they responded, "We are Catholic, but this is our tradition."

For the ceremony, the men cooked the turkeys and prepared the ritual food (*c'ol*) (see Figure 6.3). *Balché* was poured into drinking gourds. Likewise, the water from the four sacred wells was strained and poured into gourds that were hung from the four corners of the altar. Special leaves were collected and placed on the altar, as were four tin cans filled with incense. While the men bowed on their knees, the *h-men* addressed the gods. Although invoking *Chac,* much of the ritual involved Catholic saints, and the language was sprinkled with Spanish words. After the Mayan ceremony, a lengthy Catholic prayer was offered, entirely in Spanish, petitioning Jesus and Mary to bless the sacrifice.

The ceremony ended, the food was consumed. At a short business meeting, the boss for next year's *comistraje* was chosen by consensus. That evening, the clouds gathered and by nightfall, opened, drowning the parched earth with a tremendous storm. It was the hardest rain we had experienced during our stay, flooding our living quarters and forming muddy puddles in the dry, rocky roads.

According to ancient belief, the presence of women at the *comistraje* could contaminate the ritual, but modern sex role divisions necessitated the cooperation of women in the production of tortillas, an important component of the ritual meal. While my husband participated with the men in the actual ritual, I had the opportunity to share in the women's activities. Once again, this exercise allowed me to experience the camaraderie of women, and their willingness to act behind the scenes.

In 1995, I again joined the women as they made tortillas for the *comistraje*. On the night before the ceremony, the women gathered at the house of the *comistraje* boss and ground the chiles and other spices that would be used for the soup. Early in the morning, I joined the women who had been working since before dawn. Women were divided into two work groups, those who made the patties from the *masa* and those who cooked the patties on the flat griddles straddled over small fires distributed around the large *solár*. I joined the former group, receiving gentle teasing and instructions over how to shape the tortillas properly. The prepared patties were distributed to the various fire pits at which two women sat, carefully monitoring the cooking process, flipping the tortillas at precisely the right moment and them pressing them lightly causing them to puff up on the hot griddle. Several huge porcelain bowls were filled with perfectly shaped tortillas.

Several hours later, Don San came to take the prepared tortillas back to the *monte*. He brought with him a bottle of *Xtabentun* (an anise and honey liqueur), which he poured into small cups and passed around so that everyone had a taste. Don San left with the tortillas and returned once again in the late morning for the rest. By now, the summer sun was streaking brightly through the fruit trees of the *solár,* and the women were fatigued from their efforts. They packed up their griddles, extinguished their fires, and retreated to the relative cool of the thatch house, unrolling

Figure 6.3 Man preparing ritual food at the comistraje, 1977

hammocks from their hooks on the walls and collapsing, laughing and joking, into their folds—two or three women squirming to balance themselves within each hammock. Eventually, Don San and the other men returned to the *solár* with pots of food that they had prepared for the ritual and shared it with the women.

The *comistraje* is still an integral part of the annual cycle of the village. Don Teodoro, however, expresses his disappointment that he will be the last *h-men,* as no other men are interested in taking his place. Until then, this ritual continues to span two worldviews, and the *h-men,* by entreating both the ancient and Christian deities and saints, bridges these philosophies. Catholics are the primary adherents to these ancient beliefs as part of the ongoing process of syncretism that separates yet links the ancient religion to that of the conquerors. The Seventh Day Adventists, although they promote the learning of the history of the Maya, do not officially adhere to their ancient beliefs as represented in the *comistraje* or in communicating with the spirits. Villagers who convert to Protestantism are expected to abandon both worldviews.

The Annual Fiesta

The most important celebration in the Catholic calendar is the celebration for the village patron saint. Mesoamerican anthropologists have written extensively about these events and the sacrifices in time and money that villagers undertake in order to care for their patron saint and to sponsor the annual *fiesta* in his or her honor.

Unlike highland Maya regions where *fiestas* are organized and underwritten by families within a cargo system (see Vogt 1990), the *fiestas* in lowland Yucatán are organized and underwritten by volunteer groups, called *gremios*. Normally a village has several *gremios,* organized by age, gender, and occupation, each of which sponsors one day of religious activities, including the cost of Mass, candles, fireworks, and parties. *Gremio* members elect officers who are responsible for the planning and the funding of the processions (also called *gremios*) that mark each day of the *fiesta* week.

The *gremios* represent the sacred functions of the annual *fiesta,* traditionally the most important. However, in more recent times, the annual *fiesta* has also developed a secular element that has expanded over time. While the *gremio* system is embedded in the Catholic church, overseen by the clergy, most of the activities of the modern *fiesta* occur outside the auspices of the church and are organized by the municipal government. As already seen, a village president is measured at least in part by his ability to provide a successful *fiesta* and this accomplishment is gauged primarily by events external to the religious functions. It is within the context of these secular events that the intersection of Catholic/Mayan and traditional/modern occurs. The traditional component includes the celebration of Mayan ethnicity through the *jarana* The European/modern component is evident in the bullfight, the nightly carnival, and the popular dances.

The Yaxbe Fiesta, 1977 and 1998

After Christmas of 1976, my sights were set on the coming of the New Year, but especially on the upcoming *fiesta* celebration, scheduled as always for the first week of February. While I waited anxiously for *fiesta,* anticipating the dances, bullfights, and rituals, another, almost imperceptible ritual occurred of which I only gradually became aware. As the days approached, the village became more and more crowded, and a trickle, and soon a stream, of visitors came to our door, accompanied by our newfound friends and neighbors. These strangers were the children and siblings who had returned to the village for *fiesta* week and who were anxious and excited to meet the local "gringos."

It was during this time that I learned about one of the most important elements of *fiesta,* that it is a time of reunion and thanksgiving. During the weeks before and during *fiesta,* I had the opportunity to meet many of the young people who had left as migrants, young men and women who had up to that time been names scribbled in my field notes and included in my kinship charts as "lost" family. Here they were, teenage girls who were working as nannies in Mexico City, young men who were building hotels on Cancún or attending school in a distant town, or young couples with babies who had moved elsewhere to seek work and new lives.

In 1998, I was reunited with villagers who were teenagers during my earlier visit and who were now parents themselves. They came from Mexico City, Cozumel, Mérida, and Villahermosa, bringing their own children, showing them off to us as we reminisced about those earlier days when they, as children, had visited us, guided us around the village, and invited us into their homes. Meanwhile, grandmothers sat proudly in the park, their young visiting grandchildren surrounding them, tentatively playing with cousins they seldom see, a little uncertain of their surroundings.

During *fiesta,* houses are crowded and vibrant as visiting relatives invade the small one- or two-room houses. Men congregate in the front room to talk, drink, or watch soccer on television; women congregate in the kitchen and rear of the house, preparing huge pots of food and caring for the small children who scramble around underfoot. At night, brightly colored hammocks are strung from all available hooks inside and outside of the houses. Every *solár* is filled with people, excited and exhausted by the visit.

Yaxbe's patron saint is the Virgin of Candelaria, and she is celebrated at the beginning of February. In 1977, there were five major *gremios:* for men, women, young boys, young girls, and one for the village government (*ayuntamiento*). Then, as now, the processions occur in the late afternoon. They are lead by the small group of musicians playing a drum, trumpet, and saxophone, none of which have been tuned for compatibility. The resultant sound is one of tinny dissonance accompanied by an overpowering drumbeat. Behind the band, the members of the *gremio* follow, carrying religious banners, the Mexican flag, and, of course, the Virgin of Candelaria, dressed in golden-colored clothes and adorned with a wreath of flowers around her flowing blonde hair. As the virgin and her entourage pass, villagers come out from their homes and follow the procession to the home of the *gremio* president where the food is already prepared and set out on tables guarded over by relatives and young girls. The success of the *gremio* is measured by the quantity and quality of food, the availability of alcohol, and the amount of time that the band has been reimbursed for playing.

The meal and dance do not complete the *gremio's* activities and responsibilities. After the party, the virgin is returned to the church, accompanied again by the band and members of the *gremio.* By now it is nearly dark and the final event of the day, the fireworks, commence in the churchyard. The extravagance of the display also reflects the wealth of the *gremio.* Various types of fireworks are ignited, with none of the safeguards required for fireworks in the United States. The finale is the running of the wooden bull through the central plaza, with firecrackers and sparklers shooting off in all directions. Children squeal in delight and, rather than run from the dangerous shooting flares, chase the rockets as they blast through the crowd and across the park.

A villager's *gremio* is a source of pride for the group as well as the individual who serves as president, for he or she often pays for the refreshments from his or her own pocket. Groups often compete for the honor of putting on the best *gremio* and parents will heavily subsidize their children's *gremios* in order to enhance both their child's and their own status in the community. In 1977, the women's *gremio* spent 4,000 pesos on its party; the men's group spent 3,000. The president of the women's group boasted that the women have the best *gremio* every year. They always serve beer, while the men can only afford **horchata** (a nonalcoholic rice drink). The women also paid the band extra to stay at the celebration and play *jarana,* or traditional Maya, music so the participants could dance. I asked Doña Sofia why the women could put on a better party than the men and she replied, "because we control the money." She made the local gesture for "rich."

While *gremios* depend on a large voluntary group to raise funds, they are still dominated by those who can afford the dues and who are able to amass the financial and in-kind backing that will result in a successful party. Anthropologists often argue that *gremios* are another example of leveling mechanisms in which benefactors are rewarded with prestige and respect in the community.

My experience in Yaxbe did not support this hypothesis. Rather, the *gremios* themselves often were the focus of suspicion. This was particularly true in 1998, but also evident in several conversations I had with villagers in 1976. Many Catholics criticize the *gremios* and do not participate because they view them as elitist. "They are for the rich" is a comment heard frequently. Others complain that if one cannot afford to serve beer or pay the dues, then one should not have a *gremio* because people will gossip about them. As a result, a small group of affluent families tend to dominate the group membership. Similarly, the young people's *gremios* include the children of those same families. The extended families of these youth *gremios* will often subsidize their children's groups and consequently gain prestige vicariously through their children's participation. In 1998, one of the most spectacular fireworks displays was sponsored by the young women's *gremio,* but allegedly funded by the wealthy father of a group member. Also in 1998, several villagers reported that the *gremios* that year were poorly attended, and according to my hosts, only the members and their families actively participated.

The *gremios* have lost their popularity for several other reasons. First, while increasingly Catholics are skeptical about their validity, the Protestants don't participate in any of the *fiesta* activities, arguing that people should spend money on food for their families, not conspicuous consumption or *fiesta* food, alcohol, and dancing. The second reason for the decline in importance of the religious component of the *fiesta* is the expansion of the secular activities and a gradual shift in the meanings attached to *fiesta* week. We will discuss the impact of Protestantism in the next chapter. Now, we will turn to the secular activities of *fiesta*.

The village president oversees the planning of the secular activities of the *fiesta*. The extravagance and organization of the yearly event is a reflection of the enthusiasm of the president and the state of the village treasury. The *fiesta* that was held during our first stay cost the village 45,000 pesos and the president hoped for a profit of 10,000 over expenses. During *fiesta* week, few men work in the fields. With the exception of the Seventh Day Adventist School, all other schools are closed for the week. *Fiesta* is a time of heavy drinking. It is also a time for many families to interact together.

The *jarana* takes place on the first night of the *fiesta,* serving as the kick-off event. The *jarana* brings elders and young people together in a celebration of traditional culture. Women and men wear elaborate *huipiles* and *traje.* Women and young girls wear their hair in the traditional bun, if their hair is long enough, and many girls who know they will be dancing will grow their hair so that they can wear their hair in this way. Their hair is adorned with bright hibiscus flowers and their necks and arms are adorned with gold jewelry that is otherwise stashed away as women's wealth.

As the stylized costumes are very expensive, few young girls or women own one. For a young girl, fitting herself with a *huipil,* slip, shawl, shoes, and hair combs is an adventure not unlike a scavenger hunt. With the help of relatives and *compadres,* young girls scour the village trying on dresses, finding one that both fits and suits them. While all the *huipiles* are white, they are embroidered at the neck and hem in a variety of bright colors and designs. The most popular designs are brightly colored flowers, usually hibiscus. Some *huipiles* also have various layers of lace or puckered stitching, so that each layer is distinct. Once the dress is found, the girls must find or purchase the embroidered underslip. Again, there are a variety of embroidered hems and styles, from laced to scalloped. The shoes are a special challenge, as a girl must find a pair that is comfortable for dancing. Once these primary pieces of the ensemble are acquired, the remaining pieces are relatively easy. The shawls are fairly uniform in size and come in several standard base colors: green and red. The particular designs and the additional colors woven into the shawls are taken into consideration as the young women attempt to achieve the perfect color combinations. Young girls conspire among themselves to find the perfect ensemble, matching up costumes among themselves, combing each others' hair, inserting combs and flowers, and finally applying the heavy doses of make-up that complete the effect.

In this way, 15- to 16-year-old girls become transformed into living dolls, wide-eyed, and twitching with nervous excitement (see Figure 6.4). Likewise the young boys who are brave enough to participate with their fathers and uncles dress in the white *traje,* with white sandals and colorful sashes and straw hats. The young men are thus mysteriously transformed from gangly, skinny boys to serious and nervous dance partners, moving stiffly and carefully to the music. While the girls have been practicing the dance for many weeks before the event, the boys are more tentative. However, they are no less impressive as they tackle the complex rhythms and ritualized motions of the dances.

The *jarana* is not a village-only event. The president sends out invitations to all villages in the region, and dance groups come from many of these villages, towns, and *haciendas* to participate in the festivities. Before the official start of the *jarana,* each of these dance groups is introduced. Each group consists of five to eight couples and is led by a "king" and "queen," or a lead couple. As each group is introduced they walk in pairs onto the tiled promenade that runs the length of the village *palacio.* As they process, the band plays bullfight music, an interesting link between the traditional Maya procession and secular custom. In 1998, more than 20 different villages were represented, the processions and introductions taking nearly an hour to complete. This widespread participation is clearly a symbol of success for the *fiesta* and for the president who planned it.

On subsequent nights, there are popular dances, with live music performed by regionally known *cumbia* bands. Like the *jarana,* these dances bring people from other villages. However, the composition of these nightly migration groups differs markedly. On dance nights, young men come by pick-up truck and motorcycle from all neighboring villages with the goal of appraising the local girls. The atmosphere surrounding these dances also contrasts from the staid formality of the traditional dance. Young musicians who have worked all day setting up equipment and loud speakers, dominate one end of the basketball court that abuts the *palacio,* and the dancers fill both open spaces. The music is deafening and draws a huge crowd of people of all ages. Mothers and other relatives sit on folding chairs along the long wall of the government building and encircling the basketball court that has been transformed into a gigantic dance floor. While outwardly, they are conversing lightly with their neighbors, they are also alert to all of the activities in their view, observing closely the behavior of their daughters, granddaughters, and those of their neighbors.

The bright, colorful lights that illuminate the tiled dance floor cast the surrounding park and churchyard in shadowy darkness. Here, older men congregate in small huddled circles, chatting, their grandchildren tugging restlessly on their pant legs.

Figure 6.4 A young Yaxbeña represents the village for the jarana and fiesta 1998

Young couples move quietly among the trees and more secluded park benches, talking softly, their arms barely touching, and constantly aware of the attention they are drawing from those who pass by.

The *fiesta* and the popular dances in particular provide a good opportunity for courtship, and also for parents to evaluate the possible matches for their children. One of the major changes I observed between 1976 and 1998 was the behavior of the young people at these events, a shift that further reinforces the social transformations already discussed. In 1977, the young women were very reticent and shy, standing nervously along the *palacio* wall, next to their mothers, until they were unceremoniously wrenched from the safety of their mothers' shadow by an equally self-conscious young man. The dancing itself was often painful to watch, the young couple shifting stiffly from foot to foot, looking past each other, their emotionless faces reflecting their nervousness and discomfort.

In 1998, the scene was very different. Most of the young people have shed their public reticence. They perform the lively *cumbia* and salsa steps with a flourish and enthusiasm inconceivable 20 years ago. Adults also participate in these dances, creating an intoxicating atmosphere of sensual Latin rhythm. One night in 1998, when I attended the dance, the *palacio* was so crowded that there was no room to dance, even though couples and individuals had to pay a small entrance fee. Those of us who did not pay were still within view of the dancers and the band, and couples, teens, and children spread outward from the *palacio,* dancing and playing under the clear February star-lit sky.

These popular dances, then, can be viewed as a ritual that suspends local custom and social protocol relating to the demeanor of young people. During *fiesta,* young people violate several cultural norms. First, as we have seen, young boys and girls can openly interact with each other. Without movie theaters, dance clubs, or restaurants, there are few places where teens can congregate socially outside of the gaze of adults.

The second cultural norm that is violated during *fiesta* week is curfew. I was surprised to discover that the teenaged daughter in my household was allowed to stay at the dance after her parents left. Each night, the popular dances start between 11:00 P.M. and midnight and last until the early hours of the morning. The local custom is to take a nap in the evening and wake up again at 10:00 to prepare for the dance. As a morning person, this routine was impossible for me. Most nights, I simply failed to wake up once asleep for my "siesta." On the one night when I succeeded in staying awake to participate, I was too tired to enjoy the festivities. For this, I was justifiably teased by the young people in the family as a *"viejita pobre"* (a poor little old woman).

Another event that typifies the secular nature of the annual *fiesta* is the bullfight (*corrida*). In rural areas, starting several weeks before the *fiesta,* men begin to construct the arena. Several men, experts at this task, organize the building of the individual **tablados** (sections). Each section has a ground level and a second level with a ladder leading up to it. The individual sections are covered with thatch and when completed, they form a perfect circle of seats and an open arena in the center. Men who wish to have a *tablado* pay the village a certain amount and then, with relatives, construct a section according to the overall plan. The families who cooperated with the construction of the section share it for the bullfights. Any unused seats are rented or made available free to friends or relatives. During *fiesta* there are three to five bullfights, depending on the wealth of the village. The quality of the bullfighters and the bulls also reflects the prestige of the town and its ability to bring in good talent. Anyone who has seen a bullfight in Mexico City will be disappointed with the local variety—overweight bullfighters and bulls that are reluctant to enter the arena and are more disposed to snoozing than attacking.

Yet, villagers appreciate the "comic" atmosphere of the event. Children sit on the second level of the *tablado,* dangle their legs over the edge, and scream with delight when the bull rushes toward them. They lift their feet in the air as the bull runs headlong into the latticed wood beneath them where their parents and grandparents sit on folded chairs, trying to contain infants and toddlers who wriggle out of their grasp.

The most entertaining segments of the bullfights are when local men, emboldened by alcohol or youthful *machismo,* jump into the arena, seeking excitement or the attention of young women in the audience. They leap boldly, if not wisely between the matador and the bull and then scramble toward the protective wall when the bull decides they are worth the effort of chasing. The men, encouraged by the shouts and laughter of fellow villagers, try again, often avoiding injury only by the intercession of the true bullfighters, or when they are finally hauled back into the *tablado* by relatives or friends.

It is at the bullfight, however, where the sacred and profane elements of the *fiesta* merge, at least momentarily (Fernández Repetto1995: 59). During an intermission in the bullfight, the mood becomes immediately somber as a single drum beats in measured rhythm. A group of teens and women enter the bullring with Candelaria on a litter followed by several others carrying a large sheet or blanket. As the patron saint makes her way around the arena, people throw coins into the blanket. Once this procession has ended and the virgin is carried from the arena, the raucous bullfight music blares and the action recommences.

There is a practical element to the *corrida* as well, as villagers donate their own bulls for the event. Every day, the matador kills the first bull that is brought into the arena. It is immediately butchered outside the arena, and the meat is sold to villagers as they leave. The rest of the bulls are reused over the days, some are killed, and others return to their owners' herds, exhausted but otherwise no worse for the wear.

Other, more modern, capitalistic practices have come to accompany the more traditional *fiesta* activities. Vendors hawk ice cream, cotton candy, and peanuts between the entrances of bulls at the bullfight. Other venders purchase permits from the village president to set up foosball tables and carnival games in the park. Beer and food vendors proliferate, competing with the village bars and family fast-food businesses. Each booth has its own music, and one's ears and senses are overwhelmed by the cacophony caused when *cumbia* meets disco.

When *fiesta* week is finally over, there is a sense of anticlimax in the air that even the Adventists share. Trash covers the plaza from where the vendors disappeared in the dead of the night. Remnant drunks will take several days to sober up, and villagers tolerantly step over their inert bodies where they lie along the sidewalk or in the park, sometimes prodding them in the side to make sure they are indeed only sleeping. Children have the dark circles and nervous energy that comes with days of over-permissiveness and lack of sleep. Parents enthusiastically send these same children off to school, and say good-bye to the houseful of guests who one by one pack up their hammocks and leave. The Adventists can also get their lives back to order, allowing their children once again to wander safely into the park, and they can finally get to sleep at night now that the endless music has ceased.

Fiesta is a wonderful event that ties most villagers together in a tighter web of interaction. It also spans generations and worldviews, incorporating the old and the new. I foresee in time that, as the ceremony becomes less religious and more secular, that the Adventists will participate more. Although invisible at the popular dances, I observed several Adventist fathers at the game tables and food booths with their children, at the bullfights, and in one case, an Adventist couple even danced the *jarana*.

CONCLUSION

For the pre-conquest Maya, religion was not a separate institution, but rather it permeated all aspects of daily life. Religion was linked not only the natural phenomena such as the rain, which nourished the crops, but also to political and social events. While Catholicism was imposed on the Maya, it is now, in many ways, indistinguishable from Yucatecan culture and has become the source of the cohesion of the peasant community. Changing economic and social circumstances have resulted in changes within the community, expanding local networks outward, and bringing events and policies of the state and nation to the village.

The *fiesta, comistraje,* and indigenous belief systems link Maya traditional beliefs and practices to those of the Catholic faith. They illustrate the syncretism that has occurred over four centuries of contact between two distinct cultures and world-views. These two traditions have found a balance in which the boundaries between old and new have become blurred, and accepted by Catholic priest and *h-men* alike.

However, in the past 50 years, another worldview has penetrated the uneasy alliance between Catholic and Maya. The recent incursions of Protestant religions in Latin America have initiated a process of reshaping that worldview and shaking the alliance. We now turn to the impact of Protestantism on village beliefs and values.

7/A Religion for Business and One for Sunday
The Seventh Day Adventists

I remember one Saturday morning when I was very young. We lived in the other house and all eleven of us were in our hammocks. We all slept in the same room, our hammocks all lined up in a row. It was very, very early, about 3:00 or 4:00, and our father came to every hammock and woke us all up . . . up and down the room, ordering all of us out of our hammocks. It was awful. We didn't want to get up, but he kept up, going from hammock to hammock until we were all awake. We thought he was crazy for waking us up so early. It was 4:00 in the morning, a Saturday morning when we didn't even have school. When we were all awake our father told us "Today, you will decide what you will do with your life." He was talking about religion. He liked the new Seventh Day Religion [see Ethnographic Essay, this chapter], but he wanted us to make up our own minds. He told us that morning, that on that day, we had to decide if we were going to be Catholics or Adventists. If we chose to be Catholic we had to be the best Catholic—we had to go to Sunday Mass and be a good Catholic; if we chose to be an Adventist, we had to go to temple that very morning and be a good Adventist. Every one of us, except Lupe, chose to go to the temple. Lupe is a Catholic to this day, and we are all Adventists. Now, we are accustomed to getting up early every day to pray and study the Bible before the day begins. (Rosa, 1998)

PROTESTANTISM IN YAXBE

Protestantism is a relatively recent phenomenon in Latin America. Although missions were established throughout Latin America since the 1920s, they have not been a serious threat to the existing Catholic hegemony until the 1970s. Since that time, Protestant missions have made inroads in most villages and towns in Mexico and Central and South America (see Garrard-Burnett and Stoll 1993; Annis 1987). In Yaxbe, it was the Seventh Day Adventists (SDA) who were able to penetrate the Catholic stronghold and eventually find a home. The Pentecostals have also formed a congregation in the village, but they have not been successful in building a strong church. We will return to this latter group of Protestants later.

The History of the Seventh Day Adventists in Yaxbe

The Seventh Day Adventists had a difficult time establishing themselves in Mexico. The first congregation in Yucatán was formed at a *hacienda* in 1925 when the local priest failed to expel the leader, Antonio Kong.[1] They experienced the same resistance when they arrived in Yaxbe. In 1957, when two women missionaries came to the village, there was only one Adventist temple in Yucatán, located in Mérida, and several small congregations.

In Yaxbe, after several informal meetings, people began to offer their homes for regular services. According to Adventists who were among the first to attend these meetings, the local priest petitioned the governor to intervene and expel the group. The priest's petition failed, and the meetings continued. Subsequent meetings were stoned by small groups of Catholics, but eventually the harassment ceased and the Adventists established themselves in the village. In 1976, they had 180 baptized members (about 10% of the population), and Yaxbe was home of the second temple and the second religious primary school in Yucatán, both constructed entirely by villagers.

The Structure of the Seventh Day Adventist Temple

Today the Adventist temple and school are located about four blocks from the main square of the village. Unlike the imposing fortress-like Catholic church that dominates an entire block along the main square, the temple is modest in size and modern in construction. Inside the austere one-room cement block building, the only concession to luxury is a tile floor that runs its length. At the front, a raised stage, podium, and public address system are the only accoutrements. There are no statues, paintings, nor even a cross that identifies the building as a church. Only the pews

---

[1]Carlos Castellanos et al., *"Aspectos de Algunas Religiones en Yucatán"* in *Boletín de Ciencias Antropologicas de la Universidad de Yucatán* 1: 4: February 1974.

attest to its purpose. Having no church bells, parishioners are called to Saturday morning service by religious music that is blasted from the public address system. The music begins approximately one hour before the service and can be heard for about one mile in all directions, and as far as the center of the village.

The school is equally austere with small unadorned classrooms lining two sides of a central courtyard. The temple stands long the third side of the courtyard and a basketball court sits along the far side of an enclosed central plaza area, replicating the format of the central park of the village. Yet, instead of having the effect of a large arena for public activity, the Adventist enclosure separates and isolates the activities of the Adventists from the rest of the village.

In contrast to the monolithic structure of the Catholic church, the Adventist organization is both local and dispersed. It is this component of the Adventist religion that drew many people away from the centralized, authoritarian, and patriarchal organization of the Catholic Church. The temple is also inclusive, comprised of many committees that fulfill administrative functions and regulate the activities of both the temple and the school. Villagers fill all of the committee and administrative positions.

Because there is no resident pastor, the Adventist organization trains members of the congregation as lay speakers, teaching them how to plan and present sermons and lead the Bible readings and the service. These components of the service are delegated to various members of the congregation, including women and young people. An Adventist pastor comes to the village periodically for special events or as part of a circuit. It is at these times when weddings and baptisms will be performed.

There are numerous services during the week. The main service is on Saturday morning and lasts two hours. There is another, shorter service on Wednesday evenings that I attended more regularly. There are often smaller services on Sunday evenings and additional services during holidays. Villagers are further tied to the temple through frequent committee, school, and youth meetings. Families who are active in the temple will walk there nearly every day for some purpose, pertaining either to the temple or the school where their children attend.

The Sacrifices of Membership

While the members of the temple come from a variety of backgrounds, they have the reputation of being "the religion of business." This label reflects the Adventist requirement that members tithe 10% of their income to the temple. The religion has two other requirements, that members maintain Saturday as the Sabbath, and that they follow certain restrictions such as abstention from pork, cigarettes, alcohol, and secular activities such as dancing. Women do not wear jewelry or pierce their infant daughters' ears, as is the custom for local Catholics. The temple elders and the members of the SDA vigilance committee monitor the compliance of their fellow members to these rules, regulations, and prohibitions. Those who stray are admonished or encouraged to reform, but if the activity continues, the congregation decides if the member stays or is dropped from the membership.

As challenging as the dietary and social restrictions might appear, the Adventists further demand acceptance of a repertory of more fundamental prohibitions and tenets that strike very deep into the Catholic beliefs of salvation as well as traditional communal values. The Adventists prohibit such deeply engrained practices as *com-*

padrazgo and infant baptism. As we have already seen, *compadrazgo* is a crucial component to the daily life of all Mexicans, rooted in Catholicism and exemplifying the complex networks that link individuals and families in mutual assistance and shared rituals. In an attempt to deny all aspects of Catholic doctrine and practice, the Adventists reject the practice of *compadrazgo,* replacing it with new networks that link members of the temple in similar relationships, called "sponsorships." Young people choose sponsors to represent them for weddings, baptisms, and other important events. By encouraging members of the congregation to seek sponsors from among the temple, they are not only attempting to link and reinforce the ties of Adventist members, but are also hoping to recruit new converts.

The Adventists also reject infant baptism, arguing that an infant is too young to understand and accept the sacrifices necessary to become a member of the temple. For the Adventists, true baptism does not occur until a child has reached his or her teen years, and occurs after a period of church education, paralleling the Catholic ritual of First Communion. Nevertheless, to ease minds of potential converts who fear that children who die before baptism will not be accepted into heaven, the temple provides a ritual whereby infants are "introduced" into the temple. This ritual, conducted periodically as needed, is informal and resembles baptism in that the infant is brought to the front of the church, accompanied by his or her parents, grandparents, and "sponsors." The congregation offers special prayers and special music is performed. This ceremony protects children until they reach the age at which they will choose their own religion and become active members of the Adventist faith in their own right. The true Adventist baptisms, which include immersion into water, take place in special *cenotes* at other villages and are performed by regional pastors. The group of converts includes teens and adults from various villages, linking them to Adventists in a regional network that transcends the community.

While these Adventist practices do not, in and of themselves, place them in conflict with Catholics, the religions collide at one of the most deeply entrenched village celebration, the annual *fiesta* discussed in the previous chapter. In fact, the entire *fiesta,* based firmly in Catholic dogma and liturgy, is off-limits to the Adventists. Many Adventist children, however, congregate at the periphery of the festivities, bravely entering the crowd to buy tacos or soft drinks from one of the food vendors. Today, as the *fiesta* becomes increasingly secular, it is more common to see Adventist families at the evening carnivals, and even at the bullfights, although elder converts reject even these profane and innocuous activities. In addition, Adventist administrators attempt to compete with the *fiesta* activities by sponsoring special events at the temple during the week-long celebration. Thus, amid the cheers coming from the bullfight taking place in the soccer field next to the Catholic church, one hears the Adventist public address system announcing the afternoon basketball games and *kermesse.*

A second major distinction between Adventist and Catholic belief illustrates the diverse worldviews of the two religions. Many scholars have explored the characteristics of Protestant religions and sects and how these characteristics and philosophy cut deep into the veneer of Catholic doctrine and practice. Max Weber, in his classic treatise, *The Protestant Ethic and the Spirit of Capitalism* (1958), outlined the historical context in which Protestantism, with its emphasis on individual salvation and the paradoxical relationship between hard work and predestination, contributed to the spread of capitalism in the 19th and 20th centuries. While these values—

individualism and a competitive work ethic—are deeply embedded in American culture, they are not congruent with the social or economic values that permeate either Mexican traditional culture or the tenets of Catholicism.

The incongruity of peasant values and the **Protestant Ethic** are outlined in the work of Sheldon Annis (1987). In his book, *God and Production in a Guatemala Town,* Annis distinguishes between "*milpa* logic" and "anti-*milpa* forces." Annis defines "*milpa* logic" as a cluster of economic and social characteristics that are historically adaptive to peasants who live precariously day to day and season to season. *Milpa* logic is embedded in the three important categories: agriculture (*milpa*), "Indian-ness," and Catholicism (Annis 1987: 10).

According to Annis, the evangelical religions appeal to those who come from the margins of the traditional village structure. This "anti-*milpa*" faction includes villagers who are not involved directly in agricultural pursuits, but who are either "petty (small scale) capitalists" or landless peasants (Annis 1987; 63–66). The adherents to the Protestant religion are those who are attracted to an ideology that promotes economic well-being and the adage (ibid. 86–87): "*Del suelo al cielo*" (from the dirt/ground to the sky).

Annis argues that peasants do not have the capital savings that allow them to take economic risks. Even though they are not as conservative as early anthropologists and developers have believed, they choose strategies that emphasize security and minimize uncertainty rather than those that require substantial capital outlay but promise rewards in the long term. Leveling mechanisms such as *compadrazgo* and perhaps *gremios* fulfill these risk-minimizing strategies. These economic and cultural obligations, however, deplete already limited family coffers and redistribute a limited pool of wealth. In order to fulfill religious or social obligations, families place themselves in unnecessary debt. Reluctance to accept such obligations results in unfavorable judgment and criticism by their neighbors.

Protestants, because they are not depleting valuable resources into the *fiesta* complex or alcohol, are more able to invest the time and capital into more risky endeavors. This does not mean that Protestants do not form kin or intra-village networks. Adventists in Yaxbe rely on family as do Catholics. Family members contribute to economic enterprises, form cooperatives together, and assisting each other in special projects. Adventist business owners hire relatives, and they are expected to contribute food and supplies to special family and temple events. Thus, the reliance on family does not differ significantly in the two religions. What is unique about the Adventists is the networks that they forge with other Adventists within and beyond the village. Protestants feel an obligation to support temple members, by purchasing goods and services from Protestant families. They will also seek social and economic bonds extending away from the village. For example, while there is a village Catholic woman who bakes decorative cakes for birthdays, weddings, and special rituals, the Protestants purchase their homemade cakes from an Adventist woman in a village 10 miles away.

While those who are products of a primarily Protestant and capitalist country, such as the United States, may applaud the growing strength of Protestantism abroad, there are those, within and outside of Latin America, who argue that Protestantism is a major disintegrative force for these countries. Critics of evangelical religions in Latin America make two convincing arguments. First, they state that Protestantism is a foreign ideology that is antagonistic to national cultures. By requiring that their

members ignore their traditional festivals and rituals, Protestant churches are alienating individuals and families from their customs and from their communal ties and
obligations. Second, Protestantism is linked strongly to capitalism and the concomitant values of individualism and competitiveness. These values also conflict with traditional values of sharing, leveling of wealth, and communal ideologies
(Garrard-Burnett and Stoll 1993: 6–7).

While it is tempting to compare the relative virtues of Catholicism and
Protestantism, this debate will not answer important questions: Why are so many
Latin Americans choosing Protestantism? Who are these converts? What are the
future implications of Protestantism to individuals and to villages and cities throughout Latin America? Garrard-Burnett and Stoll suggest (ibid: 6) that "researchers must
look at the social clusters receiving the message. We have to ask how ordinary people choose between the religious discourses available to them, bend these to their
own purposes, and wend their way in and out of particular groups." We will now turn
to a discussion of these questions and issues of conversion to Seventh Day
Adventism in Yaxbe.

Elements in the Decision to Convert

Given these conditions of membership and the sacrifices that converts must make in
their everyday lives, why do more and more Latin Americans choose Protestantism?
Why do they risk community scorn and family criticism? We will now turn to some
of the factors that have influenced conversion to the Seventh Day Adventist religion
in Yaxbe. Some of these, inclusiveness and personal reform, have already been discussed, but we will look at them again, within the context of a larger pattern of
behavior and personal strategies.

PERSONAL REFORM   Protestantism has given many people the support and positive
reinforcement in reforming themselves and ridding themselves and their families
from the social and financial stigma surrounding drunkenness and infidelity. Many of
the current members converted as a result of personal crises that were not resolved
by one's faith in Catholicism. Don Max, a village tailor, is a notable example of the
power of conversion. He is a smiling man who prides himself in his knowledge of
the Bible as well as the history of Yaxbe. He also knows a spattering of English and
teaches Maya in Mérida. Born with a birth defect, Max walks with the aid of crutches
(see Figure 7.1). When he was young, he could not work in the fields as did other
young men his age. He testifies quite frankly that at one time he was a hopeless
drunk—that he was depressed and hated life. Because of his deformity, he would
often fall and people would have to pick him up from the road. He reports that it was
a Pentecostal man who made him realize his sinful ways by refusing to sing a song
for him. Later, he joined the Adventist church where he has been a member for nearly
40 years. He learned his trade as a tailor and today is one of the leaders and major
participants in the administration and worship activities of the temple. In 1998, he
was the principal of the Adventist school. Don Max's story is only one of many. Most
of the early converts to the religion enthusiastically share their "born again" stories.

SELF-SACRIFICE AND MORAL SUPERIORITY   Protestants are drawn together by a
sense of daily sacrifice and a moral superiority over those whom they perceive as

Figure 7.1 Don Max, 1977

still suffering because they lack the will and the strength of God that will allow them to better themselves. It is not uncommon to hear Adventists refer to drinkers, not as sinners, but as *"pobres"* or poor ones, still lost and searching for meaning in their lives. According to Adventists, the sacrifices that they make for their faith make them stronger.

INCLUSIVENESS   As we have already seen, it is the strictness and philosophy of self-sacrifice that prompted many villagers to join the Adventist religion. First, the Adventists drew many villagers who were disillusioned by the monolithic structure of the Catholic Church and who were intrigued by the inclusive organization of the Adventists who encouraged, even demanded, that their members actively participate in the day-to-day administrative duties and social events discussed above. Inclusiveness has another dimension for the Adventists. Where Catholic women are a central focus of Catholic activities and attendance at Mass, they are invisible in the Church hierarchy. In contrast, the Adventist temple has offered women, not only the opportunity, but the obligation to become involved in the daily administrative and committee duties.

Protestantism has had a special meaning for village women. Several scholars have examined the role of women as agents of conversion, as well as their subsequent roles in the organization of local Protestant churches (Brusco 1993; Green 1993). In many conversion stories, men acknowledged the role of mothers and wives in their lives. As members of important committees, women were able to utilize their extensive networks, not only to support temple activities, but to enhance temple membership. They brought their mothers and sisters, who were struggling with drinking, absentee, or abusive husbands to temple services and events. These women supported each other and many eventually brought their menfolk into the religion.

DEL SUELO AL CIELO   In the previous section, we discussed Annis's description of the sentiment expressed in Guatemala as "*Del suelo al cielo.*" This sentiment can be understood in two ways: spiritually and economically. While Yaxbeño Protestants do not use this phrase, they do express a similar philosophy of life; that Adventism allows them to live a good life—one that is productive and fulfilled, one that eschews laziness and moral vices. On the other hand, village Protestants have never indicated to me that economic success is a virtue in and of itself. It is hard work and dedication to the temple that is stressed. In the next section, we will examine how the Protestant Ethic influences those who follow the religion, despite their reticence in expressing wealth or affluence as individual goals.

THE IMPACT OF PROTESTANTISM
ON THE LIVES OF MEN AND WOMEN IN YAXBE

In this section, we will examine the impact of Protestantism on villagers using various kinds of data: economic, education, migration, and intra-village relationships.

The Protestant Work Ethic and Economics in Yaxbe

> Our father had cattle, henequen, bees, trucks, and many things, but now he has nothing. He spent everything sending his kids to school. [Our parents] had economic problems just like everyone else, but our father wanted to send us and our mother agreed with this. Thus, our mother always said, "if you want to buy a soft drink, you have to pay for it." So we began to work [at an early age], earning what money we could. (Rosa, 1998)

Even though villagers do not discuss their faith in economic terms, a definite work ethic and emphasis on individual effort and success is evident in Yaxbe. Table 3 (see Appendix) demonstrates that Adventists are less likely to be employed in either agriculture or factory work. Instead, they are represented prominently in professional and "other" non-agricultural occupations. In this section we will examine some of the reasons for these distinctive patterns of Adventist and Catholic economic strategies.

The most obvious finding from Table 3 is that Adventist men are less likely to work in agriculture. This has not always been the case. In 1976–1977, the majority of all village men, regardless of religion, worked in the *ejido*. Tensions arose, however, as men began to convert to the new religion and refused to work on Saturdays, preferring to work the plots on Sunday. Because plots are not worked individually, but as teams, the productivity of the entire group was jeopardized if the members of the group did not work together. The Saturday Sabbath also became an issue at Cordemex. Adventist men were not hired if they refused to sign the contract agreeing to Saturday hours. As a result, Adventist men were forced to be more creative in their occupations, and many opted to self-employment and other diversified sources of income that allowed them the flexibility to adhere to their religious tenets.

Today, Protestants who continue to work in agriculture have diversified and now practice a mixed strategy, combining henequen production with cattle herding, vegetable horticulture, or non-agricultural pursuits. They often form informal family cooperatives in which costs and labor are shared. In 1976, the Adventists dominated the village tailoring trade as that was one that coincided well with their religious schedule. In 1998, while many Adventist women still worked as seamstresses, most

ETHNOGRAPHIC ESSAY
BECOMING A SEVENTH DAY ADVENTIST

Don Pablo was destined to be the next *h-men*. His father, a highly respected shaman, taught him the pertinent chants and prayers necessary for the *comistraje* as well as the secrets of herbs and curing. Pablo is one of the few remaining villagers who is fluent in the Maya language and was one of the informants consulted by linguists in Mérida who were, during my 1976–1977 research, compiling a Maya dictionary. Don Pablo was also a devout Catholic who saw no conflict between the teachings of his Maya ancestors and those of the Catholic faith. He was appalled, as were his fellow villagers, when the Seventh Day Adventist missionaries arrived in the village in 1957:

> I remember . . . it was 19 or 20 years ago that two sisters came and talked to whomever would listen. The first person to let them speak in his house was Don Adelfino. Then other people came, Doña Lilia, Don Lauriano. But I was a fanatical Catholic. Don

Bernadino and I went to a meeting to hear all the bad things that the Adventists were saying. I didn't admit it to my friend at the time, but I didn't find anything bad. I went a second time for the same reason, but I found that I agreed with the religion and I began to attend meetings regularly. In July 1959, the priest gave a sermon at San Martín and afterwards, some Catholics stoned a meeting of the Adventists. They said that the priest was not involved, but he had talked to the people about the religion and he instigated it. That meeting had eight people. The next week, there were 15 people. It was stoned again and the next week there 30 people. We were not bothered in that way anymore. (Don Pablo Uc, 1977)

In 1977, Don Pablo was the major philosophical and financial backer of the Adventist religion. He was a wealthy man, owning many *hectares* of henequen

men had tapped into a newer form of employment—inter-village vending and collecting (*cobratorio*).

It was a young Adventist man, Pedro, who initiated the local idea of the traveling vendor. Having access to a small pick-up truck (a necessity for this job), he purchased vegetables, watermelons, and inexpensive clothing from the Mérida market and sold them in small villages and *haciendas,* where few people had automobiles. As his business expanded, he began to sell larger items, such as furniture and crated vegetables for sale to village stores. This expansion necessitated another innovative concept in rural sales: credit. At first, Pedro, after selling throughout the region Monday through Friday, would then make the rounds again on Sunday to collect weekly payments from his customers. Later, as his business expanded, he hired his family members, both as vendors and collectors. Young male relatives who had motorcycles were able to move quickly and relatively inexpensively on the collection rounds on Sunday when most people were at home. Thus imagination and innovation allowed a segment of Adventists to be self-employed.

land and an independent trucking business. Today, Don Pablo is retired, but he is still a dominant member of the temple, always holding a position within the organizational hierarchy (see Figure 7.2).

Ten of Pablo's eleven children are committed to the Adventist faith and have become active in the temple. Eight of his children were educated in Adventist institutions, including two sons who attended seminary and are now Adventist pastors. Others are administrators and teachers. One of these, Rosa, whose story is found at the beginning of this chapter, is a teacher at the Yaxbe Adventist school and an officer in the temple administration. One of her sons is attending an Adventist school in another town. Not all Adventists are as involved with the daily affairs of the temple. Yet, the enthusiasm and dedication of many villagers causes adherents to say: "Catholicism is a religion for Sunday; Adventism is for everyday." Many

Figure 7.2 Don Pablo, 1977

Adventists have told me, "It's not easy to become an Adventist. One must be prepared to make sacrifices."

Tables 3 and 4 (see Appendix) also indicate that Adventist men are more likely to have professional jobs than are Catholic men. This difference is not statistically significant, but it indicates an important trend in village employment, especially when we explore this tendency in the wider context of out-migration (Chapter 8) and gender, which we will do presently. For this section, we will look at how the Adventist value placed on education affects the local economic structure.

Education and Occupation

In 1977, I noted a remarkable difference in educational levels when Catholics and Protestants were compared. I first discovered this contrast as I asked families whether their children had completed the 6th grade (*primaria*). I found that while only 5% of Catholic children had attended school beyond primary, 16% of the Protestant children had (including Pentecostals).

This pattern has persisted to the present day as the children of the 1970s have grown into the adults of the 1990s. While professionals come from both religious groups, there is a tendency for Adventists to pursue higher education and to become professionals (see Table 4). Whereas the Protestants—Adventists and Pentecostals—account for approximately 10% of the population, 58% of the professionals in the village are Protestant; all but two are Adventist.

The Adventist religion promotes education in several ways. First, it encourages individual advancement and the Protestant Ethic; the road to success is defined in terms of individual striving more than commitment to family or community. Second, the SDA school promotes the various Adventist colleges and professional schools located throughout Mexico. Local students are often able to obtain scholarships to these universities, receiving degrees in teaching, nursing, and theology; third, they have always promoted the education and delayed marriage of girls. For example, in one such program I attended in 1976, primary school students performed a skit, telling a story of a village girl who chooses to attend the Adventist university. She loses her local boyfriend, but finds that there are more important things in life than an early marriage and children. Clearly this represents promotion of the Adventist ideals and SDA universities, but it also illustrates an enormous shift, not only in attitudes about education, but also in attitudes regarding women's role in this society as well.

The young village girls, as well as boys, are encouraged to attend the religious institutions. Because most education in Mexico is free or highly subsidized, it is difficult to convince parents to send their children to the Adventist schools and universities. Tuition scholarships are available to poor families, but few local families could afford even the supplementary costs of nonresident education: lodging, food, books, transportation, and clothing. It is not surprising that only one family, that of Don Pablo, sent children to Adventist universities. Juanita, one of Don Pablo's daughters, started her own chicken business to earn money to attend the Adventist nursing school. On her own, she began to purchase young chicks, fattened them up, butchered them, and sold the meat from her house.

The Adventist promotion of educational advancement may have opened many doors for young women—Catholic and Protestant. In a sense, it may have paved the way for increased acceptance of the idea that all village women could pursue their education and careers. As the first to promote education and to lessen the stigma of out-migration, Adventists families showed other village girls and young women what they can attain. This, in collaboration with the economic downturn, may well have contributed to the increase of women in the economic and social spheres of village life (see Chapters 8 and 9).

THE PENTECOSTALS

The third and least established church in Yaxbe is the Pentecostal temple, represented by five related families. Although the Pentecostal missionaries arrived in Yaxbe one year before the Seventh Day Adventists, this religion had difficulties getting organized. The church, under construction in 1976, was not completed until the 1990s.

Despite the similarities in restrictions (the Pentecostals have fewer) and the lack of tithing, the Adventists have grown more quickly. While the Adventists consider the Pentecostals unusual in their beliefs, commenting on their "speaking in tongues" and hypnotic rituals, the Catholics consider them deviant. These families are isolated from others in the village.

THE IMPACT OF PROTESTANTISM ON VILLAGE LIFE

It is not a simple task to analyze the impact of Protestantism on the fabric of village life. There are several reasons for this. First, religion is not at the forefront of village factions or politics. The two Protestant religions have been accepted (the Pentecostal less than the Adventist) with no outward hostility among the three groups. Second, people are reticent about publicly expressing their feelings regarding the other religions. I had to read into subtle gestures and offhand comments to get a feel for any animosities that might exist. I interpreted such intriguing comments as, "Yes, he is Adventist, poor soul" or "The Catholics are only for Sunday."

Third, and perhaps most crucial, is village reluctance to express their opinions to me. The ambiguous role of anthropologists is important here. I have befriended many villagers, Catholic, Adventist, and Pentecostal, so my religious allegiances are difficult for them to interpret. The two families with whom I stay, and who have become closest to me are an Adventist family and a Catholic family. Both try to understand my religious beliefs. They have not heard of the Methodists. Even though I describe Methodism as a form of Protestantism, the Catholics think that Methodism is like Catholicism because I worship on Sunday, drink beer once in a while, and have no aversion to dancing or eating pork. The Protestants, on the other hand, either think I am a closet Catholic for the same reasons, or that I am a very deviant Adventist.

My actions are even more problematic. I never drink when I am staying with or socializing with the Adventists. When I go to a Catholic event, I have always refrained from alcohol unless other women are drinking, and then I only have one beer. This is both a cultural issue, but also a gender issue for the female anthropologist, who must live according to different gender values than those to which she is accustomed in the United States. So, I am always in a precarious position, balancing both diverse gender roles and religious expectations. Once, after attending a Catholic wedding, when I imbibed my one beer, I was reprimanded by my Protestant friends who, through the ever-efficient local grapevine, knew of my sins by next morning if not before. "We heard you drank beer and danced. . . ."

Despite the subliminal animosities that might exist among these diverse groups, there are some signs of mutual acceptance. Both Protestants and Catholics participate in the school-sponsored parent groups, and such government-sponsored programs as DIF and PACR. Men who still work in henequen production are organized along family lines, so it is increasingly common to find Protestants and Catholics within these work groups. Likewise, although the women's cooperatives are made up primarily of Catholic women, all groups have at least one Adventist member.

Historically, conversion split families into painful factions, as one family member, then another converted. In a society where family is the most important institution, such splintering was devastating. Over the years, this process of conversion has continued, but it has become less fractious. Instead, it has engendered a more tolerant and accepting relationship within and between families. In families often divided by religion, children and young people of both religions play together, attend school, and learn to tolerate, if not accept, the beliefs of the others.

The social interaction of young people and the increasing leniency toward courtship in the village results in more inter-religious marriages than occurred in the past. While most young people still marry within their religious group,

FIELD JOURNAL
DORCAS

February 26, 1998: Dora asked me if I wanted to accompany the **Dorcas** women on one of their missions. Dorcas is an Adventist women's volunteer organization, the purpose of which is to visit the sick, bring food to the poor or elderly, and assist families that need help. Today, they were planning to fix up the house of Doña Pastora. I thought they meant to clean up her modest home, but I was surprised to find that they actually meant to rebuild it! According to Dora, Doña Pastora's husband, a long-time invalid, had recently died leaving her destitute. In a situation extremely uncommon in this village, Pastora's children have neglected her. Her son is one of the village drunks who sleeps in the house, but who has not done any repairs, nor does he support his mother in any way. Her two daughters are married to local men and live in the village. For reasons not entirely clear to me, Pastora would not, or could not, live with either of them. Thus, she lived in a miserable state in a dilapidated thatch and tarpaper house.

We left Dora's newly built cement and stucco home at 2:30 in the afternoon. I teased her about walking during the middle of the day when only the dogs and anthropologists venture out. Yet, this was the only time that village women have free. Dora had to accomplish several chores before we left her house such as laundry and sweeping (see Figure 7.3). I washed the lunch dishes and helped to hang the clothes on the line. The thermometer that David [my son] brought to measure the temperature for his science class read 95 degrees Fahrenheit.

Outside the house we met up with Doña Celia, Dora's sister-in-law. She had a hammer and asked Dora if we brought tools. Dora laughed, saying that she didn't have any. As we walked south on the highway out of town, we picked up other members of the group. They waited in the doorway of their homes or congregated in pairs on street corners. They were dressed in their everyday clothing—dresses and plastic sandals. I was the only woman wearing shorts and tennis shoes. Every woman had a hammer, but no other tools. I had a sense that they weren't sure what tools they needed. The women exuded a light-hearted ambiance, an intensifying sense of adventure as each new woman joined the group. We passed Silvia's corner, but she wasn't there, so I was elected to run down to her house to see if she planned to come. I found Silvia hanging her clothes on the line. She had to finish her wash, then she would come. "I'll bring a hammer," she yelled at me from the back of her house.

When we arrived, there were already several women there, walking around the outside of the wattle and daub house, surveying the job ahead. I circled the house with my camcorder recording the "before" scene and wondering what the "after" would look like. Someone asked about the "*tapas.*" Who has the *tapas*? Someone else remarked that Doña Adi, who had not yet arrived, was to bring the *tapas*. While I wondered what kind of tops (or appetizers) they were talking about and why they needed them, Doña Adi arrived with a paper bag full of pop and beer bottle caps each of which had two holes tapped through it. Doña Juana arrived next with a roll of wire and wire snips, and then Silvia came with her hammer. Doña Isabel arrived last, the only *mestiza* beside the

Figure 7.3 Dora, 1989

owner of the house, dressed in her huipil, her shawl wrapped artistically around her neck. She brought a knife.

Doña Pastora, the owner of the house, was genuinely pleased to see us, and eagerly invited us in. Hers was the poorest home I had seen in the village since my first research year. It was a traditional oval-shaped house with a stone foundation. Above the foundation the original mud had disintegrated leaving wide gaps between the vertical sticks. The walls had been covered by corrugated cardboard on the outside. On the inside, Doña Pastora had hung plastic bags, scraps of material, tarpaulin, and broken cardboard boxes to keep out the cold and rain. At one time, someone had poured a cement floor, but that was the only improvement that had been made to the house. A small wooden table and several wooden chairs were the only furniture, and a single hammock was strung up along the gaping wall. Her clothes were packed in boxes that were placed on the floor along the wall, adding additional insulation against the cold. The roof of her house was thatched with huge gaps filled in by tarpaper. Her cooking area was located, in the traditional way, outside the back door of her house, covered with additional tarpaper. She used a fire to cook food.

I surveyed the house with a sense of despair. What could we possibly do? From my perspective, the best tool for this job would have been a bulldozer, but these women were more pragmatic and optimistic. They quickly evaluated the situation and began to tear the old tarpaper from the inside and outside walls. They took pieces of an old hammock loom and loose tree branches and fashioned new cross-beams to be nailed perpendicular to the vertical branches that had formed the original walls. The new tarpaper would be nailed to these new cross-beams.

The first problem immediately arose as the women realized that they had 10 hammers but no nails. Doña Clara, whose husband is a carpenter, was dispatched to find nails and the rest of us ripped tarpaper and shaped cross branches. I was less aggressive than the others because of my paranoia about scorpions that I knew resided in the thatch and walls of old houses. By the end of the day, I was relieved that the cockroaches that scurried out of the clothes boxes were my only encounter with the insect, arachnid, or crustacean kingdoms.

When the nails arrived, our work began in earnest. As we were all inexpe-

(continued)

FIELD JOURNAL
DORCAS (*continued*)

rienced with hammers, we struggled to nail the branches together. The wood proved to be remarkably hard. Because I towered one foot above the tallest woman in the group, I was elected to stand on the rickety wooden chair and nail the top branches at the peak of the house. Once that chore was done, the truly remarkable work began.

Doña Pastora had a bundle of tarpaper that her son had purchased a year ago, but had never installed. The women began shaping the corrugated material to fit the difficult contours of the house (thus the knife). Another woman cut the wire and threaded long pieces through the bottle caps, forming a U pattern with the bottle cap at the bend. The remaining women took positions around the exterior of the house, attaching the tarpaper to the house using the wire and bottle caps. The wires were poked through the tarpaper walls on either side of a branch or cross-beam and then, with the assistance of one's counterpart on the inside of the house, was wound around the beam forming a tight binding. The bottle cap serves as a nail head/washer, being pushed into the tarpaper and wood from the outside. Again, because of my height, I was positioned at the outside of the house, working on the highest sections.

To reach the top of the outside walls, I had to stand on large limestone boulders that rocked precariously under my feet. I decided not to burden them with my fear of heights and accepted my job with grace, if not enthusiasm.

The work was difficult, especially in the heat. Perspiration clouded and stung our eyes as we pounded and poked. Despite the unbearable heat, however, the women were in good spirits. They worked as a team, as if they did this type of thing every day. Everyone had a task and women often shifted tasks, moving from inside to outside and vice versa. They joked with each other about mistakes and commented on how smart I was because I learned so rapidly how to use the bottle cap method of construction. They asked if I learned to do it by building houses in the United States. I answered "no," but that I had learned how to use a hammer.

Finally, we had used up all the tarpaper. We had covered all the gaps and holes in the outer wall. There were still areas of the inside walls that were not covered completely, and several women promised to return the next day to complete the job. When we were finished, Doña Clara's builder-husband came to the house to inspect our work. Doña

approximately 10–15% of the marriages in recent years have been interreligious. I will be interested to see how this trend shapes the village in the future. How will religious intermarriage affect the membership of the Adventist temple, for example, and how will children be raised?

One current example of an interreligious marriage will illustrate the ambiguity that still exists in the village. Elena is the 19-year-old daughter of a very strong Catholic family. Her *novio* of several years, Roberto, is the product of a family split between two religions. His mother is Catholic, but his stepfather and stepsisters are fairly active in the Adventist temple. When Elena got pregnant, Roberto asked her father for permission to marry, and plans for a wedding commenced. Because the family of the groom pays for weddings in Mexico, it became clear very early that

Figure 7.4 The Dorcas group, 1998

Rosario, one of the SDA schoolteachers, noted that the stone foundation was badly in need of repair. Indeed, it looked as if a good storm might topple the entire building. Don Ernesto offered to repair it for her.

When we finished, I was surprised to see that it was only 6:00. I videotaped the "after" shots and offered to take a picture of the entire group of women (see Figure 7.4). I wanted to suggest we go somewhere for a beer, but this was not the group that would appreciate such a suggestion. Besides, there is no place in the village for women to drink anyway. So I settled for my bottled water as they all drank from the well at the back of the house. The women all collected their tools, and we headed back as we had come, women splitting off where they had originally joined the group, returning home to pick up where they left off in their real jobs—caring for their families.

problems would arise. And they did. Roberto's stepfather did not want a wedding in the Catholic church. Rather he wanted a civil ceremony. This decision greatly disturbed Elena's family. After much anguish, Elena's parents decided on a solution. They had two weddings. Elena and Roberto were married in front of the civil judge when Elena was about three months along in her pregnancy. Roberto's family had a reception afterward in his *solár* where the couple took up residence. Later, in her sixth month, Elena's parents, Cristina and Rubio, held a wedding for her in the Catholic church. It was a very painful event for the family as only Roberto's parents attended the wedding. Elena's parents held a huge reception after the wedding in their family *solár*. I saw videotape of both weddings and receptions—the first subdued and almost lethargic, the second, a celebration with many family and friends (of the bride) attending. Roberto and Elena's daughter was born three months after the Catholic wedding. Elena's mother laments that the infant's ears are not pierced and that Elena does not attend any church. They continue to live with Roberto's family.

Consequently, even though Protestants and Catholics live and interact within the same village, it can also be said that Adventists and Catholics live parallel lives, each involved in separate days of worship, religious practices and rituals, social events, and interests. In looking to the future of Yaxbe, it will be crucial to find the intersection of these parallel worlds and explore the cultural threads that bind them together.

CONCLUSION

Protestantism is not an evil intrusion into the peaceful life of Catholic Mexico. It is merely another factor, combined with the increase in cash crop agriculture and television, which initiates the evolution that is occurring gradually, within thousands of Mexican villages and larger towns and cities. Protestantism brings with it an entire cluster of values that confront religious beliefs and social institutions that are now deeply embedded into Mexican culture, in much the same way that Catholicism confronted and conquered the earlier Mayan belief and social systems. In this chapter, we have examined how and why some Yaxbeños have converted to Protestantism and how Protestantism has contributed in bringing Yucatecans into contact with the larger society. In the next chapters, we will look at the economic factors that have further fostered the integration of rural Yucatan with the larger global society.

8/In the Ashes of the Henequen *Ejido*

PEASANTS AND THE WORLD SYSTEM REVISITED

In this chapter, we will look at the transformations that have occurred in the village since 1976. We will focus on the impact of the henequen collapse and current governmental policies on the villagers themselves. The consequences of the intersection of these two factors are visible in the choices that rural people make today. We will be investigating several of these options: diversification of income in the village, commuting, and out-migration. By examining how people make these decisions, we gain insight into rural life. We are able to see the Maya as active participants, not remnants of a glorious past or passive victims of larger global events. We are further able to learn how rural villagers formulate these strategies and how they redefine themselves and their place in the local and state system. Finally, we can appreciate their resilience and their will to persevere.

1989: The Fall of the Ejido and the Rise of the Service Sector

As we have seen, the economic system of Yucatán has depended on the integration of the individual worker, work groups, the state bank and credit institutions, the private and state factories, and the federal government. The *henequenero* was, and still is, at the bottom of the pyramid, supporting the fragile economic system. When I returned to Yaxbe in 1989, it seemed as if the delicate balance had tipped toward disaster. The decrease in demand for henequen was not new, but what I now saw was the impact of this collapse on the local economy.

JOURNAL ENTRY
THE KING IS DEAD, LONG LIVE THE KING

March 17, 1998. I am thinking about the idea of the ending of one *katun* and the beginning of another—a time of change. I am also thinking of LaVail's observation that the relationship between men and henequen was a religious one, and that henequen is worshipped like a god. Its demise is reminiscent of the death of a religion, the death of the God of Henequen. I prefer the idea of a king to that of a God, but the pervasiveness of henequen cannot be denied. Henequen demanded all of a man's energy, from predawn to midday and then again in the afternoons, six or seven days a week. Henequen demanded major sacrifices, not only in time, but in health and well-being. A *henequeneros* hands are scarred from the thorns that form the ridge of the leaves and crown each tip. There is a painting in the Governor's Palace in Mérida entitled simply "A *Henequeneros* Hands" showing the two hands, palms up in supplication, with scars and open wounds.

The henequen routine, however, allowed men to remain linked to their ancient agricultural traditions. They planted corn between the rows of young henequen plants and made a small *milpa,* producing food crops for their families. They performed their annual supplication to their ancient rain god, *Chac.* There was a place for the *h-men* in the cycle of life, linking the farmer to the gods and linking the traditional medicines to local beliefs of sorcerers and magicians. But, the henequen kingdom had no place for women. They remained invisible in their *soláres* weaving, cultivating fruits and vegetables, and raising pigs and turkeys, independent from men but linked in a complex symbiotic relationship.

The fall of henequen disrupted the routine, dislodged the rituals. Men no longer share their routine with their fellow villagers. Those who still follow the agricultural routine now work as individuals or families, taking a bicycle or pickup truck to the cooperative, to the small individual henequen field or *milpa,* to their cattle ranch at the outskirts of the village . . . following a different rhythm. Buses come and go, according to a 10-hour factory shift; taxis take workers and students to Mérida, Tixkokob, Motul, or any number of locations within the widening sphere of influence.

And women. The death of henequen has either freed women or tied them to new responsibilities, depending on one's perspective. Women have come out of the woodwork and have taken their places in the high school and college classrooms; in the factories; and in the political sphere. A young married woman rises early, drops her child off at her *comadre's* house and goes to her job in the clothing factory. A young grandmother works as a cleaning lady in a government office in Mérida and on the weekends works with a group of women friends on their own chicken farm. Two nurses, dressed in starched white uniforms wait in the plaza for the afternoon bus to take them to the Mérida hospital where they work the night shift . . . the death of one way of life and the birth of another. But perhaps it is only a cycle, not a new thing. As the Mayan calendars predict, events repeat themselves—what occurs now has occurred hundreds of times in the past and will occur again and again in the centuries to come.

In the summer of 1989, I returned to the village for the first time since 1979. As my bus bumped along the roads, I passed the familiar scenery. Henequen fields with plants in various stages of growth still dominated the landscape. But the comfortable monotony of the henequen fields was deceptive. The illusion of continuity dissolved when I arrived in Yaxbe where a closer investigation of the henequen fields revealed the harsh reality. Instead of nicely cleared rows of carefully trimmed plants, weeds grew freely among the plants and in between the rows. The plants, still in their productive years, had been cut literally "to death," leaving only the few scraggly leaves at the top.

As I talked to my friends, I also discovered the *ejido,* never a lucrative source of income, was even less so now. Most workers in 1989 were only earning about US$12.00 per week. The henequen *ejido* was clearly not worth the time spent weeding and caring for the fields if other wage work was available. My research that summer confirmed the obvious. Less than half of former *ejidatarios* were still employed in the *ejido* in 1989. Most of these were older men who had fewer options for alternate sources of income. Their strategies were influenced by several factors: their age, their relationship to land and the job market, and their freedom and willingness to leave the village.

Of the 75 *ejidatarios* who were less than 20 years of age in 1976–1977, only 4 (5%) were still *ejiatarios* in 1989. Few young men wanted to work as their fathers and grandfathers did, performing grueling stoop labor with long hours and few rewards. In contrast, younger men sought non-agricultural wage jobs. Unfortunately, few of these jobs are found in the village.

The demise of henequen was also apparent at the *hacienda* and at the Cordemex factory. The *hacienda* at Santiago was abandoned altogether by 1989. The decorticating factory and the surrounding workers' homes had collapsed under the weight of the economic decline. The *hacienda* had recently been purchased by the owner of the Mérida Coca-Cola Bottling Plant who planned to develop a cattle ranch. This enterprise came to fruition by the mid-1990s when new employee housing was built and the fields, once dominated by henequen were used for grazing cattle or for the production of **zacate,** a grass grown specifically for cattle consumption. In 1989, however, there was no evidence of either development or cattle.

Cordemex also displayed evidence of the collapse. In 1976, there were two shifts of workers at the Yaxbe plant. In 1989, there was only one, and the factory was scheduled to close entirely in the near future. Villagers blamed the managers of the plant, political appointees of the new national president who knew nothing about henequen and who mismanaged the factory through inconsistent pricing of leaves and through cronyism and top-heavy administration. Workers laid off as a result of the decline of the henequen economy in the early years earned one major benefit that to some extent compensated for their loss of employment, a severance bonus of between 2 million and 8 million pesos (US$800–$3,200) depending on seniority. *Ejidatarios* received a smaller compensation.

Ironically, there was a notable incongruity between the condition of the henequen fields and the quiet factory, and the appearance of the village itself, which appeared prosperous and modern. Between 1977 and 1989, a new elementary school had been built to accommodate the increased number of children in the village. A new kindergarten and secondary school also reflected the increased village population, as well as state and federal investment in the rural area. The success of a locally owned taxi service attested to the increased traffic between the village, Mérida, and many small towns in between. This paradox continues to the present day.

The 1990s: Economic Change in Yaxbe

In 1977, 80% of the adult men in Yaxbe gained their primary income directly from the henequen industry, either in the *ejido* itself or in henequen-related jobs in the *hacienda,* the Cordemex factory, or as truckers. Only 20% of adult men earned their primary income from other agricultural products, animal husbandry, or non-agricultural jobs. By 1995, these percentages were reversed (review Tables 1 and 2 in the Appendix). The national reforms of Article 27 and NAFTA are not the immediate reasons for these shifts. Rather, these current transformations are the consequence of a long process of decline in the henequen market. The changes in the agrarian code, as interpreted by local families and officials, are just nails in the coffin of the henequen *ejido*.

As the data in Table 2 suggest, the conditions of the henequen *ejido* have disintegrated since my initial research, culminating in 1992 with its elimination. The henequen fields were then visibly neglected and many fields were abandoned altogether. Instead of cutting leaves, men were actually extracting the plants and selling the woody portion of the stalk to a distributor for the production of tequila. Apparently the international demand for tequila has outstripped the national supply of maguey, and the stalks of the henequen plants have been found to be an adequate substitute.

Cordemex closed during my visit in 1992, and the former employees had been promised that they would have the opportunity to purchase the factory themselves. By 1995, it was clear that this had never been a realistic promise, since villagers could not possibly have raised the money necessary for its purchase. By 1998, Cordemex had reopened under a different name and was privately owned. The union wages, paid vacations, and seniority system had been replaced by poor wages, minimal benefits, and one-year contracts.

In the 1990s, despite economic decline, there were more improvements in the infrastructure and appearance of the village. Since 1989, the local government has built a new municipal market, a Conasupo (government-subsidized grocery store), a library, and a medical clinic staffed by two doctors and a nurse. In addition to new buildings, other improvements in infrastructure are evident: an expanded system of paved roads leading from the village center to its perimeter and an expansion of electrical services and potable water. The village has a single telephone line that connects to a pay phone in the president's office. Until 2001, a long distance call home necessitated a 20-minute drive to the neighboring town where I waited in a small room of a private home for my call to go through. If I was lucky, the proprietor of the long distance office was home, there was no special local festivity, and the connection was good. However, if any of these conditions occurred or if no one was home when I called, then I had wasted my time and the gas and time of the villager who transported me there. Today, several villagers have cellular phones in their homes, and I have been able to call home with much more ease. In Mérida, I can send email home from one of several Internet cafés.

Houses have become larger over the years, with separate rooms, modern appliances, and furniture. This trend has already been noted, but the speed with which it is spreading is remarkable. The demand for VCRs and cameras has increased, as has the number of families who own cars or trucks. At my last visit, the Seventh Day Adventist temple had received a computer from its parent organization with the goal of maintaining membership records and forming linkages between the headquarters in Berrien Springs, Michigan, and its mission sites. Unfortunately, no one in the village had any idea how to use the new equipment and it sat in a small locked office of the temple, awaiting a computer programmer to arrive to set it up and train temple administrators how to use it. Without any previous exposure to typewriters or electronics, it is likely to be a formidable task.

Over the years, as I returned periodically to the village, I expected to see a gradual deterioration of village life. I also expected to see a flood of out-migrants, as my 1989 research had suggested. Instead, I continued to find evidence of affluence, a decline in migration rates, a healthy increase in population, and marked village improvements. Yet my conversations with villagers often contradicted these observations. Women living in beautiful houses complain about "the crisis," young people and married men leave the village at dawn to work in urban factories, and married women add baby-sitting to their daily chores. The juxtaposition of this apparent affluence and the unkempt henequen fields and abandoned Cordemex factory presented a paradox and forced a few questions: Why was there such a contradiction between the economic deterioration and the apparent growth and prosperity of the village? Where was the money coming from that built these houses and purchased these material goods? How can a village, wrought by economic depression, support a growing population?

The answer to these questions is complex and related to several factors, which we will examine in the remainder of this chapter and in Chapter 9. In this chapter, we will explore the economic strategies that have emerged for men and women in the past 20 years: (1) diversified sources of income and the increased participation of women in the wage economy; (2) commuting; and (3) out-migration. In Chapter 9, we will examine the attempts by the national government to win the hearts and minds of rural people by improving infrastructure and providing social programs. These programs are particularly important for women, as we will see. In the last chapter, we will examine how these factors have resulted in transformations both within the village and within the family.

ECONOMIC DIVERSIFICATION IN THE VILLAGE

Case Study: The New Campesinos

Justo and Jesus Chan (Journals, June 11, 1995, and Feb 23, 1998):

Justo Chan and his sons are the epitome of the new *campesino* (farmer). Justo and Jesus both worked in the *ejido* in 1976. Justo also owned a *parcela* on which he cultivated additional henequen. In 1992, Justo solicited the *socio* for former *ejido* land. He was granted about three acres of land that he holds in usufruct (see Figure 8.1). While other men abandoned their henequen fields or allowed them to be overrun with weeds, the Chans planted henequen and maintained three immaculate fields at different stages of maturity. When I visited his field in 1995, they were planting a new field of *hijos* in a field they had recently burned. A group of men worked in each row, lining up the plants, digging the holes, placing the plants, and securing each with rocks.

Figure 8.1 Don Justo, 1998

Justo and Jesus were also planting additional crops in newly cleared and burned areas: watermelon, *camote* (sweet potato), and squash. In addition, they had built a small corral for their small herd of cattle and a caretaker's house at the edge of the field. Every section of the farm was utilized. The area surrounding the caretaker's house abounded in fruit trees—orange, tangerine, banana—and various types of grasses for their cattle. Don Jesus guided me through his garden, a large area of abundant bushes and trees laden with colorful flowers and fruit. As I followed him through the maze of still young trees, he pointed out and identified numerous flowering plants and herbs. He tenderly picked leaves for me to smell or taste. ". . . this one is oregano, this is pimiento, this is tabasco, this is mint . . . can you guess what this is?" I was surrounded by a myriad of brilliant colors, fragrances, and greenery.

In 1998, I returned to Don Justo's farm. I was accompanied by Reymundo, his son, Hector, and my own son, David. Don Justo, now in his 60s, worked less at the farm. Don Jesus was now the principle agriculturist. His younger brother, Daniel, who returned recently from Cancún, was the newest partner in the expanding enterprise. There were now 30 head of cattle, more than 100 chickens, and 60 mature turkeys. Daniel was in charge of their most recent acquisition, a 10-stall pigsty with more than 30 pigs. He insisted that I take many pictures of his prize possessions.

Don Jesus was proud of their henequen field, greatly enlarged over the past three years. They now had several fields of mature plants, ready for cutting. The *hijos* I watched them plant three years before were thriving. He had since planted more *hijos* and interspersed with these younger plants was his *milpa,* the stalks now brown and bent down in Mexican fashion to protect the corn from birds and the heat of the sun. As I watched, he poked and prodded the rocky earth and uncovered mounds of sweet potato, handing several of the large vegetables to Hector.

As we wove around henequen plants of various sizes, I regretted having worn a skirt as my legs became badly scratched from the thorns as well as from the other prickly vines that are part of the Yucatecan landscape. As we walked back to our truck, Reymundo approached a tree, which to me was indistinguishable from the others that lined the path to the road. He pulled a handful of leaves from the tree and instructed me how to extract the juice from their veins and rub it on my cuts. The bleeding stopped immediately and I could feel the pain lessen.

"What is this?" I asked.

"*Ek balám,*" he answered. "The medicine of the *henequenero.*"

Current Economic Occupations in Yaxbe

When critical changes occur in an economic system, they do not affect all individuals in the same way. This is true in the Yucatán. Middle-aged married men have limited options given the decline in the agricultural sector. Displaced *ejidatarios* are especially hard hit since they do not have the training or education necessary to take up a skilled or semi-skilled occupation. These men who are not able to continue in henequen production have begun to invest in other forms of agricultural labor, such as vegetable cropping or raising domesticated animals. Older men, in their 50s and 60s, are particularly vulnerable. Unable to find new work, they will often work as laborers for younger village men who have private parcels, work family gardens, or possibly work for their children who now own stores. While this type of diversification illustrates their industriousness and flexibility, the reality is that these local sources of income pay very poorly and often offer only part-time employment.

AGRICULTURE   Some villagers have maintained ties to agriculture by forming cooperatives. Cooperatives were not very successful in the early years of my research, as they were incompatible with the demanding routine of henequen production. However, beginning in the 1990s, village men began to form cooperatives, sponsored by national peasant organizations. The supporting organizations assist the men in dynamiting wells and in purchasing seeds. The men share the labor of planting, weeding, harvesting, and guarding the field. Unfortunately, these cooperatives continue to be only marginally successful, and do not promote real development. There are constant problems: theft of their produce, malfunctions of their wells and water shortages, and conflicts among the men that center on the fair distribution of labor. Because the cooperatives are normally supplemental to other forms of employment, men are often unable or unwilling to put the necessary time and labor into them. Those men for whom the cooperatives are a primary source of income often complained about the lack of commitment from the others.

The most interesting development in the village since the early 1990s is the initiation of women's agricultural and factory cooperatives that have allowed women to supplement family incomes, and, as will be seen, have empowered rural women in various ways. These will be discussed in detail in the next chapter.

NON-AGRICULTURAL OCCUPATIONS   In the remaining sections of this chapter, we will look at some of the new non-agricultural occupations within and outside the village. Tables 1 and 2 illustrate this shift from agriculture to non-agricultural occupations since 1976. Because Yaxbe is a large village, there has always been a diverse economic structure. In 1976, 16% of adult men worked in non-agricultural occupations, such as construction, tailoring, and shopkeeping. In 1998, 70% of the men in my sample worked in non-agricultural positions. While many of these men are employed in the above occupations, the range of occupations has expanded since the 1980s.

Shifts in economic participation of women are also remarkable. Referring again to Table 1, note that in 1976, only 12% of the women in my large sample earned an income from their labor. In contrast, in 1998, 21% of the women in my sample earned an income or participated in a family business. Women's participation is much more difficult to gauge, as already noted, because a substantial percentage of their income is earned in the home—sewing or weaving hammocks. Nevertheless, the numbers reflect a marked increase in the dependence of family on the earnings of women. Much of this new money is earned outside of the home and even, as we will see in the next section, outside of the village.

Innovative villagers with access to capital have developed new strategies that allow them to pursue entrepreneurial alternatives to wage labor. The source of capital for these local businesses has been, ironically, the severance pay allotted to workers laid off from the *ejido* and from the decorticating factory. While both *ejidatarios* and factory workers received severance pay, that received by Cordemex workers was much more substantial than the compensation paid to agricultural workers. This benefit catapulted the factory worker far beyond the average villager and entrenched his position in the new middle class.

Several farsighted men used part of their severance pay to purchase private parcels or *soláres* in the village. The most obvious change in the village in my 1989 visit, however, was the proliferation of small house-front stores, financed primarily by severance payments. These enterprises, often secondary sources of income, are managed on a daily basis by the members of the immediate and extended family. Other men invested in vans that formed the core of the taxi service. Another purchased a flatbed truck and started his own transport business. Those who did not start businesses added to the material prosperity of the village through the construction of new homes or the purchase of the consumer goods already described. All of these investments, short or long term, attest to the continued commitment to the village.

Women and Income Production within the Home

As stated in Chapter 3, women have traditionally earned income through a variety of means within the household. These strategies still exist for many women, and even those who have jobs outside of the home continue to earn money in these ways, as do other female household members. Living with families during my subsequent visits has afforded me the opportunity to observe these various supplemental sources of income. At one home in 1998, there was a steady stream of children at the door, purchasing soft drinks, ice pops, and chunks of ice from the family refrigerator/freezer.

At another house, I peeled, sliced, and packaged papaya and watermelon, and weighed tomatoes, limes, and chile peppers to sell to women and children who came to the door while my hostess was out back doing laundry or running errands herself. This informal economy is not lucrative in and of itself, but compounded provides supplemental income to the family.

The household responsibilities of many women have been expanded in many homes where men have invested their severance pay into house-front stores. While men may do the purchasing and will dedicate some hours to the store, for them it is often a second source of income, supplementing a factory job or agricultural labor. Instead, the women and children contribute the bulk of the labor to the store, sharing housework, and taking turns attending customers. The success of this endeavor depends largely on the life cycle of the family: the age of the children, the time available to the mother, and the cooperation of the husband and his family members.

Between 1995 and 1998, I noticed that few homes had hammock looms. I was surprised to see unused looms hanging from the beams of houses or leaning against dilapidated out-buildings. In response to my inquiries, I learned that women now saw the hammock "putting-out" system as an inefficient means of income production. Increasingly sophisticated about the value of their labor, women realized that the hammock contractors and distributors had been taking advantage of them. "We know how much they sell for in Mérida," was a common response.

The hammock industry is reliant on a compliant and indigent work force. Currently, in Yaxbe, only the poorest families continue to pursue this option. One exception is a hammock cooperative formed by several elderly village women. These women bypass the Tixkokob marketers; they purchase their own skeins, weave, and sell their own products. Their hammocks are huge, and made of the best materials. Best of all, the women are being rewarded for the value of their labor.

Women and Income Production outside of the Home

Generally, employed women are single, but increasingly, married women with children are entering the workforce, working in factories or as teachers, secretaries, or nurses (see Table 5, Appendix). The expansion of opportunities for women in professional jobs and the participation of women in the job market has implications for other women in the family as well, as these working women seek childcare for their children. Women in rural Mexico have an advantage over most working mothers in the United States in that they live with or near their mothers or mothers-in-law and have built-in baby-sitters. While the sharing of childcare is an intrinsic part of Mexican culture, there are indications that the increased reliance on grandmothers and other female relatives is having negative ramifications on the children and on the caregivers themselves. This phenomenon will be discussed further in Chapter 9.

Case Study: Pedro Chac

Manuel Chac is the patriarch of a family of nine children. He and his wife, María, portray the image of the indigenous Maya, wearing the traditional Maya *huipil* and *traje* and speaking Maya. Nonfluent in Spanish, they spoke only Maya to their children, who are now grown and have children of their own—children who do not speak Maya. During the Revolutionary years, Manuel worked at the *Hacienda* Santiago.

He is known as an authoritarian father whose wife seldom left the house alone and always walked behind him. He is a man of stern disposition who seldom smiles. In 2000, María passed away, and Manuel lives alone in his small stucco house at the edge of the village, near his daughter.

Over the years, we have become close friends with two of Manuel's sons and one of his daughters. Unlike their father, these three individuals are outgoing and have egalitarian marriages. Like their father, all three have a strong work ethic and have used diverse strategies to survive the economic "crisis." Miguel and Pedro work together in various economic endeavors and Paula, their sister, is the president of the *horchata* cooperative (Chapter 9).

In 1976, all of Manuel's sons were employed in the *ejido,* but in addition, Manuel owned 100 *mecates* of private henequen land. In 1989, two of Manuel's sons worked at Cordemex, but by 1995, they had both lost those jobs and had resumed work in the *ejido* and on the family parcel. During the 1970s, two of his sons, Pedro and Miguel, converted to the Seventh Day Adventist religion. They both married Adventist women and escaped their father's authoritarian sphere.

The youngest son, Pedro, married a young woman from one of the founding SDA families, and moved into her extended household. When I met them, Pedro and Dora were childless after three years of marriage and had filled their life with religious activities. They were members of one of the best a cappella choirs I have ever heard, and, despite their youth, participated actively in the church administration. Dora and her brother were both tailors, and Dora continued to sew in their home until she injured her hand in a sewing machine accident. Pedro was supplementing his *ejido* work with an incipient traveling sales career, selling produce from his family land and reselling small household items he bought in the Mérida market. My earliest memories of Pedro are of him sitting in the park surrounded by watermelons, strumming his guitar, and practicing his music.

In 1989, Pedro was very successful in his sales enterprise, and he no longer worked in the *ejido.* He was now selling good quality furniture from town to town in his own truck and had hired Miguel as *cobrador,* or payment collector. In 1992, Pedro and Dora were building a new house across the road from her family, a multi-room stucco house with carport, louvered windows, gas stove, and indoor kitchen and plumbing. They had adopted a child and were an integral part of the Adventist temple.

By 1995, the tide had turned somewhat for Pedro as the national "crisis," penetrated the countryside. His business was very slow, and he was having a difficult time collecting on outstanding debts. Unable to afford a full-time *cobrador,* he was now doing much of the collecting himself. He expanded his economic activities by collaborating with his father and Miguel in a cattle ranch located on a portion of their private land (see Figure 8.2). He also joined a horticultural cooperative, which—when operating—provided the men with fresh vegetables for family consumption and sale. Despite the downturn, Pedro and Dora were still affluent by local standards. Besides the new house and truck, their possessions included a completely furnished living and dining room, refrigerator, a color television, and, in 2001, a cellular phone. Dora shops in Mérida for groceries, as well as for clothing and toys for their only child and does not earn an outside income.

In 1998, Pedro had become entrenched in this mixed strategy. Besides his ranch and his agricultural cooperative, he had a contract with a local agricultural college to

Figure 8.2 Pedro at his ranch, 1998

sell their produce in Mérida. Every day, he left his house early in the morning, traveling either to his fields or to the college. Some days, he would do both. First, he would work in his field—clearing, weeding and harvesting whatever crop was in season. Then he would drive the 15 miles to the college, fill his truck with limes, tomatoes, watermelons, sweet potatoes, chiles, and transport his load the 30 miles to the Mérida market where he would sit all afternoon until he sold the produce. He preferred to sell the items in bulk to store and restaurant owners and others like him who buy in the city and sell in their own villages.

Once he sold his produce, he returned home, often arriving after the family had eaten dinner. On other days, he would return home early so he could tend to the family's cattle. Because his sister and father-in-law also kept cattle at the ranch, the chores surrounding them were more widely dispersed. Together, they had also hired an elderly widower to sleep at the ranch at night. Some evenings, after showering and eating the meal that Dora had saved and reheated for him, the family attended the evening temple activities. On Saturdays, Pedro did not work, but he and others from the temple often traveled to other villages to visit the sick or to attend special events. On Sunday, he took his motorcycle and his credit sheets and collected his weekly payments for whatever items he sold in his spare time—wooden tables, chairs, and dressers.

While Pedro was involved in these various activities, Dora was also very busy. Her father, a widower for many years, lives in the family *solár* across the street and she feeds and cares for him. Until they were grown, she also prepared food for her teenage nephews who lived in the family *solár* with her divorced brother. Her day was filled with cleaning and cooking; she washed by hand all of her family's clothes as well as those of her father, brother, and nephews. Her day was constantly disrupted as neighbors came to her door to purchase Pedro's produce: tomatoes, chile, squash, oranges, limes, papaya, watermelons, and whatever was in season.

As of 2001, Pedro still had an association with the agricultural college. As the only remaining member of the cooperative, he now purchases all of the seeds and starter plants and cultivates 100 *mecates* of papaya, in addition to other fruits and vegetables. He hires seven young men to work the field with him and he sells his papaya to a distributor who transports it to Mexico and the United States. When I visited in 2002, he had just lost an entire crop of papaya trees to disease and he estimated a loss of 10,000 pesos. He continues to harvest vegetables on his land and at the college, but he has incurred a tremendous loss.

Pedro and Dora have recently obtained another piece of land through the new PROCEDE program, which he is clearing for production. Dora's nephews have moved out of the *solár,* as has her brother. She still cares for her father who is now 90 years old. Carlos is 10, and Dora no longer has the same demands on her time; she still works in the home, selling produce from her living room. She dotes on her husband and son, and takes all of her pleasure from their well-being, as well as from her work at the temple. Pedro is clearly one of the more affluent members of the community, but one who is generous and unassuming. His self-effacement and simple demeanor are characteristic of the older generations of peasants. Theirs is a stable, loving household, and one that has been generous to me and my family over the years, accepting us into their household, and treating our children as their own.

COMMUTING AS ECONOMIC STRATEGY

In the predawn hours, an ancient ritual is replicated. Workers stumble down poorly lit, rock strewn roads toward the center of town where transportation to their jobs awaits them. In 1976, these workers were men climbing onto the bed of pick-up trucks or onto horse-drawn wagons that took them to the henequen fields at the outskirts of the village. Today, these workers have a very different appearance and destination. Instead of wagons and trucks, buses line up along the plaza to await the new workers. In addition, many of the workers converging on the plaza from all directions are women. Some climb on the bus that will take them to the foreign-owned brassiere factory in Mérida; others board the bus that takes them to the American-owned Jerzees factory in Tixkokob. The men board a bus that will take them to a concrete factory on the highway to Mérida. The ritual repeats itself in the early evening, when the buses return and release their passengers, exhausted, to return to their homes. In addition to the company-owned buses, public buses and taxis also provide transportation for the new workers, as men and women leave the village daily to work in restaurants, stores, hospitals, schools, factories, and urban offices.

In 1976–1977, only 14 of 197 households (7%) had at least one family member commuting from the village. By 1998, Yaxbe had become a bedroom community, with more than half of the households sending at least one member out of the village to work. These daily commuters represent a vital transformation in village economics and family dynamics. In this section, we will examine the impact of commuting on village life.

Factory Jobs

Wage labor is not a new development in Yucatán, as we have seen. Because *henequeneros* have earned wages for their labor since the 1930s, the shift from reciprocal exchange to market economies is not a recent one. What is new is the shift in the relationship between the worker and employer. Whereas, historically, the henequen workers were employees of the paternalistic state, modern laborers work for private corporations. As such, they are often invisible laborers often far removed geographically or experientially from their employers.

While the *ejido* and Cordemex employed only men, factory work today is defined largely as female work. This is also true in Yaxbe. Of 59 villagers who worked in factories outside Yaxbe in 1998, 22 (37%) were women and 16 of these were single. Men are primarily employed in two factories, one that produces rugs and another that produces cement blocks. The factory that employs the most women is a brassiere/ lingerie factory near Mérida. Here, women and other employees work from 7 A.M. to 5 P.M. five days a week with a half-hour lunch and two breaks. They earn a base wage and additional pay for anything produced beyond their daily quota. They also earn a bonus every year and have a one- or two-week paid vacation every year. As with many piecemeal systems, however, the quotas are constantly being raised and the women earn a minimal amount of money for their time in the factory. One young woman told me in 1995 that she earned 116–120 pesos per week. This equates roughly to US$20–$25 (1995) per week. In comparison, a henequen farmer, working every day earned about 150 pesos (US$30) per week. Although painfully inadequate, the income earned by a young woman can greatly augment a family income or pay for her own education.

By 2001, even more factories have proliferated in the countryside, providing low-paying jobs for villagers and high profits for their parent companies. Another example will suffice to illustrate this point. In 2001, Reymundo's wife, Sonia was employed at Jerzees, a factory that produces casual clothing, shirts, and sweatshirts. She worked a shift cycle called 4 × 4 in which women work four straight 12-hour days and then have four days off. These 12-hour days don't include travel time between Yaxbe and Tixkokob where the factory is located, about half hour each way. For one four day shift, Sonia earned 500 pesos (about US$45), or less than $1 dollar an hour (including lunch). After my 2001 visit, Sonia and Reymundo's daughter returned to Michigan with me for a short visit. We were excited and pleased to be able to do this for her. While shopping in the mall one day, we happened on a rack of Jerzees sweatshirts, and Carmen was shocked to see that they cost $20 each. Doing the calculations, she realized that it would cost her mother almost two days' wages to purchase one of the shirts that she made in the factory.

Professional Occupations

As discussed in Chapter 4, few children in 1976–1977 attended school beyond primary, or 6th grade. Secondary school attendance (equivalent to junior high) or *prepa* (high school) was limited to those children whose families could afford, not only the loss of their labor, but their transportation and living costs. After the secondary school was built in the village, attendance increased. Improved access to transportation has likewise increased the number of children who now attend high school or technical school. As a result, numerous villagers today have earned degrees in higher education and vocational licenses (review Table 1).

The most common professions for men are business, accounting, and administration; for women, they are teaching and nursing. Professional careers in the village run the gamut from a doctor (woman) and a veterinarian (man) to a violinist in the Yucatán State Symphony Orchestra (woman). Because there are few opportunities for professionals in the village, most educated villagers must either migrate or commute to their jobs. In the past few years, more of the local teachers are Yaxbeños, including the director of the secondary school and several of the elementary schoolteachers—both public and SDA. One exceptional case is that of the Ek Ake family (a Catholic family) in which five of the seven children (four daughters and one son) are all teachers. Two of the daughters live and teach in the village, two live and teach elsewhere, and the son lives in the village and commutes to a nearby town.

While commuting has become a dominant employment pattern for both married and unmarried men and women, the meaning of work is not identical to all categories of workers. For women, the work itself is a novelty, a vast and dangerous leap into new economic and social territory where the ramifications to self and family are just beginning to be felt. For men, commuting is an extension of their previous wage labor that nevertheless necessitates a shift in their economic and social ties to the larger society. In this section, I will discuss briefly the different meanings attached to work and commuting for men and women in Yaxbe.

Men and Commuting

Growing from 2% of working men in 1976 to 44% in 1998, it is apparent that commuting is expanding as a strategy for both married and single men. For married men, it represents a less risky alternative to migration that will separate them from kin and their established social networks. Villagers live within walking distances to family, friends, church, school, and stores. Men and women all assert that they prefer to live in the village where life is "quiet and agreeable." For most men, commuting is less disruptive to their family and it preserves the desired quality of life. It follows then that commuting is a strategy chosen most often by married men. In fact, since 1977 when only 10 men commuted (five married, five single), approximately 65% of those who commute today are married, divorced, or widowed; in other words, men who have obligations and connections to the village.

The sources of employment for unmarried and married men depend on their level of education and skills. Both unskilled married and unmarried men will be likely to find work in one of the factories where skills are learned on the job. Men who have learned a skill, such as carpentry or mechanics, are able to obtain more highly paid employment in the urban areas. Young men often strive to find employment in the tourist area of Mérida in the hotels, restaurants, and stores. These jobs pay well, but the employee must have a working knowledge of English and perhaps a little French or German. For young men (and women) the ability to speak English is a growing avenue out of the unskilled job market and into a more lucrative and enviable occupation.

Women and Commuting

One day as I waited in the plaza for the taxi, I realized that all of those waiting with me were women. An informal poll informed me that most of these women were on their way to work or school. Several were on shopping expeditions. I have found that commuting is an important new strategy for women. In 1976 only 12% of working women commuted to their jobs, compared to 52% in 1998.

As we have already seen, there are limited means available for women to earn money within the village, and the income earned in these endeavors is insufficient to meet the growing economic needs of the family. For unmarried women, the opportunities for employment in the village are few, since businesses such as stores and *tortillerías* will employ family members before tapping the local labor pool. Although the potential exists for a future market in childcare and housekeeping, these responsibilities are still primarily fulfilled within the family.

Contrary to what Westerners might expect, half of the commuting women in both 1976 and 1998 were married, divorced, or widowed and half were single. However, married and unmarried women differ in the types of jobs they obtain. Because of their flexibility and lack of family commitments, most unmarried women found jobs in the factories. Surprisingly, the married women who commute from the village tend to be educated, professional women, such as the teachers and nurses already described. As we have seen, village women do not suffer the angst that many U.S. women feel leaving their children with strangers or day-care centers. Most working women in Yaxbe know that their mothers or mothers-in-law will be loving (and inexpensive) caregivers. Additionally, most villagers, even the more cosmopolitan-oriented women, agree that it is better to raise their children in the village where they are loved and where they learn the proper values.

MIGRATION AS ECONOMIC STRATEGY

Case Study: Estéban

In 1976, Estéban was one of Reymundo's best friends. Estéban was a fun-loving young man, seldom seen without his guitar and his ragged shirt made from the remnants of an American flag. Yet, like all young men, Estéban also worked hard, employed like many of his age, in the Cordemex factory. At 20, Estéban still had no plans to marry and had amorphous ambitions to learn English and work in the city. Unfortunately, his desire to learn English outweighed his discipline to actually do so. In the 1980s when the Cordemex factory closed, Estéban invested his severance pay in the purchase of a small store on the main street of the village. By that time, he was married and had two small children. He and his wife worked the store, taking turns at shifts, working around the care of their young children. By the time their fifth child was born, the older boys were able to help out in the store and relieve their mother somewhat so that she could spend more time at home with the youngest. During my visits, it was a joy to watch this family thrive, marveling at the resemblance between the sons and their father.

In 1998, I was dismayed to see the store closed and to find out that Estéban and Berta had left the village to join her family on Cozumél. Over the years, Berta's siblings have, one by one, moved to the island to seek other fortunes. Her parents had left after her marriage to Estéban and now Berta was the only child to remain in Yaxbe. I had wondered if the pull of family would eventually draw them away.

During the *fiesta* of 1998, I was in my room, or rather, I was in Carmen's bedroom, on loan to me during my stay. I was writing in my journal when my concentration was diverted by a very familiar voice and cheerful laugh. Following the sound to the living room, I found Estéban sitting on the wooden couch, looking only a little older than when I had seem him last. He had come to visit Reymundo and to give me his new address so I would visit him on Cozumél. He told me that being a storekeeper was boring work. He complained that while the rest of the village was celebrating, dancing, or simply being home with family, he would be working in the store. Knowing Estéban's personality, I knew that this would be difficult for him.

Indeed, his in-laws had offered to help them get settled on Cozumél, and they had finally succumbed. Now, he works at a factory that makes the plaster ornaments commonly found on the modern houses and walls. His oldest sons both have jobs on the island, and he was proud that he now owned a car. The chain migration continues still as Estéban's younger brother has now joined them on Cozumél and is living with Estéban and his family. Estéban's parents still reside in Yaxbe—at least for the time being.

Migration Strategies

To leave one's village of birth is a major decision, one that is not taken lightly. The decision to migrate and the strategies employed depend on such variables as gender, age, and marital status. In this section, we will review several common migration strategies. These scenarios will allow us to understand the complexity of decision making for those who leave and the impact of these decisions on those left behind.

TEMPORARY MIGRATION   Most migrants, especially young people, leave the village with the intent to return. They live with relatives while they attend high school, vocational school, or university. Others leave to pursue jobs. Parents prefer that their children stay within the Yucatán peninsula so that they can return home on weekends, maintain their ties to family and friends, and share their wages with their parents. Despite their best efforts, however, some young people stray further away in search of that better job, or to follow someone that they met. The longer that a migrant stays away, the more likely that temporary migration stretches into years and the young person becomes lost to the family and community.

Some individuals don't plan to migrate at all, but find that it happens by accident. Carolina's husband died while we were in the village the first time, leaving her a young widow with four children. She sold her house and moved with her children into her parents' home. To support her family, she initiated a number of enterprises, such as hammock weaving and tailoring. She also became the village's first (and only) Avon Lady. Carolina is a feisty woman, exuberant, and humorous. She speaks so rapidly that I never, in the entire period I lived in Mexico, understood exactly what she said to me. I was always several sentences behind, and she enjoyed my confusion.

Eventually, Carolina moved to Cancún to work during the week. She took the money from the sale of her home and purchased a small parcel on the island (in the town center, not where the tourists stay), and built a small house. Her children remained in the village with her mother, their grandmother, Doña Isabel. This was a burden on Isabel who had small children of her own. At first, Carolina returned every weekend, paid her mother for baby-sitting and left money to purchase food and clothing for her children. Ultimately, she married a man from Yaxbe, and they had several more children who, once weaned, were also left with Doña Isabel. While she felt justified in leaving her children in the village so that she could work full-time, her siblings criticized her for taking advantage of their mother who already had oppressive responsibilities, including young children of her own and an alcoholic husband. Carolina, however, was unperturbed, convinced that her decision was the best for her and for her children who would otherwise be cared for by strangers in a dangerous and dirty environment.

As Carolina's children grew, they were able to assist their grandmother, but one by one, just when they were able to do so, they joined their mother on Cancún. At my last visit in 2001, I found that the last child had left, and Doña Isabel was finally free from childcare responsibilities, after almost 25 years. In this story and that of Carla (Chapter 4), the temporary migrant ultimately became a permanent migrant. But also, in both cases, the migrant family maintains close ties to the village (see Figure 8.3).

CHAIN MIGRATION   Both Carolina's story and that of Estéban are examples of chain migration. This is a very common pattern in Latin America and elsewhere. Estéban's wife, Berta, was the last sibling to leave Yaxbe for Cozumél. Carolina's pattern of taking her children one by one to Cancún is another. It is most common for the oldest child to leave, establish him or herself with other family members, and send for younger siblings. One by one, they follow the leader, live together, share expenses, and often work at the same location. This pattern becomes complete when the parents leave the village to join their children. Once this occurs, it is likely that migrants will remain permanently in the receiving area. There are exceptions, however, as we shall now see.

RETURN MIGRATION   Once villagers leave the village permanently, it is unusual for them to return except for occasional visits. This was especially true in the past when the village offered little in terms of employment that could lure villagers back home. Consequently, the most highly educated and skilled individuals became lost to the village. This pattern is reversing itself as the village expands and as communication and transportation between Yaxbe and the outside world improve. Slowly and cautiously, young professionals and skilled workers are returning to the village. One such man earned an accounting degree. He and his family lived and worked in Mérida until he was appointed by a newly elected village president to be the village Civil Registrar. Another young man moved to Valladolid after finishing veterinary school. However, his wife, also from Yaxbe, was homesick and unhappy. Attempting to please her, he eventually obtained a position as an animal inspector, traveling throughout the region, inspecting domesticated cattle and goats, and giving inoculations. He was thus able to move his family back to Yaxbe and use the village as his home base.

Migrant remittances have always been considered an important contribution to rural households. While most families noted that their migrant relatives send money, they always added that it was not a lot of money. Numerous resident families

Figure 8.3 Author with Carla and her children, 1998

complained that their children sent little if any money home since it is very expensive to live on Cancún and Cozumél. The longer that the family members are gone, and once they become established with families of their own, the less that is sent home, and the more tenuous the bonds become. This is even more true in cases where the migrant marries a person from the receiving area or from another region of Mexico. Connections become strained, networks are neglected, and families lose touch.

THE NEW SOCIAL CLASS SYSTEM, 1977–1998

As we have seen, the wealthiest individuals in the village in 1976 were the merchants and a few families (often also store owners) who were diversified economically— producing and transporting henequen. These families, while wealthy, were not a leisure class, nor did they set themselves apart from other villagers. Their wealth was not symbolized by material possessions, Western dress, or consumption, but in the hard work of the entire family. They were also expected to be generous with their wealth, contributing to village projects, *gremios,* and other social events. Because of their position in the village, however, they attained a certain political stature, and all village presidents until 1975 were part of the merchant class.

The prestige and political hegemony of the merchant class was threatened in the 1970s by the new emerging middle class. This "nouveau riche," not only developed a political base, as we have seen, but displayed the material wealth that has come to symbolize one's position in the new social class system. An emerging value placed on conspicuous consumption battled the traditional communal values of reciprocity and generosity. New houses became more extravagant and were filled with furniture and luxury items. Husbands bought refrigerators for their wives so now they could shop weekly in Mérida and store food, making them less dependent on the village stores for daily food supplies. As the traditional power of the *socio delegado* and his appointees evaporated with the collapse of the *ejido,* the power vacuum is being filled by younger leaders who are not tied economically or politically to the traditional power structure.

The former Cordemex contingent is likewise being threatened in recent years by yet another emerging class made up of educated villagers. With urban, professional salaries, they set an even higher standard of consumerism as they purchase cars, cell phones, VCRs, camcorders, hot water heaters, and microwave ovens. They represent an articulate and potentially politically active group in the village, as we have already seen. So far these new players have not been successful politically because their individualistic and somewhat elitist worldviews are still inconsistent with local values.

A new working class is also emerging in Yaxbe, comprised of factory employees, construction workers, and semi-skilled laborers. While these men do not earn much money and are dependent on multiple sources of income, they are a growing contingent in the village. Aspiring to middle class status, these families demonstrate their success by purchasing televisions and other consumer items, most of which are purchased on credit.

The new affluence of the village is conspicuous in two ways. First, it reflects the pervasive influence of Western advertising and television, as the above list of consumer items illustrates. Evidence of this consumerism is not only apparent by items found inside the house. Villagers are willing to display their wealth by means of such exterior displays as carports, tile patios, and most recently, pretentious 8-foot cement walls and gates that simultaneously hide wealth and display it (see Figure 8.4).

The second symbol is social exclusivity. This is less apparent visibly, but it has struck to the heart of the basic village values of egalitarianism and family. Two examples will illustrate this.

The Wedding of Clara Dzib and Jorge Morales

Clara's family owns one of the village stores. Her nuclear family is part of a large, wealthy extended family, native to the village. Jorge's family roots extended to the pre-Revolutionary era when his ancestors were caretakers of a nearby *hacienda.* After the Revolution, his ancestors remained and intermarried with the local population, and today, his family has no special prestige in the village, nor are they any richer than their neighbors. What they share is part of that history which makes Mexico so unique.

Jorge's parents were not particularly wealthy, but his father did own private parcels and was a successful henequen producer. Part of a large Catholic family (10 children), Jorge was the only child to attend college. He was now a professional, living in the village, and commuting to work.

Figure 8.4 A modern house in Yaxbe, with two stories, barred windows, and a metal gate

Both of these families were well-regarded, but their wedding, long anticipated, violated long-standing values of egalitarianism and reciprocity. As such, it was remembered for all the wrong reasons. In Yaxbe, custom dictates that all weddings are public and all villagers are invited. Until recently, no one sent out invitations to a wedding. People learned of the event through their participation as supporters and *compadres,* or from friends, and family. Word spread from these sources to all villagers and anyone who wanted to attend was welcome. Weddings were often performed as part of a Mass, as we have seen, and receptions were informal.

New protocol has altered the custom, and this particular wedding was the first that reflected a new set of social expectations and boundaries. Not only did the couple have a closed wedding, by invitation only, but their guest list consisted primarily of Jorge's professional colleagues from Mérida and Valladolid. Villagers were scandalized because many of the couple's own aunts and uncles were not invited. I was told that villagers were so angry and insulted that they "closed their doors on the wedding day."

The couple first moved to Valladolid. This allowed tensions to heal somewhat, but later they returned to the village, and Jorge commuted daily to work. People in small towns have long memories, as Jorge learned when he decided to run for village president. He was surprised when few villagers supported his candidacy.

During one of my trips to the village, Jorge and Carla had a party for their daughter's baptism. I was invited and was excited to attend. Reymundo, one of Jorge's cousins who (unknown to me) was not invited to the wedding, equivocated about attending, but didn't explain the reason to me. Reymundo's wife, Sonia attended with me, but Reymundo never arrived. Sonia was visibly upset about his absence, watching the gate nervously for his entrance. He returned to his own house much later that evening and it was clear he had been drinking, but not at the party. It was not until many years later, in events related to the next story, that I learned that his absence from this seemingly innocuous event had very deep roots.

The Wedding of Omar Dzib and María from Nolo

It was during my 1998 visit to the village that Reymundo revealed the reason for his actions years before. The occasion for this confession was an invitation I received to the wedding of Carla's younger brother, Omar. He was marrying a young woman from a nearby village. The wedding was in her hometown, but Omar's parents were sponsoring the reception in the large *solár* beside and behind their store, the same location as Carla's wedding and the baptism party. Excited about the invitation, I asked Reymundo and Sonia if they were going. My assumption was that I would go with them, but I was shocked to learn that they had not been invited. In fact, only immediate family had received invitations.

It was within this context that Reymundo related the story of the earlier wedding and the hard feelings that it brought to the village. It became clear to me that my presence would be a status symbol for the family, as the Dzib family was not one to which we had been particularly close over the years. I announced to Reymundo and Sonia that I would not attend the reception. Unexpectedly, they encouraged me to attend. "Look around," Reymundo remarked cynically, "and see how many Yaxbeños are there."

I did attend the reception. It was an extravagant affair with a large *cumbia* band and 20 tables set up with white cloth tablecloths. A bottle of brandy sat on each table, and bottled beer was served to the guests, one after the other. Huge plates of tacos were brought to each table and immediately replaced when empty. To one side of the dance floor there was a large table for the cake and gifts. The cake was tall, multilayered, and bedecked with flowers and ribbons. The gifts were wrapped, according to local custom, with clear plastic wrap so everyone can view them and assess their quality. While the majority of the gifts were the standard wedding gift fare, household items, dishes, bowls, and glasses, more lavish gifts included the newly coveted small appliances such as toasters, blenders, and coffee makers.

The guests were more intriguing than the gifts, however. Reymundo was correct. There were few villagers in attendance. It was impossible to know if their absence was due to lack of invitation or personal reluctance to set themselves up for criticism or accusations of snobbery. The guests in attendance stood in sharp contrast to the groom's family. They were predominantly light skinned, as was the bride. The men were dressed in fine suits that few, if any, villagers own. The women wore elegant dresses and high heels, their faces made up in bright rouges and lipsticks, and their hair professionally styled. I was hard pressed to reconcile the event and the guests with its location—a large dirt yard, surrounded by a tin fence, and a gate first opened, then closed to the outside. I now understood the ire of the villagers.

I felt very uncomfortable at this celebration—the first time ever that I have felt this way in the village. Although I received a tremendous amount of attention, I felt as if I did not belong there. More beer than I could possibly drink was placed in front of me, and I was urged to dance, though I had no partner. While I sat, making small talk with Carla and some of her family members, a young man—obviously intoxicated—wandered into the party from the street. I recognized him as a relative of the groom, but could not think of his name. Immediately, Jorge intercepted him and coaxed him out of the *solár,* closing the large metal doors behind him. That act sufficiently shut the event off from the outside, and symbolized more than any one particular action of the entire evening, the growing segmentation of the village.

The next day when I visited Reymundo and Sonia, I found them suspiciously unconcerned and disinterested about the wedding. They had, I am sure, already heard about the reception from those more knowledgeable about the social dynamics and more articulate in the story rendering than I could ever hope to be. Sonia was interested, however, in the clothing and how people acted toward me, her concern, as always, with my best interest and my acceptance in the village.

These two weddings and a baptism provide excellent examples of how social class is acted out in daily life, and how the aspirations of the upwardly mobile can affect their relationships with family and friends. It also illustrates how deeply embedded are the rituals of life. Every act of exclusion has meaning; every door closed in anger screams "outrage," and every minute modification in decorum leads a village further away from tradition and inches closer to segmentation and social tension.

CONCLUSION: THE NEW YUCATECAN FAMILY

That all is not perfect in Yaxbe is evident as one looks closely at those who have not been able to reap the benefits of wage jobs and advanced education. While some families are purchasing microwave ovens and automobiles, other families have ceased using their stoves, reverting to open fire cooking as the cost of propane skyrockets in the inflationary times. In 1998, I observed a sight that I had not seen for 20 years— a family using a horse-drawn cart was cutting down branches and small trees in the *monte* and selling firewood door to door. The *henequenero* and the *milpero* define the lower class today. As the *ejido* is displaced, more of these laborers will find themselves working for larger landowners or more successful skilled laborers. They will continue to live largely at the outskirts of the village, beyond the paved roads and potable water. The success of these villagers in providing for their families will depend on their ability to integrate themselves into the newly defined wage economy. Their hope lies in the ability of their children to attend school or to obtain viable employment outside of the agricultural sector. A life that used to be defined as egalitarian is no longer viable.

9/Mayan Women
Beyond the Stereotypes

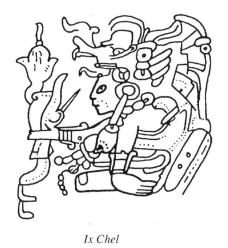

Ix Chel

In Chapter 8, we explored the integration of men and women within a changing economic environment where they have struggled to adopt new strategies that will allow them to adapt to shifting economic realities. In this chapter, we will peek into women's lives, encountering their particular adaptations and examining how their own strategies have created new relationships within the family and how women are making a place for themselves in the public sphere.

THE ANTHROPOLOGY OF GENDER ROLES AND STATUSES

Feminist anthropologists have shown that gender roles and male-female relationships are not just one component of society, but that they permeate all aspects of a culture and that they are rooted in the history and tradition of that society. Anthropologists have also learned that gender roles are not determined by biology or physiology, but rather are socially constructed. They are reinforced daily by religion, kinship and family systems, and the economic division of labor. Consequently, when shifts occur within a society such as the inclusion of women in the workplace, the ramifications will be felt in all other social institutions, from the family to religion. As these shifts occur, tensions inevitably arise as individuals are forced to question previous assumptions and to fit new realities into an existing framework. This tension between traditional and modern patterns of family and gender roles was evident in the 1960s in the United States as women began to question the roles delegated to them in post–World War II American society.

Once patterns of gender relations become embedded within a society, they are often employed as cultural markers, defining roles and statuses of all individuals from the inside and also from the outside. Westerners often form stereotypes of Middle Eastern women based on the cultural and religious markers associated with Islam, even though many of the customs in dress and demeanor associated with these women predate Islam by thousands of years. Likewise, Westerners have a tendency to stereotype Mexican women as submissive and under the control of men, first their fathers and then their husbands. Westerners perceive them as shadows quietly serving husband and children, hidden in houses—invisible and uninvited into the public sphere. The reality is much more complicated and hinges on many factors: ethnicity, urban or rural residence, personality, and social class. In this chapter, we will examine the context in which the diversity of women's roles can be explored, and in which women's status can be understood. To probe beyond the stereotype, we must place Mayan women's roles and statuses within an historical, economic, and social context.

The Historical Context of Maya Women's Gender Roles

The true history of the pre-conquest Maya is shrouded in mystery, to be deciphered from hieroglyphs and the few documents that survived the book-burning pyres of the Spanish conquerors. From these sources, we know that the Maya had a complex polytheistic religion that was dominated by a pantheon of gods and goddesses that set the parameters of daily life. The rain gods, *Chacob,* dictated to priests the requirements for their services; the *chilamob* (prophets) determined the agricultural cycle and advised the king as to the best days for warfare.

Yet, female deities also ruled in certain domains. Experts believe that one goddess, *Ix Kanleox* (the word *"ix"* means woman), was the mother of the other gods. Her name is often invoked in current Maya prayers (Roys 1972: 77). Probably the most important goddess for the Yucatec Maya was *Ix Chel,* the moon goddess, consort to the Sun God, and the patroness of weaving, divination, medicine, and childbirth (Henderson 1981: 64). *Ix Chel* was so important that she has a shrine on the island of Cozumél. Reports indicate that the ancient Maya made the pilgrimage by foot and boat to Cozumél to consult the oracle of *Ix Chel,* represented by a large pottery idol. A priest, hidden behind the shrine, answered the questions posed to the image by the supplicants (Henderson 1981: 64; Roys 1972: 78). Bishop Landa, in his description of the Yucatec Maya (in Thompson 1975: 135), compared the pilgrimages to Cozumél with the Christian pilgrimages to Rome and Jerusalem.

Ancient Maya social life has not yet been totally deciphered. **Stelae** (stone markers) depicting noblewomen at Cobá and Tikal indicate that there were close networks and intermarriage between these two ceremonial centers (Henderson 1981: 189; Friedel and Schele 2001: 89–93). According to Henderson (ibid: 165), marriage was used as a means of uniting political families or ceremonial centers. Smaller regional leaders could increase their personal influence or that of their city by arranging marriages with daughters of more powerful nobility. Women are also known to have ruled ceremonial centers on the death of their husbands or brothers (Henderson 1981: 165).

Early accounts of the life of Yucatec Maya come to us from Diego de Landa, first a friar assigned to Yucatán (1549–1562), and later a bishop. It was Landa, who in his zeal to convert the Maya to Catholicism, burned all of the existing Maya chronicles that he could find and ultimately brought the Spanish Inquisition to Mexico. Ironically, we now turn to his chronicle to glean clues as to the status of women in those years just prior to the conquest. From Landa we learn that Maya women were both modest and assertive. While they deferred to their husbands and taught their daughters to serve their families, they would "pull their husbands' hair for the least infidelity" (Landa 1978 [1566]: 55).

Women were also full participants in the daily economic life, both in villages and later in colonial towns and cities. In the villages, cotton was the major cash crop demanded by the Spanish for tribute, and it was the women who wove the cloth, both for Spanish consumption and for that of their families. Later, women provided many services for urban Spanish families. Like modern village women, many young Maya women migrated to Mérida (T'ho) and other cities and towns to earn money for their families. Also, like their modern counterparts, they were employed as nannies, housekeepers, and weavers for wealthy Spanish women (Hunt and Restall 1997: 236). Landa himself writes:

> They [Maya women] are great workers and good in all the domestic economies, for on them rest the most, and most important, work of alimentation, housekeeping and education of their children, and the payment of the tributes; with all this they bear heavier burdens if it is necessary, working the fields and harvesting the crops. They are great economists, watching at night in what time is left them after their domestic labors, attending the markets to buy and sell their things. (Landa: ibid: 55)

Women also had some control over land and possessions that they both held and passed on to their heirs. According to Restall (1995: 587), men among the post-conquest Maya had control over nonresidential lands, large domesticated animals such as cows and horses, and tools. Women, in contrast, usually had ownership and control over plants and animals found within the *solár,* including pigs, chickens, turkeys, and bees, and may have been able to bequeath house plots to their heirs. Restall notes that "women are recorded as buying, selling, inheriting, and bequeathing land" (ibid: 581). In another example (Hunt and Restall 1997: 250), a Maya woman from Cacalchen listed in her will a fortune that she had earned through loaning money to others in the town. Her private enterprise as a "banker" had made her a wealthy woman, and she passed this wealth down to her children in her own name.

The documents available to us indicate that Mayan women were strong, and that they resisted the advances and sexual aggressiveness of the Spanish conquerors and clergy (Restall 1995: 583). In one case (Hunt and Restall 1997: 251), a priest refused to give confession to a woman unless she gave herself to him. Her complaint to her local governmental leaders protected her from this abuse. Landa relates the following story about the strength and conviction of Maya women:

> The captain Alonso López de Avila, father-in-law of the admiral Montejo, captured a handsome and graceful Indian girl during the war in Bacalár. She, in fear of death for her husband, had promised him never to yield herself to another, and for this nothing could persuade her, even the fear of death, to consent to violation; so that they threw her to the dogs. (Landa 1978 [1566]: 54)

There is no strong evidence of a sexual double standard among the Maya comparable to that which we associate with Latin American cultures today. According to

Landa (1978 [1566]: 51–52), a man convicted of adultery was brought to the chief's house and tied to a piece of wood. The woman's husband could pardon him for the crime or kill him. "For the woman a sufficient punishment was the infamy, which was great; and commonly for this he left her."

Women formed alliances with Spanish men, both to position themselves in Spanish society and to obtain property and wealth that they could pass on to their children. Hunt and Restall (1997: 234–236) offer several examples of Maya noble-women who married Spanish merchants. These marriages of convenience benefited newly arrived Spanish men by linking them to noble Maya families and, at the same time, offered the privilege and power of Spanish descent and society to ambitious Maya nobility. The Maya noblewomen could offer these young men the money and property that they needed to establish themselves in the New World.

Machismo and Marianismo

These patterns of male and female interaction, as scant as our knowledge may be, contrast with the gender role stereotypes that define our perceptions of Latin American culture today. The stereotype of the submissive woman and the aggressive man in Mexico is embedded in the ***machismo-marianismo*** model. *Machismo* refers to a pattern of male dominance whereby a man proves his manliness in careless or dangerous behavior that is often pursued at the expense of women who become victims of violence and social oppression (Stevens 1994: 4). *Marianismo* is the complement pattern, characterized by the passive, silently suffering woman whose lack of power in the public realm is balanced by her domestic role and the cultural ideal of Madonna-like moral superiority (ibid: 4). While we associate *machismo* with Latin American men, the phenomenon itself has its roots in the Old World, and, like Catholicism, has been reworked to fit New World economic and social realities (ibid: 4).

According to Evelyn Stevens (1994: 5–6), the dominant concepts of male honor, virility, and bravado permeated the Mediterranean cultures and those of Southern Europe, such as Spain, North Africa, and the Middle East. It was transported to the New World in the guise of conquerors and European aristocracy. *Marianismo* was derived from the patriarchal nature of Christianity, which disavowed the female orientations of earlier religions and which used as the model for female behavior the sacrificial, submissive, and virginal Mary. According to Tracy Ehlers (1991: 3), *marianismo* was introduced by the Catholic hierarchy to foster the virtues of the Virgin Mary, establishing a tradition of female subordination, but placing it in the context of religious martyrdom. Mary was reborn in Mexico as the Virgin of Guadelupe in a vision revealed to a poor peasant. The Virgin of Guadelupe has been adopted and finally accepted by the Catholic Church as a legitimate religious figure (Stevens 1994: 5–7).

Nevertheless, even though the traditional Maya culture was patrilineal and male-oriented, the *machismo* model was not present at the time of the conquest. Nor does it permeate all ethnic groups. Rather, the pattern came to be associated with urban, *mestizo* or *Ladino* males, and those of the lower classes. Indigenous villages, especially those far removed from Spanish influence, did not develop the characteristics of *machismo-marianismo,* and where the pattern does exist, as it does in Yaxbe, it is developed to a lesser degree than elsewhere. Today, "[i]ndigenous communities, while patriarchal in structure and value orientations, do not seem to share the *machismo-marianismo* attitudes as long as they retain their cultural 'purity'" (Stevens 1994: 5).

According to various anthropologists (e.g., Bossen 1984: 46), *catrín* males have the economic advantage over indigenous males, yet they are more likely to neglect their families economically, and be preoccupied with demonstrating dominance through the *machismo* mechanism of sexual prowess. In contrast, indigenous males, although economically weak, have a greater social prestige in their daily lives, and their social roles emphasize a strong husband-father role that minimizes the *machismo* effect (Wolf 1966: 64). Bossen further argues that urban *catrín* women may have lower status than women in indigenous communities and may be victims of the *machismo-marianismo* complex. Her argument is compelling. In urban, middle class homes, the wife's focus is the care of the home and the family while the husband works and socializes independently of the home and family. This estrangement perpetuates a philosophy of male disloyalty and a diminishing of the husband-father role in the household. In rural Guatemala, in contrast, Bossen found that because women are crucial to the economic success of the family unit, and subsistence is located within the family and household, that the husband-father role is highly valued. Consequently, men are rooted in the household and women do not see themselves in the image imposed on them from the outside (Bossen 1984: 316–317). In recent years, then, the *machismo-marianismo* duality has been defined within a larger context, that of economic participation. It is no longer viewed as an isolated cultural unit, but part of a larger system of understanding. We will now examine women's roles and statuses in Yaxbe, returning to *machismo-marianismo* in the conclusion.

FROM THE WOODWORK TO THE DOUBLE DAY

The Transformation of Women's Production

In Chapter 8 we saw how men and women have devised diversified sources of income within the village, found jobs within commuting distance, and have sometimes left the village altogether. We also saw how both women and men have taken advantage of educational opportunities to increase their skills (review Tables 1 and 5). In this section, we will look at economic opportunities that women have initiated and how men and families have adapted to the new economic positions of women and how economic shifts may result in more political opportunities and higher status for women.

While the transformation of women's production from household to village and beyond has its roots in the overall shifting economic conditions, outside forces have affected the direction of women's participation. Women in Yaxbe and elsewhere have become involved in various government-sponsored cooperative programs that have altered women's roles within the village and in the household.

The Mexican government, as we have seen, has long provided myriad social and economic programs designed to ameliorate poverty in the rural areas. While none of these programs provides real economic development, many have had a positive impact on rural life. Some of these, such as the DIF and PACR, have provided milk and nutritional programs; other agencies have brought the health clinic, the library, and potable water. Since the late 1980s and the early 1990s, the federal government has intensified its investment in rural areas for purposes of supplementing the incomes lost during the instigation of the land reform (Collier 1994b: 141). I am intrigued by two of these programs in particular. The first is **Solidaridad** (Solidarity), an antipoverty program administered as part of an umbrella program called **PRONASOL.** Solidarity consists of four packages of programs that target a menu of social and economic ills—education, health, agricultural training and development, and rural infrastructure. Programs also target specific groups, one of which is Women in Solidarity (Collier 1994b: 139–141; Laurell and Wences 1994).

The second program is **UAIM** (the Women's Agro-Industrial Unit), which allows women to form cooperatives within the structure of the *ejido* to farm collectively or carry out small development projects. Obtaining UAIM status allows women to receive land equivalent to that held by one *ejidatario* (Stephen 1994a: 16; see also Robles 1993). This program is often the only way women can gain access to land under the new privatization procedures, which do not guarantee a woman's joint rights to her husband's land during his life or upon his death (Stephen 1994a: 28–29).

Because these programs were developed by the PRI after the 1992 reforms, critics argue very effectively that they further reflect the attempts by the government at that time to deflect the opposition parties and increase the dependence of the poor on government programs. Critics also argue that the underlying agenda of these programs was to compensate the rural poor for the elimination of economic subsidies and for the increased poverty that results from the massive privatization efforts associated with NAFTA.[1] Yet, regardless of the national agenda, women in Yaxbe have taken advantage of these initiatives and have organized four cooperatives. We will look at three of these cooperatives so we can learn about these women, and perhaps gain insight into the emerging roles of women in Yucatecan society.

CASE STUDIES

UAIM

Sara Morales Gonzales is the fourth child of Isabel and Jose (see also A Woman of Substance, Chapter 1). In 1992, she organized a small group of married women friends and relatives, and, aided by a sympathetic village president, petitioned the government for UAIM funds.

The group received funds to start a chicken cooperative, contingent on their ability to raise 5,000 pesos for start-up money to purchase their chicks, blast a well, and build a structure. The village president provided most of the start-up money, and Reymundo, Sara's brother, volunteered to blast the well. They were successful at first, but several disasters had threatened their business by 1995. First, they had the misfortune of obtaining a batch of chicks that had failed to thrive despite large quantities of food given them. They were forced to sell them at a loss, and then had to raise money so they could purchase another batch. To do this, they had attempted a number of projects. First, they had raised two pigs for sale; unfortunately one of them died of trichinosis, and the other ate half a bag of fertilizer and came to a messy end.

[1]For a discussion of these programs and their critics see: Collier 1994a, 1994b; Cornelius, et. al. 1994; Laurell and Wences 1994; and Stephen 1994a, 1994b.

In 1995, I helped them clear a portion of a 75-*mecate* parcel on which they planned to cultivate vegetables for sale and also for themselves. In 1998, the women again had chickens, but the interest in the group was waning, as they worked very hard and earned very little reward for their labor. In 2001, the women had given up on chickens altogether. Instead they were growing *pitahaya (Hylocereus undatus H.)*, an agave whose red flowering fruit is used in juices and sold in the local markets. A female agrarian agent stayed in the village for several months to teach the women how to plant, care for, and harvest the fruit. In 2002, the young woman was still visiting the village weekly, staying with one of the UAIM women for several days each week. Their plants are still too young to give fruit and they have the additional hazard of villagers entering their field at night and stealing their crop.

Although not the most successful cooperative, the UAIM has proven to be the initial impetus for female activism in the village, culminating in the formation of a women's political party led by Sara. In 1995, Sara was the first woman to hold public office in the village.

Women in Solidarity: The Horchateras

In the early 1990s, a government promoter came to Yaxbe to recruit women to start an *horchata* factory in the village. *Horchata* is a beverage made from rice and caramel that rural families substitute for cow's milk. Several women attended the meeting, and ultimately 14 women initiated a cooperative through the *Mujeres en Solidaridad* Program. The government provided them with a *molino* and an initial supply of ingredients. At first, the women produced the milk in the home of one of the women, Doña Paula, the current president of the cooperative. Later, they were allowed to put their *molino* in the *casa del pueblo,* in the same room where my husband and I lived in 1976–1977.

By 1995, the factory was in full operation. Fourteen women worked three days a week, grinding the rice in the *molino,* mixing in the other ingredients, stirring (with their hands), and finally straining the liquid into cleaned liquor bottles that they had solicited from friends and relatives. Although not physically demanding, the work is challenging. They worked long hours in a hot room, fighting flies that are drawn to the sweet liquid. During one visit, I purchased two fans that allowed them to circulate the air without opening the windows to the flies, but it was a minor improvement as the room was small, cramped, and unbearably hot.

At 6:00 in the evening, their work was still not completed. After the bottles were filled, the women departed in different directions to sell their milk. Some traveled by bicycle, bottles rattling in metal bike racks, to nearby *haciendas* and villages. Others carried plastic carrying cases of bottles by bus and taxi to villages more distant. After one woman was injured in a bicycle accident and was stranded on a lonely road for several hours, the women started traveling in pairs, a less efficient, but much safer option for them. Then, after working a long and exhausting day, the women returned home to do their household chores.

In 1998, all but one of the original group still worked in the factory. One elderly woman had to quit for health reasons, but another woman, age 72, was still active. The group had divided into two shifts by 1998, solving the dual problem of having too many women in the small factory room and not having enough work to keep all

14 busy. The groups now work 10-hour shifts on alternate days, producing *horchata* six days a week, instead of three, and their business has expanded all the way to Mérida. They produce 500 bottles a week, and finally, they have begun to purchase new, sterile bottles and have their own label. They also obtained a small truck (*camioneta*) from the government that they use to transport their *horchata* to other villages. That none of the women knows how to drive is an insignificant problem, as husbands take turns transporting the women on their rounds.

When I arrived in 1998, the women were preparing to move to a new building about one block away. Their account of how this move came about provides an excellent example of the perseverance of these women. Once their business began to thrive, the women became concerned about the size of their factory, and the fact that it had no ventilation. They approached the village president for assistance in soliciting the state governor for a larger facility or money to expand the size of the current building. The president (Don Alberto, Chapter 5), was not responsive to the women's proposals. He canceled meetings and ignored their requests. In a mood of frustration and determination, the women took a very brave step on their own behalf and went directly to the governor. All 14 women took the bus to Mérida and coaxed each other into the intimidating entrance of the governor's palace, a daunting colonial structure guarded by soldiers with semiautomatic rifles. They all entered the governor's office without an appointment and requested a meeting. Despite the secretary's insistence that the governor was busy, they decided to wait. And wait they did, middle-aged women with *huipiles* and their hair tied in tight buns at the back of their heads, younger women in worn polyester skirts and plastic shoes, sitting in the governor's waiting room.

Finally, they did see the governor, and they explained their predicament and what they wanted to do. The governor gave the women money for their lunch and transportation and promised that he would send someone out to look at their building and assess their need. The women, skeptical and not very hopeful, returned to the village and were very surprised when, about one week later, a man did come and agreed with them that their factory was inadequate. Inquiries within the village resulted in the purchase of a *solár* and building across the street from their current location. The governor bought the building and *solár* for $20,000 and paid for half of the cost of a new roof and other construction necessary to meet the requirements of the new factory. The women were to pay the remaining cost for the roof and build a bathroom in the back. When I returned to the village in 2001, the factory was in operation. The women had a well-lit and amply ventilated factory, and their business was thriving.

Today the women laugh when they tell the story. They are very proud of their accomplishments and are very critical of the president who spurned their requests. They speak affectionately of Don Vicente, the governor, who calls the women "his *horchateras de Yaxbe*." According to the women, the governor told them that he prefers to promote women's economic endeavors because "the money women earn will go to their families and not to the *cantinas*." I asked the women if they knew when Don Vicente leaves office. Again they laughed, understanding my question. "He leaves office in three years. We have a lot of time to get a new *molino* before he is gone." (See Figures 9.1, 9.2, and 9.3.)

Figure 9.1 Group I of the horchata cooperative in front of the camioneta, 1998

Figure 9.2 Group II of the horchata cooperative in front of the new factory, 1998. This group has changed membership since 1998.

*Figure 9.3 Doña Paula,
president of the horchata
cooperative, 1998*

The Tortillería

Doña Juana is a force to be reckoned with. In 1976, she was the president of the DIF milk program that she commanded with the resolve of a marine sergeant. Now in her 60s, Juana is still a dynamic presence in the village, despite the fact that she is crippled with rheumatoid arthritis and in constant pain. A staunch proponent of the PRI, she is the only villager who has met a Mexican president. In 1998, she was the treasurer of the tortilla cooperative. This cooperative, like the others, also had an inauspicious beginning. Their first attempt to solicit a UAIM grant was rejected by President Eduardo (Chapter 5), who feared that the cooperative would compete with his own *tortillería* and *molino.* Despite this barrier to their success, the women persisted and finally, with the election of the next president, obtained their grant, and set up their business in the back room of the *casa del pueblo*. It was a successful business from the early 1990s until 1996 with Doña Juana as the president (see Figure 9.4).

In 1996, according to Doña Juana, the *molino* developed a serious malfunction. *Masa* (tortilla dough) was spurting out from the machine in all directions (*¡un disastre!*). The cost of repairs was estimated at nearly a million pesos, an amount far beyond the means of the small cooperative. The women approached the current president, the same one who refused to assist the *horchata* ladies. With no surprise, he

Figure 9.4 Doña Ana and Maria work at the tortillería cooperative in 1995. In 2002, the cooperative was not in operation.

also rejected their claim for village assistance in repairing or replacing their machinery. The *tortillería* was out of business for more than one year as the women continued to press the president for loans. Finally in late 1997, they found a credit bank willing to loan them the money with a manageable pay back schedule, contingent on proof that they had supplies to start immediate production of *tortillas* once the machine was functioning. So the women returned to the president to request money to purchase the start-up supplies but he refused them even in this small request. In frustration, and a conspiratorial mood, the women enlisted the assistance of the president's mistress, who was also a member of the cooperative. As the story goes, she was able to convince him that the women needed the supplies in order to get their loan, and the president finally complied. The *tortillería* reopened early in 1998 with a heavy debt but hopes of succeeding once again in their endeavor. Unfortunately when I returned to the village in 2001, the *tortillería* was closed for reasons I was not able to ascertain.

WOMEN AND ECONOMIC PRODUCTION

Obstacles to Women's Local Production

Women must overcome a variety of obstacles in their quest for economic security. Before they can even initiate their project, purchase their first chick, or their first *molino*, they must surpass the daunting hurdle of convincing the village elders, all men, that their enterprise has merit. The village president must give the project his approval and must be willing to assist the women in preparing the paperwork and promising to provide them some kind of initial support, in start-up costs or land. We have already seen how one president obstructed both the *tortillería* and the *horchata* factory by refusing assistance, or by merely stonewalling and ignoring their requests.

This is not to say that governmental support is never forthcoming. The UAIM chicken ranch (*granja*) was initiated under the auspices of a very supportive and generous president who not only co-signed on their project, but assisted them in obtaining land and in the construction of their small ranch house. Another sympathetic president provided the *horchata* co-op a rent-free room in the *casa del pueblo*. Yet these examples of both benevolent and antagonistic presidents serve to illustrate clearly that women are still indebted to the village authorities and are vulnerable to changes in village leadership.

Commitment to cooperative labor not only places women in an ambiguous position with local leaders, but also with men within their own households. Many men, although they do not object to women earning money within the context of the home, are reluctant to see their wives working outside of the home. Husbands often object to their wives' employment for two reasons. First, men feel that it reflects poorly on them if their wives work outside of the home. One young man, Jose, expressed this idea to me in this way: "Men aren't accustomed to having their wives work, especially if the wife is the only one in the family with a (wage earning) job. Men suffer from '*vergüenza*' (shame) if their wife has more authority in the family."

Second, many men disapprove because jobs, even cooperative labor in the village, takes women away from their household chores. The same man told me that when he works all day, he doesn't want to wait for his supper. As a transporter, his schedule is not consistent from day to day and he comes home at different times, eats, and then leaves again. "How can I do my work if I come home to an empty house without food to eat? If I have to wait for lunch, I miss my deadlines. Besides, we do not need more money. I earn enough to support my family." This man's wife has turned down several opportunities to earn money outside of the home because of her husband's attitude. She once earned money taking care of Jose's grand-niece, but when they were named *compadres* to this niece and thus *padrinos* to the child, Jose would not let his wife receive payment for the service. Instead, she cared for the infant full-time in her own home for no pay while the niece worked in a Mérida factory.

Women in the cooperatives have had to negotiate with their husbands, most of whom shared the feelings expressed by Jose in the above example. However, unlike Jose, few men can support their families on their income alone and thus face a glaring contradiction between their traditional values and current economic circumstances. The chicken cooperative lost some of its early members because the husbands resented the time their wives spent away from home caring for the chicks and guarding them at night. This latter obligation was critical because the *granja* was located about one mile from the village along the highway, and women took turns spending the night there. While some husbands were accommodating to this arrangement and children often liked to accompany their mothers "to the *monte*," this was not the case for others.

Likewise, the *horchata* factory faced similar resistance in the beginning. All of the married women I interviewed agreed that their husbands did not want them to work at first, but necessity forced them to acquiesce. Now, the women say, their husbands are accustomed to their work schedules. They especially like the income, an average of 100–150 pesos per week. Many husbands even assist the women by hauling the 50-pound bags of rice, transporting the product to villages, and especially by driving the *camioneta.*

Other husbands, however, may undermine women's economic activities in malicious ways. When the *tortillería* was first organized, the treasurer lost all of the cooperative money because her unemployed husband was spending the funds for his own expenses. The woman, afraid to confront her husband, said nothing until the money was gone, hoping that she could replace it. When the cooperative president, Doña Juana, found out, she took over the treasury position, solicited money from the village and other members, and collected enough money to cover their next purchase of corn.

Who Joins Cooperatives?

While there is diversity among the women who participate in the various cooperatives, they do share certain characteristics. First, the majority of women in all of the cooperatives are married. Husbands hold a wide variety of jobs, but most of them are employed in non-agricultural activities. Second, all of the married women have children who are still in the home. The cooperative is appealing to these women because they can remain in the village and work around their children's school schedules. In 1998, the 14 members of the *horchata* cooperative had, combined, 53 children, although two of them have eleven each, skewing the numbers considerably. Of these 53 children, a total of 29 still lived at home, averaging 2.2 children per household.

Third, most members were between the ages of 30 and 45 years old in 1998. This category has the most diversity, however, as women in the three cooperatives range in age from the mid-20s to 75. Fourth, cooperative members tend to be related to one another through blood or marriage. This is a logical finding as women who attend organizational meetings will likely do so with a family member and will also begin to recruit from among those in their personal sphere.

Fifth, women who are involved in cooperatives are also involved in other community activities, the short-lived women's political party of 1993 (see *Sí, Podemos Mandar,* this chapter) and other government sponsored programs such as DIF, PACR, and local school committees. Sixth, the majority of the women involved in cooperatives in 1998 were Catholic, but Adventists were represented in all organizations. Because most women will do cooperative labor on Saturdays, Adventist women have to make special arrangements in order to participate.

Last, all women from the various cooperatives who were interviewed stated that their motivation for joining was economic. Nevertheless, many women also added that they enjoyed their work and liked getting out of the house. The *horchata* women were particularly enthusiastic about their work. One woman who had seldom left the village before joining the co-op said, "I get to see other villages and people. I like going to markets and seeing how other places look. It's nice talking to people from other towns. People know us as the '*horchata* ladies.'"

Economic and Social Costs of Women's Employment

It is difficult at this juncture and at this stage in the acculturation process to ascertain whether these changes are beneficial or detrimental to women and their families in the long term. There are some indications, however, of incipient shifts in family dynamics. Let's examine some of these early indicators of future transformations within the Yaxbe family.

GENDER-BASED DIVISION OF LABOR   In the early days of the women's movement of the 1960s and 1970s in the United States, one of the major issues that emerged as a result of women's participation in the wage labor force was the "Double Day." Women often found that they were putting in 40 hours in the office or factory and then returning home and putting in another 30–40 hours a week in the home. As the cultural norms that dictated the gender-based division of labor within the American home began to shift, men and children began to take on more of the work traditionally performed by women, but the complaint is still pertinent for many working American women. In Mexico in general, and Yaxbe in particular, this shift has still not taken place. Women's work and men's work are clearly demarcated within the home. It is a division of labor conducive to the agricultural system by which women's activities are centered in and around the home and include caring for children and domesticated animals, gardening, cooking, and cleaning. Unfortunately, as women take on more responsibilities outside of the home, they are still expected to maintain their same level of home-based occupation. I have never seen a man in Yaxbe wash clothes (still done primarily by hand), wash dishes, or cook. These are women's activities. Men used to tease my husband for being the Mexican equivalent of henpecked because he assisted me by washing dishes and doing hand laundry.

Housekeeping chores are not as oppressive for Yaxbeñas as for the average American woman, as the former live in extended households and have children who are expected to help them with chores. Yaxbeñas also have networks of kin outside of the household who can be counted on to assist in various ways. Yet, it is up to the woman to make sure that someone is there to assist her with childcare, to make sure that her husband's food is ready when he comes home from work, and that the household chores and cooking are done. A woman's success in joining the labor market is often dependent on her ability to recruit labor, her husband's flexibility, and the extent to which he considers her employment crucial to the household survival.

IMPACT OF EMPLOYMENT ON THE FAMILY   Although few would deny that additional income is a positive result of women's work, the disappearance of women from the household does have consequences that some people consider detrimental to the social fabric. As we have seen, women's employment takes them further from the home for longer periods of time. Increasingly, grandmothers, aunts, sisters, or even children are enlisted as childcare providers for the absent mother. While this extended pool of caregivers has always been available to women, many individuals have lamented that the growth of this trend over the years is having negative ramifications for children. One major complaint is the apparent lack of supervision that often accompanies the new childcare arrangements. Grandmothers, while they are willing to watch their grandchildren, often have their own children at home or are very elderly and unable to adequately supervise their wards. Likewise, young childcare providers—nieces and siblings—may be negligent in watching younger children as they socialize with their own friends.

Laxity in supervision often continues once the parents come home in the evening. Not unlike American homes, both parents return home tired. The mother may have to cook dinner on her arrival and clean up afterwards. Consequently, in many homes, television has replaced more social forms of evening entertainment. Previously, most families walked to the park in the evenings, children in tow. During this social time, young boys play park soccer, girls play tag, and teens, carefully supervised, visit with their female friends. While this custom has not disappeared altogether, it has slowly transformed as children run to the park unattended or under the supervision of older siblings or other relatives. The behavior of children has changed considerably as a result of this shift in custom, as I have observed over the years.

In 1976, a young girl would not dare be seen talking to a young boy lest she be the subject of cruel gossip. In fact, a young girl did not even go to the park unless she was accompanied by a mother or perhaps an older sister. Girls above puberty never wore shorts, and no one wore blue jeans. In 1998, I was surprised as I sat in the park and watched the young people. Teen girls, wearing shorts and tank tops, crowded in small circles and shuffled in barely contained excitement toward a similar, though more restrained, group of young men. In my host's house, their teenage daughter went out every night to meet her friends. Sometimes we adults would follow and sit in the park socializing with the other parents, but other times, we did not.

When I informally tried to elicit commentary on these observations, women and men agreed that, yes, things are different now. But instead of expressing displeasure, mothers defined these changes in a positive light, relieved that their daughters have more freedom than they themselves did. The exception to this sentiment came from an unlikely source, the local teachers. In two interviews, one with three Catholic teachers and another with two Seventh Day Adventist teachers, I heard the same complaints. They were all concerned with the lack of supervision of children, both after school and in the evenings, noting an increase in discipline problems and a general lack of respect toward the teachers. Parents, for their part, didn't have time to come to school to discuss their children's problems and seemed to expect more from the teachers in terms of discipline.

As with many elements of cultural change, the impact is difficult to measure, and opinions are based on perceptions not shared by all members of a community. Those who lamented the transformations in the behavior of young people draw on a fear that community values and morals were being threatened. This assessment stands in contrast to that of others, including some mothers who view the relaxation of social constraints in a positive light, as evidence of more independence and personal freedom.

Benefits of Women's Production

CONTROL OF RESOURCES   One discovery that surprised me is that women are often the caretakers of the family money. The stereotype of male dominance in the household may apply to other regions of Mexico or in urban areas, but not to Yaxbe. Although there is much variation among families in Mexico just as there is in American families, I was interested to learn that many women controlled the family finances. While not all men agree, most men I talked with concur that it is best if they turn their wages over to their wives for safekeeping. Women themselves argue that they spend money wisely, for household expenditures and the needs of their children. Their husbands, in contrast, cannot be trusted to bring their wages home. Likewise, women normally have control over the money they earn selling domesticated animals (or their by-products), factory work, or cooperative earnings. In discussing this

ETHNOGRAPHIC ESSAY
SÍ, PODEMOS MANDAR (YES, WE CAN LEAD)

In 1976 when I first studied in Yaxbe, Sara was a 17-year-old wife and mother of one infant daughter (see UAIM, this chapter). She was the daughter of an alcoholic father who had, as a younger man, spent 11 years in prison for murder (see A Woman of Substance, Chapter 1). Destined to follow in her mother's footsteps, Sara married young and married a man who was also prone to drinking, and when I returned to visit in 1995, I was dismayed to find that Sara's husband, Marcos, was having difficulty keeping jobs. Sara, however, had been transformed from a painfully shy child-mother to an economic and political activist. The mother of five children ranging in age from 20 to 3, Sara was then the president of the UAIM chicken cooperative, and she was the secretary of the village, the first woman to hold public office in Yaxbe (see Figure 9.5).

In 1976, Marta, also a Catholic, was the 16-year-old single woman described in Chapter 4, whose confrontation with Doña Juana had surprised me so much (Figure 4.4). In 1992, Marta was the mother of five children. Her husband had one of the desired jobs at Cordemex, and they lived with Marta's parents. Marta worked as a domestic in Mérida and her mother cared for her children. She was also the president of DIF. In 1998, she still worked as a domestic, but she had left her husband (or rather, had kicked him out of the house because of his drinking), and was still active in DIF, although she was no longer an officer.

In 1976, Rosa was 21 years old, the fifth child of Don Pablo, the SDA convert who had earlier been in line to become the next *h-men* (Chapter 7). Rosa was one of three teachers in the Adventist elementary school and lived at home until she married. In 1991, her husband was killed in an electrical accident leaving her a widow with three young children. Since 1992, Rosa continues to teach at the village SDA school, the only sibling out of 11 who remains in the village. Currently, she is a member of the *municipio* committee and is active in the SDA temple activities.

In 1976, I did not know Sonia, although she lived close by. She was very young, one of the mass of 10- to 12-year-old children who visited and played around our house. Yet, she is one of my closest friends in the village since she married Reymundo, Sara's brother. Sonia's family was unique in that her mother and grandmother were both divorced; she was raised in a matrifocal environment in which both her mother and grandmother worked outside of the home at one time or another. While Sonia's mother, Claudia, worked in Mérida as a domestic, her grandmother took care of her. Sonia's grandmother is Doña Juana, the former president of the *tortillería* and Marta's nemesis.

Sonia and Reymundo have two children. In 1995, Sonia was the president of the PACR, the parents' group for the school, an officer in DIF, and was an inactive member of the UAIM women's cooperative. She is also a seamstress, and in 2000, was working as a seamstress in the Jerzees factory in Tixkokob. So what is the connection between these four women: Sara, Marta, Rosa, and Sonia?

In 1993, they formed the core of a woman's political party in which Sara was candidate for village president. Through this group, Sara solicited the support of her female friends, from the Catholic church, the cooperative, and from her family. She had a very strong backing and was able to raise some money from her supporters. As described in Chapter 5, the state PRI organization demanded that the candidate pool be reduced to two candidates, and a committee was formed to decide which of the candidates were the strongest. Even though Sara's brother

Figure 9.5 The original UAIM group at their chicken ranch, 1995. Sara is at the far right in the back.

was on this committee, it became clear that the women's party did not have a chance of being chosen as the party's representative. So Sara, always astute, encouraged her group to back one of the two strongest male candidates, one who was very sympathetic to women's issues. This candidate ultimately became the PRI candidate, winning the election. Don Carlos, a soft-spoken unmarried man showed his appreciation to the women by appointing Sara as village secretary, the first woman to have a political office in Yaxbe. In addition, all but one of the other women in Sara's party were given positions as heads of committees. Because Carlos was not married, he appointed Marta as the president of DIF, and she in turn appointed Sonia and three other women as officers. Rosa was appointed to the *municipio* committee and another woman was appointed as caretaker for the new small park recently built at the edge of the village. In addition to their political positions, all of these women continued to be involved in local politics, even after their terms expired.

When I arrived in 1995, Don Carlos's term of office was coming to a close and new elections were about to take place (*see* Figure 5.1). When I asked Sara why she had run for village president, she answered as a true feminist. She told me that women understand better than men the problems in a community. She argued that men get their money and go to the bar, whereas women are in the home and in the street and they know what needs to be done. She knew also that five villages in the state of Yucatán had women presidents at that time, and she thought that Yaxbe should also have that distinction. I asked if she was going to run again and she said, "Of course. Men laughed at me before because they said that a woman cannot lead, but we will show them that yes, we can lead . . . *sí, podemos mandar.*"

issue with various families, I have learned that husbands and wives discuss and agree on major household expenditures. This is particularly true when the wife is earning wages.

STANDARD OF LIVING   As women enter the wage labor market (Chapter 8 and Tables 1 and 5), they are contributing to an overall improvement of family economic status. The wages earned by these women also facilitate the purchase of consumer goods and the reimbursement to those who care for their children and perform household chores. Added income also provides a buffer for unexpected costs. It trickles down through the kinship system providing care to the elderly and generous gifts to family, and allows men and women to fulfill traditional obligations to *compadres* or *gremios*.

EMPOWERMENT   Another positive, yet elusive, benefit to women is the development of **empowerment,** or the realization that women have power in the home and in social life and that they can effect change. Yaxbeñas have proven that they are creative. They have gone beyond the confines of their social position and beyond the bounds of local power. The ethnographic essay on pp. 162–163 explores how increased economic participation has resulted in political empowerment.

WOMEN IN YAXBE

Empowerment Revisited

In this chapter, we examined three stories of resistance, where women bucked the patriarchy and went beyond the local authorities to achieve their goals. These small acts of resistance to local authority are not new expressions of women's participation in local-level politics. Rather, they are merely the most recent reflections of a growing sense of empowerment of women in the village. In my 20 years of visiting Yaxbe, I have watched women organize the grandest of the *gremios* for the annual *fiesta;* I have watched women head various DIF programs, often standing up to the men who questioned their authority to be the leaders. I have observed women speak out in public parent-teacher meetings and Seventh Day Adventist meetings. It is the women who plan and coordinate village fund-raisers and when an elderly widow's alcoholic son refused to fix his mother's house, it was the women of the SDA Dorcas committee who replaced the ragged tarpaper and cut and hung tarpaper panels over the dilapidated stick and daub walls. It did not matter that the old woman was Catholic.

I have found that village women have a strong sense of pride in their work. In the many conversations I have had with women, I have learned that they are aware of their subordinate status. But rather than accept their subordination, they now question the validity of the paternalistic system that envelops them. When I interviewed Sara about her candidacy for village president, she articulated her interest in politics within two contexts—community and feminism. In the first context, she argued that women should be leaders. Because women raise the children, and because they are active in the village, they know the needs of the village and will be more likely to make improvements that will benefit the community as a whole. Sara was also cognizant of the many women who have held elective office in Yucatán, from a former mayor of Mérida, former governor of the state, to various municipal presidents, including one in the closest town to Yaxbe (see Massolo 1996). Sara told me emphatically that women can (and should) lead.

Estelle Disch (1996: 12–13) states that empowerment can be defined on three levels, which can also be envisioned as stages. First, empowerment begins with a sense of awareness that inequality exists and that society's directives are suspicious and unfair. Women in the cooperatives expounded on the corruption in the local political system (also a topic among men), but in their case, the corruption was defined in terms of how women were treated by the system. They recognized that the avoidance strategies employed by the village presidents were symptomatic of their disregard for women and not evidence that the women were in any way innately inferior to the men.

Second, individual awareness is reinforced through participation with groups that are politically or socially marginal. In Yaxbe, the marginal groups are represented by the cooperatives. Men were reluctant to accept them as viable economic endeavors and considered the work of women in these groups as insignificant, to be accomplished in such a way as not to interfere with women's "real" work in the home. The cooperatives, however, have raised women's awareness of their vulnerability. The process of having requests denied or delayed and the persistent silencing of their voices in the public arena contribute to the development of a collective identity.

In the third stage, women take their empowerment to the level of political activism. This occurred during 1992 when the women's party emerged from the chicken cooperative, but it has not maintained momentum, and the party no longer exists as an activist group. This stage of empowerment is not strongly developed at the present time and it will be interesting to see if it re-emerges, and from where. Will it rise from the lower economic levels of the cooperatives or from the newly emerging women's professional class made up of teachers and nurses whose attentions, as of now, are turned outward to the urban workplace?

Machismo and Marianismo Revisited

The above discussion should entice us to examine the *machismo-marianismo* model within a more complex rubric. Particular cultural traits cannot be transferred wholesale from one society to another. As we have seen with Catholicism and *compadrazgo,* institutions forced on a group will be diluted, transformed, and molded to fit local custom and tradition. The evolutionary process started as the conquerors and missionaries interpreted their own religion and social patterns, such as *compadrazgo* and *machismo,* within a colonial context and molded them as a means of gaining control of the indigenous population. The introduced traits then are strained through additional filters as the indigenous population itself either rejects these traits or refashions them again to their own advantage, as an adaptation to critical transformations in their lives that are beyond their control. The way in which the pattern is refashioned depends on many factors: economics, social class, ethnicity, and residence.

In Yucatán, the *machismo-marianismo* relationships are apparent but not deeply entrenched despite the male-dominated political structure. The role of women, though admittedly subordinate, is not one of silent submission to brutal or even subtle oppression. The indigenous pattern of strong assertive women permeates the patriarchal political system. In this case, the *marianismo* stereotype is simplistic and applies only weakly to daily life. For example, women are typically very diffident. They congregate in the kitchens and in the background of many rituals. Yet, they dominate other rituals in the public sphere such as weddings, church, and school activities. These are not contradictions, but evidence of complexity, symbiosis, and tradition.

The activism of women in rural Yucatán cannot be analyzed solely within the context of Western theoretical concepts. While they portray many of those characteristics Disch has enumerated, we cannot assume that the women themselves view their own actions in terms of "power" or in opposition to men. Rather, women are primarily acting within the confines of their established worldview, though they are stretching those borders perceptibly. Every time they defy male authority, go above the village president's authority, or protest the actions of men, they are questioning authority and asserting their place in the social sphere.

Likewise we cannot understand these women within the feminist construct as they would deny any association with feminism. Instead, they would insist that men are the heads of the household, but would admit that they (the wives) control the money and set the family routine. They would insist that men are the breadwinners, while at the same time, they are aware that they are providing a substantial amount of the household income. They would argue that men are better leaders, while they quietly manipulate public officials, run school and church organizations, and hold leadership roles in the DIF, the largest state program present in rural villages. Sara's statement about the leadership abilities of women is an exception to the rule of female self-effacement. She is a woman ahead of her time in the village, and one of several women who are leading the fight against patriarchy.

Finally, in contrast to much of the literature stating that development projects marginalize women, in Yaxbe, the economic decline has resulted in increased participation of women in the public sphere. I am not arguing that women are not exploited within the process of capitalization—they are. Both men and women are exploited. Yet, the participation of women in the village has succeeded in integrating them into the public arena even more than before. While they have never been invisible, they were in the background of daily activities. Today, the women's factory, located on the central square, is a constant reminder that women will not be silenced. When I go into a store in another village and see a bottle of *Horchata de Yaxbe,* I feel a sense of pride, even though I had nothing to do with its birth or success. It was born from a strong sense of camaraderie, pride, and persistence, evidence that the women of Yaxbe are indeed bucking the patriarchy.

CONCLUSION

In this chapter, we have seen how women's roles in even a small village are complex. Their decisions to seek jobs in the city, join a cooperative, or indeed to stay home, are based on myriad factors, including, but not limited to, their responsibilities to home and husband. They, with their husbands, are entering a brave new world, an uncertain place where all of their assumptions about their lives are being questioned, where fathers and sons and mothers and daughters no longer share the same experiences or even hold the same values. Yet, in this, as in all other eras of the Maya, they will persevere, despite conditions far beyond their control and outside of their experience. The economic transformation has been swift; the social transformation will be more gradual. But because of the historic flexibility and resilience of the Maya, the next *katun* will demonstrate that they have once again succeeded in maintaining what is important to them: their families, their villages, and their identity.

10/From Tortillas to Bread

In this ethnography, my goal was to share a 20-year journey with you—a journey in which you could learn, as I did, how societies can become transformed yet maintain important elements of shared culture and values. In leading you in this journey of time and place, I hoped to impart knowledge about the economic and social matrix within which people live; I also wanted to put a face on the people of Yaxbe and put their own words into print. This has been a long-term, intensive, and awesome task.

To conclude, instead of reiterating the ideas put forth in the previous chapters, I would like to offer one more ethnographic essay. The topic of this essay came to me as Cathy, my student-research assistant, and I wandered the streets of Yaxbe one day in 1992, looking for a woman who could make tortillas.

This essay illustrates the holistic and integrative nature of society. It shows that shifts in national and state economic conditions and policies can have implications in the most intimate and routine rituals of daily life. It also demonstrates, I hope, the importance of food, family, and home in the daily life of Yaxbeños, past and present.

FROM TORTILLAS TO BREAD:
THE TORTILLA AS METAPHOR
FOR ECONOMIC AND SOCIAL CHANGE

Some of my most pleasant memories of my first year in the village revolve around the ritual of making tortillas (which Yucatecans have turned into a verb—*tortillar*). On many occasions, I sat awkwardly on a wobbly three-legged stool, inches off the ground, trying to imitate the way in which the women modestly tuck their *huipiles* around their legs as they worked. Giving up, I would stretch my legs outward and pull my skirt down to cover my knees. This position impeded my ability to both work at the small table or to work closely at the *comal* (griddle) that was balanced over the fire by three large stones.

There was a soothing rhythm to the patting of the *masa* into perfect circles of identical size, placing them on the large *comal,* and turning them at the perfect time, watching in delight as they puffed up like balloons. The steaming hot tortillas were then folded into a large gourd and covered with a clean towel in preparation for the next meal. Burned or imperfectly formed tortillas (usually mine) were torn into small pieces and thrown to the chickens and turkeys that scurried around us, nibbling at my exposed ankles as they awaited such morsels. This was women's space, and conversations were casual. It was during these moments, as I fumbled with *masa* or burned my fingers on the *comal* that I learned many Maya words and captured glimpses of family life (see Figure 10.1).

It was with great dismay that I returned to the village in the 1990s and found that most of the cooking huts had disappeared and few women performed the tedious and time consuming task of *tortillando.* I didn't fully realize the extent to which this activity had disappeared until I took one of my anthropology students to the village in 1992. Cathy was anxious to watch and videotape women making tortillas, and we blissfully set out to one, then another neighbor, only to be told the sad news—that they no longer made tortillas. Not wanting to disappoint us, each woman would say, "Check with Doña so-and-so. She makes tortillas." Finally, early one Sunday morning, as we were still lazing in our hammocks, a woman whom I recognized but did not know well knocked on our door. "Doña Sofia said you want to watch tortilla-ing" (there is no appropriate translation for this form of the verb). Groggily, but excitedly, we dressed and followed the woman to her *solár* where her mother-in-law and sister-in-law were already making tortillas for the Sunday meal. According to our hostess, Sunday was the only day of the week that they make tortillas. "It is the only day that we have time. We wouldn't make them at all except my father-in-law and husband want them."

It is difficult for Americans, a nation of borrowers, to understand the significance of one particular food to a society. Americans do not have a food that identifies it as nation, a food that is embedded in their culture and psyche. Corn is such a food for Mexicans. Maize is native to Mexico and represents the core value of all Mexicans. According to the *Popul Vuh,* the Quiché Book of Prophesy, humans were formed from a corn plant. Cornfields are sacred, and corn forms the basis of every Mexican meal, either in the form of tortillas or beverages. Tortillas are an integral part of the only Mayan ceremony that is still performed in the village, the *comistraje.* Thus, a shift in the relationship of villagers to the tortilla is a vital one. The traditional practice of making tortillas, from the shucking of the corn, grinding it by hand, soaking it in water and lime, forming the *masa,* and making the tortillas, is disappearing. It is being replaced by a ritual that is performed almost as an afterthought . . . as easily as sending one's daughter to the corner *molino* for a kilo of tortillas.

My reaction to the disappearance of this ritual was a terrible sense of the irreparable loss of an integral part of Mexican culture. My second response was one of self-pity, since I loved the hot corn tortillas and I craved them whenever I ate a bland flour tortilla in a "Mexican" restaurant in the United States. Since then, I began to see a

*Figure 10.1 Doña Fidelia
making tortillas, 1977*

parallel between this women's ritual and one in which I was involved in my own rural community of Chippewa Lake, Michigan. When I first joined the Young Women's Club, the monthly meetings were held in members' homes and each hostess, in her turn, served home-baked desserts and coffee. As more women, in response to failing farms and underemployment in the 1980s, found jobs outside of the home, the women no longer had time to clean their houses in preparation for guests, so the meetings were moved to the local community building. For a while the designated hostess still brought homemade desserts, but this custom also faded, as women brought boxed or prepared desserts instead. Finally, the desserts were discontinued altogether, and each woman brought her own coffee in a thermos mug or a soft drink. Thus, as modern American families are increasingly dependent on prepared foods and meals on the run, so is the Yucatecan family making a similar shift, and the two family types are beginning to look uncomfortably similar. Renalto Rosaldo (1993: 201) makes a similar observation as he recounts the story of the anthropological fieldworker who travels the world to discover the "exotic other," but finds instead that "the other" lives just like him.

Once I recognized these parallels, I was able to view the loss of tortilla making as symbolic of the many changes occurring in Yucatecan life, and particularly within the family. I began to see how this event, this loss of ritual, represents a kind of microcosm of events that are occurring at the national and international arena beyond the control of the Yucatecan peasant. This loss of ritual further symbolizes changes that are occurring within the village itself, embedded in social and familial interaction.

I suggest that there are several reasons for the loss of this custom. These factors represent symbolically the overall transformation of the village on various levels—economic and social. The economic decline that is the focus of this ethnography has had many ramifications for families in Yaxbe, as we have seen. One of these ramifications is the necessity for women and unmarried children to enter the wage earning market either in or outside the home. Traditionally women and their daughters cooperated with household chores. But now as married women have entered the Double Day and their daughters have found a place in the wage market or the college classroom, this symbiotic relationship has weakened.

While the extended household is still the ideal family form, the new opportunities and obligations of women within these households have made a marked impact on production within the *solár*. In addition, however, there has been a gradual shift in the meaning attached to family in recent years. As *soláres* become crowded, families are more willing to split off from the extended family and move elsewhere in the village. As the village expands outward, and less land is needed for agricultural pursuits, there is a trend on the part of young people to set up their own nuclear families. Thus, as the extended family contracts and nuclear families evolve, women's time becomes more valuable in all households.

Another factor influencing the decline in importance of the homemade tortilla may be the transformation of the modern Mayan house and especially of the modern kitchen. As we have seen, the new cement block houses not only introduced indoor bathrooms, but indoor kitchens as well. While many villagers attached outdoor kitchens to their new homes to accommodate cooking fires, many others did not. The lack of a cooking fire further distances young women from the traditional cooking styles of their mothers and grandmothers.

The introduction into the village of the first *tortillería* in 1977 gave women a choice. I was living in the village when Don Justo installed the first *molino* and *tortillería*. A great amount of excitement was generated, but there was some reluctance to take advantage of the new technology because women who purchased tortillas were considered a bit lazy. As the *tortillería* became more accepted, however, local practice shifted. At first, the store-bought tortillas supplemented the daily needs of the family and released women somewhat from the time-consuming task of making tortillas several times a day. Eventually, as economic and social factors shifted the roles and responsibilities of women within the household, the machine-made tortillas became more and more appealing and convenient.

Shifts in economic and educational patterns, then, resulted in a subtle transformation at the local level. Women, for a variety of reasons, decided not to make tortillas. Because this transformation occurred over a period of time and because I am not privy to the private conversations that took place in countless homes over the past 20 years, I cannot say what the men of these families had to say about this silent revolt. Yet, it has occurred. Village women are now divided into two categories: those who know how but no longer make tortillas over the fire, and those who watched their mothers make tortillas, but never learned the skill themselves. Today, when women make tortillas for enchiladas or tacos, they use metal presses to shape the *masa* patties and cook the tortillas on stove-top *comals*. This technique produces a hand-made tortilla but without the social interaction and intimacy of the original.

One of the paradoxes with which I have struggled over the years is the incongruity between the national economic decline and the apparent affluence of the village. Few people have migrated, as I had predicted they would. Instead, families have adopted the mixed strategies summarized above, which include the incorporation of women and young people into the workforce. As families have adapted to new economic values, such as set work hours and a new work ethic, there has been a concomitant metamorphosis in traditional values and ideologies: from communal to individual; from reciprocity to accumulation and consumerism; from an egalitarian ethic to an acceptance of social class. Today, with exposure to broader Mexican and American culture through television and the ever-present tourists in Mérida, villagers are exposed to the wonders of material goods and have accepted the consumer ethic.

Social class is also evident in such sumptuary items as food. Children, who used to irritate me by spitting their orange seeds on my cement floor, now litter the streets with potato chip wrappers and pop cans. As rural Mexicans are introduced to Western foods, through television and local availability, these higher status (and more expensive) foods become preferable and desirable to the rural poor. Likewise there is a connection between tortillas and social class. For example, my husband and I were invited to numerous dinners during our stay in which our hosts offered us white bread instead of tortillas. We tried to hide our dismay as our gracious hosts attempted to serve us the food they thought we preferred. Increasingly, affluent families will eat bread, while the poor continue to eat tortillas, a more nutritious, yet socially inferior food. As modern families have access to bread and as bread is perceived as a sign of high status, the importance of tortillas will continue to decline as a social food, and this in itself will further undermine the value of making tortillas by hand. Thus, the integral relationship between food and culture may be starting to unravel as the Western world impinges more and more on the lives of Mexican people.

Finally, while releasing women from a time-consuming and tedious job, the loss of this skill and activity has implications for the social bonding of women, especially bonds that cross generations. Making tortillas is not only a food preparation activity but also a social activity. It was an activity that women performed with their daughters or daughters-in-law, sisters and sisters-in-law, that grandmothers taught to their granddaughters. It provided social time, time for sharing, learning, and teaching. It also linked husband and wife in their symbiotic economic and social relationship that centered on the production and consumption of maize.

Anthropologists are interested not only in the material aspects of life—tools, food, and shelter, but how people construct their worlds and what kinds of items or events have special meanings. The making of tortillas has that type of symbolic meaning. Not only is the tortilla made from the primary food in the Mexican trilogy, maize, but it is the primary form in which corn is consumed. That the tortilla is slowly disappearing as the primary food source is indicative of other changes that are also occurring in Yucatán: the entrance of women and girls into the workforce; the increasing trend of nucleated families; the roles of women in the household; the availability of other sources of grain fiber; and the status attached to the consumption of Western foods.

Thus *tortillando* can symbolize not only the Mexican relationship with corn and agriculture in general, but it represents a whole series of economic and social relationships as well. As the meaning of the symbol changes, so do the relationships that it represents. Yet it is important that women themselves define the meaning of the symbol, not the anthropologist. Thus, for me the tortilla defines tradition, household, and female bonding. For older women, it is a primary symbol linking past to present, mother to daughter, and home to village. In contrast, to young girls, it means poverty, tedium, and old-fashioned hard work. (1998)

Epilogue
Return to Yaxbe, 2001

On a hot and muggy June day, I return to Yucatán with my two sons, Nathan and David. This is my sixth trip to the village, the second for Nathan, now a university student, and the third for David, a freshman in high school. We arrive in the Mérida airport, minus one suitcase that was lost somewhere between Chicago and Mexico. As we fill out the required paperwork and submit our remaining luggage to the customs search, we look out into the terminal where a crowd of people presses expectantly against the huge glass doors. I smile as I recognize Reymundo and his two children, Hector and Carmen, and Pedro Chac, his wife, Dora, and their son Carlos and other assorted nieces and nephews. Reymundo had commissioned a taxi-van from his nephew so that they could bring a large group to meet us. It was a crowded van that took us back to Yaxbe. Above the noise of traffic and the van that, like most other vehicles, lacked a functioning muffler and tailpipe, we got the highlights of village life since my last visit. Reymundo's brother, Ernesto, who was president during our first stay had died in the past year, a young man who unfortunately had inherited his father's alcoholism. I learned of several other funerals and weddings. Sonia, Reymundo's wife, was not at the airport because she had a job at the Jerzees factory. Carmen had graduated from high school and was hoping to attend university in the fall.

As I listened to the hum of conversation, I tried to take in the landscape as it passed us by. We passed through familiar neighborhoods of Mérida, but with a clustering of new businesses. My sons pointed out the McDonald's and Internet cafes in excited anticipation, while I gazed in awe and dismay at a shopping mall and a

Wal-Mart. As we left the narrow, congested streets of the capitol, we merged onto a new, widened highway that led us from city to countryside. It was a countryside transformed. Although it was only three years since my last visit, the changes were tremendous. Instead of miles and miles of henequen fields, our van passed by new housing developments serving the expanded urban area, huge cattle ranches, and a proliferation of factories. Finally we left the new highway and traversed through the familiar villages that were also experiencing their own transformation. Slowly, the thatch houses along the side of the road were being replaced by cement block houses and tin laminated roofs. Cars were parked helter-skelter along the road and in makeshift driveways. In Tixkokob, we passed the factory where Sonia works, a monstrosity of modern technology.

As we approached Yaxbe, we passed a new housing development that had been uninhabited in 1998. Now, it was beginning to look like a community. Clothes hung from clotheslines in back yards, cars were parked along curbs, and children played in the street. Further, on entering the village proper, my heart lurched, like it always does when I see the familiar houses and the faces of so many friends. As people recognized us in the van, they smiled and waved, and I could hardly wait to start my now routine visiting rounds.

It did not take long for me to realize that there were critical changes in the daily round of village life. In the past, I conducted my visits and interviews in the mornings, when women and children were working in the home. Women would pause in their work to talk to me individually or in small groups. They were very gracious in conversing with me, very lively and open. It was a cherished time, when I could talk to women while the men were working in the fields. I was disappointed now as I found house after house closed up. The women were working, and the children were in school or staying with a relative who was caring for them. During the three weeks I was in the village, I only visited Sonia two or three times a week instead of daily as would be my normal practice. At the factory she worked four straight days of 12-hour shifts and then had four days off. During her days off, she caught up on her housework and visited family and friends. I hated to impose on her limited leisure time, though she often sought me out on her off-days and invited us to dinners where we fell easily into our routine of sharing news and reminiscing about the past.

Another woman whom I know well works as a custodian at one of the government buildings in Mérida. She returned home late in the evenings, and I only was able to visit her on the weekends. This pattern was repeated throughout the village. Women were busy, and houses were often left empty during the day as both husband and wife went off in different directions to work.

Other changes reflected the shift in consumer patterns over the years. In most *soláres* at least one house would have a refrigerator, television, and indoor kitchen and plumbing. Some families had computers, microwaves, and VCRs. However, there was still only one telephone line in the village and that was linked to a pay phone in the president's office. Several families had cellular phones in their homes, paying the exorbitant price of communication with the outside world. These families charged an inadequate fee for neighbors to call relatives living in other parts of Mexico and even in the United States. Pedro Chac's aunt used his phone several times a week to check up on her brother who was getting cancer treatments in Mexico City.

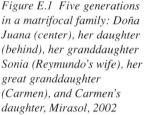

Figure E.1 Five generations in a matrifocal family: Doña Juana (center), her daughter (behind), her granddaughter Sonia (Reymundo's wife), her great granddaughter (Carmen), and Carmen's daughter, Mirasol, 2002

We learned early in our visit that Reymundo wanted us to take his daughter back to the United States to visit with us for a month. This request was very special for us, as Reymundo had come to visit us in Michigan in the fall of 1977, several months after we had left the village. At that time, we were living in a small upstairs apartment in Grand Rapids, expecting our first child. I was writing my dissertation and LaVail had just started a new job working with migrant workers as a legal aid attorney. Reymundo enjoyed his visit, but suffered extreme culture shock, coming from Yaxbe to Grand Rapids. He always remembered his visit with us and recalls things about his stay that we had forgotten. In our turn, we have stories of his stay that we could tell his children, such as the time he took off walking to a major department store that was about 10 miles away. Because it was a short drive in a car, he thought that he could walk there in a few minutes. He was rescued by my brother-in-law, who happened to see him walking in the October cold, wearing only a light jacket.

I assisted Carmen in getting her passport and visitor's visa, a difficult feat as immigration officers assume that Mexicans, on arriving in the United States, will do anything to stay. Carmen had plans to attend university when she returned to Mexico and had paid her entrance fees in order to assure U.S. Immigration that she planned to return. It was a joy having her stay at our house and our cottage. Her experiences were very different than those of her father: jet skiing, horseback riding, a baseball game, and a family vacation to Mackinac Island. When she returned to the village, however, she did not start at the university. Instead she married and moved in with her husband's family, per the local pattern (see Figure E-1).

Now, once in a while the phone rings and it is Pedro and Dora, calling to check up on us. I told them that my ethnography was going to be published, and I would be returning in the summer of 2002 to get permissions for photographs. As Pedro passed this information on to Dora whose voice I could hear in the background, she grabbed the phone and asked a favor. She asked me if I would bring her a new *comal* for making pancakes. The one I had bought her earlier had broken. She also wanted some instant coffee packets for her father. These items are very expensive in Mexico, and it is my pleasure to bring things for them that only begin to repay them for their hospitality as they will not accept rent money from me.

These random phone calls, letters, and occasional email messages from Hector remind us of our other life, in the rural Yucatecan countryside. It is a life very different, yet in some ways very similar to life in rural Michigan. I see my farming neighbors in Pedro and Reymundo and glimpses of my women friends in Sonia, Sara, and Dora. Whenever I leave Yaxbe, I am already anticipating my next visit.

Appendix

TABLE A-1   Sources of Income for Resident Men and Women:
1976 and 1998

Primary Source of Income	Males				Females			
	1976–1977		1998		1976–1977		1998	
	Number	%	Number	%	Number	%	Number	%
Henequen/ Agriculture[a]	200	65	41	25	0	0	7	4
Factory (including Cordemex)	55	18	37	22	0	0	22	13
Professional[b]	0	0	12	7	1	.002	17	10
Sales/Collecting	0	0	28	17	0	0	0	0
Family Store/Bars	12	4	9	5	—	—	14	8
Miscellaneous[c]	40	13	40	24	51	12	35	21
Unemployed/ Homemaker[d]	0	0	0	0	360	88	76	44
Total	307	100	167	100	412	100	171	100

[a]Includes retirees who receive pensions based on their years in henequen production.
[b]Residents of the village. Other professionals live elsewhere and others don't earn a living from the career for which they are trained.
[c]Includes construction, tailoring.
[d]Individuals in this category may earn money through hammock weaving, raising of domesticated animals, etc., but income is sporadic and they do not earn a wage.

TABLE A-2   Henequen Occupations as a Percentage
of Total Occupations: 1976 and 1998

Occupation	1976–77[a]		1998[b]	
	Number	Percentage	Number	Percentage
Henequen	250	81	41	25
Ejido[c]	*171*	*56*	*32*	*20*
Henequen related	*24*	*8*	*0*	*0*
Cordemex	*55*	*18*	*9*	*5*
Non-Henequen	57	19	126	75
Misc. agriculture/ Animal husbandry	*10*	*3*	*9*	*5*
Other non-henequen	*47*	*16*	*117*	*70*
Total	307	100	167	100

$$X^2 = .0001 \ (147.5)$$
$$Q = .86$$

[a]N = 307 adult males in 200 households
[b]N = 167 adult males in a sample of 86 households
[c]Since 1992, the *ejido* no longer exists; these numbers refer to men who work on former *ejido* land that they own or on which they work as day laborers.

TABLE A-3 OCCUPATION AND RELIGION: MALES, 1998

Occupation	Catholic Men		Adventist Men	
	Number	**Percentage**	**Number**	**Percentage**
Agriculture/Henequen	32	29	9	16
Non-agricultural:				
Factory	*31*	*28*	*6*	*11*
Professional	*6*	*5*	*6*	*11*
Other	*43*	*38*	*34*	*63*
Subtotal–Non-agricultural	80	71	46	85
Total	112	100	54	101

$X^2 = .05$
$Q = .62$

TABLE A-4 PROFESSIONALS[a] BY RELIGION AND GENDER, 1998

Religion	Male	Female	Total	Percentage
Catholic	10	15	25	42
Protestant[b]	17	18	35	58
Total	27	33	60	100
Percentage	45	55	100	

$X^2 = .34$
$Q = 48$

[a]Professionals include such vocational occupations as secretarial and lower administrative positions that are considered professional by villagers.
[b]Protestants include both Seventh Day Adventists and Pentecostals.

TABLE A-5 EMPLOYED WOMEN: MARRIED, DIVORCED/WIDOWED, AND SINGLE: 1976 AND 1998

1976

Occupation	Married	Divorced/Widowed	Single	Total	Percentage
Non-Professional	37	5	9	51	12.5
Professional	0	0	1	1	.5
Total Employed	37	5	10	52	13
Homemaker[a]	N/A	N/A	N/A	360	87
Total	—	—	—	412	100

1998

Occupation	Married	Divorced/Widowed	Single	Total	Percentage
Non-Professional	43	4	31	78	45
Professional	10	1	6	17	10
Total Employed	53	5	37	95	55
Homemaker[a]	66	5	5	76	45
Total	119	10	42	171	100

[a]Does not include various sources of income such as raising and sale of food and domesticated animals or hammock weaving, all of which are sporadic and difficult to document.

Glossary

ahijado/a godchild

aguardiente a hard liquor produced from henequen or other local grains

alux(ob) trickster spirits that inhabit nature

Ayuntamiento collective term for the local government and officials

bagazo the pulp that results when the fibers are stripped from the henequen leaves

balché (Lonchocarpus longistylus) a tree whose bark is used to make a ceremonial wine

batab(ob) Mayan town leader or governor

bilateral kinship a pattern of descent in which both the mother's and father's line are used in reckoning inheritance and genealogy

bride service a residence pattern in which the husband lives with the wife's family for a period of time and provides for her family

cacique an indigenous ruler who is appointed by the colonial government to act as an administrator; mediates between the colonial government and the indigenous community

campesino a farmer

cash crop a crop, such as henequen, that is grown for the market, not for family consumption

catrín a person who wears Western clothing and speaks Spanish

ceiba type of cedar tree, sacred to the Maya

cenote (*dzonot* in Maya) pools of fresh water that form when the limestone karst collapses

Chac(ob) Mayan rain god(s)

Chachac (comistraje in Yaxbe) annual rain ceremony

checador political appointee in the henequen *ejido* who sets the daily quota and oversees the workers

chilam(ob) Mayan religious leaders who specialize in prophesy

cobratorio occupation in which men travel between villages collecting weekly payments from villagers on behalf of independent vendors or stores

comistraje see *Chachac*

compadrazgo system of ritual co-parenthood introduced by the Spanish

compadre/comadre co-parents to the parents of the child/godchild

conquistadores Spanish conquerors of Mexico

consejo viligancia elected position in the henequen *ejido*; the man in charge of inspecting the fields and reporting to the *socio delegado*

Cordemex the state-owned decorticating factories (see *disfibradora*)

corrida bullfight

Creole people of Spanish descent who were born in the New World

cultural relativism the idea in anthropology that other customs and beliefs should be understood within the context of culture, and not judged by one's own culture and beliefs

Day of the Dead (Día de los muertos) celebration that takes place between October 31 and November 2 that acknowledges the ancestors

debt peonage a colonial system under which peasants accumulated debt to the *hacendado* that passed on to their children; families were not free to leave the *hacienda* until the debt was paid

Del suelo al cielo from the ground to the sky (heaven): a phrase that Adventists use to describe the conversion process

DIF (Desarrollo Integral de la Familia) government agency that delivers welfare and family based programs to rural areas

disfibradora decorticating plants that strip the fibers from the henequen leaves

Dorcas an Adventist voluntary association for women; it assists the poor, ill, and elderly

double descent system of inheritance and kinship found in pre-conquest Maya society in which men and women gain status and rank from both their mother's and father's descent groups

ejido/ejidatario   communal land held by individuals or villages/men who work in the *ejido*

empowerment   idea that one has power over his or her life and that he or she can effect change

encomienda/encomendero   land holdings and the indigenous people who lived on the land/owner of an *encomienda*

endogamy   marriage to someone within the same ethnic, racial, or social category or village

exogamy   marriage to someone from a different group, clan, lineage, or social category

granja   a chicken/turkey ranch

gremio   a volunteer organization that cares for the village patron saint and sponsors the *fiesta*

hacienda/hacendado   land tenure system oriented toward the production of a cash crop and self-sufficiency

halach uinic   hereditary Mayan regional chief or "true man"

hectare   unit of measurement—1 acre = 2.49 hectares

henequen (agave fourcroydes)/henequenero   cactus-like plant grown for the production of rope and twine, also known as sisal/a man who works in henequen production

hetzmek   Mayan ceremony that marks the time when a child is carried on the mother's hip

hijo   Spanish word for "child." Here it refers to the henequen starter plants.

h-men   Mayan religious leader and curer who leads the *comistraje* (*chachac*) ceremony

horchata   rice milk drink produced in Yaxbe

Huay Pop   an animal spirit associated with sorcerers who allow storekeepers to amass large inventories

huipil   white smock-like dress with embroidered neck and hem, worn by Mayan women

Itzamná   creator god; sun god

Ix Chel   goddess of weaving and childbirth; moon goddess and consort to *Itzamná*

Ix Kanleox   mother of the gods

Ix Tab   patroness to those who commit suicide

jarana   traditional dance associated with the annual *fiesta*

karst   topography of Yucatán, characterized by porous limestone surface and underground waterways

katun   a 20-year cycle in the Maya calendar round

kermesse   a fund-raising festival with food and games

Kukulkan   the "Feathered Serpent" god or ruler equivalent to the Aztec God-human Quetzalcoatl

ladino   descendants of Spanish conquerors who hold a dominant social position in Mexican society

leveling mechanisms   means by which those who are affluent contribute more to the community economically in return for prestige

machismo   cluster of values that emphasize male virility and dominance

madrina   godmother

mal aire   bad air that can cause illness

mal ojo   evil eye

mal viento   evil wind that can cause illness or death

maquiladora   foreign-owned factory; also *maquila* industry

marianismo   cluster of values that emphasize female submissiveness and moral superiority

masa   corn dough from which tortillas are made

matrilocal   post-marital residence pattern in which married couple lives with or near the wife's family

mestizo/a   in general usage, individuals of mixed Spanish and English heritage; in Yucatán, those who speak Maya and wear traditional clothing

milpa   corn field

molino   mill that grinds grains such as corn or rice

mono-crop   the production of one dominant crop for the market, on which an entire region's economic success depends; often a cash crop.

monotheism   religions in which a single powerful god controls the natural and supernatural environment

monte   thorny, dense semi-tropical brush

municipio   municipality; roughly equivalent to a county in the United States

NAFTA   the North American Free Trade Agreement between the United States, Mexico, and Canada

neolocal   post-marital residence pattern in which a married couple lives separately from both sets of parents

novio/a   boy/girlfriend

nuclear family   family that is comprised of a mother, father, and children

PACR (*Programa del Alimentacíon Complementaria Rural*)   government-sponsored food and nutritional program

padrino   godfather

palacio   administration building of a village

PAN (National Action Party)   current ruling party in Mexico

pantheon   gods of a particular religion who are considered collectively

parcela/parcelario   private plot of land/ owner of a private parcel

patrilineal   descent system in which inheritance and kin are reckoned through the male line

patrilocal   post-marital residence pattern in which the husband and wife live with the husband's family

patrón   wealthy individuals who sponsor or assist poor families

peasant   a generic term referring to agriculturists who are linked economically to the larger market economy

polytheism   religion comprised of a pantheon of gods and goddesses that share power over the natural and supernatural environment

posada   procession, usually related to religious events

PRI (Institutional Revolutionary Party)   the dominant political party from 1946 to 2000

PROCEDE   procedure instituted by the national government to facilitate the land reforms and privatization process initiated in 1992

PRONASOL   umbrella government agency for Solidaridad and UAIM

Protestant Ethic   historical context in which the Protestant emphasis on individual achievement and salvation was the impetus for the development of capitalism; the idea was introduced by Max Weber

quinceñera   fifteenth birthday party; "coming out" for young girls

reducciones   colonial pattern of incorporating small populations of Maya into larger villages for the purpose of administration and conversion

sacbe(ob)   "white road"; the ancient Mayan raised roads, some of which still exist between major archaeological sites

sindicato   trucking organizations

socio delegado   president of the *ejido*

solár(es)   enclosed yard where a collection of related nuclear families reside

Solidaridad   a governmental program part of PRONASOL that promotes rural cooperatives and development programs

stela(e)   ancient Mayan inscribed stone markers

swidden   technique of horticulture in which land is cut and burned to return nutrients to the soil, followed by a long fallow period; also called "slash and burn"

syncretism   process through which opposing beliefs become reinterpreted and reconciled

tablado   sections in the bullfight arena purchased by individuals and families

traje   traditional clothing for Mayan men, consisting of white shirt, white pants and apron, and sandals

UAIM (Women's Agro-Industrial Unit)   government-sponsored program that promotes women's agricultural based projects

Uay Pop   see *Huay Pop*

usufruct   a system of use rights in that a person may hold a piece of property indefinitely and pass it on to children, but cannot sell it

World Systems Theory   the paradigm that non-Western societies are embedded economically and socially within a global system in which they hold a peripheral position

Xtabai   Mayan female spirit who lures men into the *monte* and kills them

yerbatero/a   curer who uses herbs and traditional healing methods; also called *curanderos/as*

zacate   a type of grass cultivated for cattle feed

References

Annis, Sheldon. 1987. *God and Production in a Guatemala Town.* Austin: University of Texas Press.

Bossen, Laurel. 1984. *Redivision of Labor: Women and Economic Choice in Four Guatemalan Communities.* Albany: Albany State University.

Brannon, Jeffery, and Eric Baklanoff. 1987. *Agrarian Reform and Public Enterprise in Mexico: The Political Economy of Yucatán's Henequen Industry.* Tuscaloosa: University of Alabama Press.

Brockway, Lucille. 1979. *Science and Colonial Expansion: The Role of the British Royal Botanical Gardens.* New York: Academic Press.

Brusco, Elizabeth. 1993. The Reformation of Machismo: Asceticism and Masculinity among Colombian Evangelicals. Garrard-Burnett and Stoll, eds., *Rethinking Protestantism in Latin America.* Philadelphia: Temple University Press.

Carmack, R., J. Gasco, and G. Gossen, eds. 1996. *The Legacy of Mesoamerica: History and Culture of a Native American Civilization.* Upper Saddle River, NJ: Prentice-Hall.

Carrasco, David. 1990. *Religions of Mesoamerica: Cosmovision and Ceremonial Centers.* Prospect Heights, IL: Waveland.

Castellanos, Carlos, et al. 1974. Aspectos de Algunas Religiones en Yucatán. *Boletín de Ciencias Antropologicos de la Universidad de Yucatán* 1:4:1974 (Feb).

Chamberlain, Robert. 1948. *The Conquest and Colonization of Yucatán.* Washington, DC: Carnegie Institution.

Chardon, Roland. 1961. *Geographical Aspects of Plantation Agriculture in Yucatán.* National Research Council Publication 876. Washington, DC: National Academy of Sciences.

Collier, George. 1994a. Reforms of Mexico's Agrarian Code: Impacts on the Peasantry in *Research in Economic Anthropology* 15: 105–127.

Collier, George (with E. Lowrey Quarantiello). 1994b. *Básta! Land and the Zapatista Rebellion in Chiapas.* Oakland, CA: Food First Books. Institute for Food and Development Policy.

Cook, S., and W. Borah. 1974. *Essays in Population History: Mexican and Caribbean* vol. 2. Berkeley: University of California Press.

Cornelius, Wayne, A. Craig, and J. Fox, eds. 1994. *Transforming State-Society Relations in Mexico: The National Solidarity Strategy.* U.S.-Mexico Contemporary Perspectives Series, 6. Center for U.S.-Mexican Studies, San Diego: University of California.

Disch, Estelle. 1997. *Reconstructing Gender: A Multicultural Anthology.* Mountain View, CA: Mayfield.

Edmonson, Munro S. 1986. *Heaven Born Mérida and Its Destiny.* Austin: University of Texas Press.

Ehlers, Tracy B. 1991. Debunking Marianismo: Economic Vulnerability and Survival Strategies among Guatemala Wives. *Ethnology* 30:1: 1–16.

Fernández Repetto, Francisco. 1995. Celebrar a los Santos: Sistema de Fiestas en el Noroccidente de Yucatán. *Alteridades* 5 (9): 51–61.

Foster, George. 1965. Peasant Society and the Image of the Limited Good. *American Anthropologist* 67: 293–315.

Frazer, Sir James G. 1911–1915. *The Golden Bough* (12 Volumes). London: Macmillan.

Freidel, D., and L. Schele. 2001. Maya Royal Women: A Lesson in Precolumbian History in Brettel, C., and C. Sargent, eds., *Gender in Cross-*

Cultural Perspective. Englewood Cliffs, NJ: Prentice-Hall, pp. 89–93.

Fuentes, Carlos. 1996. *A New Time for Mexico.* New York: Farrar, Straus, and Giroux.

Garrard-Burnett, Virginia, and David Stoll, eds. 1993. *Rethinking Protestantism in Latin America.* Philadelphia: Temple University Press.

Green, Linda. 1993. Shifting Affiliations: Mayan Widows and Evangélicos in Guatemala. In Garrard-Burnett and Stoll, eds., *Rethinking Protestantism in Latin America.* Philadelphia: Temple University Press, pp. 159–179.

Helms, Mary. 1975. *Middle America: A Cultural History of Heartland and Frontier.* Englewood Cliffs, NJ: Prentice-Hall.

Henderson, John. 1981. *World of the Ancient Maya.* Ithaca, NY: Cornell University Press.

Hunt, Marta Espejo-Ponce, and Matthew Restall. 1997. Work, Marriage, and Status: Maya Women of Colonial Yucatán in Schroeder, Wood, and Haskett, eds., *Indian Women of Early Mexico.* Norman: University of Oklahoma Press, pp. 231–252.

Jordan, Brigitte. 1993. *Birth in Four Cultures: A Cross-Cultural Investigation of Childbirth in Yucatán, Holland, Sweden, and the United States.* Prospect Heights, IL: Waveland.

Kintz, Ellen. 1990. *Life under the Tropical Canopy.* Fort Worth: Holt, Rinehart & Winston.

La Botz, Daniel. 1995. *Democracy in Mexico: Peasant Rebellion and Political Reform.* Boston: South End Press.

Landa, Friar Diego de (Translated with Notes by William Gates). 1978. *Yucatán before and after the Conquest.* New York: Dover. (Original 1566, entitled *Relación de las Cosas de Yucatán.*)

Laurell, Asa Cristina, and Maria Isabel Wences. 1994. Do Poverty Programs Alleviate Poverty? The Case of the Mexican National Solidarity Program. *International Journal of Health Services* 24:3: 381–401.

Littlefield, Alice. 1978. (August) Exploitation and the Expansion of Capitalism: The Case of the Hammock Industry in Yucatán. *American Ethnologist* 5:3: 495–508.

———. 1979. The Expansion of Capitalist Relations of Production in Mexican Crafts. *Journal of Peasant Studies,* vol. 6: 471–488.

———. 1990. The Putting Out System: Transitional Form or Recurrent Feature of Capitalist Production? *The Social Science Journal* 27:4: 359–372.

Massolo, Alejandra. 1996. Mujeres en el espacio local y poder municipal. *Revista Mexicana de Sociologia* 58:3 (July–Sept.):133–144.

Morgan, Lewis Henry. 1964 (1877). Leslie A. White, ed. *Ancient Society.* Cambridge: Belknap Press of the Harvard University Press.

Ortner, Sherry. 1984. Theory in Anthropology since the Sixties. *Comparative Studies in Society and History* 26:126–166.

Raymond, N. 1968. Land Reform and the Structure of Production of Yucatán. *Ethnology* 7: 461–470.

re Cruz, Alicia. 1996. *The Two Milpas of Chan Kom: A Study of Socioeconomics and Political Transformations in a Maya Community.* Albany: SUNY Press.

Redfield, Robert, and Alfonso Villa Rojas 1990 [1934]. *Chan Kom: A Maya Village.* Prospect Heights, IL: Waveland.

Reed, N. 1964. *The Caste War of Yucatán.* Stanford: Stanford University Press.

Restall, Matthew. 1995. He Wished in Vain: Subordination and Resistance among Maya Women in Post-Conquest Yucatán. *Ethnohistory* 42: 4 (Fall): 577–594.

Robles, Rosario, et al. 1993. La Mujer Campesina en la Epoca de la Modernidad. *El Cotidiano* 53 (March–April): 25–32.

Rosaldo, Renato. 1993. *Culture and Truth: The Remaking of Social Analysis.* Boston: Beacon.

Roys, Ralph. 1957. *The Political Geography of the Yucatán Maya.* Washington DC: Carnegie Institution.

———. 1972 [1943]. *The Indian Background of Colonial Yucatán.* Norman: University of Oklahoma Press.

Shuman, M. 1974. *The Town Where Luck Fell: The Economics of Life in a Henequen Zone Pueblo.* Unpublished Ph.D. Dissertation, Tulane University.

Simpson, E. 1937. *The Ejido: Mexico's Way Out.* Chapel Hill: University of North Carolina Press.

Stephen, Lynn. 1994a. *Viva Zapata: Generation, Gender, and Historical Consciousness in the Reception of Ejido Reform in Oaxaca.* Transformation of Rural Mexico, #6. Ejido Reform Project. Center for U.S.-Mexican Studies. San Diego: University of California.

———. 1994b. Accommodation and Resistance: Ejidatario, Ejidataria, and Official Views of Ejido Reform. *Urban Anthropology* 23 (2–3): 233–265.

Stevens, E. P. 1994. Marianismo: The Other Face of Machismo. In Gertrude M. Yeager, ed. *Confronting Change, Challenging Tradition: Women in Latin American History.* Wilmington, DE: Scholarly Resources.

Strickon, A. 1968. Hacienda and Plantation in Yucatán. *America Indigena* 25:1: 35–61.

Thompson, J. Eric. 1970. *Maya History and Religion.* Norman: University of Oklahoma Press.

———. 1975 [1966]. *The Rise and Fall of Mayan Civilization.* Norman: University of Oklahoma Press.

Tylor, E. B. 1958 [1871]. *Primitive Culture.* New York: Harper Torchbooks.

Vogt, Evon. 1990. *The Zinacantecos of Mexico.* Fort Worth: Holt, Rinehart & Winston.

Wallerstein, I. 1974. *The Modern World System: Capitalist Agriculture and the Origins of the European World Economy in the Sixteenth Century.* New York: Academic Press.

Weber, Max. 1958. *The Protestant Ethic and the Spirit of Capitalism.* New York: Charles Scribner's Sons.

Willey, Gordon. 1996. *Essays in Maya Archeology.* Albuquerque: University of New Mexico.

Wolf, Eric. 1955. Types of Latin American Peasantry: A Preliminary Discussion. *American Anthropologist* 57: 452–471.

———. 1957. Closed Corporate Peasant Communities in Mesoamerica and Central Java. *Southwestern Journal of Anthropology* 13 (1): 1–18.

———. 1966. *Peasants.* Englewood Cliffs, NJ: Prentice-Hall.

Yoder, Michael. 1993. The Latin American Plantation Economy and the World Economy: The Case of the Yucatecan Henequen Industry. *Fernand Braudel Center for the Study of Economies, Historical Systems, and Civilizations* 16:3: 319–337.

Credits

All photographs taken by Cindy or LaVail Hull, or the Hull children.

All illustrations drawn by Valerie Hover.

Figure 1.1—Map reprinted from Philip DeVita, ed., *The Naked Anthropologist*, Wadsworth, 1992, p. 131.

Figure 4.1—Original map drawn by Juan Cervantes; adapted and updated by author and Valerie Hover.

Figure 9.1—Reprinted from John S. Henderson, *The World of the Ancient Maya*, Second Edition. Copyright © 1981 by Cornell University. Used by permission of the publisher, Cornell University Press.

In this textbook, I have used pseudonyms for the name of the town and villagers to protect their privacy.

Index

Agency, 22–23
Agriculture, 15, 16, 23–24, 59, 126, 129–130,
    131–132, 153. *See also Milpa*;
    Occupations
Ahijado, 6, 44, 64–65. *See also Compadrazgo*
Ah Macan Pech, 37
Alcohol use, 10, 32–33, 34, 45, 48, 49, 51,
    62–63, 78, 80–82, 84, 85, 101, 106, 145,
    159
  Adventists and, 45, 84, 110, 113–114, 119,
    123
  ritual use, 60, 98
  women and, 32, 49, 81, 84, 154
Alux(ob), 91–93
Animal husbandry. *See* Occupations
Annis, Sheldon, 112, 115
Anthropological research
  ambiguous role, 35, 119, 173, 174–177
  community studies, 13
  feminist anthropology, 147–148, 150–151
  focus of ethnography, 13–14
  longitudinal research, 8–9
  objective and subjective, 7–8
  "the Other" in anthropology, 35
  participant observation, 54–58, 62–65,
    120–122, 168–173
  on religion and symbolism, 88, 91, 169, 172
Ayuntamiento, 70, 101

Batab(ob), 16
Boas, Franz, 7
Bossen, Laurel, 151

Cárdenas, Lázaro, 17, 19, 67–68
Caste War. *See* Yucatán, political development
Catholicism, 12, 38, 40, 42, 44, 47, 49, 50,
    51, 52, 57–58, 64, 70, 87–106, 108–109,
    110–113, 119, 122–124, 148–149, 150,
    161, 164, 165. *See also* Religion; Family
    planning
  baptism, 46, 63–64, 144
  contrast with Adventists, 42, 46, 47, 50, 54,
    108–109, 110–113, 119, 122–124, 161
  local structure, 90
  and politics, 70, 73
  ritual, 44, 46, 47, 50
  roots in Mexico, 89, 148–149
  syncretism with Maya, 90–91, 95–99
  and women, 12, 90
Chac(ob). See Mayan religion, gods
Chachac, 28, 60, 91, 95–99, 107, 116, 169

  and Adventists, 99, 116
  syncretism with Catholic saints, 98
  and women, 97, 98–99
Checador. See Ejido, structure of
Cobratorio. See Occupations
Colonialism. *See* Yucatán, political
    development
Comadre. See Compadrazgo
Comistraje. See Chachac
Commuting, 20, 58, 126, 136–137, 138–139
Compadrazgo, 5, 6–7, 43, 44–45, 46, 48, 50,
    52, 54, 69–70, 72, 85, 91, 102, 110–111,
    112, 158, 164, 165
  becoming a *compadre,* 62–64, 158
  vertical, 45
Compadre. See Compadrazgo
Consejo de vigilancia. See Ejido, structure of
Construction. *See* Occupations
Cooperatives. *See* Occupations
Cordemex, 10, 18, 24, 26, 27, 28, 68, 115,
    127, 128, 129, 132, 137, 139, 143. *See
    also* Occupations
  description, 27
  and social class, 28, 68, 132, 139, 143
Cortés, Hernán, 15, 89
Crónica de Yaxbe, 37

Day of the Dead, 91(fn)
Debt peonage, 16, 17, 19
Decorticating plants, 10, 17, 18, 19, 27, 127
  description, 10, 17
Del suelo al cielo. See Seventh Day
    Adventists
Desarrollo Integral de la Familia (DIF). *See*
    Mexico, economic programs
Díaz, Porfirio, 18
Disch, Estelle, 165, 166
Disfibradoras. See Decorticating plants
Divorce. *See* Marriage and family
Dorcas. *See* Seventh Day Adventists
Double Day. *See* Women

Education and schools, 18, 24, 45, 46, 47,
    52–53, 56–59, 76–77, 102, 127
  and Adventists, 56, 58, 102, 109–110,
    117–118
  and occupation, 58–59, 117–118, 137–138,
    143, 179
Ehlers, Tracy, 150
Ejidatarios. See Ejido; Occupations

Ejido, 19, 20, 24, 25–27, 34–35, 38, 56, 59,
    115, 125–129, 133–134. *See also*
    Occupations
  definition, 19
  ejidatarios, 20, 25–26, 27, 35, 127,
      133–134, 152
    defined, 25
  structure of, 25–26
    checador, 25–26
    consejo de vigilancia, 25–26
    socio-delegado, 25–26, 27, 34–35, 69,
        72, 143
Empowerment, 164–165. *See also* Women
Encomienda (encomenderos), 16, 17, 37
Endogamy. *See* Marriage and family
Ethnicity. *See* Race and ethnicity
Exogamy. *See* Marriage and family

Factory labor. *See* Occupations
Family planning, 61, 64. *See also* Health and
    illness; Marriage and family
Fiesta for the Virgin of Candelaria, 7, 38, 42,
    54, 62, 70, 82–84, 90, 91, 99–106, 111,
    140. *See also Jarana*
  bullfight as part of *fiesta,* 54, 62, 105–106
Foster, George, 94
Fox, Vicente, 68, 75, 94
Frazer, Sir James, 88

Garrard-Burnett and Stoll, 109, 113
Globalization, 13–14, 22–23, 125, 143, 172
  and henequen, 16–20, 128–129
    and *maquiladoras,* 20, 136–137
    and tourism, 20
Godparenthood. *See Compadrazgo*
Gods. *See* Mayan religion, gods
Gremios, 62, 82, 90, 100, 101–102, 112
  definition, 90
  and social class, 101–102
Guadelupe, Virgin of, 40, 90, 150

Hacienda (Hacendado), 16–19, 23, 25, 27,
    28, 38, 42, 53, 127–128, 143. *See also*
    Occupations
  Yaxbe *haciendas,* 10, 11, 16–17, 23, 27, 28,
      38, 42, 127, 133
Halach Uinic(ob), 16, 89
Hammock weaving. *See* Occupations
Health and illness, 59–66, 152. *See also*
    Family planning; Syncretism
  midwives, 36, 46, 60
  nutrition and, 65–66
  traditional concepts of health and healing,
      59–61, 89, 95
  Western medicine, 61–66
  yerbateros (curers), 60
Henderson, John S., 43, 148
Henequen, 1, 2, 9, 16–19, 23–24, 28, 32, 59,
    74, 80, 115, 125–131, 134, 143, 146, 175
  decline, 9, 19–20, 125–129, 175

  life cycle, 24–25
  structure of. *See Ejido,* structure of
Henequeneros, 24, 125–128, 146. *See also*
    Occupations
Hetzmek, 41, 46
H-men(ob), 36, 59, 60–61, 91, 93, 95–99, 116,
    126, 162
Horchata, 101, 134, 153–156, 158–159, 166
Huay Pop (Uay Pop, Uay Cot), 92–93, 94
Hunt, M., 149–150

Illness and health. *See* Health and illness
Image of the limited good. *See* Limited good,
    image of
Itzamná. See Mayan religion, gods
Ix Chel. See Mayan religion, gods
Ix Kanleox. See Mayan religion, gods

Jarana, 41, 57, 70, 100, 102–103, 104, 106.
    See also Fiesta for the Virgin of Candelaria

Katun, 126, 167
Kinship, 43, 68–69, 72, 171. *See also*
    Marriage and family; Residence
  colonial, 43
  fictive kinship. *See Compadrazgo*
  naming, 43
  pre-conquest, 43
Kintz, Ellen, 43, 44
Kong, Antonio, 109

Landa, Fr. Diego, 1, 87, 148–150
Leveling mechanisms, 45, 102
Life cycle, 46–55
  adolescence, 47–49
    and *fiesta,* 103–104
    and gender roles, 48–49, 160–161
  birth, 46
  death, 52
    funerals, 54–55
  early childhood, 46
  marriage. *See* Marriage and family
  old age, 52
Limited good, image of, 94
Littlefield, Alice, 33

Machismo and *marianismo,* 64, 105, 150–151,
    165–166
  defined, 150
Madrina. See Compadrazgo
Maquila (maquiladora). See Occupations,
    factory
Marianismo. See Machismo and *marianismo*
Marriage and family, 43–52, 68–69, 110–111,
    157–161, 175. *See also* Family planning;
    Kinship; Life cycle; Residence
  abuse in, 51, 81
  colonial patterns, 43, 150–151
  divorce, 51, 70, 92, 138, 139, 162, 180
  endogamy, 51, 85

exogamy, 43
nuclear family, 11, 43, 143, 171
pre-conquest patterns, 43, 148–150
    bride service, 43
role of women in, 51, 157–158, 160
types of marriage, 50
weddings and social class, 45, 143–146
Maya
archaeological sites, 1
gods. *See* Mayan religion, gods
language. *See* Yaxbe
location, 3, 14–15
pre-conquest chronology, 15–16
women. *See* Women
Yucatec Maya, 1–2
    contrast with highland Maya, 14, 100
Mayan religion, 37, 89, 90–99, 148–149
cosmology, 89, 126, 148
gods, 28, 36, 89, 95, 98, 148
syncretism with Catholicism, 87–88, 90–99
women and, 114, 120–122, 148–150
Merchants. *See* Occupations
Mérida, 1, 4, 10, 16, 17, 18, 27, 30, 45, 58,
    63, 70, 83, 85, 109, 116, 126, 128, 134,
    136, 138, 141, 143, 149, 154, 162, 164,
    174, 175
Mexican Revolution. *See* Yucatán, political
    development
Mexico, economic programs, 67, 70, 74,
    77–78, 85, 119, 151, 152–157, 158, 159,
    162–163, 164
Mexico, political parties, 67–68, 75, 78–79,
    85, 94, 152, 156, 163
Migration, 9, 100, 117–118, 129, 138,
    139–142, 149
endogamy and, 51
types of, 140–142
Milpa, 1, 23, 24, 27–28, 46, 169
cycle, 27–28
milpa/anti-milpa forces, 112–113
milperos. See Occupations
Montejo, Francisco de, 15, 89, 149
Morgan, Lewis Henry, 87

North American Free Trade Agreement
    (NAFTA). *See* Yucatán, political
    development

Occupations, statistics, 23, 127, 132,
    178–180. *See also* Cordemex;
    Decorticating plants; *Ejido*; Henequen;
    Parcelas; Women
agriculture/*milpa,* 24, 28, 29, 129–131,
    146, 153, 169
animal husbandry, 12, 28, 40, 115, 126,
    127, 130, 134, 149, 152–153
cobratorio, 116, 134–135
construction, 28–29, 132
cooperatives, men, 115, 134–135, 136
cooperatives, women, 74, 76, 119,
    131–132, 134, 151–159, 162, 166

education and, 56–59, 117–118
factory work (*maquiladoras*), 10, 20, 27,
    115, 127, 128, 136–137, 160
    women in, 136–137, 160, 166
hammock weaving, 10–12, 24, 33, 46, 132,
    133
henequen related
    decorticating factories as occupation, 10,
        16–19, 24, 26, 27, 68, 115,
        127–128, 129, 132, 162
    ejidatarios/henequeneros, 5, 16–19,
        23–24, 25, 26, 115, 125–127, 128,
        134
    trucking *sindicato,* 24, 27, 128
merchants (store, restaurant owners),
    30–33, 68, 73–75, 85, 92–94, 132
parcelarios, 25, 26–27, 85, 129, 132, 134
professionals, 58–59, 76–77, 117, 126,
    137–138, 143–145
religion and, 111–113, 117
tailoring/seamstresses, 10, 29–30, 57, 113,
    115, 132, 134, 162
taxi service, 126, 132, 136, 139
transport, 73–74, 117, 128, 132, 142
women and. *See* Women
Ortner, Sherry, 22

Padres de Familias, Sociedad de (Parents'
    Groups), 52–53, 75, 77, 80
Padrino. See Compadrazgo
Parcela, 24, 25, 26, 31, 129, 132, 134
Parcelarios. See Occupations
Partido del Acción Nacional (PAN). *See*
    Mexico, political parties
Partido de la Revolución Democrática (PRD).
    See Mexico, political parties
Partido Revolucionario Institutal (PRI). *See*
    Mexico, political parties
Pentecostals, 42, 109, 113, 117, 118, 119.
    See also Religion
Popul Vuh, 169
Post-marital residence. *See* Residence
Privatization. *See* Yucatán, political
    development
PROCEDE. *See* Yucatán, political
    development
*Programa del Alimentacíon Complementaria
    Rural* (PACR). *See* Mexico, economic
    programs
PRONASOL. *See* Mexico, economic
    programs
Protestant ethic. *See* Seventh Day Adventists

Quinceñera, 29, 45, 47–48, 83

Race and ethnicity, 10, 23, 41–42, 43, 86,
    100, 148, 150
re Cruz, Alicia, 93
Redfield, Robert, 60, 93–94
Religion, 12, 23, 42, 44–45, 46, 47–48,
    59–61, 62–64, 85–106, 108–124, 134,

147–148, 150–151. *See* Catholicism;
    Seventh Day Adventists; Pentecostals;
    Syncretism
  polytheism and monotheism, 60, 88–89,
    147, 148
Residence. *See also* Kinship; Marriage
  matrilocal, 81
  neolocal, 81, 171
  patrilocal, 43, 51
Restell, M., 149–150
Roys, Ralph, 14, 15, 16, 148

Salínas de Gortari, Carlos, 19–20, 68
Schools. *See* Education
Seventh Day Adventists (SDA), 7, 42, 45, 46,
    47, 54–55, 56, 58, 70, 73, 84, 90, 99,
    102, 106, 108–124. *See also* Religion
  Chachac (comistraje) and, 99
  contrast with Catholicism, 45, 46, 47, 90,
    109, 110–113, 119, 122–124
  conversion, 84, 108, 113–114, 134
  del suelo al cielo, 112, 115
  Dorcas and, 120–122
  education and SDA schools, 56, 58,
    117–118, 161
  fiesta and, 102, 106
  history in Yaxbe, 109
  milpa and *anti-milpa* forces, 112
  occupation and, 115–118, 133–136, 138,
    159
  politics and, 70, 162
  Protestant ethic and, 111–113, 115, 117
  rules and dogma, 110–113
  structure of, 109–110
  women and, 114, 162, 164
Sindicato (trucking). *See* Occupations
Social class, 23, 27, 41, 42–43, 68, 72, 73–75,
    85, 137–138, 142–146, 150–151, 172
  gremios and, 101–102
Social control, 84–85, 91–95
  spirits and, 91–95
Sociedad de Padres de Familias (Parents'
    groups). *See Padres de Familias*
Socio delegado. See Ejido, structure of
Solidaridad. See Mexico, economic programs
Stevens, Evelyn, 150–151
Swidden, 14
Syncretism
  definition, 90–91
  health and, 59–61
  religion and, 46, 87, 90–91, 95–106

Tylor, E. B., 88

UAIM. *See* Mexico, economic programs
Uay Pop (Uay Cot). See Huay Pop

Voluntary associations, 52–53.
  See also Dorcas; *Padres de Familias*

Weber, Max, 111–112
Women, 147–167, 178–180
  ancient Maya gender roles, 148–149
  empowerment and, 164–165
  gender roles, 46–50, 148–150, 171–172
  income production, 178–180
    commuting and, 139
    cooperatives, 152–157, 159, 162–163
    Double Day and, 151–152, 171
    economic costs and benefits of
      production, 159–164
    factory work and, 28–29, 136–137
    in the home, 10–11, 28, 29, 33, 132–133,
      178, 180
    obstacles to production, 157–159
    outside the home, 10–11, 30–33, 126,
      133, 136–138, 139, 178–180
    tortillas and, 168–173
  machismo/marianismo, 64, 150–151,
    165–166
  marriage and divorce. *See* Marriage and
    family
  politics and, 70, 73, 77–78, 162–165
  professional women, 137–138, 178–180
Women's Agro-Industrial Unit (UAIM). *See*
  Mexico, economic programs
World Systems Theory, 14, 22–23, 125

Xtabai, 92–94

Yaxbe
  description, 2–7, 38–43
  history, 13–21, 37
  location, 14
  the people
    language, 5, 41–42, 133
    race and ethnicity, 10, 41. *See also* Race
      and ethnicity
    surname, 10, 42
  population, 23, 38
Yerbateros (curers). *See* Health and illness
Yucatán, location, 1, 3
Yucatán, political development (chronology)
  colonialism, 2, 13–14, 16, 37–38, 57, 85,
    87
    compadrazgo and, 44–45
    family and, 43, 149–151
    religion and, 87–88, 89–90, 148–149
  independence, 16–18, 58
    Caste War, 17
    United States and, 18
  Mexican Revolution, effects on, 5, 18–19,
    25, 27, 67–68
  post-revolutionary reforms, 19, 27. *See also*
    Cárdenas
  reforms of 1992, 19–20
    North American Free Trade Agreement
      (NAFTA), 20, 128
    PROCEDE, 20, 136

Chicago

A guide to recent architecture

Chicago

● ● ● ellipsis
KÖNEMANN

Susanna Sirefman

A guide to recent architecture

Susanna Sirefman 1994

•••

CREATED, EDITED AND DESIGNED BY
Ellipsis London Limited
55 Charlotte Road London EC2A 3QT
E MAIL ...@ellipsis.co.uk
www.http://www.ellipsis.co.uk/ellipsis
PUBLISHED IN THE UK AND AFRICA BY
Ellipsis London Limited
SERIES EDITOR Tom Neville
SERIES DESIGN Jonathan Moberly
LAYOUT Pauline Harrison

COPYRIGHT © 1996 Könemann
Verlagsgesellschaft mbH
Bonner Str. 126, D-50968 Köln
PRODUCTION MANAGER Detlev Schaper
PRINTING AND BINDING Sing Cheong
Printing Ltd
Printed in Hong Kong

ISBN 3 89508 284 8 (Könemann)
ISBN 1 874056 81 1 (Ellipsis)

Chicago: a guide to recent architecture

Contents

Introduction 6
O'Hare International Airport 13
Lakeview and Uptown Ravenswood 27
Lincoln Park 35
Gold Coast and Old Town 53
River North 73
Near North and Streeterville 87
North Michigan Avenue 101
East Loop 127
West Loop 165
Near West Side and South Loop 213
Plisen 231
Near South Side and Bridgeport 239
Hyde Park 249
Suburbs South-West 255
Suburbs North 271
Gurnee and Zion 295
Index 303

Introduction

This book covers exactly 100 schemes, all designed and built within the last decade. While it is not meant to be a comprehensive guide, I hope the work I have chosen cumulatively represents the current trends of architecture in Chicago and is a diverse representation of both well-established firms and the new, fresh, up-and-coming design stars.

Beginning chronologically with 333 West Wacker Drive and The Associates Center, both significant projects from 1983 and ending with the Cesar Chavez Elementary School opened in autumn 1993, I have attempted to include a cross section of the diverse commercial, residential, industrial and public projects, both large and small, throughout the city and its suburbs. It is worth noting that the two earliest schemes are downtown office towers and the most recently completed project I have included is a public education facility in one of the less affluent areas of town. The crazy 1980s' boom of speculative commercial skyscrapers has definitely come to a screeching halt and is being replaced with an emphasis on civil work. It is very encouraging that the largest public project of the decade is the Harold Washington Library. Whether you care for the building or not, it is undeniably of huge social significance. Its location should go some way to reverse the dire recreational decline of the Loop area, where there is now a conspicuous shortage of restaurants, cinemas or entertainment activities, particularly at night-time.

The other recent federally funded building, the Thompson Center, is significant for the difference in its appearance, not so important for its aesthetic value but for the very fact that it was allowed to be built. It is depressing to witness the obvious difference in financial resources between a federal project such as the Thompson Center and the super lush, marble and granite extravaganzas along Wacker Drive. Contemporary and experimental architecture must be encouraged and supported and given the funding it deserves. Ideas must be given a chance. I believe the current somewhat reactionary vogue for historicism or contextual buildings must be tempered with a bit of daring and outrageousness. Fitting into the existing typology is of the utmost importance but has unfortunately been the cause of too many bland, nondescript structures. This is why it is so pleasing to happen upon projects such as Bertrand Goldberg's River City or Hartshorne Plunkard's Peter Elliott Productions Studios. Their very merit is in attempting something new and different, almost regardless of their success or failure.

North Michigan Avenue, one of America's poshest strip malls, also tells a fascinating story about the state of architecture (and economics) in the 1990s. The large and formidable complexes – 900 North Michigan Avenue, City Place and Chicago Place – are next door to the diminutive but fun Banana Republic, Crate & Barrel and the nondescript Escada Plaza. It would be refreshing but unrealistic to think that smaller, free-standing shops will replace the monstrous vertical malls being erected like mad just a couple of years ago.

The middle belt of residential properties ringing the downtown centre, most notable architecturally on the North Side of Chicago (Lincoln Park, Gold Coast and Old Town), is also of great interest as Chicagoans clearly have an affinity for living in houses. Most of the city is surprisingly flat, allowing for the family home to flourish along quiet residential streets. Accurately known as a city of neighbourhoods, sadly this clear division and delineation emphasises Chicago's extraordinary and unfortunate segregation. It was no surprise that there were no new architectural delights in the South Side residential areas. I hope the move towards less commercially motivated projects will spur some decent low-income public housing plans in the 1990s.

The decentralisation of downtown Chicago is in part a direct result of an enormous demographic shift over the last 20 odd years, the city oozing and seeping outwards and into the suburbs. For this reason I have included eighteen schemes located in the north and south-west Greater Chicago areas. As in most North American cities, the 'burbs are currently one of the most important growth and expansion areas of Chicago, as the trend of large corporations moving their offices out of downtown requires not only the creation of industrial parks (or the first skyscraper in Chicago's suburbia – Oakbrook Terrace Tower) but also infrastructure and housing for employees. Post-urban Chicago is continuously generating outwards, slowly urbanising an ever-increasing ring around its epicentre.

Aside from being America's best-known city of architecture, Chicago's spectacular geographical setting lends it a unique air of elegance. Considered world-wide the 'Home of the Skyscraper' (as a result of rebuilding after the Great Fire of 1871), the Chicago River and the lake surrounding the entire eastern half of the city (beaches and all!) creates a tranquil backdrop for this all-American city. The skyline is a spectacular mixture of industrial warehouses and factories; Beaux-Arts buildings, linear Mies juxtaposed with the many new and astounding forms the most contemporary buildings have taken on.

Standing on the top of the Sears Tower or the John Hancock Tower and surveying the rooftops is a wonderful way to enjoy the diversity of Chicago's buildings. The public transport system, in particular the 'L', is another good way to get an overview of Chicago. Snaking past many of the new buildings that I mention is as exciting as the boat ride down the river, another must do for all enthusiasts of contemporary architecture.

Acknowledgements

Thank you:
to all the architects I met with or spoke to for their time and the materials they so enthusiatically supplied; to all the photographers who so kindly contributed their work; to the Marketing Department at the Chicago Transit Authority for their advice on public transport; to my great friends in Chicago, Edward Moore and the Exley family; but most of all to Carol and Josef Sirefman for their tireless support, generosity and encouragement.

SS 1994

Using this book

The city has been divided into sixteen geographical sections, starting at the O'Hare International Airport and running roughly north to south before covering the suburbs. Bus and rapid transport train (RTT) routes from downtown are listed under each entry, and road directions for buildings outside the city's rapid transport system. I have given the station listing closest to each destination.

A useful number to have for emergency details is the CTA Travel Information Center. They will provide directions, schedules and fare information for the CTA bus, rapid transit system, Pace suburban buses and Metra trains. Open 05.00--01.00 daily, including holidays, their telephone number is 312 836 7000.

The CTA System Transit Map (constantly being updated) is available at the major transit stations, O'Hare Airport, all major hotels downtown and Visitor Information Centers. Passes and tokens are sold at banks and currency locations.

Chicago is also a wonderful city for walking, provided the weather is fair enough. If you are unfamiliar with the city do ask advice on where not to wander into, particularly on the South Side.

If you would like more architectural information, The Chicago Architecture Foundation (CAF), has a shop, gallery and tour center which offers over 50 walking, bicycle, boat and bus tours. They are located at 224 South Michigan Avenue at East Jackson Boulevard.

15, 16

1

1 O'Hare International Airport
2 Lakeview and Uptown Ravenswood
3 Lincoln Park
4 Gold Coast and Old Town
5 River North
6 Near North and Streeterville
7 North Michigan Avenue
8 East Loop
9 West Loop
10 Near West Side and South Loop
11 Pilsen
12 Near North Side and Bridgeport
13 Hyde Park
14 Suburbs South-West
15 Suburbs North
16 Gurnee and Zion

2

3

4

5

7 6

9 8

10

11

12

13

14

O'Hare International Airport

United Airlines Terminal One Complex **14**
O'Hare Rapid Transit Station **20**
International Terminal **22**

United Airlines Terminal One Complex

O'Hare International Airport opened in 1963 and is currently the nation's busiest with over 72 million passengers passing through in just one year. In 1982 Chicago's Department of Aviation initiated the $2 billion development plan due for completion in 1995. This master plan for rejuvenation and expansion was drawn up by a team composed of Murphy/ Jahn, Environdyne Engineers, Inc., and Schal Associates. The strategy called for two new terminals, additional roadways, a new rapid transit station, services and a 240 acre cargo area. Murphy/Jahn, whose firm has had a historical link to the airport (throughout the airport's development the various stages of design and construction have been headed by the same architectural firm in its several incarnations: Naess & Murphy, C F Murphy & Associates and now Murphy/Jahn led by Helmut Jahn), designed the United Terminal and the peripheral transportation station linked to the new terminal.

Located on the same site as the former International Terminal, the new plan is designed to serve 70,000 travellers a day. Constrained by previously set rules – 747 wide-body jet size, taxiing patterns, site lines from the control tower and the already set length of the two pre-existing parallel concourses – Helmut Jahn has created a superb, calm, easy-to-negotiate terminal.

The structurally expressive terminal is entered under an industrial square-cornered stainless steel canopy that extends its entire length. Passengers leave the access roadway at the curb and enter a transitional vestibule leading to the light-filled Ticketing Pavilion. This grand open space was inspired by the magnificent waiting rooms of Victorian railroad sheds, exhibition halls and arcades with visible iron and glass skeletons. Treated as an island, the 1.2 million square foot terminal is focused around the two long, rectangular concourses, B and C, that run parallel

Murphy/Jahn 1982–1988

O'Hare International Airport

Murphy/Jahn 1982–1988

to the pavilion. The vast column-free Ticketing Pavilion is only an ante-room, albeit huge and capacious, leading to these terminal centres. The lower level below the ticketing area is the baggage claim. The free-span of 120 feet created by the folded truss system roof frame allows total flexibility for the 56 flow-through ticketing/baggage check counters in the pavilion. According to the architects 100 per cent of the lighting requirements during the day are met naturally. This is achieved by 5-foot-wide linear skylights placed at the peaks of the folded truss roof. Gull-wing baffles suspended underneath the skylights filter direct sunlight and house flourescent lamps and a relatively new type of low-wattage compact metal halide lamps for night illumination.

The monumental concourses are vaulted corridors constructed using a system of aluminium sandwich panels (which incorporate an acoustical inner surface) and glass units secured to the steel purlin substructure. The glazed units, varying between clear insulated, tinted insulated and clear-fritted glass, were arranged according to the most beneficial natural light and solar gain configurations. A ceramic frit pattern was fired directly to the inside surface of the inner lights in the system to allow transparency while reducing solar penetration and also effectively creating a reflective interior surface for indirect lighting at night. This innovative use of fritted glass in such quantity is a first in America.

The beautifully detailed structure of the vaults is accentuated by curved rolled steel beams placed at 30-foot intervals. Painted white and punched with circular holes to achieve lightness and transparency, the beams are supported on clusters of bundled columns (steel pipes in groups of one to five tubes depending on the load each column supports). These continue the length of each concourse, both of which terminate in semi-domed spaces. The effective sequence of spatial events culminates in the

O'Hare International Airport

Murphy/Jahn 1982–1988

concourse connection; the most wonderful 52-foot-wide and 815-foot-long pedestrian tunnel. Evocative of a New Age *Logan's Run* movie set, this novel corridor is entertaining and relaxing. The 800 foot, below-grade link, reached by an escalator, has a moving walkway surrounded by futuristic magical lighting, art and music. Undulating translucent glass walls and ceiling are backlit with a delightful range of colours. Stylistic steel 'trees' support the curvy, glowing membrane walls and ceiling plane. Above the four parallel moving sidewalks is a constantly changing light sculpture created by Michael Hayden. The neon light tubes hanging from a mirrored surface are controlled by a computer that generates patterns of light pulses that are never repeated. These changing colours, coordinated with the colours of the walls, are synchronised with atonal synthesised music composed by William Kraft and amended by Gary Fry. Great fun, this corridor brings a smile to even the most jaded passenger.

O'Hare International Airport

ASSOCIATE ARCHITECTS A Epstein & Sons
STRUCTURAL ENGINEERS Lev Zetlin Associates and A Epstein & Sons
RTT Blue Line
ACCESS public areas open

Murphy/Jahn 1982—1988

Murphy/Jahn 1982—1988

O'Hare Rapid Transit Station

Very much a gateway, this station is the primary public transport link between downtown Chicago and O'Hare Airport.

Allowing two column-free platforms, a system of large post-tensioned concrete girders constructed around the parking garage columns are set in an open-cut excavation. This configuration resulted in sloping berms running the length of the station. These earth mounds were concrete sprayed and concealed behind undulating glass block walls. Ribbed glass blocks alternate with translucent bricks behind which the berm has been painted in a progression of colours. The changing pattern of blocks, from transparency to opacity and back, is reinforced by the intensity of pastel colour. The combination of the 30-foot curving wall, gradated, incandescent colour and backlit glass blocks creates a warm, kinetic ambience. The rippling walls also reduce the noise level from the trains. The vocabulary of materials throughout the station – stainless steel benchs, handrails, platform carrels and the black rubberised flooring – revolve around the underground train theme and heavy usage requirements.

The long, curving concourse has been treated as a transitional space and is in muted tones of grey, black and white. Horizontal bands of glazed brick reverse in colour at the terminal entrances and symbolic gateways are marked by bright red columns supporting a tiled glazed brick entablature that are derivative of classical patterns.

ASSOCIATE ARCHITECT Murphy/Jahn
STRUCTURAL ENGINEERS Alfred Benesch & Co.
SIZE 105,000 square feet (9750 square metres)
CLIENT City of Chicago, Department of Public Works
RTT Blue Line
ACCESS public

O'Hare International Airport

City of Chicago, Dept of Public Works, Bureau of Architecture 1984

City of Chicago, Dept of Public Works, Bureau of Architecture 1984

International Terminal

The final large piece of the $2 billion O'Hare redevelopment scheme, the International Terminal accommodates foreign-flag departures and all international arrivals. It houses a ticketing pavilion, twenty-one gates, concessions, support facilities, a transit station and Federal Inspection Services. The terminal is organised around three primary levels: the upper contains the departure hall, the lower level is the 'meeters and greeters' area and the middle, intermediate level is for baggage processing. Administration occupies a fourth mezzanine level. The 100-acre triangular site determined the boundaries of the design as it is bordered by taxiways, runways, and the entrance roadway. Set at some distance from the other terminals and parking facilities at O'Hare, there is a delightful above-ground light rail transit system that follows a dramatic curvy track and provides a spectacular approach to the new terminal.

A soaring vertical arch, the terminal is beautiful and streamlined. As at the United Terminal, the inspiration was early 19th-century railway stations although here it has been given a completely different twist. An 800-foot-long ticketing pavilion has a gently arched roof that curves up from 14 to 50 feet. The departure hall benefits the most from the exposed structural steel system, enclosed by expansive glazed sidewalls. From this hall, passengers enter the galleria which is directly under the curving roof, functioning as a guide towards the airline departure gates.

The major materials – glass curtain wall and skylights, fluted metal and metal panel siding, painted concrete block, plastic laminate and precast terrazo tile – all speak an industrial language appropriate and familiar from airport structures such as hangars and warehouses.

Security has put a fair amount of restraint on circulation within the terminal and unfortunately movement through the building is not as streamlined as the overall structure. Surprisingly small, the dimensions

Perkins & Will 1993

Perkins & Will 1993

of such a new and ambitious facility seem extremely restricted and there is talk of further expansion. Perhaps more energy should have gone into the initial masterplanning phase to produce an overall scheme capable of properly accommodating future growth.

ASSOCIATE ARCHITECTS Heard & Associates, Consoer Townsend & Associates
STRUCTURAL ENGINEERS Wells Engineering
CLIENT City of Chicago Department of Aviation
COST $618 million
SIZE 1,145,000 square feet (106,000 square metres)
RTT Blue Line
ACCESS to public areas

Perkins & Will 1993

O'Hare International Airport

Perkins & Will 1993

Lakeview and Uptown Ravenswood

Chicago City Day School Addition   **28**

Chicago Public Library, Conrad Sulzer Regional Branch   **30**

Chicago City Day School Addition

This very smart addition to a private elementary school houses a gym, auditorium, labs and a dining room. Set against the back of the triangular site, this stylish extension blends well into its posh residential surroundings. The existing three-storey classroom building dates from the 1960s.

The new exterior is of limestone, in stark contrast to the old building's dark brick. The architects were clearly inspired by Eero and Eliel Saarinenn's Crow Island School. An assymetric clock tower sheathed in stainless steel adds a vertical element to the façade. Windows at a child's scale and a low protective entrance canopy rhythmically energise the limestone façade.

ADDRESS 541 West Hawthorne Place
STRUCTURAL ENGINEERS Robert L Miller Associates
COST $2.64 million
SIZE 22,800 square feet (2100 square metres)
RTT Belmont on Red Line, Brown Line, Purple Line Express
BUS 8, 36, 77, 135, 145, 146, 152, 156
ACCESS none

Weese Langley Weese 1990

Weese Langley Weese 1990

Chicago Public Library, Conrad Sulzer Regional Branch

The firm of Hammond, Beeby and Babka has quite a track record in building libraries, having designed them throughout suburban Illinois in Champaign, Skokie, Tinley Park, Northbrook and Oak Park as well as for the Kansas State University in Manhattan, Kansas. Best-known is the Harold Washington Library, smack in the middle of the Loop.

One of the highest circulation branches in Chicago's regional library system, the Conrad Sulzer holds 250,000 books. The design was five years off the drawing board before it was actually constructed because of bureaucratic red tape.

The triangular site, bounded by the diagonally bisecting Lincoln Avenue and east–west Sunnyside Avenue, is directly opposite a city park. The building is intended to be a link between commercial Lincoln Avenue and the ethnically rich residential surrounding neighbourhood. Treated as an object, the building is a long rectangle with a semicircular front. The façade on Lincoln Avenue comes to the pavement edge and continues the height level of the existing stores and shops. The back of the building, which contains the non-public services, has less assertive massing.

Head designer Thomas Beeby describes the library as 'hybrid Mies and Schinckel'. The nod to German neo-Classicism was an acknowledgement of the ethnic flavour of Ravenswood. The heavy façade is evocative of traditional civic institutions. The thick brick walls give the impression of substance as well as housing mechanical systems. There is very little interior visibility from the street and, for security reasons, the steel-outlined setback windows are barred and locked.

The interior is filled with natural light and is as friendly as the exterior is imposing. The entrance lobby, a beautiful elliptical rotunda two storeys

Hammond, Beeby & Babka

Lakeview and Uptown Ravenswood

Joseph Casserly/Chicago City Architect 1985

above a terrazzo floor, provides access to the auditorium and a public meeting room. These spaces can be used when the rest of the library is shut, creating an important neighbourhood gathering place.

As you walk up the stairs to the second level there is a marvellously powerful view of eight 20-foot columns parading down the centre of the room. These fabulous giant black pillars are also exposed function – they are the air-circulation system. A large fun clock hangs in the middle of the space over a circular computer station.

Another enjoyable element of this public facility is the furniture. Architect Tannys Langdon has created charming folk chairs that celebrate the Teutonic theme. Dotted throughout the library, they tell mythical tales based on German fables and mythology. In the children's section, child-sized chairs and a special combination chair-table are constructed of plywood and surface paint.

The local community was closely involved in the development and decoration of the library. In fact, a fresco by Irene Siegal entitled 'Aenead' had to be removed from the meeting room as the text the artist had painted into the mural was interpreted by the neighbourhood as graffiti. There was general outrage that public money was paying for what the neighbourhood perceived as illegal and disrespectful!

ADDRESS 4455 North Lincoln Avenue
CLIENT Conrad Sulzer Regional Library
COST $7.6 million
SIZE 62,700 square feet (5800 square metres)
RTT Western on Brown Line
BUS 11, 49, 49B, 78
ACCESS public

Hammond, Beeby & Babka

Lakeview and Uptown Ravenswood

Lakeview and Uptown Ravenswood

Joseph Casserly/Chicago City Architect 1985

Lincoln Park

BMT Offices 36

Florian Twoflat 38

Mohawk Street House 42

Scoozi! 44

Cairo 46

Luminaire 48

Embassy Club 50

BMT Offices

This uppermost floor of a 1910 industrial warehouse has been renovated for a small toy-design company. Fragmented drywall planes, unexpected angles and colourful cubic partitions in primary colours – red, blue and yellow – create a complex anti-orthogonal plan. A yellow wedge is visible on the exterior rear façade bursting out of the thick red brick wall signalling the office's existence to the passing world.

Security and the fear of industrial espionage caused the public areas and the design laboratory space to be separated. Included in the programme is a toy demonstration stage for the unveiling of new playthings. After journeying through a succession of doors in the common rooms there is an open-plan design studio with the confidential toy-making workshop. The whole loft is then connected by an overhead miniature train keeping to the toy theme permeating the 30-person office.

ADDRESS 750 North Orleans
CLIENT Rouben Terzian and BMT Design
SIZE 4800 square feet (445 square metres)
RTT Chicago on Brown Line, Purple Line Express
BUS 37, 41, 66
ACCESS none

Lincoln Park

Pappageorge Haymes 1988

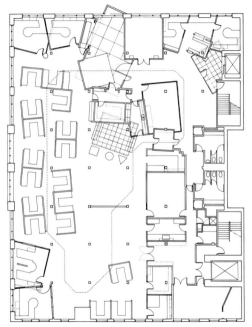

Pappageorge Haymes 1988

Lincoln Park

Florian Twoflat

The striking cream and grey street elevation of this two-storey wooden-frame house is descriptive of the building's structural history and reflects the designers' preoccupations. A juxtaposition of two urban building types, attention is called to the twenty odd years between the construction of the top and bottom of the house. The downstairs is a straightforward post-and-beam rowhouse while the top, added on later, is a typical balloon-frame Chicago bungalow.

The lower half of the façade has three perfectly proportioned window columns placed within a raised rectilinear grid. This topographical geometry is repeated in the horizontal ornament of the front garden enclosure. Representative of urban order, these silhouettes of classical configuration are playful gestures suggesting formality. The simple top half, a vernacular bungalow perched on the stripped classical base, is punctuated by irregular fenestration. One square window is unexpectedly placed directly on top of the cornice line and the other is just a narrow hint of an opening. In the centre is a vertical pillar of windows and a miniature balcony with a charming linear balustrade that links the two halves.

The upper apartment's interior, reached by a staircase to the second floor, is a colourful combination of Russian Constructivist, Deconstructivist and De Stijl influences. Various planes have been pulled, shifted and reoriented, giving this small 750-square-foot studio apartment an open and spacious air.

The layout is one long rectangle centred around a free-standing cube. A skewed red triangular slab slices through the top of the white floating kitchen wall, and connects all the elements of the space. Extending diagonally through the apartment, this level plane, which is the structural support for the sleeping loft, juts into the shower room and transforms into the kitchen ceiling. This element connects all the functionally sepa-

Florian-Wierzbowski 1986

Lincoln Park

Florian-Wierzbowski 1986

rate areas of the apartment.

An arcade of repeating green doors lengthens the perspective of the white entry wall. Windows have been placed quite high for privacy as the lot is enclosed by buildings on either side. There is a wonderfully subtle match between the green wall and the next-door roof slats that is visible out of these raised windows, and changes with the daily travel of the sun. All the carefully chosen colours throughout the project – greens, brilliant yellow, an orange pink and blue – highlight specific forms and therefore call attention to their interaction. An example of this is the yellow kitchen shelf that penetrates into the living room, creating a fabulous composition of linear colour and form.

A condition that is repeated at all scales, the floor of the apartment extends as a deck, hanging over the backyard, and is treated as a breakfast nook. This cantilevered treehouse deck is shaded by a pear-tree. Form, function and process have clearly been intellectually explored and most delightfully expressed.

Lincoln Park

ADDRESS 1816 North Cleveland Street
CLIENT Paul Florian
SIZE 750 square feet (70 square metres)
RTT Sedgwick on Brown Line (B stop)
BUS 11, 37, 72, 73
ACCESS none

Florian-Wierzbowski 1986

Florian-Wierzbowski 1986

Mohawk Street House

Rigorous symmetry, inside and out, characterises this contemporary three-storey city house. Adjacent to an empty lot and surrounded by older weathered threeflats, this private home is located in a slightly rundown residential neighbourhood. The simple vertically oriented exterior of brick and concrete has an unexpected cupola on top. The apparently narrow façade, with a recessed entranceway, actually hides a surprisingly spacious interior. This illusion is intentional and Frederick Phillips plays with this theme throughout the project.

Each floor is 900 square feet, a studio flat occupying most of the first floor. The remaining two levels are each divided into three. The second floor revolves around a central dining space, separated from the kitchen and living room by frames with doors that can slide out if desired. The lack of solid enclosure between areas produces a feeling of space and openness. A skylight at the top centre of the house not only lets sunlight in (there are no side windows) but becomes an organising element for the three bedrooms on the upper storey. Curved walls caused by the insertion of a spiral staircase leading to the cupola add character to these bedrooms.

The interior is finished in subtle shades of white and cream. Natural light makes lovely shadows throughout. Everything seems to be perfectly placed, fitting together just so, like a super-neat sock drawer.

ADDRESS 1518 North Mohawk Street
STRUCTURAL ENGINEERS Beer Gorski & Graff
CLIENT Frederick and Gay Phillips
SIZE 2700 square feet (250 square metres)
RTT Sedgwick on Brown Line (B stop)
BUS 37, 72
ACCESS none

Lincoln Park

Frederick F Phillips & Associates 1989

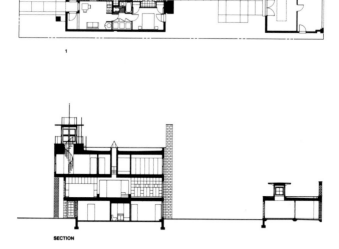

1

SECTION

Frederick F Phillips & Associates 1989

Scoozi!

Jordan Mozer and Rich Melman, president of Lettuce Entertain You Enterprises, have transformed a former auto-repair garage into a spacious warehouse restaurant, easily identifiable by the huge 652 pound fibreglass tomato hanging on the façade. A pleasantly crowded dark wood bar is theatrically set against the front wall as the focal point of the three-tiered 320-seat dining area. There are excellent people-watching views from most vantage points. The bright and cheery kitchen is at the back of the large, open space. The ambience is very New York vogue.

Distressed walls, mosaic floor, Renaissance-style moulding combined with antique fixtures lend a fashionable pseudo-historical feel. The discoloured, cracking walls look as though they have met with a great deal of aggression. The tormented result was achieved by overplastering, over-heating, and then smashing at the plaster with sledge hammers.

Mozer kept the existing ceiling trusses, allowing the 100-foot clear span, and used these wooden planks to hang industrial chandeliers, an odd addition, particularly the rectangular Art Deco fixtures, as they diminish the well-worn, traditional image, as do the Italian magazines haphazardly wallpapered onto the low space dividers.

ADDRESS 410 West Huron Street
CLIENT Lettuce Entertain You Enterprises, Inc.
COLLABORATORS Aumiller Youngquist p.c.
COST $1.9 million
SIZE 13,000 square feet (1200 square metres)
RTT Chicago/Franklin on Brown Line, Purple Line
BUS 37, 41, 66
ACCESS lunch Monday through Friday and dinner seven nights

Lincoln Park

Jordan Mozer & Associates, Limited 1987

Jordan Mozer & Associates, Limited 1987

Cairo

Another trendy Mozer-designed nightspot, the theme for this jazz club is Egypt. Legend has it that Mozer was struck by the loaded symbolism and fantasy of the client's girlfriend's goldleaf earrings. Mozer then spent over a year steeped in Egyptology. From the naming of this two-level establishment through to the downstairs dance floor with private catacombs, the sarcophagus-like entry and the generous distribution of lapis lazuli inlay, the Egyptian notion has inspired the plan, materials and details. Lacquered wood, oxidised copper and the expected decaying walls add that archaeological touch. Even the maple zigzag bar takes the form of the hieroglyph for water.

As in all his imaginative and inventive spaces, Mozer adds novel contemporary touches. At Cairo the piano is hiding in a wonderful curving free-standing partition and the light fixtures are Art Deco. The furniture – in particular the Cairo chair, a pudgy upholstered seat on a steel frame held together by automotive lug nuts – is quite charming. This chair is now being manufactured in a limited edition by Shelby Williams.

In admirable merchandising style Mozer has expanded into home furnishings; the furniture at other Mozer-designed venues (Sabrina, Neo, Scoozi! and Vivere) besides Cairo is now being made to order.

ADDRESS 720 North Wells Street (at West Superior Street)
CLIENT John Abell
COST $840,000
SIZE 5500 square feet (510 square metres)
RTT Chicago/Franklin on Brown Line, Purple Line Express
BUS 11, 22, 36, 37, 41, 135, 136, 156
ACCESS Tuesday–Friday 20.00–04.00; Saturdayand Sunday 21.00–04.00

Lincoln Park

Jordan Mozer & Associates 1988

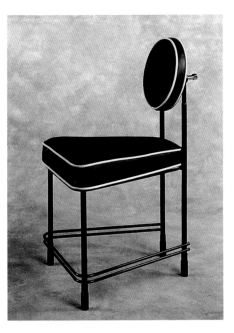

Jordan Mozer & Associates 1988

Luminaire

This converted loft shop is designer furniture heaven. An industrial steel bridge leads through a floating glass entranceway into a quiet interior that shows off the beautiful chairs, beds, lighting fixtures and art/architecture books at their best, allowing them to be splashes of colour against the store's predominantly neutral palette. Sandblasted glass partitions hover over the white wood floor in between stretches of exposed brick wall creating little niches for the various categories of display in this studiously chic ambience. A serious, trendy place in which many young architects spend their lunch hours dreaming of owning all these gorgeous designer wares.

ADDRESS 301 West Superior
CLIENT Nasir-Kassamau Luminaire
COST $247,000
SIZE 12,455 square feet (1160 square metres)
RTT Chicago/Franklin on Brown Line, Purple Line Express
BUS 37, 41, 66
ACCESS open during normal shopping hours

Lincoln Park

Pappageorge Haymes 1992

Pappageorge Haymes 1992

Embassy Club

The Embassy Club is the latest of Pappageorge Haymes' monopoly of Lincoln Park housing developments. City Commons (intersection of Willow, Orchard & Vine) was the first complex completed in 1985, and Larrabee Commons (intersection of North Avenue, Larrabee and Mohawk), Altgeld Court (1300 West Altgeld) and the Clybourn Lofts (1872 North Clybourn) followed.

The Embassy Club luxury homes are a witty, solidly built play on the English townhouse. Lined up in straight (or the odd curving formation) terraced rows, the ornamentation on the façade and size of the bay windows seems to reveal the house's cost, setting up a rather feudal little enclave.

ADDRESS intersection of Wrightwood, Greenview, Southport
CLIENT MCL Construction Corporation
STRUCTURAL ENGINEERS Samartano & Co., Abatangelo & Hason
COST $15 million
SIZE 412,262 square feet (38,300 square metres)
RTT Fullerton on Brown Line, Red Line, Purple Line Express
BUS 9, 74, 76
ACCESS none

Lincoln Park

Pappageorge Haymes 1993

Pappageorge Haymes 1993

Gold Coast and Old Town

House of Light 54

Chicago Historical Society Addition 56

Victorian Townhouse Extended 60

Playboy Enterprises Corporate Headquarters 62

Steel & Glass House 64

House with a Bay 68

Schiller Street Town Houses 70

House of Light

Nicknamed by the architects Casa della Luce, not only because of the extraordinary amount of natural light pouring in through skylights and huge windows but also because of the playfulness of the designed lighting fixtures floating throughout the house. At night the house has the capacity to be flooded with as many subtleties of light as during daylight hours. Delicate, elegant and radiant, everything about this house glows.

A green wrought-iron fence is the first announcement connected to the cool façade (limestone veneer over masonry) that supports a glazed vestibule (the only questionable space, this lobby is extremely formal, a bit too impersonal in comparison to the warmth of the rest of the house).

The house is organised symmetrically around a central three-storey skylight core with stairways wrapping round a rectangular opening. The dining room surrounded by columns and architraves is at the bottom of the atrium, set a few inches above the living room. These split-level floors elongate the plan, opening up the already voluminous-feeling space. The second floor has the master bedroom and a formal library/study with a giant oculus that is part of the intricate lighting plan, creating internal sunshine. The third floor, continuing the theme of understated colour modulations for each space (adding another lovely dimension to the play of light), has a children's bedroom with a comforting low ceiling and an informal guest bedroom.

ADDRESS 1828 North Orleans Street
STRUCTURAL ENGINEERS Chris P Stefanos Associates
SIZE 5124 square feet (476 square metres)
RTT Sedgwick on Brown Line (B stop)
BUS 11, 22, 36, 37, 73
ACCESS none

Booth Hansen & Associates 1983

Booth Hansen & Associates 1983

Chicago Historical Society Addition

Founded in 1857, in 1931 the Chicago Historical Society moved into a 105,219 square foot Georgian Revival building designed by Graham, Anderson, Probst & White. This grand redbrick and limestone building sits on the south-west corner of Lincoln Park. In 1971 a 53,875 square foot annex was built, designed by Alfred Shaw & Associates. The main access was shifted to Clark Street, but the white marble entrance created an intimidating image. The latest addition has a welcoming street façade and neutralises the stylistic differences of the old and new. Gerald Horn led the Holabird & Root team in establishing a new identity for the building and improving its programmatic functions.

The 1988 addition conceals the 1971 edifice, wrapping the west elevation in a skin of red brick, Indiana limestone, glass and steel. These materials, and the scale of the new structure, although stylistically unassociated, meld well with the original. As the museum is situated on city park land the available new space was quite restricted, with any addition pretty well contained within the existing building's perimeters. This required extensive structural modifications, and cladding from the building was removed to reduce the load on structural members. The second floor, originally 23 feet high, was divided into two floors, doubling the gallery space within the same enclosure.

The public entrance, of glass curtain wall grid and white steel trusses, has a pointed steel pediment from which bright banners announcing the exhibits are hung. Grids are everywhere. The black, rust and white gridded marble lobby floor is enclosed by a wonderful grid wall installation on either side of the main staircase (which has a gridded railing), and a gridded viewing bridge over the entranceway. Twenty square niches forming a grid parade some of the Society's 20 million artefacts. These are all objects used or made in Chicago. Life-size exhibits about Illinois

Holabird & Root 1988

Holabird & Root 1988

pioneer life and frontier Chicago continue in the galleries. There are rooms full of dioramas depicting Chicago's swift growth in the nineteenth century, an hands on interactive gallery, and a time capsule sitting in the lobby waiting to be unsealed in 2038.

A public restaurant, staff lounge and the Historical Society gift shop are housed in the three-storey curving glass wall facing south towards North Avenue.

ADDRESS 1601 Clark Street (at West North Avenue)
CLIENT Chicago Historical Society
SIZE 93,820 square feet (8700 square metres)
COST $11 million
RTT North/Sedgwick on Brown Line B, Clark/Division on Red Line
BUS 11, 22, 36, 72, 135, 136, 151, 156
ACCESS Monday–Saturday 09.30–16.30; Sunday 12.00–17.00 (entrance free on Monday). Closed for Thanksgiving, Christmas Day and New Year's Day

Holabird & Root 1988

Holabird & Root 1988

Victorian Townhouse Extended

The wide alleyways between streets are an intrinsic part of Chicago's plan. Usually simply passageways to garages, back gardens, or depositories for rubbish, the alleyway between Dearborn and Clark Streets has a remarkable architectural surprise. An extension of a demure Victorian townhouse juts out in colourful glory. One of the few examples of Deconstructivism in Chicago, this addition is a wild paroxysm of clashing angles, planes, colours and forms. Starting with hints of fragmentation in the interior, the house explodes into the alleyway in a flash of blue, gold and pink glass, battered/warped aluminium and mirrored curling stairways. A spectacular, dizzying sight!

ADDRESS 1522 North Dearborn
STRUCTURAL ENGINEERS Gullaksen, Getty & White
SIZE 5000 square feet (465 square metres)
RTT edgwick on Brown Line B, Clark/Division on Red Line
BUS 11, 22, 36, 37, 72, 135, 136, 151, 156
ACCESS none

Krueck and Olsen 1985

Krueck and Olsen 1985

Playboy Enterprises Corporate Headquarters

The first thing you see as you step out of the lift at Playboy's elegant and modern penthouse offices is a giant bronze Rabbit Head sculpture, Richard Hunt's interpretation of the famous logo. The groovy energetic 30-foot-high lobby is anchored by a freeform reception desk, a lunar pearl Black Andes granite and sand-blasted elliptical top supported by wavy poured concrete wiggles. The exterior of the elevator bank clad in an exotic, warm, African wood, avodire, that resembles washed silk, offsets the cold terrazzo floors inlaid with stainless steel lines.

The central atrium, a long galley designed to be the central circulation spine as well as an art gallery for Playboy's art collection, is carpeted in a sumptuously camp purple. A 160-foot-long skylight from the second storey sends sunlight bouncing off bowed stainless steel canopies and aeronauticalish curved steel soffits into the back office spaces. A huge Tom Wesselman painting of crimson smiling lips waits at the top of one of the terrazzo staircases. Perforated metal fins pivot to display more art and to separate work areas from common ground. Most of the office space is open plan, but the executive offices have translucent panels separating them from the long, rectangular atrium.

ADDRESS 680 North Lake Shore Drive
STRUCTURAL ENGINEERS Kolbjorn Saether & Associates
SIZE 100,000 square feet (9300 square metres)
CLIENT Playboy Enterprises, Inc.
RTT Grand/State or Chicago/State on Red Line
BUS 3, 29, 56, 65, 66, 120, 121, 157
ACCESS none

Himmel Bonner Architects 1989

Himmel Bonner Architects 1989

Steel & Glass House

Mies van der Rohe's rectangular glass and steel house was a starting point for Krueck and Olsen's first project together. Both trained in Chicago (ITT). They have reverently incorporated many Mies ideals, adding their own special twist.

A two-storey steel-frame structure (a prefabricated steel angle framing system) forming a U-shaped plan, the house is 5000 square feet located on a 67 x 127 foot corner plot. The flat plane of the steel lattice is accentuated by the narrow red metal stripe following the grid line. To create an ambience of privacy the centre of the house (with access to the rest of the building) is reached by passing through a series of parallel layers. The circular drive, partially hidden behind an iron spot brick wall, leads up to the industrial–style façade. A screen of subway grating camouflages the back of the cylindrical glass block stair tower. This façade is illuminated by a continuous neon billboard tube at night to spectacular effect. The entrance is on the west side of the horseshoe and off the terrazzo-floored foyer is a cloakroom and the garage with the master bedroom suite above on the second level and a stairway off the first level leading to the basement gym. The focal point of the U is the 70 x 22 foot living room.

Materials differentiate the four exterior sides of the house, the front and rear elevations are glass and the sides are metal allowing privacy from the dense residential neighbourhood. The front south-facing wall of the living room is floor-to-ceiling glass looking out on the small courtyard and allowing natural light to fall on the wonderful Richard Long wall painting covering the entire rear wall. The entire house is currently filled with contemporary art, including Claes Oldenburg sculpture and Barbara Kruger collages.

A housekeeper's quarters, kitchen and dining room occupy the eastern

Gold Coast and Old Town

Krueck & Olsen 1985

Krueck & Olsen 1985

section of the U on the ground floor with a guest bedroom, bathroom, and study above. The study masks a wet bar behind it, useful for entertaining. A skylit steel and glass-block walkway hangs over the living room connecting the two wings.

Interior surfaces are softer and more luxurious than the cold façade. Greys, maroons and dark greens are explored in marbles, velvets and lacquered woods. This steel and glass house is an elegantly precise and voluptuous container, a satisfying modern balance of urbanity and homeliness.

ADDRESS 1949 North Larrabee
STRUCTURAL ENGINEERS Gullaksen & Getty
SIZE 3000 square feet (280 square metres)
RTT Armitage on Brown Line
BUS 8, 11, 37, 73
ACCESS none

Krueck & Olsen 1985

Krueck & Olsen 1985

· **House with a Bay**

Squeezed into a 24-foot-wide lot, this small townhouse's most remarkable feature is the large bay on the front façade. The building is a tribute to the art of ornamentation and the Chicago School.

The structure is masonry, using 'Chicago Common', hard-faced red brick on the elevations. The front façade functions as a modest background for the marvellous geometric bay stuck smack in the centre. The framework is constructed of moulded fibreglass that resembles metal. Curved and straight glass sections are set into it. The ornament is based on a Victorian composition of circles in a square, used by Sullivan in his early work, and common to the Lincoln Park neighbourhood. The smooth red brick is also a familiar sight. The embellishment is repeated in three different sizes, on the red terracotta mouldings, the cornice and the plain terracotta sills. Similiar decorative circles appear in the iron picket fence. This motif persists throughout the interior. The fireplace and the kitchen have ornamental tiles made from the same moulds and even the layout of the internal spaces has been loosely based on this theme.

The ground floor has a guestroom at the front and a children's playroom at the back, opening onto the garden. The bay allows natural light into the living room, and together with the ten-foot high ceiling creates an airy, open, ambience.

ADDRESS 1873 North Orchard Street
STRUCTURAL ENGINEERS Beer Gorski & Graff
SIZE 3200 square feet (300 square metres)
RTT Armitage on Brown Line
BUS 8, 73
ACCESS none

Nagle, Hartray & Associates 1986

Nagle, Hartray & Associates 1986

Schiller Street Town Houses

Nagle, Hartray & Associates received the commission for this project after the client saw a house they had designed in Lincoln Park in 1985. This house (1852 North Orchard Street) became the prototype for the Schiller Street development. Oriented towards the quiet, residential Schiller Street, the brick townhouses are located on the corner of busy LaSalle Street. An exercise exhibiting the lyrical potential of repetition, all five of the townhouses have an identical front elevation and plan.

The garage and main entry face north, allowing the back garden to face south. A rhythmic series of two-storey bays protrude symmetrically from the flat grey brick veneer façade, overhanging the driveway. These cylinders contain two sets of curved gridded glass windows set in limestone sills. This manipulation of bold forms is similar to local 1930s' residences in the Chicago Modern style. Glass block detailing, metal piperail fences and metal entry gates add a layer of detail. The first level is organised around the service space, garage, entry and garden room. Living, dining and kitchen areas are on the second storey. On the second level there is an internal double-height skylight central court, allowing natural light in. Bedrooms are on the top floor, organised around the skylit space and linked by a bridge.

ADDRESS 141–149 West Schiller Street
STRUCTURAL ENGINEERS Beer Gorski & Graff
COST $1.66 million
SIZE 3500 square feet (325 square metres) each
RTT Clark/Division on Red Line, Sedgwick on Brown Line (B stop)
BUS 11, 22, 36, 135, 136, 145, 146, 147, 156
ACCESS none

Nagle, Hartray & Associates 1988

Nagle, Hartray & Associates 1988

River North

Hard Rock Café **74**
Commonwealth Edison Substation **76**
American Medical Association Headquarters **78**
River Cottages **82**

Hard Rock Café

A giant electric guitar rotates on the corner of the Hard Rock parking lot – you are now in Tacky Theme Park, Chicago. To be fair, the Hard Rock was built about eight years before the official River North Corridor Gimmick Invasion. Now its pseudo-orangerie façade seems positively serious. Designed to relate contextually to the original neo-Georgian Commonwealth Edison Substation next door, the Café has Tuscan proportions and neo-Palladian fenestration. All the measurements for entablatures, pedestal, die, collonettes and the windows in the building were informed by the 1929 substation. Painted green trellises decorate the façades, reinforcing the 18th century grand conservatory imagery.

There are three recent buildings in the area, which is already home to the Rock'n'Roll McDonald's, Ed Debevic's and Oprah Winfrey's Eccentric restaurant amongst others, creating an enclave of Disney-inspired architecture. Directly adjacent to the Hard Rock is the most disturbing new building of all, Capone's Chicago, a one-room polychromatic box dedicated to immortalising the gangster. Façades are bright yellows and blues with framed portraits slapped on in the most tawdry fashion. The new, completely over-the-top, Planet Hollywood a bit further up the street sports plastic palms, pink and green canopies, roving spotlights and a gigantic, gaudy posterboard Godzilla.

ADDRESS 63 West Ontario Street at North Dearborn Street
SIZE 12,000 square feet (1100 square metres)
RTT Grand/State on Red Line
BUS 15, 22, 29, 36, 65, 135, 136, 156
ACCESS Monday–Thursday 11.00–24.00; Friday 11.00–01.00; Saturday 10.30–01.00; Sunday 11.00–23.00

River North

Tigerman Fugman McCurry 1985

Tigerman Fugman McCurry 1985

Commonwealth Edison Substation

A few years after the Hard Rock Café was designed to complement the old substation, roles were reversed and the new substation (replacing the original) now takes its design cues from the Hard Rock. This duplicate reciprocity has resulted in two adjacent buildings with a similiar frame of reference and a close contextual relationship.

The new building incorporates actual fragments of the old as well as being stylistically similiar. Medallions and a plaque from the original façade, along with portions of the wrought-iron fence, are prominently displayed in Tigerman's scheme. The Indiana limestone elements, pilasters and entablatures are constructed through the wall, not just stuck on.

The only clue that this building's function is as an industrial utility is that large mechanical vents instead of glass fill the limestone window surrounds.

Part of the brief was that the building should be maintenance free. Therefore the architects chose to use dense and dimensionally stable FBX brick laid in English cross-bond.

ADDRESS 600 North Dearborn Street at West Ontario
STRUCTURAL ENGINEERS Beer Gorski & Graff
CLIENT Commonwealth Edison
SIZE 33,297 square feet (3100 square metres)
RTT Grand/State on Red Line
BUS 15, 22, 29, 36, 65, 135, 136, 156
ACCESS none

River North

Tigerman McCurry 1989

Tigerman McCurry 1989

American Medical Association Headquarters

Impressive use of negative space is evident in this Modernist building. A square, four-storey chunk of skyscraper has been cut out near the apex of this thirty-storey trapezoidal tower. Evocative as a refined, practical version of Gordon Matta-Clark's famous work – in particular 'Day's End' and 'Conical Intersect' (both 1975) in which Matta-Clark sliced large-scale geometrical sections from existing buildings – the hole in the American Medical Association Headquarters was designed to make the building an easily identifiable landmark. Such powerful spatial manipulation not only makes the project unique, it becomes exciting and thought-provoking. Removing a cube from an off-centre section of the upper middle of the building creates an ambiguity of scale. It is a powerful architectural gesture that forces the viewer to recognise the structure as a volumetric form in its own right.

The AMA owns eight blocks, roughly 12 acres in the River North region. The headquarters building is phase one of an ambitious urban redevelopment scheme. Kenzo Tange Associates (who title themselves Urbanists-Architects) were commissioned to draw up a masterplan for the entire site. This is Tange's first large commercial venture in the USA.

The new edifice is the first of a future pair. Both have been designed as trapezoids to 'maximise the sense of space and minimise the visual exposure to each other', according to the firm's publicity.

Structurally, the foundation is steel frame and the tower itself is steel frame with reinforced concrete. A glass and aluminium curtain wall rises elegantly from the flecked granite base. The exterior landscaping echoes the sharp, angular shape of the building. The dignified lobby has bonsai plants and a wonderful clear crackle-glass partition separating the

Kenzo Tange Associates 1990

elevator banks.

Part of the project brief was to provide public exhibition space. The ama accommodates one of the three galleries of The Chicago Athenaeum, an independent international museum of architecture. Founded in 1988, the proclaimed aim of the foundation is to educate the public about good design. They could not have chosen a more apt location.

ADDRESS 515 North State Street and Grand Avenue
CO-ORDINATING ARCHITECTS Shaw & Associates, Inc.
STRUCTURAL ENGINEERS Cohen Barreto Marchertas, Inc.
CLIENT American Medical Association in a joint venture with developers Buck Company and Miller-Klutznick-Davis-Gray and Company
RTT Grand on Red Line
BUS 15, 29, 36, 65
ACCESS public lobby and gallery

River North

Kenzo Tange Associates 1990

Kenzo Tange Associates 1990

River Cottages

With a working drawbridge to one side and elevated train tracks to the rear, these posh townhouses are situated in one of the most interesting, atmospheric locations in Chicago. This piece of prominent riverfront, across from Wolf Point, was the site of Chicago's first railroad depot. Completed in 1848, it was the final destination of the Galena and Chicago Union Railroad. Freight trains would transport grain from all over the Midwest to this spot where the cargo was loaded onto schooners and shipped down the river. Disused railroad tracks are still charmingly visible, half buried among pathways and the greenery around the site. Adding to the mood, boats float past under the lifted authentic Kinzie Avenue drawbridge.

River Cottages is a project of personal interest to the architect, Harry Weese, who originally intended to live in one of the townhouses. The scheme allowed Weese to explore nautical themes and their architectural interpretations, a long-time interest.

Built symmetrically around an existing tree, River Cottages consists of four luxury townhouses in two attached buildings. Two of these family homes have 4400 square feet of space on six levels and two have 2200 square feet of space on five levels. The long, narrow floors of all four are connected by stairs as well as individual elevators. The ground-floor entry is on North Canal Street but all the homes are oriented toward the river. From the inside, the views out at the Chicago skyline are spectacular. The interiors of the units were kept unfinished so that the buyers could do as they liked. This was not as great a success as expected, although the units went very quickly. Apparently the buyers would have preferred finished interiors. The suggested layout which most of the units follow is the living room, dining room and kitchen on the first floor, the master bedroom on the second, with additional bedrooms on the third, a study on the fourth

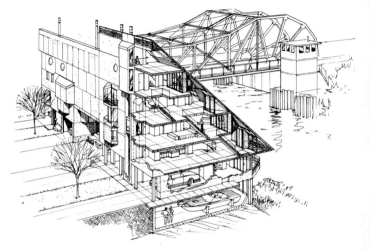

Harry Weese & Associates 1990

and a roof deck on the fifth.

All of the steeply sloping units have triangular balconies, spiral staircases, green metal decks, skylights and angled windows. These were inspired by schooner sails, boat riggings and lookout posts. The lovely curliqued stairs, juxtaposed with the severe angles of the sloped roof, present a fascinating, avant-garde façade. This complicated building suits its ideal site well. Surrounded by poplars, silver maples and flowering crab trees, it is a perfect retreat.

The exterior of the first three storeys is rubberised stucco. The geometrical upper half of the structure is steel and glass. The entire structure is cantilevered off the back concrete wall. Exposed tubular steel crossbracing is evident on the top floors of the two shorter homes. These mechanics have allowed the river façade of the building to have large triangular windows and peaked roofs.

This recently rejuvenated area has another Harry Weese & Associates' project (completed in 1981) a bit further down the river at number 345 North Canal Street. The Fulton House Condominium building is a converted warehouse. Built originally for the North American Cold Storage Company, the thickly insulated walls now house residential units.

ADDRESS 357–365 North Canal Street
STRUCTURAL ENGINEERS Harry Weese and Seymour Lepp & Associates
CLIENT Harry Weese
COST $2.5 million
SIZE 14,600 square feet (1360 square metres)
RTT Merchandise Mart on Brown Line, Purple Line Express
BUS 16, 37, 41, 44, 56, 61, 125
ACCESS none

Harry Weese & Associates 1990

Harry Weese & Associates 1990

Near North and Streeterville

North Pier 88
Northwestern University Law School Addition 92
Onterie Center 94
NBC Tower 96

North Pier

Containing roughly 450,000 square feet of space, this solid red brick and timber warehouse designed by Christian Eckstorm was completed in 1920 after fifteen years of construction. Devoted entirely to wholesale merchandise display, the Pugh Warehouse (after developer James Pugh) was the predecessor of the massive Merchandise Mart and the American Furniture Mart. Conversion of the old warehouse was the initial project of the Cityfront Center complex. The first stage of development for the adaptive reuse of the site involved redirecting the road along Lake Shore Drive to ease automobile access.

North Pier, as it is now called, has been transformed into a trendy, popular retail and office facility. The lower three floors (200,000 square feet) are devoted to small shops and restaurants and the remaining four levels (250,000 square feet) are office lofts. The fact that the floor plates were restricted to 10,800 square feet dictated the size of the boutiques. The entire building is essentially a row of seven inter-connected structures, each 120 x 90 feet. The masterplan for Cityfront Center allocated the site's eastern end for a residential tower. As a result, part of the original 900 foot warehouse was demolished, leaving it just 630 feet long.

Semicircular suspended dark green steel canopies hang above all the entrances on Illinois Street. Windows have been fitted into the old loading dock openings retaining the original dock number stamped on the steel frames. The Ogden Slip elevation has had a white steel and glass curtain wall added, bringing the edge of the building up to the waterfront. Decorative lookouts at either end of the galleria enhance the nautical theme displayed throughout the entire Pier. Outdoor cafés, a wooden boardwalk and docks for tour boats have created a lively location on the north bank of the Chicago River.

Internal circulation in the lower retail portion of the Pier is organised

Booth Hansen & Associates 1990

Booth Hansen & Associates 1990

around a central three-storey rotunda. Escalators at either end of the long layout are fit into curved atriums, visually opening up the space. A thin concrete coat had to be laid over the floor timbers to cut down on noise, but the sandblasted timber frame (it had been covered with white paint) is still visible. The original posts are reinforced with concrete columns with exposed brick capitals. These, along with the remaining heavy timber and brick structure, maximise the rugged maritime tableau.

To emphasise the new and contrast with the existing wood the architects made a point of adding mostly metal elements. Metallic materials are used throughout the interior, perforated or burnished sheet metal, visible clamps, steel mullions and the super original stainless steel floor tiles. All the interior street furniture – lamp posts, rubbish bins and railings – accentuate this industrial vocabulary.

Spots of planned colour enliven the atmosphere; a giant circular lamp suspended from the ceiling in the centre of the building is painted with the bright North Pier motif and then repeated in the floor tiles at the main entrance. This wavy maritime design is also incorporated into some of the metal door handles, a sign of the attention paid to the details of the scheme. The real colour is provided by the crowds who flock to this very popular spot every day.

ADDRESS 435 East Illinois Street (at North McClurg Court)
ASSOCIATE ARCHITECTS/STRUCTURAL ENGINEERS The Austin Company
SIZE 450,000 square feet (41,800 square metres)
COST $20 million
RTT Grand/State on Red Line
BUS 29, 56, 65, 66, 120, 121
ACCESS usual shopping hours

Booth Hansen & Associates 1990

Booth Hansen & Associates 1990

Near North and Streeterville

Northwestern University Law School Addition

The existing neo-Gothic building housing the Law School (designed by James Gamble Rogers in 1927) has been joined to a twelve-storey addition by a grey glass and aluminium framed five-storey enclosed atrium. The interior of this recessed atrium juxtaposes the original limestone of the eastern façade and the aluminium and tinted glass walls of the new cascading curtain wall. This central space is dramatically pierced by bridges and a rather grand central staircase that follows the axis of the entryway. The programme for the new building (on an irregular trapezoidal site) encompasses both the national headquarters of the American Bar Association, and facilities for the Law School – an 800-seat auditorium, a library with a 600,000-volume capacity, a moot court room, and three classrooms.

The ABA is the high-rise portion of the extension, physically differentiating it from the four-storey Law School addition. The decorations on the old structure are imitated by drywall buttresses on the new building, just one of many examples of the successful effort made to synthesise elegantly the new with the old. Rigorous attention to detail adds to the finish of the building. The only regrettable feature is the dark reflective glass used on the exterior, which at night is lovely, but somehow during the day does not do justice to the form of the building.

ADDRESS 357 East Chicago Avenue
COST $25 million
SIZE 360,000 square feet (33,000 square metres)
RTT Chicago/State on Red Line
BUS 3, 15, 66, 125, 157
ACCESS public lobby

Holabird & Root 1984

Holabird & Root 1984

Onterie Center

The playful name Onterie, a combination of Ontario and Erie, the two streets this 60-storey tower sits on, is its most notable feature. The last joint effort of the famous SOM team, architect Bruce Graham and the engineer Fazlur R Khan (responsible for the design of the Sears Tower and the John Hancock Tower), looks positively 1960s'. Using a blend of their innovative structural designs from previous showstopper towers, reinforced concrete bracing is visible on the exterior. This is a bland building with very little to redeem its dated appearance.

Near North and Streeterville

ADDRESS 446–448 East Onterie Street/441 East Erie Street
CLIENT PSM International Corporation
SIZE 1,100,000 square feet (102,000 square metres)
RTT Grand or Chicago on Red Line
BUS 3, 29, 56, 65, 66, 120, 121, 151, 157
ACCESS public lobby

Skidmore, Owings & Merrill, Inc. 1986

Near North and Streeterville

Skidmore, Owings & Merrill, Inc. 1986

NBC Tower

Defining the edge of Cityfront Plaza, the National Broadcasting Company Tower was the first structure to be erected at the new 50-acre office, retail and residential complex. This 900,000-square-foot building consists of a 38-storey office tower with a four-storey radio and TV broadcasting facility. Other sites such as in the Illinois Center or behind Quaker Tower were considered by NBC, but Cityfront Center won out.

Begun in 1985, the complex, bordered by Grand Avenue, the Ogden Slip turning basin, the Chicago River, Michigan Avenue and St Clair Street, is an ongoing project. A far more urbanly sensitive scheme than the earlier Illinois Center, the plan appreciates the recreational possibilities of the river.

Before construction of the building started the site had to be rearranged and the necessary infrastructure set up. North Water Street was realigned; services were all re-routed. Circulation and both pedestrian and automobile convenience were important in creating a market for the scheme. An important urban element of NBC is the marble and bronze arcade that runs through the ground floor. Used by the local residents to avoid the freezing Chicago winter, it is part of a plan that hopes to create an interior pedestrian system connecting Columbus Drive to future buildings.

The Cityfront development masterplan, drawn up by Cooper, Eckstut Associates and SOM, set specific architectural guidelines. The building was required to be primarily stone or masonry, measurements for setbacks were specified, and the top 10 per cent of the tower had to be distinctive. The rules for the setbacks were based on 1923 zoning laws, an attempt to be historically contextual. One setback was required at 265 feet above grade to recognise the traditional height of buildings along the Chicago River and a setback at 20 storeys was required where the Tribune Tower has a setback.

Skidmore, Owings & Merrill, Inc. 1989

Near North and Streeterville

Skidmore, Owings & Merrill, Inc. 1989

NBC Tower is recognisably derivative of the RCA (now GE) Building at Rockerfeller Center in Manhattan. The series of setbacks, emphasis on elegant verticality and classical materials are a romantic throwback to the skycrapers of the 1920s and 1930s. The neo-Gothic Tribune Tower, built in 1923–1925 by Raymond Hood, also receives homage. Flying buttresses at the 21st floor of the NBC echo those of the Tribune. But the buttresses are functional members, transferring load from the exterior column of the highest portion of the structure to the lower levels outside the column line.

The structural system is post-tensioned, pour-in-place concrete. The curtain wall is of Indiana limestone attached to 2600 precast concrete panels. Patterned precast spandrels alternate with tinted glass, emphasising the verticality of the building. A steel spire soars 130 feet above the roof, making the entire structure rise 602 feet above street level.

Conservative and reactionary, this building is nevertheless graceful, and affable. Perhaps it seems familiar as it is a romantic hybrid of several already traditional façades, or more probably because the building is a nightly TV star as the Channel 5 News icon.

ADDRESS Cityfront Center, 200 East Illinois Street at North Fairbanks Court
CLIENT Tishman Speyer Properties
SIZE 1,098,515 square feet (102,000 square metres)
COST $65 million
RTT Grand/State on Red Line
BUS 2, 3, 11, 29, 56, 65, 66, 120, 121, 145, 146, 147, 151, 157
ACCESS public lobby and arcade

Near North and Streeterville

Skidmore, Owings & Merrill, Inc. 1989

Near North and Streeterville

Skidmore, Owings & Merrill, Inc. 1989

North Michigan Avenue

900 North Michigan Avenue 102

Barnett Apartment 106

Oilily 110

Boogies Diner 112

Banana Republic 114

City Place 116

Sony Gallery 118

Niketown 120

Terra Museum of American Art 122

Crate & Barrel 124

900 North Michigan Avenue

North Michigan Avenue has undergone a steady transformation over the last sixty years. In the early part of the century Pine Street (as it was then known) was part of a middle-class residential neighbourhood. The street was broadened into a boulevard and renamed Michigan Avenue as part of Daniel H Burnham's 1909 Grand Plan for the city. Gradually Michigan Avenue became commercial, and by the end of World War 2 this major shopping street was nicknamed Magnificent Mile. Continual commercialisation and upscaling in the 1960s, 1970s and the 1980s occurred as a direct result of changing demographics. Water Tower Place, erected in 1976 (architects Loebl, Schlossman, Dart & Hackl; associate architects C F Murphy & Associates), was the beginning of a new typology along the avenue. This monolithic shopping emporium set the tone for the behemoth vertical malls that dot the Avenue.

Stretching across an entire block, 900 North Michigan Avenue is slightly to the north and on the opposite side of the avenue from Water Tower Place. A more sensitive design than the Tower, the eighth-floor base of its tripartite composition is meant to address the pedestrian, maintaining the low proportions of the street wall. The remaining 58 storeys are set back twice and end in a central arch decorated by four corner pavilions and lanterns. The lanterns are striking against the skyline when lit up at night. Cream limestone, granite and marble are combined with light reflective green glass for a Deco-inspired façade. Decorative vertical striations, large circles and square grids embellish the exterior.

The ubiquitous, supposedly soothing piano player (a baffling must for all posh shopping malls) is audible when passing through the grandiose two-storey entrance that opens out into a six-storey marble, polished steel and bronze trim atrium. The other atmospheric essential, an elaborate water fountain, dominates the second floor.

Kohn Pedersen Fox 1989

Kohn Pedersen Fox 1989

The tripartite compositional organisation and geometric theme visible on the exterior has been continued inside. Columns that evolve into light fixtures emphasise verticality and the brass spherical ornaments slightly liven up the restrained, over-pampered environment.

The tower is frequently referred to as the Bloomingdale's Building because Bloomies is the anchor retail store occupying part of the first six levels. The famous New York department store is housed at the rear of the building and luxury boutiques such as Gucci, Henri Bendel, Aquascutum and Charles Jourdan line the atrium. Escalators are strategically placed so that the consumer has to walk by the 100 smaller shops.

Above the retail space is the Four Seasons Hotel, office space and luxury condominium residences on floors 48 through 66. The hotel and private residences have an entrance on Delaware Street while the offices have their own side entrances on Walton Street.

ADDRESS 900 North Michigan Avenue (between East Walton Street and East Delaware Place)
ASSOCIATE ARCHITECTS Perkins & Will
CLIENT JMB Urban Realty
SIZE 2,700,000 square feet (251,000 square metres)
RTT Chicago/State on Red Line
BUS 11, 15, 66, 125, 145, 146, 147, 151
ACCESS public

Kohn Pedersen Fox 1989

Kohn Pedersen Fox 1989

Barnett Apartment

Planned around a private contemporary art collection, this duplex is the owner's personal gallery and city *pied-à-terre*. The first step in the design process was to photograph and document the collection which includes Mirò aquatints, large Warhol silkscreens, one being the famous 'Marilyn' tapestry, and colourful flag paintings by Ronnie Cutrone. This exciting two-storey open space (there are no conventional rooms) is all angles, curves, soffits, niches, and floating walls bearing paintings and sculptures.

Sited over sixty storeys high in the north-east turret of the 900 North Michigan building and directly across from the John Hancock Tower, the apartment's skyline views are simply spectacular. The city context has been treated as an artwork of equal magnitude and Chicago's grid system is continued in the floor pattern. 5 x 5 foot square floor slabs of highly polished black granite articulated with zinc strips are a luxurious component of the basically neutral palette of the apartment, creating a backdrop for art. From the entranceway, with an alcove housing a sculpture by Beverly Mayeri ('Realignment 1990') the flat unfolds itself, teasing and tantalising with varying views of different artworks set against the spectacular double-height windows. The central focus of the flat is a concrete column (smack in the middle of the atrium) that has been transformed into a replica of the Saturn V rocket. Relevant to the client's profession, aeronautical engineering, this rocket is a structural column supporting a glass and stainless steel elevator. The four-person lift, decked out in industrial checker plate stainless steel flooring, is attached to the cylindrical shaft by a cross-braced steel structure that absorbs all lateral stress. The glass elevator and the overlapping panels of glass in the railings surrounding the upper level allow continued viewing of the paintings and the city. Fragments of the rocket are visible through many of the cutaway partitions.

North Michigan Avenue

Hartshorne Plunkard, Limited 1992

The second level of the apartment has large pneumatic doors pocketed into sculptural walls that slide out to create a bedroom, guestroom and private study. These walls also contain paintings! Even the master bath has been decorated with exquisite hand-made tiles commissioned especially for this project.

The furniture is mostly artwork as well, including a Ron Arad stainless steel number. The home entertainment centre on the first level is contained within a cabinet painted by Neraldo de la Paz to match and act as a continuation of a Kurt Frankenstein moonscape painting, 'Bureaucratic Planet', hung above it.

ADDRESS 132 East Delaware entrance of 900 North Michigan Avenue
STRUCTURAL ENGINEERS Stearn-Joglekar, Limited
SIZE 3500 square feet (325 square metres)
RTT Chicago/State on Red Line
BUS 11, 33, 66, 125, 145, 146, 147, 151, 153
ACCESS none

Hartshorne Plunkard, Limited 1992

Hartshorne Plunkard, Limited 1992

Oilily

This is a pure geometrical composition. Labelled by the architects as a neo-plastic landscape, two-dimensional patterns on the floor, ceiling and storefront are interlocked with the three-dimensional display furniture.

The playful and colourful exploration of vertical and horizontal linear structure make this small retail space both fun and chic. Shocking pink, yellow, and blue rectilinear volumes create a three-dimensional version of Mondrian's work. Floating cubic display surfaces are set in asymetrical configurations. The solid forms, limited to planes, and round or square shafts are reminiscent of nursery building blocks. The bold colours and textured surfaces complement the wild ethnic motifs of the clothing. Different materials appear in the same colour or pattern, transforming from two to three dimensions and adding another layer of texture.

Narrow vertical shelving for socks, gloves and foldable items offset the horizontal forms. There is no consistent registration of perimeter height, each separate display is at a varying level with its neighbour. The shelves within the cases are all height coordinated and aligned, creating a sense of balance. The epoxy-stabilised floor is an abstract grid that is complemented by the orthogonal lighting fixtures and meshes with the intersecting planes and volumes of the cashwrap and display furniture.

North Michigan Avenue

ADDRESS 900 North Michigan Avenue
CLIENT Oilily
SIZE 1600 square feet (150 square metres)
RTT Chicago/State on Red Line
BUS 3, 11, 15, 33, 66, 125, 145, 146, 147, 151, 157
ACCESS open

Florian-Wierzbowski 1988

Florian-Wierzbowski 1988

Boogies Diner

Vibrant primary colours, intersecting angular planes, neon signs and industrial vinyl carpet give this clothing shop-cum-eaterie a snappy, snazzy rock'n'roll atmosphere. Bright track lighting sheds an artificial glare on the leather jackets and cowboy boots for sale on the ground level, while diners devour juicy burgers and special curly fries on the upper level. An eclectic mix of vernacular influences dating back to 1950s-style drug store soda fountains and roadside coffee shops, this is the Chicago outlet of the Aspen-based chain. This youthful, super-friendly joint is striving for a clubby mentality. Boogies' own baseball hats signed by music and film celebrities hang in a row above the long lunch counter, indicating the great desirability of being part of the Boogies crowd. Blaring juke box music completes the fun, partytime atmosphere.

North Michigan Avenue

ADDRESS 33 East Oak Street (at North Rush Street)
SIZE 13,000 square feet (1200 square metres)
RTT Chicago/State on Red Line
BUS 11, 15, 22, 33, 36, 66, 125, 145, 146, 147, 151
ACCESS open

Himmel Bonner Architects 1990

Himmel Bonner Architects 1990

Banana Republic

This free-standing two-storey hut is a romanticised version of a small tropical plantation villa. Robert Stern's first central Chicago commission is this clothing store, suggestive of turn-of-the-century colonial prefabricated metal structures. Stern has created a prototypical make-believe exotic backdrop for this fashionable retailer.

Lead-coated copper panels form the barrel-vaulted roof, and the bronze façade has teak-framed windows complete with pretend tropical shutters. The exterior is beautifully detailed with solid bronze strapping woven round lead-coated copper piers reminiscent of sheaves of bamboo. (Bundles of real dried grasses dot the interior.)

The French colonial settlement motif continues inside. The main focal point is a sophisticated suspended double-return glass and steel staircase, hanging from guyed cables underneath the gabled skylight. The materials are extremely warm and luxurious – leather strapping is woven round the white oak handrail and the laminated glass stairtreads are sandwiched with rice paper. The cross-lashed leather basket-weave theme recurs throughout. Two lacquered particle-board tents laced with steel cable disguise the cash counter areas.

ADDRESS 744 North Michigan Avenue
ARCHITECT OF RECORD Robert W Engel of The Gap
STRUCTURAL ENGINEERS Charles E Pease Associates
SIZE 14,360 square feet (1330 square metres)
RTT Chicago/State on Red Line
BUS 3, 11, 15, 33, 66, 125, 145, 146, 147, 151, 157
ACCESS open

Robert A M Stern 1991

Robert A M Stern 1991

City Place

A curiously two-dimensional building, City Place had to be wedged into its narrow corner site. As a result of its narrow profile, broadened width and flat, smooth façade this structure looks as though it was poured into a mold or shaped by a cookie cutter. The thin, wide form required an innovative lateral resisting system with post-tensioned columns to check movement and drift of the building caused by extreme wind loads.

Adjacent to the far gaudier Chicago Place (700 North Michigan Avenue), another complex completed in 1990, City Place is a shiny combination of Imperial red granite and reflective blue glass. Visually divided into three sections, this tripartite organisation – base, shaft and top – is a direct result of programme. The Hyatt Hotel has floors five through twenty-five (special suites are available, decorated in the styles of Mies van der Rohe, Frank Lloyd Wright and Charles Rennie Mackintosh). This area of the façade has punched windows. The top twelve floors, marked by ribbon windows, house the office space. In a reversal of the standard placement, the offices are at the top of the tower and have larger windows. The arch at the top contains the most glass. Its 70-foot diameter barrel vault has a space frame, visible from the sides (if you happen to be forty storeys high), that supports the façade much like a billboard.

ADDRESS 678 North Michigan Avenue (at East Huron Street)
STRUCTURAL ENGINEERS Chris P Stefanos Associates
CLIENT Fifield Realty Corporation and VMS Realty Partners
SIZE 482,000 square feet (44,780 square metres)
RTT Chicago/State on Red Line
BUS 3, 11, 15, 33, 66, 125, 145, 146, 147, 151
ACCESS none

North Michigan Avenue

Loebl, Schlossman & Hackl 1990

North Michigan Avenue

Loebl, Schlossman & Hackl 1990

Sony Gallery

State of the art is the overall image of this sophisticated adult toy store. Punctuated by steel-framed floor-length windows and three navy canopies suspended by cables from the third floor, the four-storey façade is a simple limestone affair. The elegant entrance has a black granite floor inlaid with reflective stainless steel bars. This leads onto bleached oak on which brushed metal pedestals display Sony's latest electronics. All items are available at retail price, but the goal here is for shoppers to experience electronics in a simulated lifestyle setting. A home-theatre display on the first floor demonstrates TV in a pretend living room, complete with Missoni rug and Le Corbusier furniture. A beautiful grey, metal and fabric undulating ceiling wave conceals the system components and audio speakers.

The Boston-based architectural firm Elkus Manfredi chose a neutral palette to highlight and frame the black and white merchandise. The constant video imagery supplies background colour. Semi-transparent perforated metal backdrops separate different product type areas. A central two-way perforated metal and glass staircase passes through the second-floor curved ceiling cutaway, allowing continuous visibility.

ADDRESS 669 North Michigan Avenue
STRUCTURAL ENGINEERS Weidlinger Associates, Inc.
CLIENT Sony Corporation of America
SIZE 10,000 square feet (930 square metres)
RTT Chicago/State on Red Line
BUS 3, 11, 15, 33, 66, 125, 145, 146, 147, 151
ACCESS open

North Michigan Avenue

Elkus Manfredi Architects Limited 1991

North Michigan Avenue

Elkus Manfredi Architects Limited 1991

Niketown

Smack next door to the Sony Gallery is the Nike Museum. A combination of Disneyland meets Smithsonian Institute, this is the sneaker hall of fame, dedicated to the glorification of anything Nike. The basic concept is a three-level pretend-outdoor shopping extravaganza, complete with manhole covers, cement pavement, brick walls, and the piped-in sounds of nature. Far less subtle than the Sony Gallery, although with equal attention to quality of detail, Niketown has a superb element of fun.

The lobby area is the Nike Museum, lined with *Sports Illustrated* covers featuring athletes who endorse Nike. A statue of Michael Jordan and a pair of his autographed shoes accompany plexiglas display cases with information about technological innovations in fitness gear. The amusement park atmosphere is heightened by oversized floats. My favourite display is a video pond, nine television screens installed in the floor and covered with a protective layer of plexiglas that show continuous seascape images.

New, bold and interactive, both the Sony and Nike showcase stores have become consumer cynosures on Magnificent Mile.

ADDRESS 669 North Michigan Avenue at East Erie Street
STRUCTURAL ENGINEERS Chris P Stefanos Associates
SIZE 68,000 square feet (6300 square metres)
CLIENT Nike, Inc.
RTT Grand on Red Line
BUS 3, 11, 15, 33, 125, 145, 146, 147, 151, 157
ACCESS Monday–Friday 10.00–20.00; Saturday 09:30–18.00; Sunday 11.00–18.00

North Michigan Avenue

Gordon Thompson, III and Nike's in-house design team 1992

Gordon Thompson, III and Nike's in-house design team 1992

Terra Museum of American Art

Established in 1980, this collection of American art was originally located in Evanston. The new site, three adjacent buildings, was aquired in 1985. No. 664, the corner building, had its façade cleaned and the interior was transformed from offices to four floors of loft-style galleries. The next-door building has been completely made over. Clad in grey-veined white Vermont marble with a five-storey glass curtain wall insert, this façade is a sophisticated addition to the street. The elegant pavilion elevation is the highlight of the project. At night an elliptical light fixture at the fifth floor makes a spectacular effect.

Past the cosy pale mahogany lobby the building is a big disappointment. The design is baffling: the primary concern seems to be about circulation and not appropiate picture display. Faced with mismatched floor levels and vertically oriented exhibition space, wide, shallow ramps with thin white railings lead to tiny exhibition spaces within No. 666. Obviously inspired by Frank Lloyd Wright's Guggenheim Museum, here the ramps are purely for circulation and do not display any artwork. If No. 670 North Michigan is eventually used, then the ramps can be read as a central circulation point, joining all the buildings, and making a far more sensible scheme.

ADDRESS 666 North Michigan Avenue (at East Erie Street)
STRUCTURAL ENGINEERS Beer Gorski & Graff
CLIENT Ambassador Daniel Terra
SIZE 28,000 square feet (2600 square metres)
COST $3.5 million
RTT Chicago/State on Red Line
BUS 3, 11, 15, 33, 66, 125, 145, 147, 151
ACCESS open

North Michigan Avenue

Booth Hansen & Associates 1987

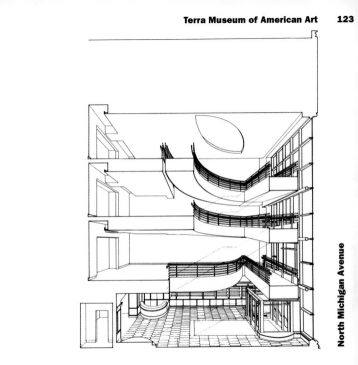

North Michigan Avenue

Booth Hansen & Associates 1987

Crate & Barrel

The national headquarters for this culinary wares and home furnishings store has a sleek exterior expressive of the products it contains. Suggestive of contemporary kitchen machinery, this dynamic flagship building resembles a giant Cuisinart food processor sitting on North Michigan Avenue. A shiny five-storey container with an attached rotunda housing diagonal escalators, this relatively small building stands out against its older and grander masonry-clad neighbours.

Clear glass and glossy white, powder-coated, ribbed aluminium panels create continuous bands of windows on a cube that has a cylindrical attachment. These main forms are literally a crate and a barrel.

The transparency of the glass-enclosed skylit rotunda is a successful commercial ploy. Vertical visibility entices passers-by to look up at the displays on all four retail floors. The entry is adjacent to the rotunda which contains the building's principal means of circulation: escalators. Natural light in the interior of light, knotty pine walls and oak floors creates a relaxed atmosphere. The Midwestern image continues onto the street. The sidewalk is a diamond-patterned smooth-finish concrete that extends from the curb to the store's curtain wall, transforming into oak in the same pattern leading into the interior.

ADDRESS 646 North Michigan Avenue at East Erie Street
STRUCTURAL ENGINEER Chris P Stefanos Associates
SIZE 44,000 square feet (4000 square metres)
RTT Chicago/State or Grand on Red Line AB
BUS 2, 3, 11, 15, 29, 33, 65, 125, 145, 146, 147, 151
ACCESS open

Solomon Cordwell Buenz & Associates 1990

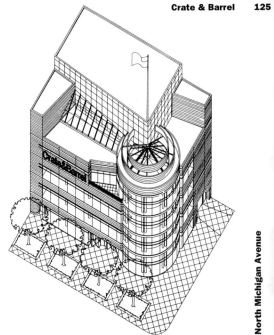

North Michigan Avenue

Solomon Cordwell Buenz & Associates 1990

East Loop

Associates Center 128

Self Park Garage 132

Athletic Club, Illinois Center 134

Two Prudential Plaza 136

Leo Burnett Company Headquarters 138

R R Donnelley Building 140

Chicago Title & Trust Center 142

Thompson Center 144

Vivere 148

Ralph H Metcalfe Federal Center 152

Daniel F and Ada I Rice Building 156

Japanese Screen Gallery 158

Harold Washington Library 160

Associates Center

The Associates Center (officially the Stone Container Building) was the ninth collaboration between the architectural firm A Epstein and Sons and New York developers Collins Tuttle & Company. The architects did not have a design team at the time they received the commission for this project. Sheldon Schlegman was appointed project designer for the Associates Center.

The top of the building is oriented towards Burnham Harbor and the Grant Park lakefront, and the base of the building follows the existing grid. Schlegman's main design aim was to create a space where as many of the upper offices as possible could have a view over the lake. The site, the gateway to the Loop, is on the north-west corner of Michigan Avenue and Randolph Street. The split in the middle of the base allows pedestrians a shortcut, an odd amenity as the building is already on the corner. The idea was that the top should make the transition and point eastward, symbolising dynamism and the entrance to Randolph Street, once a Mecca of nightlife. The entranceway is marked by a multicoloured vertical sculpture by Yaacov Agam, 'Communication x9'.

An underground pedestrian walkway, now closed, was designed after a study of existing sewer systems and utilities, under contract with the City of Chicago. The pedway ran under Randolph Street at Michigan Avenue connecting the 150 North Michigan Building to the Illinois Central Railroad Station.

Forty-one storeys, 582 feet overall, the top third of the Associates Center has been canted 45 degrees. Split down the centre, a 'composition of two forces coming together', according to Schlegman, the top half resembles a diamond made up of two sloped triangles. The sloped atrium is faceted in silver reflective insulating glass as is the curtain wall of alternating bands of white polymer-finish spandrel aluminium panels,

polished stainless steel trim and the reflective glass.

The basic structure is a flat-slab reinforced concrete frame and floors. The central service core has been oriented asymmetrically on a south-east–north-west axis. Although setting the record for perimeter window area per square foot of interior space, the turned core combined with the diagonally angled apex creates some very awkward rooms. These residual spaces must make for difficult interior planning.

Up close, cheap materials and crude detailing exacerbated by the unfortunate white façade make the building clinical and cold. This is, sadly, a no-frills product.

Despite these shortcomings and the fact that much has been written about the building's unflattering proportions (the original plan was intended to be five storeys higher), time and familiarity have made the Associates Center a well-loved element of the skyline. At night, the illuminated diamond with 'Go Bulls' written across its clumsy façade seems like a goofy relative. A well-known albeit clutzy landmark.

ADDRESS 150 North Michigan Avenue
STRUCTURAL ENGINEERS A Epstein & Sons
CLIENT Collins Tuttle & Company
COST $55 million
SIZE 714,000 square feet (66,300 square metres)
RTT Randolph/Wabash on Orangle Line. Purple Line Express
BUS 3, 4, 6, 56, 145, 146, 147, 151, 157
ACCESS public lobby and underpass

East Loop

A Epstein & Sons 1984

A Epstein & Sons 1984

Self Park Garage

Heralded by a giant bronze hood ornament gracing its pediment, this twelve-storey grille of a classic touring automobile is snugly wedged in between two early 20th-century skyscrapers. The result of a private competition among three architects, this is a whimsical example of literal symbolism. The alucobond metal-clad exterior with stylised fenders in a baked enamel finish is a turquoise shade taken from the 1957 Chevy colour schedule. The façade has two acrylic prefabricated dome head-lights disguising skylights, bumpers, and black vinyl canopies that resemble tyres, treads and all. The lower two levels are retail and the car park has 199 parking spaces. The finishing touch is the metaphorical license plate signage, SELF PARK.

ADDRESS 60 East Lake Street (between North Wabash and North Michigan Avenues)
ASSOCIATE ARCHITECT Conrad Associates
CLIENT A Ronald Grais and Hersch M Klaff
SIZE 98,000 square feet (9100 square metres)
RTT State/Lake on Brown Line, Orange Line, Purple Line Express
BUS 2, 3, 6, 11, 16, 56, 145, 146, 147, 151, 157
ACCESS public

East Loop

Tigerman Fugman McCurry 1986

Tigerman Fugman McCurry 1986

Athletic Club, Illinois Center

Aside from possessing the tallest (116 feet) indoor climbing wall in Chicago and allegedly having Michael Jordan as a member, the Athletic Club can also claim fame as America's first building designed by Kisho Kurokawa. The gym is a small white structure, almost swallowed up by its neighbours in the dense 83-acre mixed-use development known as the Illinois Center. The Illinois Center is so large that it apparently has several zip codes! Conceived in 1967 by Mies van der Rohe, construction began in 1975 and expected completion is in the late 1990s. Built around an incredibly confusing tri-level street system and incomprehensible pedestrian concourses, the Center is dark and overpowering. Indifferent to Michigan Avenue or the river, the complex is architecturally incoherent. Looming, oppressive tower blocks are packed around gloomy plazas. The light and airy Athletic Club is definitely the highlight.

Only two of the Club's six storeys are visible from Stetson Avenue, the rest are below grade. The exterior is an aluminium and glass curtain wall caged in a white, wide-flange steel framework. The main entrance is at the fifth floor. A whimsical decorative element has been added onto the top level, presumably to draw the eye to the sunken building: steel pedestals support 17-foot kinetic wind sculptures by Osamu Shingu.

ADDRESS 211 North Stetson Avenue
ASSOCIATE ARCHITECTS Fujikawa, Johnson & Associates
STRUCTURAL ENGINEERS CBW Engineers, Inc.
RTT Randolph/Wabash on Brown Line, Purple Line Express, Orange Line
BUS 3, 4, 6, 16, 56, 145, 147, 151, 157
ACCESS private club; try calling

East Loop

Kisho Kurokawa 1990

Kisho Kurokawa 1990

Two Prudential Plaza

At 920 feet, Two Pru is the world's second tallest reinforced concrete building. Similiar in design to Helmut Jahn's Philadelphia skyscraper One Liberty Place (1987) the 63-storey tower has chevron setbacks and a diamond-faceted apex. Its spire seems quite stubby in relation to the vertical length of the building. Sitting between the old Prudential Plaza (a 44-storey Miesian building: Naess & Murphy, 1955), and the very tall Amoco Building (82 storeys, completed 1973: Edward Durrell Stone and Perkins & Will, famous for the accidental loss of its marble cladding), the height of the new Pru makes it appear a logical vertical progression.

The project also involved renovation of the old Pru building, a new 1 acre landscaped public plaza and a five-level parking garage. The two buildings share a common mezzanine and are joined by two five-storey atriums. The award-winning outdoor plaza with two fountains is a popular, flower-filled space. Its concrete structure also functions as the roof for the complex's mechanical equipment.

The new tower is clad in grey and red granite alternating with grey reflective glass. The motif is repeated to death in the entranceway and layered elevator banks. 230 exterior lighting fixtures strategically positioned in the setbacks on the north and south faces and around the chevroned top and spire are illuminated for a dramatic effect at night.

ADDRESS 180 North Stetson Avenue at East Lake Street
SIZE 1,200,000 square feet (111,000 square metres)
STRUCTURAL ENGINEERS CBM Engineers, Inc.
RTT Randolph/Wabash on Brown Line, Orange Line, Purple Line Express
BUS 4, 60
ACCESS public lobby and plaza

Loebl, Schlossman & Hackl 1990

East Loop

Loebl, Schlossman & Hackl 1990

Leo Burnett Company Headquarters

Structurally quite exciting, this building has a perimeter tube of steel columns on 15-foot centres, with a reinforced cast-in-place concrete service core and trusses supporting the floors. This enables a column-free span of 45 feet. This deep interior space was a requirement for the major tenant, Chicago's largest advertising firm.

Essentially a steel structure with a thin cladding of stone, the building gives the impression of a 50-storey skyscraper wearing an unflattering plaid suit. The granite checkerboard pattern covering the entire height of this free-standing tower destroys its verticality, visually shortening and broadening the building. Three cornice levels continue the pattern, and imitate the base. Three different treatments, thermal stippling, polishing, or honing, were given to the green granite to create a pattern in the building's veneer. Corners, edges and the base of the building are polished granite and the tick-tack-toe pattern of the stuck-on pilasters is outlined alternately by honed and stippled stone. The deeply recessed windows are of dark reflecting glass, adding to the ominous effect.

The overdone pink marble lobby has an incongruous sculpture by John Chamberlain that celebrates materials in a way the building nullifies.

ADDRESS 35 West Wacker Drive at North Dearborn Street
STRUCTURAL ENGINEERS Cohen Barreto Marchertas, Inc.
COST $100 million
SIZE 1,460,000 square feet (135,640 square metres)
RTT State/Lake on Brown Line, Orange Line, Purple Line Express, Clark/Lake on Blue Line, Washington on Red Line
BUS 2, 6, 11, 15, 16, 22, 24, 29, 36, 44, 62, 62 Express, 99, 99M, 125, 146, 162, 164
ACCESS public lobby

East Loop

Kevin Roche-John Dinkeloo & Associates 1989

Kevin Roche-John Dinkeloo & Associates 1989

R R Donnelley Building

From a distance this prominent skyscraper appears amusing but the closer one gets the less funny the pun seems. In fact my final impression is of bewilderment: what is the joke? Spaniard Ricardo Bofill directed the design and DeStefano & Partners were the architects for this 50-storey office tower. Categorised as Modern Classicism, the building is not popular amongst the architectural profession, being jeered at as everything from fascist to trivial and silly!

Apparently meant to be a giant column recalling Giotto's campanile in Florence Cathedral, Bofill wanted his tower to 'reestablish a dialogue between the classicism of stone and the high-tech of glass'. Portuguese white granite abstracted pilasters, arches and entablatures appear to be wallpapered onto the façade. Silver reflective glass windows exacerbate the building's shiny, unreal impression. The patina-green roof inspired by Classical temple proportions sticks to the trend of nighttime illumination.

The self-important base is 42 feet high and houses a grandly proportioned atrium. Giant white marble twisted candy sculptures by Bofill sit alongside a beautiful Tapies and sculptures by Xavier Corbero in the richly marbled lobby. Dramatic elliptical chandeliers hang from the white oak ceiling.

ADDRESS 77 West Wacker Drive
SUPERVISING ARCHITECTS DeStefano & Partners
STRUCTURAL ENGINEERS Cohen Barreto Marchertas, Inc.
RTT State/Lake on Brown Line, Orange Line, Purple Line Express, Clark/Lake on Blue Line, Washington on Red Line
BUS 2, 6, 11, 15, 16, 22, 24, 29, 36, 44, 62, 62 Express, 99, 99M, 125, 146, 162, 164
ACCESS public lobby

East Loop

Ricardo Bofill Taller d'Arquitectura 1992

Chicago Title & Trust Center

Part of a two-phase project, the second planned tower of this scheme has been postponed because much of the existing tower is still vacant.

Tall and white, the completed portion of the scheme is a 55-storey monolith that gives the impression that someone got overexcited and went wild with decorating ideas. Ornaments have been stuck all over the façade in a decidedly haphazard fashion – there is far too much icing on this vertical cake. Although well constructed and detailed, excessive varieties of signage, patterning, materials (the main lobby alone is faced with three types of marble) and styles combined with confusing asymetrical planes at the apex generate an uncomfortable restless feeling. The exterior, clad in sterile white marble, glass and metal has (off-putting) separate entrances that appear lopsided because they are on different levels and have completely contrary canopies.

The top of the building is ornamented by three sculptural glass and metal pylons. Extended from a 70 foot wide aluminium shaft attached to the tower's western façade are steel bridges that brace the three pylon embellishments. Irregular, overdesigned, and as described in the *Chicago Tribune* (by Blair Kamin), '... there's simply too much going on ...'.

ADDRESS 161–171 North Clark Street
CLIENT The Linpro Company
SIZE 2,300,000 square feet (213,700 square metres)
RTT Clark/Lake on Brown Line, Orange Line, Purple Line Express
BUS 16, 22, 24, 36, 42, 44, 62, 135, 136, 156
ACCESS public lobby

East Loop

Kohn Pedersen Fox 1992

Kohn Pedersen Fox 1992

Thompson Center

Commissioned by Republican Governor James R Thompson and recently renamed in his honour, this controversial building was originally known as The State of Illinois Center. The anchor project for a 30-acre redevelopment plan to rebuild the Central Business District in the North Loop area, the idea was to gather together 56 different state agencies into one central building. Three thousand state employees are housed in this mixed-use facility, with a million square feet devoted to government offices and 150,000 square feet of commercial space. The inclusion of shops and galleries is intended to bring people in who do not need to renew their driver's license or sort out a tax formality.

The Thompson Center takes up an entire street block. Its unconventional massing basically consists of a low rectangular box with one curved inwardly stepped façade and a diagonally truncated glass cylinder projecting above. This rejection of orthogonal order breaks up the downtown Cartesian grid, diverging from the expected rectilinearity of the rest of Chicago. Although a definite landmark and tourist magnet, the Thompson Center has an uncomfortable and indecisive appearance. The abstract Jean Dubuffet sculpture, 'Monument with Standing Beast', standing on the corner of Randolph and Clark, proclaims pride in its own amorphic form, pointedly mocking the heavy glittery wedge it is meant to complement. The building's bulkiness is exacerbated by its vertically striped polychromatic and mirrored glass skin. Silicone glazing was originally intended, eliminating the need for mullions, but the story has it that the contractors were scared of the possible liabilities. Instead a 2 foot 6 inch vertical division governs alternating strips of reflective glass vision panels and opaque coloured glass panels on the north, east and west façades. The vast heavily lined glass exterior initially caused numerous problems with extreme interior temperature fluctuations.

Murphy/Jahn 1985

Murphy/Jahn 1985

For me, the overriding, far more serious difficulty with this building is that Helmut Jahn's well-intentioned concepts about the reinvention of public space have not survived translation into a built structure. The link between idea and execution has not been successful. References to the centrality of government and the importance of openness in the central piazza-style atrium are diluted by the lack of appreciation for detailing and materials throughout. There has been an enormous amount of understandable criticism concerning the tacky shades of symbolic red, white, and blue that were chosen. Salmon, silver, and powder blue immediately date and cheapen the building. The constantly moving kaleidoscope that one encounters upon entering the atrium is dominated by these trivialising colours topped off by orange structural steel beams that criss-cross the front façade and the roof. All of this, combined with the exposed mechanics of the escalators, mirrored panels and the spinning, geometric rosette-motif patterned marble and granite floor, creates instant vertigo. Perhaps the building succeeds on the level that it is a realistic representation of the merry-go round chaos of bureaucracy – truth in architecture!

ADDRESS bounded by North Clark, North LaSalle, West Lake and West Randolph Streets
ASSOCIATE ARCHITECTS Lester B Knight & Associates
SIZE 1,930,000 square feet gross (179,000 square metres)
CLIENT State of Illinois Capital Development Board
COST $172 million
RTT Clark/Lake on Brown Line, Blue Line, Orange Line, Purple Line Express
BUS 22, 24, 42, 135, 136, 156
ACCESS public

Murphy/Jahn 1985

Murphy/Jahn 1985

Vivere

Layers of sensual spirals in a soft rusty palette create a magical neo-Baroque ambience in this lovingly renovated restaurant. Each romantic surface and voluptuous object – tableware, door handles, chairs, walls, tables – has been custom-designed by the hotshot designer Jordan Mozer. Involved at every level and stage of design and execution, Mozer has been called a throwback to the days of the masterbuilder. Working directly with artisans, he had practically everything in Vivere handmade. His method of working sometimes consists of blowing-up freehand drawings to life-size and having craftsman build directly from these.

The omnipresent spiral motif was inspired by a detail in the original space (known as the Florentine Room), and seized upon as representative of Italian Baroque architecture. This was pertinent because, as the third of three restaurants housed in one building, called Italian Village, Vivere serves delicious though eclectic, gourmet, regional and seasonal Italian cuisine, and has a renowned wine list. The spiral metaphorically represents the genealogical history of the restaurant's ownership, having been founded three generations ago in 1927 by an Italian immigrant, handed down to his children and currently run by their grandchildren.

This super-meaningful helix is evident everywhere in the long, narrow, split-level space. A curvy iron entry gazebo, behind the large mahogany front door, paves the way for endless twisty, bulgy forms. 13-foot, copper, internally illuminated corkscrews descend like fat slinky toys from the ceiling. In the centre of the rear main room an 8-foot-wide chandelier supposedly fabricated by an aeroplane nose-cone company is inlaid with a leaded glass whorl. The chairs, bar stools and booths finish in twists, and the bar itself is a spiral.

These ripe, organic shapes are complemented by rich surfaces on the walls, mosaic floors, and stained-glass panels. Silk drapery hangs above

Jordan Mozer & Associates 1990

Jordan Mozer & Associates 1990

narrow mirrors on textured walls that have had streaks of different coloured plaster applied with a cake icer. The snailshell-shaped lighting fixtures are particularly wonderful, made of handblown glass set in copper.

Drama and theatricality are appropriate here; the restaurant has always been patronised by opera stars and fans from the nearby Lyric Opera.

ADDRESS 71 West Monroe Street (between South Dearborn and South Clark Streets)
SIZE 5500 square feet (510 square metres)
COST $980,000
CLIENT the Capitanini Family
RTT Monroe on Red Line, Blue Line
BUS 1, 7, 22, 24, 36, 42, 60, 62, 126, 129, 130, 151
ACCESS Monday–Saturday 11.00–14.30, 17.00–21.45

Jordan Mozer & Associates 1990

Jordan Mozer & Associates 1990

Ralph H Metcalfe Federal Center

A competition for this federal project was held in 1988 among architect/developer/contractor teams. This is the first building constructed under the auspices of a new programme run by the General Service Administration, the government agency responsible for property management. The Design Build programme is economically advantageous as private developers become responsible for delivering an entire package at a fixed cost. Siting, design, construction, long-term financing, and guaranteed occupancy were all part of the specifications. An unusual ownership contract is involved as well. After thirty years of paying regular monthly rent the government gets full ownership.

The interesting twist to this arrangement was that the siting of the building was part of the competitive scheme. Property rights narrowed the field down, and it was probably due to luck, not a masterplan, that the building ended up adjacent to three other federal buildings, in the Chicago Federal Center, creating a small centralised governmental enclave. The winning scheme was designed to complement the Miesian structures surrounding it. The Post Office and the nearby Dirksen and Klucynski Buildings were begun in 1961 by Mies van der Rohe and completed by 1974.

The new building is named after US representative Ralph Metcalfe (also at one time an Olympic star) and is home to the Environmental Protection Agency, US Department of Agriculture, Social Security Administration and the Department of Housing and Urban Development.

Twenty-seven storeys with a two-storey annexe, this tall, rectangular building has 600,000 square feet of office space. The bustle houses amenities such as a staff cafeteria, a daycare centre, a health club and a 9000 square foot conference centre. Serious and dignified, this understated tower has a 27-foot-high lobby similar to its neighbours. The curtain wall

Fujikawa, Johnson & Associates 1991

Fujikawa, Johnson & Associates 1991

and structural columns are clad in black-grey thermal finish granite creating a sombre Modernist ambience. Structurally a straightforward poured-in-place reinforced concrete beam/slab system using post-tensioning tendons in the east–west direction, this building had a couple of unusual technical requirements. The type of soil the building sits on required that the caissons had to be very wide in diameter (some are 9 feet across) under the high-rise section of the building. The need for computers and sophisticated communication equipment required an exorbitant number of power outlets. The electrified floordeck system has one outlet per 90 square feet as compared to the average of one per 175 square feet.

In summer 1993 a Frank Stella sculpture commissioned by the GSA as part of their art in architecture series (under the national scheme a half per cent of construction cost is set aside for art) was installed. This 118-foot-high steel and aluminium work, 'The Town-Ho's Story', is one in a series of 135 different sculptures, each based on a chapter in *Moby Dick*.

ADDRESS 77 West Jackson Boulevard
STRUCTURAL ENGINEER Cohen Barreto Marchertas, Inc.
CLIENT US General Services Administration and Stein & Company Federal Center, Inc.
COST $95 million
SIZE 800,000 square feet (74,300 square metres)
RTT Jackson/State on Red Line, Jackson/Dearborn on Blue Line, La Salle/Van Buren on Brown Line, Orange Line, Purple Line Express
BUS 1, 7, 22, 24, 42 60, 62, 126, 129, 130, 151
ACCESS public lobby

East Loop

Fujikawa, Johnson & Associates 1991

Fujikawa, Johnson & Associates 1991

Daniel F and Ada I Rice Building

It is easy to miss the austere historicist exterior of this addition to the Art Institute. The Spartan Indiana-limestone-clad façade with mere suggestions of ornament and practically no windows is neo-Classical. Hiding at the south corner of the original Beaux-Arts building, the extension is overshadowed by the Illinois Central Railroad tracks. The main entrance is through the grand old building so the Rice addition's public face (the south façade) is only used as an occasional exit.

The project included renovation of the existing building (completed in 1987) and relocation of the museum's central cooling tower. The three-storey addition provides exhibition and storage space. The internal entrance to the new galleries is on a cross-axis with the original building. The formality of the overall design is emphasised by the serene colours used throughout. The first floor is focused around an elegant, unashamedly Classical, two-storey skylit sculpture court framed by colonnades. Axial views allow peeks into the surrounding American art galleries.

The structural layout has repeatedly been described as a 'Thermos bottle' design. Services have been sandwiched into thin spaces running along the inside perimeters of the building, creating a passive vapour barrier. With incredible respect for its contents, this extension has been very literally treated as a container for the precious objects within.

ADDRESS Michigan Avenue at Adams Street
STRUCTURAL ENGINEERS Cohen Barreto Marchertas, Inc.
SIZE 130,000 square feet (12,000 square metres)
RTT Adams/Wabash on Brown Line, Orange Line, Purple line Express
BUS 1, 3, 4, 6, 7, 14, 60, 126, 127, 129, 145, 147, 151
ACCESS Monday, Wednesday, Friday 10.30–16.30, Tuesday, 10.30–20.00, Saturday 10.00–17.00, Sunday 12.00–17.00

East Loop

Hammond, Beeby & Babka 1988

Hammond, Beeby & Babka 1988

Japanese Screen Gallery

A mixture of traditional Japanese architecture and geometric minimalism characterises Tadao Ando's first project in America. This signature space is the last room in the recently renovated 16,500 square foot Chinese, Japanese, and Korean wing of the Art Institute.

Access is through glass doors, necessary for proper temperature and humidity control. A symmetrical forest of sixteen free-standing oil-stained oak columns, a foot square and 10 feet high, forms a grid directly in front of the entrance. According to Ando, '… the pillars obstruct the viewer's gaze and yet help to suggest depth and resonance of the space. As the visitor moves through this space, the static pillars change their relationships. At times the pillars overlap and unite'.

The display cases containing the screens and ancient ash-glazed stoneware jars seem oddly placed, winding in an L formation along the back and right side walls. They are actually placed to make a point. Physical metaphors for the expansion of space, the panels' purpose is the division of space for privacy yet the art they sport suggests spatial depth.

ADDRESS The Art Institute of Chicago, South Michigan Avenue at East Adams Street
ASSOCIATED ARCHITECTS Cone Kalb Wonderlick
STRUCTURAL ENGINEERS Knight Architects Engineers Planners, Inc.
SIZE 1850 square feet (172 square metres)
RTT Adams/Wabash on Brown Line, Orange Line, Purple Line Express
BUS 1, 3, 4, 6, 7, 14, 60, 126, 127, 145, 147, 151
ACCESS Monday, Wednesday–Friday 10.30–16.30; Tuesday 10.30–20.00; Saturday 10.00–17.00 Sunday and holidays 12.00–17.00

East Loop

Tadao Ando Architect & Associates 1992

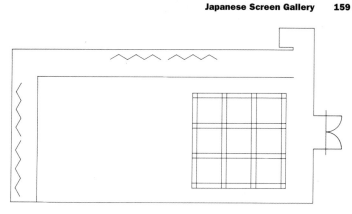

East Loop

Tadao Ando Architect & Associates 1992

Harold Washington Library

Love it or hate it, Chicago's first central library is dichotomous in many respects, not the least in the reaction it elicits on first viewing. The largest municipal library in America it is one of the largest public libraries in the world, second only to the British Library in London. Controversial from its inception, a design/build competition (financed by a bond issue), relatively rare in the States, was held in 1988 to decide the architect. Drawings by six teams were exhibited and the public became involved.

Named after the city's first black mayor, it is significant that one of the most important buildings to be erected in Chicago in the early 1990s is a civic space. The library houses approximately 2,000,000 circulating volumes and has ten floors, each devoted to specific topics. The programme includes an orientation theatre, language-learning centre, 385-seat auditorium, video theatre, public restaurant and a bookstore.

While this is all very good, once again the coin has two sides. It is very reassuring that a repository for books, a sanctuary in fact, exists in a post-urban environment, but has any thought been given to the nature of a contemporary library, or of a library for the future? Information technology is changing so rapidly that the question must be posed: is such a retrograde building (architecturally and functionally) appropriate? Need a library be a memorial?

The building has inspired extreme criticism leaning in all possible directions. Called everything from a monstrous behemoth to the best civic building in 60 years, the most important critic is the public and the overwhelming reaction seems to be one of enthusiasm.

There is no mistaking this as a bold and brawny monolithic public building. The Beaux-Arts/neo-Classical exterior is massive in scale, the rusticated granite base looming powerfully (verging on the threatening) over passers-by. Monumentally heavy walls are emphasised and exag-

East Loop

Hammond, Beeby & Babka 1991–1993

Hammond, Beeby & Babka 1991–1993

gerated by recessed five-storey arched openings containing windows of several floors. Durable deep red brick (the familiar colour enhances the solid image) faces the building from the third floor up, the floor levels marked externally by horizontal bands of cast stone.

Decoration is an intrinsic part of the library's vocabulary. The façade is covered with stone iconography based on historical Chicago themes. Reminiscent of Greek temples, the ornament starts as an intertwined chain-patterned strip (guilloche) around the base, with foliated scrollwork above. Huge cast-stone corn stalks, oak leaves, swords and shields, Ceres (a popular Chicago theme also adorning the 1930 Board of Trade Building), and other harvest symbols cover the exterior, surrounding 22 allegorical medallions on the seventh floor. A glass curtain wall emerges at the ninth floor, forming massive pediments topped with seven over-scaled aluminium gargoyles. Designed and sculpted by Kent Bloomer and Raymond Kaskey, these ornaments are breathtaking from far away but seem plastic and Disney-like up close.

There is something oppressive about the massive over-scaling of this building and its ornaments. It is as though the gigantic owls on the roof could swoop down and gobble up the tiny mortals at the structure's base.

ADDRESS 400 South State Street between West Congress and Van Buren
ASSOCIATE ARCHITECTS A Epstein & Sons
COST $144 million
SIZE 760,000 square feet (70,600 square metres)
RTT Jackson/State on Red Line
BUS 2, 6, 11, 15, 29, 36, 44, 62, 62 Express, 99, 99M, 146, 162, 164
ACCESS Tuesday to Thursday 09.00–19.00, Friday to Saturday 09.00–17.00

East Loop

Hammond, Beeby & Babka 1991–1993

Hammond, Beeby & Babka 1991–1993

West Loop

One Financial Place 166
Chicago Board Options Exchange 168
Savings of America Tower 170
Holabird & Root Offices 172
190 South La Salle Street 176
Chemical Plaza 178
Helene Curtis Corporate Headquarters 180
222 North La Salle Street Addition 182
181 West Madison Street 184
Chiasso 186
AT&T Corporate Center, USG Building 188
311 South Wacker Drive 192
Chicago Mercantile Exchange 194
333 West Wacker Drive 196
225 West Wacker Drive 200
Morton International Building 204
Northwestern Atrium Center 206
T W Best Newsstand 208
Presidential Towers 210

One Financial Place

The centrepiece of a new trio of financial structures that is physically and electronically linked with the gorgeous Art Deco Chicago Board of Trade. State-of-the-art provisions have been made to distribute necessary data/telecommunications services vertically and horizontally throughout the complex.

This 39-storey structural steel tower clad in Imperial red granite with bronze tinted vision glass sits on what used to be the train shed and railroad tracks of the LaSalle Street Station. An integral part of the complex is an obscurely placed plaza with a fountain and bronze horse sculpture by Ludovico de Luigi, a tribute to the piazza of all piazzas – St Mark's in Venice - with which this plaza has nothing in common except air.

ADDRESS 440 South LaSalle Street
CLIENT Financial Place Partnership
COST $62 million
SIZE 1,147,350 square feet
(106,600 square metres)
RTT La Salle Van Buren on Brown Line,
Orange Line, Purple Line Express
BUS 11, 37, 135, 136, 156
ACCESS public lobby and plaza

West Loop

Skidmore, Owings & Merrill, Inc. 1985

Skidmore, Owings & Merrill, Inc. 1985

Chicago Board Options Exchange

Affectionately called the CBOE amongst insiders, this building houses the growing facilities of The Chicago Board of Trade. Lined by sidewalk arcades, this ten-storey box secretively shelters a 44,000-square-foot trading floor and another columnless, capacious floor to be used for future expansion. An Exchange Bridge (added in 1987) links the Chicago Board of Trade with the CBOE, making the biggest adjacent trading area in the United States. This exposed steel truss supported by a large pier serves to regulate interior circulation.

Located on one side of One Financial Place, the financial complex is completed by a third structure, the Midwest Stock Exchange, flanking the other side of One Financial Place. All three buildings are clad in red granite and have bronze-tinted windows although the CBOE has a negligible number of windows, hence the private, furtive effect.

ADDRESS 141 West Van Buren Street
CLIENT One Financial Place Partnership
SIZE 348,000 square feet (32,300 square metres)
RTT La Salle Van Buren on Brown Line, Orange Line, Purple Line Express
BUS 41, 60, 157
ACCESS none

West Loop

Skidmore, Owings & Merrill, Inc. 1985

Skidmore, Owings & Merrill, Inc. 1985

Savings of America Tower

A curved grey-tinted glass bay extending over LaSalle Street is topped by an extraordinary projecting cantilevered trellis. This architectural element then transforms into a ladder and finally culminates in a wall sitting on the quarter vault pinnacle. This adds to the asymmetrically arranged façade of this narrow 40-storey building.

A fine example of texture, materials and geometrical form, this is one of Helmut Jahn's finest buildings. The curved entrance gallery, also placed off centre, has a wonderful 20 x 50 foot curved mosaic, 'Flight of Daedalus and Icarus' (by Roger Brown) flying above. Ingredients intrinsic to the building's design are echoed in the mural. Clearly some collaboration between artist and architect occurred, and it is refreshing to see artwork incorporated in a building's design.

ADDRESS 120 North LaSalle Street
CLIENT Ahmanson Commercial Development, Mitsui & Co.
STRUCTURAL ENGINEERS Martin/Lam, Inc.
SIZE 400,000 square feet (37,000 square metres)
COST $48 million
RTT Randolph/Wells on Brown Line, Orange Line, Purple Line Express, Washington on Blue Line
BUS 20, 23, 56, 127, 131, 135, 136, 156, 157
ACCESS public lobby

West Loop

Murphy/Jahn 1991

Murphy/Jahn 1991

Holabird & Root Offices

Founded in 1880, Holabird & Root is one of the oldest architectural firms in America. Originally established as Holabird & Roche, the partnership was handed down to the next generation in the late 1920s. The firm's title was altered when Holabird's son John was joined by John Root, Jr, whose own father had been Daniel Burnham's partner. They had met while finishing their studies at the Ecole des Beaux Arts in Paris and returned to Chicago to take over the well-established firm. The founding designers were known for their powerful Chicago School buildings. Amongst their definitive steel-frame edifices are the McClurg and Old Colony buildings. The younger partners became famous for such spectacular Art Deco buildings as the Chicago Board of Trade and the Palmolive Building, and civic institutions such as the magnificent Soldier Field.

The present partners recently decided to renovate their own offices. Based in a 70-year old courtyard building, their dominant aim was to make full use of the central light court. The clever solution was to insert a steel and glass bridge diagonally spanning this open area. Internal circulation could be reorganised and opened up by functional use of the light court. This dynamic hanging walkway leads across from the elevator exit to the walled-in reception area. As the office plan is an L, those afraid of heights can take the longer route around the bridge.

Structurally, the bridge floor is hung from its roof structure and outrigger-type brackets minimise its load on the existing concrete frame. These brackets are tied to two concrete columns with steel jackets. The actual construction involved shop-fabricated members being lifted by crane into the office through a window, put together and pulled across the light court by a winch and then hung in position.

An industrial quality defines the drafting and work areas. The exposed mechanical services, electrical ducts and power drops are intentional

Holabird & Root 1992

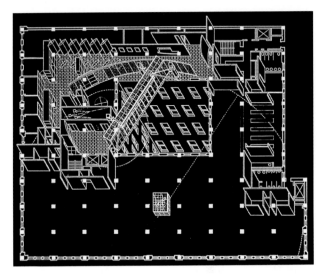

Holabird & Root 1992

references to what the firm refers to as the machine aesthetic. The administrative area is more refined, with slate floors and curving glass walls. Executive spaces are separated by fritted glass partitions. Six pivoting, perforated metal screens rotate to serve a double function as display panels and space dividers, creating a semi-private conference space. The meeting room opposite has a wonderful, curved, heavy sliding door on a giant track. This is the slide show room and affords greater privacy.

In 1992 the firm won an Honor Award (Divine Detail category) for the bridge and a Citation of Merit for the whole scheme from the Chicago Chapter of the American Institute of Architects.

ADDRESS 300 West Adams Street
STRUCTURAL ENGINEERS David Ekstrom
CLIENT Holabird & Root
SIZE 22,500 square feet (2100 square metres)
RTT Quincy/Wells on Brown Line, Orange Line, Purple Line Express
BUS 1, 7, 37, 60, 61, 126, 129, 130, 135, 136, 156
ACCESS on request

West Loop

Holabird & Root 1992

Holabird & Root 1992

190 South La Salle Street

Philip Johnson and John Burgee's only project in Chicago stands on the corner of the La Salle Street canyon in the heart of the financial district. Classified as both Postmodern and historicist, this 40-storey tower is a study in formal pastiche. Elegant and graceful, it has often been criticised as pretentious. Inspiration clearly came from Burnham & Root's 1886 Rookery building. The overall design is loosely based on John W Root's Masonic Temple, built in 1892 and demolished in 1939.

Like two completely different buildings, the top of 190 South La Salle differs drastically from the bottom. The five-storey rusticated base is built of red granite and is a direct reference to the Rookery. The 35-storey tower of pink granite and tinted glass is much lighter and more refined. The roof, reminiscent of the Masonic Temple, has six copper-clad, aluminium-crested gables housing a law library and reading room. Set on each side of the gables are whimsical concrete balls, evidence of Johnson's penchant for paraphrasing historical references. The 50-foot-high entrance arch leads into an over-scaled barrel-vaulted lobby. Even the elevator cabs have goldleaf-covered vaulted ceilings and marble floors! Huge bronze chandeliers hang above the black and white marble checkerboard floor, dwarfing a sculpture by Anthony Caro, 'Chicago Fugue'.

ADDRESS 190 South La Salle Street
ASSOCIATE ARCHITECT Shaw & Associates, Inc.
SIZE 9,000,000 square feet (836,100 square metres)
STRUCTURAL ENGINEERS Cohen Barreto Marchertas, Inc.
RTT Quincy/Wells or LaSalle Van Buren on Brown Line, Orange Line, La Sale/Congress on Blue Line
BUS 1, 7, 2 2, 24, 37, 42, 60, 65, 62 local, 126, 135, 136, 156
ACCESS public lobby

West Loop

John Burgee Architects with Philip Johnson 1987

West Loop

John Burgee Architects with Philip Johnson 1987

Chemical Plaza

The original 1912 structure standing on this LaSalle Boulevard site was the Otis building designed by Holabird & Roche. The Classical Revival granite and terracotta base was preserved in order to continue the traditional streetscape and to allow the new structure to retain a relationship with its neighbours. Adding a 33-storey office building on top, the Canadian firm Moriyama & Teshima left the north and east walls of the four bottom storeys intact. The load of the new building's columns was simply transferred to some of the large caissons of the original building.

There are only two demarcations of the changeover between old and new. The tower glazing directly above the base is set back slightly and a semicircular seven-storey lobby has been inserted behind the historic façade. This creates a transitional space as one passes through the old thick walls and progresses into the newer lobby. To accommodate as many corner offices as possible (ten per floor) the north-west and south-west corners are stepped back in phases.

An otherwise unremarkable office building, the cobalt blue painted frame, bright green detailing and blue-silver tinted windows make this tower block noticeable, inappropriate and out of place.

ADDRESS 10 South LaSalle Street
ASSOCIATE ARCHITECTS Holabird & Root
STRUCTURAL ENGINEERS Cohen Barreto Marchertas, Inc.
CLIENT Fidinam (USA), Inc.
COST $43 million
SIZE 844,000 square feet (78,400 square metres)
RTT Quincy/Wells on Brown Line, Orange Line, Purple Line Express
BUS 14, 20, 23, 56, 127, 131, 135, 136, 156, 157
ACCESS public lobby

West Loop

Moriyama & Teshima Architects 1986

LA SALLE STREET ELEVATION

Moriyama & Teshima Architects 1986

Helene Curtis Corporate Headquarters

At the junction of the Wells Avenue Bridge and the north bank of the Chicago River, a 1912 warehouse designed by L Gustav Hallberg has been renovated to become home to America's second largest cosmetic manufacturers. The company was founded in Chicago in 1927 and still maintains its world headquarters in the windy city. The extensive overhaul of the 168,000-square-foot building has been jokingly dubbed a facelift or beauty makeover by many architectural critics. And a most successful makeover at that!

The rehab began with the gutting of the interior, leaving only the brick shell, support columns and stair tower. A floor was added at the top, making the structure 10 storeys tall, emerging as a green glass cylinder surrounded by two glass squares capping the building. The glass is a sumptuous green and consistent from the bottom of the structure up so it seems as though the fenestrations at the top have broken free from their brick constraints. The flags waving from the roof slam home the nautical theme. This tenth floor is a two-storey boardroom surrounded by smaller executive spaces. The oval conference room, complete with Saarinen furniture, is serene and posh. The entire interior is geared towards promoting an ambience of individual importance. Bleached oak-panelled workstations throughout the offices have been designed according to user needs. The monotony of the ceiling is alleviated by puffs of acoustical tiles.

ADDRESS 325 North Wells Street
SIZE 163,000 square feet (15,000 square metres)
COST $13 million
RTT Merchandise Mart on Brown Line, Purple Line Express
BUS 37, 41, 44, 61, 125
ACCESS public lobby

West Loop

Booth Hansen & Associates 1984

222 North La Salle Street Addition

An elegant renovation and limestone clad addition to the Builders' Building erected in 1927, designed by Graham, Anderson, Probst & White. The addition on the western side of the existing building retains the proportions and compositional principles of the existing façade.

Significant energy and expense has been spent on redesigning the entryway. A three-storey, three-bay-wide loggia leads to a two-storey lobby that terminates at the restored rotunda. This four-storey atrium, the link between the old and new structures, is artificially backlit, and redecorated in the original 1927 colour scheme complete with gold-leaf detailing. A grand staircase is the central focus of the space as the elevators have been moved to the addition. Wooden spandrels replace the decaying decorative iron spandrels and a new marble floor extending into the addition (a further connection between the two structures) replaces the previous terrazzo. The entire roof has been replaced by a four-storey glass sloped penthouse, visually connecting the two buildings.

ADDRESS 222 North LaSalle Street
CLIENT Tishman Speyer Properties
SIZE 1,030,000 square feet (96,000 square metres)
COST $46,750,000
RTT Clark/Lake on Blue Line, Brown Line, Orange Line, Purple Line Express
BUS 135, 136, 156
ACCESS public lobby

West Loop

Skidmore, Owings & Merrill, Inc. 1986

Skidmore, Owings & Merrill, Inc. 1986

181 West Madison Street

Vertical and vast describe Cesar Pelli's only Chicago tower. A seemingly straightforward glass (and granite-clad pier) curtain wall has been subtly modified to add dimensionality. Vertical ribs of granite express the 5-foot interior floor modules, and metal accent mullions (set slightly away from the windows) are centred between the vertical ribs, reinforcing the tower's verticality. The piers end in metal finials 9 inches from the top of the glass line and are meant to reflect sunlight and add height when lit at night.

The vastness occurs in the interior, a vaulted coffered ceiling lobby preceded by a four-storey glass roofed loggia on the Madison Street front. In the deliberately overscaled five-storey lobby even at lunch hour the space feels deserted and the lone receptionist looks lost amidst miles of white, grey and green marble in this ghost town room.

The developers of Paine Webber Tower, as 181 West Madison is known, Miglin-Beitler and Cesar Pelli & Associates have an extraordinary proposition for another building. A 125-storey tower was planned as the tallest building in the world to be located at the south-west corner of Madison and Wells Streets. Elegant as the model and plans appear, the need for such macho architecture is elusive.

ADDRESS 181 West Madison Street at Wells Street
ASSOCIATE ARCHITECT Shaw & Associates, Inc.
STRUCTURAL ENGINEER Cohen Barreto Marchertas, Inc.
COST $75 million
SIZE 1,000,000 gross square feet (93,000 square metres)
RTT Quincy/Wells or Randolph/Wells on Brown Line, Orange Line, Purple Line Express
BUS 20, 23, 37, 56, 61, 127, 131, 157
ACCESS public lobby

Cesar Pelli & Associates 1990

West Loop

Cesar Pelli & Associates 1990

Chiasso

Adjacent to the lobby of the glossy Skidmore, Owings & Merrill 303 Madison Street office tower (completed in 1988) is an amusingly witty store. Packed with trendy designer objects, accessories and toys for the modern executive, the shop points a gently mocking finger at the dead serious building it inhabits.

Conceived as a stage set in the process of either being constructed or disassembled, the shop consists of fragmented forms placed in an unfinished space. Amongst exposed ductwork and an unusually furry ceiling (most likely faux insulation!) only synthetic-faux materials have been used. The 'industrial look' has taken a new twist with exposed standard scaffolding supporting fragments of display tables covered, of course, in faux pigskin laminates.

Faux granite, faux bronze, faux brushed aluminium, faux ebonised oak and even faux paint texture laminates create this anecdotal environment. The contrast between the very serious, shiny, dark, marble lobby and the sleek corporate toys available in the shop is extremely clever.

West Loop

ADDRESS 303 Madison Street
SIZE 870 square feet (81 square metres)
RTT Quincy/Wells on Brown Line, Orange Line, Purple Line Express
BUS 14, 20, 37, 56, 61, 127, 129, 131, 157
ACCESS open

Florian-Wierzbowski 1988

Florian-Wierzbowski 1988

AT&T Corporate Center, USG Building

The lavish foyer of this temple to the telephone is appropriately cathe-dralesque. Costing approximately $3 million, almost everything in the 40-foot vaulted lobby was custom designed. The skylit central hall covered with marble and exotic woods serves as the connection between the two buildings. The second floor of this hall is part of the building's public space and has restaurants and shops as well as an amazing vista of the vast, richly detailed and beautifully crafted lobby. Marble, gold leaf, and American oak walls are complemented by the elaborately patterned Italian marble floor. Satin finish bronze grilles and feature strips line the ceiling from which three massive chandeliers dangle.

Covering an entire block and almost 900 feet tall, the two buildings together contain over 2.4 million square feet. A combination of Art Deco, Modernism and what some critics call Revivalism, this building has been inspired, like much of architect Adrian Smith's work, by the Tribune Tower and other 1920s' skyscrapers. The tripartite granite façade emphasises verticality. The AT&T building rises 60 storeys and the USG is somewhat smaller at 34 storeys.

An interesting technique was used to pattern the 2600 decorative aluminium panels that separate the windows. Meant to evoke turn-of-the-century ornamental ironwork, imprints were photographed onto each panel, bypassing the more usual stencilling process.

This very prolific firm, SOM, founded in Chicago in 1936 as Skidmore and Owings, has several other recent towers in the Loop worth mentioning. A 28-storey red granite clad, rather petite skyscraper can be found at 225 West Washington Street (1986). One North Franklin (1991) is another Art-Deco corporate pageant and 303 West Madison (1988) has a beautiful stained-glass wall facing Franklin Street. 500 West Monroe (1992) has a dramatic nine-storey base topped by a 36-storey

West Loop

Skidmore, Owings & Merrill, Inc. 1989, 1992

West Loop

Skidmore, Owings & Merrill, Inc. 1989, 1992

series of setbacks and is yet another record holder as the current tallest office tower on the west bank of the Chicago River.

ADDRESS 227 West Monroe Street and 125 South Franklin Street
CLIENT Stein & Co.
COST $250 million and $94 million
SIZE 1,750,000 square feet (162,600 square metres) and 1,100,000 square feet (102,000 square metres)
RTT Quincy/Wells on brown Line, Orange Line; Purple Line Express
BUS 1, 7, 37, 60, 61, 19, 129, 130, 135, 136, 151, 156
ACCESS public lobby

Skidmore, Owings & Merrill, Inc. 1989, 1992

Skidmore, Owings & Merrill, Inc. 1989, 1992

311 South Wacker Drive

Another record-breaking building, this 959-foot-tall skyscraper is the world's tallest reinforced-concrete office tower. The first phase in a three-tower development on the South Wacker Drive site, the projected complex (estimated to be 4,000,000 square feet in total) will be focused around the recently built Wintergarden plaza. This is a vast 80-foot barrel-vaulted space intended as a pedestrian hub with pedways linking the building with transportation systems. The skylight corridor is supported by white painted steel rising from granite piers and once the remaining towers are built will unfortunately be hidden from the sun.

The 65-storey tower is clad in a pinky shade of Texas red granite with shiny horizontal strapping increasing in density at the lower levels.

The top of the building is its most extraordinary feature. It has been nicknamed 'White Castle' for the giant (105 feet tall) translucent glass cylinder surrounded by four smaller glass cylinders perched on the 51st floor. Not well liked by the architectural community, the drums, especially when lit at night by 1852 florescent tubes, seem a trifle medieval, and unnecessarily territorial.

ADDRESS 311 South Wacker Drive
ASSOCIATE ARCHITECTS Harwood K Smith & Partners
CLIENT Lincoln Property Company
SIZE 1,400,000 square feet (130,000 square metres)
RTT Quincy/Wells on Brown Line, Orange Line, Purple line Express
BUS 1, 7, 60, 121, 123, 126, 130, 135, 136, 151, 156
ACCESS public lobby

Kohn Pedersen Fox 1990

Kohn Pedersen Fox 1990

Chicago Mercantile Exchange

Two 40-storey granite and glass twin office towers stand on either side of the ten-storey Carnelian granite clad structure that houses the 40,000-square-foot trading floor of the project's major tenant. A floor above the trading area also has 30,000 square feet of column-free space, an admirable structural feat. This was achieved by cantilevering a substantial section of the top 34 storeys of the two towers over the low-rise building, allowing loads to be carried to the ground without columns in the trading spaces. Built in two phases, the first tower was in use and the trading floor was occupied by the time the second tower was erected. Fronting the Chicago River (affording spectacular views), the entire structure presents a calm, solid ambience, quite the antithesis of the interior activities.

It is possible to view the trading floor, a fascinating and colourful experience as the different colour coats run and gesticulate frantically. The fourth floor visitors' gallery is reached via a separate elevator shuttle, bypassing the many escalators carrying runners and traders back and forth.

ADDRESS 10 and 30 South Wacker Drive
STRUCTURAL ENGINEERS Alfred Benesch & Co.
CLIENT Metropolitan Structures/JMB Urban Realty
COST $350 million
RTT Quincy/Wells or Randolph/Wells on Brown, Orange, Purple Lines
BUS 20, 23, 56, 127, 131, 157
ACCESS public viewing gallery on the fourth floor

West Loop

Fujikawa, Johnson & Associates 1983, 1988

Fujikawa, Johnson & Associates 1983, 1988

333 West Wacker Drive

Only ten years old and already an icon of the city, this is easily the most beautiful recent skyscraper in Chicago. Site sensitive, elegant and moving to look at from all angles this is an architectural *tour de force*. This dramatic 36-storey office tower is delightfully curved on one façade and angular on the other. The 365-foot-wide curve is a contextual response to the twisting of the Chicago River on which this façade fronts, and the rectilinear Loop front suits the triangular site perfectly.

Having swept up all possible awards and compliments this is one building it is impossible not to get excited about. The taut curve of the river-front façade is a reflective green glass curtain wall, reinforced by horizontal bullnoses at 6-foot intervals. The sheer green colour deepens and changes shade (sometimes seeming almost silvery) according to the river and the sun, always dramatically reflecting the urban landscape. This elevation has a calmness and meditative quality appropriate to an aquatic and urban setting. It is marvellous to stand, drive or sit on the El and watch the world curving by on this smooth surface as the location of 333 West Wacker makes it highly visible from many vistas. The top of the curve is set against a bevelled surface (chamfers), the slim flatness adding a tension to the fluid bend of the north façade as well as calling attention to the buildings crown. This curtain wall is supported by an elegant horizontally banded polychromatic granite base with highlights of black, grey and green marble or granite and brushed stainless steel.

The base houses mechanical facilities, cleverly disguised by the Art Deco stripes. Large medallions resembling ship portholes serve as ventilation louvres, a theme repeated in later KPF buildings. The steel bars of these round slatted windows are echoed in the Art Deco style railings along the serrated edge of the south-east façade. The downtown façade is geometrically set on the city grid, softened by the circular steps leading

Kohn Pedersen Fox 1983

Kohn Pedersen Fox 1983

up to the circular two-storey lobby. The materials of the exterior base are used in the green and silver lobby, continuing the lush ambience. There are many thoughtful touches such as the octagonal black columns that support the base echoing those found across the river at Merchandise Mart. The usual tower block amenities are found on the lobby level. Hidden below grade is a two-level parking garage.

ADDRESS 333 West Wacker Drive
ASSOCIATE ARCHITECTS Perkins & Will
CLIENT Urban Investment & Development Company
SIZE 800,000 square feet (74,000 square metres)
RTT Clark/Lake on Blue Line, Brown Line, Orange Line, Purple Line Express
BUS 16, 37, 41, 44, 61, 125
ACCESS public lobby

Kohn Pedersen Fox 1983

Kohn Pedersen Fox 1983

225 West Wacker Drive

The 1980s' economic boom created such a wide market for speculative office buildings that a flood of out-of-town architects arrived on the scene in Chicago. Amongst the most successful of these has been the New York-based firm Kohn Pedersen Fox Associates. KPF have certainly made their mark on the city. Aside from 333 and 225 West Wacker, they have recently designed 900 North Michigan Avenue, Chicago Title & Trust and the 65-storey 311 South Wacker Drive, all very substantial schemes.

Completely different (apart from the repeated although modified porthole motif), but in its own fashion as successful as its superlative neighbour, 333 West Wacker Drive, 225 is a rectilinear masonry box crowned by four aluminium spires. Within the base for these twinned spires is a barrel-vaulted roof and penthouse executive offices. Needless to say the lanterns are illuminated at night. This narrow tower is 31 storeys high and the straightforward exterior is a blend of granite and marble with an aluminium and insulated glass wall.

Set on a protracted, slender site, the building is bounded by West Wacker Drive, Franklin and Lake Streets, with entrance lobbies on both West Wacker Drive and Franklin Street. A riverfront arcade complements the dignified marble and granite clad vaulted lobby, planned, according to KPF's literature, as the building's formal front door and a transitional space between the exterior and interior of the building.

The stainless steel portal in the centre of the arcade is intended to pay reference to the metal construction of Chicago bridges. The two lobbies are decorated using the same sophisticated vocabulary and are connected by a vestibule. The Franklin Street atrium is 125 feet long and 35 feet wide and leads off into the requisite shops housed within the building. Behind the building and above the elevated train tracks is a six-storey parking garage.

Kohn Pedersen Fox 1989

Kohn Pedersen Fox 1989

While it is nowhere near as spectacular as 333, this is a well built and gracious structure that allows its illustrious predecessor to shine.

ADDRESS 225 West Wacker Drive
ASSOCIATE ARCHITECTS Perkins & Will
CLIENT The Palmer Group Limited
SIZE 710,000 square feet (66,000 square metres)
RTT Clark/Lake on Blue Line, Brown Line, Orange Line, Purple Line Express
BUS 16, 37, 41, 44, 61, 125
ACCESS public lobby

Kohn Pedersen Fox 1989

Kohn Pedersen Fox 1989

Located on an asymmetrical delightfully urban plot along the west bank of the Chicago River, this edifice was built on an unusual 53,225-square-foot air-rights site. An extraordinary engineering design allows part of the building to partially hang over active railroad tracks. This south-west corner (55 x 150 feet encompassing twelve floors) is suspended by steel rolled section trusses which are cantilevered from the eastern part of the building. The exposed trusses have been likened to bridge elements seen on the Chicago River, adding a contextual element to this massive office block.

The two basic volumes forming the building, one a horizontal rectangle and the other a vertical rectangle, conspicuously reveal their programmatic functions. The shorter block houses a two-storey lobby, six-level parking lot and 250,000 square foot computer centre for use by Illinois Bell Telephone; the upright tower is obviously offices. A 30-foot-high covered promenade leads to the main entrance and a two story lobby. An arcade and an open air plaza overlook the river.

The exterior glass and aluminium curtain wall has been jazzed up with varying patterns of grey granite. Functional stipulations dictated the shade of grey (one of three) or its absence altogether in the intricately patterned façade. This visual stimulation somewhat alleviates the size and mass of these large rectilinear blocks.

ADDRESS 100 North Riverside Plaza
CLIENT Orix Real Estate Equities, Inc.
SIZE 1,100,000 square feet (102,000 square metres)
RTT Randolph/Wells on Brown Line, Orange Line, Purple Line Express
BUS 20, 23, 56, 127, 131, 157
ACCESS public lobby and arcade

Perkins & Will 1990

Perkins & Will 1990

Northwestern Atrium Center

A combined commuter terminal and 40-storey office complex, this building replaces the 1911 Beaux-Arts Chicago and Northwestern Train Station. Another glossy, glassy tower designed by Helmut Jahn, from a distance the cascading layers of blue-grey mirrored glass on the southern façade are quite beautiful, but the closer one gets the more the unfortunate shopping mall effect takes over. Designed originally as an addition for the Board of Trade, the scheme was shelved and later dusted off and adapted to its new site and function.

The reflective glass and steel walls are constructed as waves rhythmically repeating the same curves, inspired by a luxury train, 'The Twentieth Century Limited'. The overall tripartite configuration is accentuated by bands of dark blue enamelled aluminium running down the streamlined façade. Inside lighting fixtures, elevator details and coloured glass decorative elements continue the Art Deco motif. The two-level terminal, with its main entrance on Madison Street, is a series of atriums. The dramatic arched entranceway opens onto exposed structural steel criss-crossing the glazed roof. At ground level a 270-foot-long concourse incorporates 60,000 square feet of retail space. Escalators in the middle of this level lead to a third-floor elevator dock charmingly called a Skylobby, evocative of Jetsonian travel. The name is more exciting than the space.

An enclosed commuter bridge at the second floor of the atrium crosses Canal Street, providing access to Wacker Drive and the Central Loop.

ADDRESS 500 West Madison at North Canal Street
SIZE 1,600,000 square feet (150,000 square metres)
RTT Randolph/Wells on Brown Line, Orange Line, Purple Line Express
BUS 20, 23, 41, 56, 120, 122, 125, 127, 129, 130, 131, 157
ACCESS atriums accessible to public

Murphy/Jahn 1987

Murphy/Jahn 1987

T W Best Newsstand

This prototype newsstand was designed as a model environment capable of being adapted and reinterpreted in different settings.

A grey chequered floor and black modular units are offset by laminated architectural elements which serve a dual purpose as compositional ingredients and attention grabbers. The main focal point is a bright red frame cutting across the centre of the space, terminating in a delightful giant blue cone. This primary-coloured form is a witty peanut and potato-chip display. Yellow perforated metal banners hanging from the ceiling delineate the traffic flow. The colourful and efficient organisation make the items on sale easily accessible for the commuter rushing through.

Eva Maddox has designed another, later installation for T W Best at the Hotel Nikko (320 North Dearborn Street). This variation retains the progenitor's economical unit display although here entirely in wood and planned around a central counter. The Hotel Nikko branch has a calmer and more leisurely ambience suitable to its less trafficked surroundings.

Maddox is known for her extraordinary temporary installations, particularly at Merchandise Mart, the massive Art Deco showroom complex built in 1931 (desinged by Graham, Anderson, Probst & White) and renovated from 1986 to 1991. Located between North Wells Street and North Orleans Street and normally only open to architects and designers, it is worth asking whether there are any current showrooms (they are very short-lived affairs) designed by Maddox.

ADDRESS Northwestern Terminal Building, 500 West Madison Street
INFORMATION ABOUT MERCHANDISE MART telephone 312-644 4664
RTT Randolph/Wells on Brown Line, Orange Line, Purple Line Express
BUS 20, 23, 41, 56, 120, 122, 125, 127, 129, 130, 131, 157
ACCESS open

West Loop

Eva Maddox Associates 1989

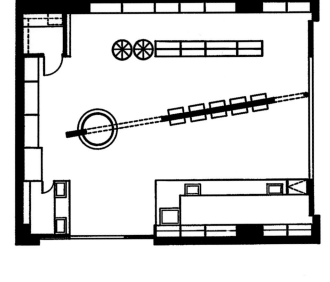

West Loop

Eva Maddox Associates 1989

Presidential Towers

Notable primarily for the financial mess the scheme has created, Presidential Towers has been a fiscal disaster since completion. Hoped to be the seed of a posh residential community in downtown Chicago capable of transforming a down-and-out neighbourhood into prime real estate, Presidential Towers has now become an icon of urban renewal failure. The developers, McHugh Levin in partnership with Dan Shannon Associates, received subsidies of one quarter of the overall cost from the federal government's Department of Housing and Urban Development. The City of Chicago also offered aid in the form of tax-exempt interim financing. This did not prevent the project from going into default.

Designed as a series of four identical 49-storey blocks, the towers have 2346 residential units linked at the base by an enclosed pedestrian mall. This covered walkway allows for 90,265 square feet of commercial space. These rather dull, light brown octagonal towers cut diagonally across two city blocks divided by a street. There are multilevel walkways connecting the complex over this street. Nothing about the exterior of the buildings identifies them as residential. It is their repetitive quality that makes these expensive apartment towers so visually unappealing. Only the luxurious amenities (health club, sun deck, rooftop track and basketball court) and expensive rent differentiate this design from welfare housing projects.

ADDRESS 555, 575, 605 and 625 West Madison Street (bordered by West Monroe, North Desplaines and North Clinton Streets)
STRUCTURAL ENGINEERS Chris P Stefanos Associates
COST $125 million
SIZE 2,000,000 square feet (186,000 square metres)
BUS 20, 23, 41, 56, 125, 131, 157
ACCESS public lobby and thoroughfare

West Loop

Solomon Cordwell Buenz & Associates 1986

Near West Side and South Loop

Peter Elliott Productions 214
Greyhound Bus Terminal 216
Canal Center 218
River City 220
John G Shedd Oceanarium 224
Burnham Park Harbor Station 228

Peter Elliott Productions

Plunked directly opposite the rather dull Oprah Winfrey Harpo Studios (remodelled 1989, Nagle, Hartray & Associates) in this predominantly industrial neighbourhood is a gem of a building. A few blocks west of the Kennedy Expressway, it is a charming surprise to stumble across this classy façade of alternating smooth and rusticated precast renaissance stone, glass block and insulated glass. A solid rectilinear structure, it is topped by three metal bowed trusses supporting an elegant brushed aluminium canopy. The canopy is echoed in the reception area by an artful floating desk fabricated by a local sculptor.

The new facility is an expansion of one of the nation's leading tabletop commercial film director's studios. It includes a 70 x 70 foot central shooting space (with an enclosed tinted glass gallery walkway for observation of the ads being shot) with a high-tech temperature control system (in case the shoot involves ice-cream) and state-of-the-art electrical and mechanical systems. Sleek white, grey and the odd splash of red demarcate curved walls hiding a kitchen, client lounge and conference room. Terrazzo floors alternate with checker plate aluminium stairways; most of the trimmings are steel. The extra-large kitchen (allowing space for clients to observe preparations – when I visited hundreds of unwrapped chocolate bars were being prepped) is equipped with video monitors so shoots can be easily co-ordinated.

ADDRESS 1111 West Washington Boulevard
CLIENT Peter Elliott Productions
STRUCTURAL ENGINEERS Stearn-Joglekar, Limited
SIZE 10,000 square feet (930 square metres)
BUS 20, 23, 131
ACCESS none

Near West Side and South Loop

Hartshorne Plunkard, Limited 1993

Hartshorne Plunkard, Limited 1993

Greyhound Bus Terminal

A prototype facility for Greyhound Lines, part of an effort to revitalise their passenger terminals throughout the country, this building replaces a 35-year-old terminal in the Loop. Oddly relocated to a less central address, Greyhound and Trailways buses from all over the States now arrive at the new consolidated terminal.

A graceful architectonic structure, the depot is smaller than photographs suggest. Masonry clad, with alternating horizontal bands of brick and concrete, this two-level building is 35,000 square feet. Two canopies (suspended extensions of the roof) provide 10,000 square feet of sheltered space for 24 bus stalls. Refuelling and mechanical service facilities are housed underneath the canopies.

This programmatic requirement resulted in a structurally expressive roof that spans 45 feet. This technically sophisticated roof is supported by ten 50-foot dark blue steel masts connected to 3-inch-diameter steel rods and then stabilised with white cable crossbracing. Uplift caused by wind loads is controlled by additional steel tube compression members. Deliberately unfinished steel joists and perforated girders are visible on the underside of the covering. The second storey of the building has a serrated perimeter, designed to complement the visible crossbracing and limit solar heat gain.

ADDRESS 630 West Harrison Street at South Desplaines Street
STRUCTURAL ENGINEERS Cohen Barreto Marchertas, Inc.
COST $6.5 million
SIZE 58,400 square feet (5400 square metres) including bus canopies
RTT Clinton on Blue Line
BUS 60
ACCESS open

Nagle, Hartray & Associates 1989

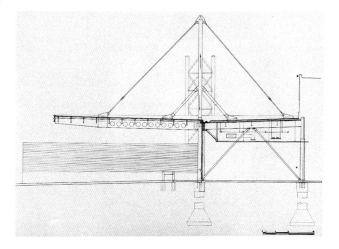

Nagle, Hartray & Associates 1989

Canal Center

This building, the Northern Trust Company Operations Center, was erected to house the bank's 'back office' operations. Relocated from several Loop locations, 2700 employees are now housed here on a 24-hour schedule. Although within a few blocks of the Chicago Union Station, the building is cut off from central downtown by the Chicago River and the Congress Expressway. The lack of local amenities resulted in a surprisingly suburban and self-sufficient building including a staff cafeteria, fitness centre, a car park, and daycare facilities.

Space in this non-high-rise building is equivalent to that in a 25-storey skyscraper. The long elevations and overall bulk have been mitigated with recesses at the Canal Street entry on the west and terracing on the east. Sandblasted grid work and a system of reveals wrap around the precast concrete perimeter, emphasising horizontality.

The formal lobby is quite dramatic, highlighted by a three-storey crystalline structural glass wall. The precast concrete skin traces an outline across this lobby window, weaving both sides of the building together. The main focal point of the lobby is a terraced glass block waterfall. The plan is organised around a central spine that serves as a 'main street' and connects all major areas on each level. Colour finishes and ceiling patterns change on each floor, serving as instant symbols of location and enlivening the otherwise identical 300-foot-long hallways.

ADDRESS 801 South Canal Street between Polk and Taylor Streets
CLIENT Northern Trust Company
SIZE 530,000 square feet (49,200 square metres)
RTT Clinton on Blue Line
BUS 37, 60
ACCESS none

Near West Side and South Loop

Eckenhoff Saunders Architects 1991

Eckenhoff Saunders Architects 1991

River City

Bertrand Goldberg, a seminal architect of late 20th century Chicago, is one of the last true idealists. The designer of the Marina City 'corncob' towers (1967), Goldberg continued his quest for the perfect urban agglomerate at River City. The motivation behind the endeavour is Goldberg's conviction that Chicago needs middle-income housing. The influx of middle-class residents propping up the tax base was an' attempt to change downtown's demographics that did not win much government enthusiasm. All sorts of political obstructions followed the initial proposal in 1976 and it was not until Mayor Jane Byrne arrived on the scene in 1981 that planning permission and funding were allowed. Goldberg has written a great deal on the decline of our cities and his Utopian philosophy is, unfortunately, considered by many today to be antiquated. Fragmentation has become such a way of life that the idea of a self sufficient environment seems sadly alien and perverse. Goldberg states, 'As our cities shrink and atrophy, so does the life within them. If our cities are to remain a centre of civilisation they cannot serve as a 35 hour a week city inhabited by our poor. The original American vision of the city is one of synergy, growth and community'.

River City is a marvellous and poetic idea; sadly, construction details have not been treated as religiously as the concept and overall design. It is also a shame that the financial infrastructure was too weak to allow the project to be completed. Just Phase One (of a proposed five phases) is finished on the mile-long site directly on the bank of the south branch of the Chicago River. This is within walking distance of the financial district, the Sears Tower and other areas in the Loop. The overall megastructure consists of two parallell s-shaped residential blocks connected by a glazed atrium that rests on a rectilinear four-storey commercial base. Inspired by a mythical River Snake and Goldberg's

Bertrand Goldberg Associates, Inc. 1987

interpretation of chaos theory, the curvy cast-in-place concrete is simultaneously structural and sculptural. Computer research allowed the economic planning of cost-effective multiple use of internally fibre-glass lined standard steel formworks to cast the complex forms.

The stunning circular geometry was achieved by using a series of vertical concrete tubes spaced at intervals along the bending perimeter of two adjoining half-circles. Single columns have been placed at the halfway mark to support the floor slabs. As the tubes follow the S curve the form of the spaces between them varies, creating 22 varieties of apartments divided between 446 units. The glass-covered ten-storey atrium forms a kinetic internal street. Meandering between the two towers, intentionally evocative of a European street, with park benches, street lights and trees, it is an area designed for neighbours to meet. There is a park for residents on top of the jutting four-storey base. Amenities also include a grocery store, health centre, drugstore and parking facilities. One third of the existing plan is the 70-slip marina.

The exterior concrete façade, composed of juxtaposing curves and cantilevered balconies, has either rough-finish concrete or vertically fluted concrete fabricated by pinning glass-reinforced plastic strips to the custom-designed steel forms that the concrete was cast into.

ADDRESS 800 South Wells Street (at Polk Street)
STRUCTURAL ENGINEERS Bertrand Goldberg Associates, Inc.
COST $45 million approximately
SIZE 900,000 gross square feet (83,600 square metres)
RTT LaSalle on Blue Line, Brown Line, Orange Line, Purple Line Express
BUS 11, 22, 24, 36, 37
ACCESS public lobby and some commercial space

Bertrand Goldberg Associates, Inc. 1987

Bertrand Goldberg Associates, Inc. 1987

John G Shedd Oceanarium

The world's largest indoor marine mammal pavilion is an elegant, giant receptacle for an artificial Pacific Northwest outdoor environment.

The site, 1.8 acres of landfill on Lake Michigan, was already home to the Oceanarium's parent building, the 1929 neo-Classical Aquarium designed by Graham, Anderson, Probst & White. A shell-shaped extension at the rear of the old structure, the addition is respectful of the axis, scale and massing of the grand civic building. The aged white Georgia marble cladding from the existing back eastern wall was removed and it now covers the new structure, maintaining continuity of materials. Facing towards the lake, the Oceanarium's rear façade is a spectacular and enormous gently curved glass and steel curtain wall (an inch thick) that opens up the building, literally drawing Lake Michigan inside.

Divided into three levels, the centre of the facility is a 1000-seat steel-trussed column-free amphitheatre facing the main whale tank and the Lake (entering from quite a height, at the top the simulated harbour seems to amalgamate with the Lake). Hidden services, both mechanical and administrative offices, are cleverly placed beneath the theatre's tiered seating.

To the left of the central space are two restaurants and an orientation centre; to the right is a smaller auditorium. The dolphins, Beluga whales, seals, otters and other creatures can be observed both from above and under the water.

The entire interior simulates the coastal habitat, with painted concrete boulders, along 400 feet of twisting rugged nature trails with a jarrah wood path, passing 70 varieties of (real) trees and excellently executed papier-mâché props.

Although controversial amongst animal-rights activists (a gang of protesters carry their banners reading 'Welcome to Whale Hell', etc. past

Lohan Associates 1991

Lohan Associates 1991

the beautiful glass wall every time there is an hourly animal demonstration), the Oceanarium is a new breed of zoo infinitely more humane than the outdated facility it adjoins.

ADDRESS 1200 South Lake Shore Drive at Solidarity Drive
STRUCTURAL ENGINEERS Rittweger & Tokay
CLIENT The John G Shedd Aquarium
COST $43 million
SIZE 170,000 square feet (15,800 square metres)
BUS 6, 130, 146
ACCESS daily 09.00–17.00 March to October and 10.00–17.00 November to February; Thursday is free

Lohan Associates 1991

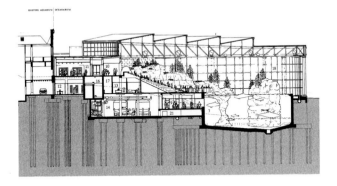

Lohan Associates 1991

Burnham Park Harbor Station

Redolent of Cape Cod or Long Island, this small maritime station conjures up mouthwatering thoughts of fresh lobster, clams and blueberry buckle. A white clapboard facility crested by a weather vane, this building could have been transplanted by a mysterious hurricane to Chicago from any site along the North Atlantic Coast. It makes a most pleasant and curious juxtaposition against the downtown post-urban skyline.

The straightforward, one-storey, bipartite L-shaped plan houses public restrooms, a food stand, public laundry and offices for the charter-boat director and a two-storey suite for the harbour master (with a super 360-degree view of the harbour). A gated breezeway separates the public amenities from those held for prearranged visitors. Built of unquestionably durable materials, the building is heavily insulated to withstand bad weather.

An adjacent sturdy shed provides an elegantly functional tabletop and water hoses for cleaning fish, very popular with the fishing public, particularly from May to October.

ADDRESS Burnham Park
CLIENT Chicago Park District
Marine Department
COST $628,898
SIZE Harbor Master Building,
1800 square feet (170 square metres);
Fish Cleaning Station,
200 square feet (19 square metres)
BUS 130, 146
ACCESS open to the public

Bill Latoza/Chicago Park District 1990

Near West Side and South Loop

Bill Latoza/Chicago Park District 1990

Pilsen

Cesar Chavez Elementary School   **232**
Harrison Park Cultural and Recreational Center   **236**

Cesar Chavez Elementary School

The Back of the Yards has traditionally been a port of entry neighbourhood. Adjacent to the former Chicago Union Stockyards, this heavily industrial area, bounded by railroad tracks and a canal, inspired Upton Sinclair's 1906 muckraking novel *The Jungle*. Originally the largest meatpacking base in America, the Back of the Yards' main industry has been decentralised since the advent of trucks and interstate highways. Today the area is still heavily populated by immigrants, currently Mexican-Americans.

In the midst of this urban fabric, on a small, shallow site (121 x 456 feet) sits the Cesar Chavez Elementary School. Wedged into this partial city block surrounded by the rear façades of commercial buildings, two-storey woodframe single-family residences and an empty lot, this is a school building that successfully addresses and attempts to engage the community.

The three-storey structure is divided into three separate masses. The library, gym and cafeteria blocks are extensions of the linear classroom/circulation spine. The entire structure is set back on the site, concealing the alley from view. Three separate playgrounds face the street, allowing visual supervision from surrounding houses. A children's palette of bright primary colours applied to masonry units and exterior steel components signals the school as a vibrant place of importance within the community.

The library – housed in a pyramid chosen, according to the architect Carol Ross Barney, for its 'visual impact as well as its non-colonial significance' – is lit at the apex at night, serving as a 'beacon in the neighbourhood'.

Once you enter the building, the hierarchy and three-tier separation of the primary, intermediate and upper grades is reinforced by the gradual loss of colour in the classrooms. This is a calculated attempt to represent

Pilsen

Ross Barney + Jankowski, Inc. 1993

Pilsen

Ross Barney + Jankowski, Inc. 1993

the activity of learning as one of increasing seriousness and a result of the students' own involvement. The classrooms are meant to be the students' personal canvas, no longer the domain of the architect.

ADDRESS 4747 South Marshfield Avenue
CLIENT Chicago Public Schools
STRUCTURAL ENGINEERS Martin/Lam, Inc.
CONTRACT VALUE $5.2 million
SIZE 64,000 square feet (6000 square metres)
TRANSPORT probably safest to drive or cab it
BUS 9, 47
ACCESS none

Pilsen

Ross Barney + Jankowski, Inc. 1993

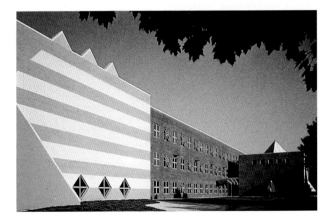

Ross Barney + Jankowski, Inc. 1993

Harrison Park Cultural and Recreational Center

Motivated by the Great Depression of the early 1930s, the conglomeration of Chicago's parks occurred when the federal government issued $6 million in bonds for WPA's expansion programmes. The Chicago Park District was incorporated in 1934 as the governing body of all parkland in Chicago.

The new building at Harrison Park is essentially a field house, a building type originating in 1888–1930 from the neighbourhood parks movement. As Chicago has such bitterly cold winters the field houses were designed as community clubhouses. Set in an existing park in a predominantly Mexican-American neighbourhood (the Mexican Fine Arts Museum is across the green), the centre serves a densely residential area. Designed as a crescent symbolically embracing the community, the new centre required new tree planting and landscaping. Rust-coloured concrete, green painted steel and copper columns in the entryway relax the fortress-like effect of very high windows (necessary for security). A gymnasium, boxing arena, music room, ping-pong room and art spaces adjacent to the already existing swimming pool are well used and appreciated by the locals.

ADDRESS 1824 South Wood Street at West 18th Place
CLIENT Community and Advisory Council of Harrison Park Chicago Park District, Department of Recreation
COST $3.39 million
SIZE 23,000 square feet (2100 square metres)
RTT 18th, Blue Line
BUS 9, 18, 50
ACCESS public

Pilsen

Julie Gross/Chicago Park District 1993

Pilsen

Julie Gross/Chicago Park District 1993

Near South Side and Bridgeport

McCormick Place North 240

Chinatown Square 242

Comiskey Park 244

McCormick Place North

An expansion of McCormick Place On-the-Lake, the new convention centre, a low-rise steel building, also accommodates a second exhibition hall allowing two major trade shows to occur simultaneously, doubling the size of the older facility. The two buildings are connected by an enclosed pedestrian tunnel and a bridge with fanciful cupolas that are visible from the highway. Designed around stacked halls, a result of the restrictive site, the exterior cable-suspended roof-truss system is spectacular to see, particularly when driving past. Constructed on air-rights, this allows the structure to hang over active commuter and freight railroad tracks.

This roof covers the main hall, measuring 480 x 780 feet. Cables are hung from twelve concrete pylons (inside, the pylons serve a double purpose and also contain the air-circulation systems) spaced in 120 x 240 foot bays, creating flexibility for different exhibitions. The pylons are joined to stiffener plates that then connect to tie-down pipes securing the roof to a podium. This podium, an elevated slab of 600 x 1350 feet, spans the working railways, supporting the main exhibition area and a warehouse space.

Clad with silver-grey aluminium panels attached to polished stainless steel mullions, the diagonal pattern of the roof trusses is repeated on the façade by patterning on the glass band of windows at the top.

ADDRESS 450 East 23rd Street
COST $170 million
SIZE 1,500,000 square feet (140,000 square metres)
BUS 3, 4, 21, 127
ACCESS varies from show to show

Skidmore, Owings & Merrill, Inc. 1986

Near South Side and Bridgeport

Skidmore, Owings & Merrill, Inc. 1986

Chinatown Square

The first, commercial phase of an ambitious scheme, 7.8 acres of the 32-acre project have been completed. Roughly $3.5 million was spent on infrastructure. The site was once the yards of the Sante Fe Railroad and required an extensive clean-up. Traces of creosote and benzene by-products meant a clay barrier had to be laid down and planting of edible vegetation has been restricted. Chinatown has needed to expand for quite a long time. Across the street from the old railroad yards, the new site is a natural area to spread onto. The outside perimeter is the Chicago River, and a bridge or link to the other side is hoped for in the far future. McCormick Place, the expo complex, is also expected to become part of the community, attracting conventioneers. A quarter (approximately 20,000) of Chicago's Chinese American population live in Chinatown: the new scheme hopes to provide housing for 2000. There is a master plan spanning the next decade accommodating the construction of townhouses, apartments, a Chinese television station, an Oriental Garden, a community center and a trade centre.

The new complex has red and green pagoda-style elevators and stair towers, bilingual street signs, diamond shaped windows, and ornamental seals periodically inserted into the brickwork to continue the dialect of the existing bordering Chinatown.

ADDRESS Archer Avenue, Cermak Road, Chicago River, 18th Street and Wentworth Avenue
STRUCTURAL ENGINEERS Seymour Lepp & Associates
SIZE 200,000 square feet (18,600 square metres)
RTT Cermak/Chinatown on Red Line
BUS 21, 42, 62, 62 Express
ACCESS open

Near South Side and Bridgeport

Harry Weese & Associates 1993

Harry Weese & Associates 1993

Comiskey Park

In 1908 Charles Comiskey purchased 15 acres of land that had supposedly been used for athletic activities since the 1860s and had a ballpark built on the property for the Chicago White Sox. This Major League stadium, the oldest in the nation, was designed by Zachary Taylor Davis.

Eighty years later, when the White Sox were contemplating relocating to St Petersburg, Florida, the Illinois State Assembly and the current Mayor, James R Thompson, created legislation for a public-private partnership to fund the construction of a new stadium to keep the team in Chicago. A reciprocal financial arrangement was reached, funding for construction being generated by a 2 per cent hotel/motel tax in Chicago and the government getting a percentage of the White Sox's revenue. This earns Chicago and the State of Illinois around $180 million annually.

The new Comiskey Park is directly opposite the 1910 original, which was deemed too costly to rehabilitate and was therefore torn down and replaced by a parking lot. All that remains of the original is home plate.

The first stadium devoted solely to baseball to be built in the USA since 1972, Comiskey Park is a both an economic feat and a step backward for urban planning. Completely oblivious to the city life surrounding it, this project was conceptualised in shopping-mall mode. Admittedly the site is in a rough neighbourhood. It is across the Dan Ryan Expressway from the Robert Taylor Homes and a few blocks east of Stateway Gardens, two of the city's most rundown, crime-ridden, gang-infested housing projects. Yet this is no excuse for the scheme's complete lack of engagement with its environment. The building is stranded in an ocean of 7000 parking spaces and the exterior pedestrian circulation ramps look like barricades against an invasion. All programmatic functions, such as food stalls or souvenir shops, are internalised, exacerbating the lonely fortress effect. No reference to the relevant historical importance of the

Near South Side and Bridgeport

Hellmuth, Obata & Kassabaum, Inc. 1991

Hellmuth, Obata & Kassabaum, Inc. 1991

site is evident, a real shame, as it would have been so appropriate to incorporate a fragment of the old stadium into the new.

Philip Bess, a Chicago architect who proposed an alternative, more urbane scheme, has been an outspoken critic of the New Comiskey: 'In terms of ballpark and urban aesthetics, the outstanding and overwhelming fact about the new Comiskey Park (and its adjacent surface parking lots) is the way it requires the city of Chicago to do all the adjusting; it is essentially anti-urban and does not accommodate city life'.

Although the architects hoped that the beige concrete panels and the series of arched windows would be reminiscent of the original building, the blue spandrels, green mullions, tinted glass and unfortunate street furniture dotting the parking lots, speak a bland suburban language.

All this aside, the stadium is comfortable, well-functioning and has no obstructed-view seats. The upper decks are at quite an angle, a 35-degree slope, but there are most definitely no pillars anywhere in the 160 feet between the viewer and the field! Commendably, there is seating for 400 handicapped spectators and access to all levels. Forty ticket windows are available, eight escalators, a Sony Jumbotron exploding scoreboard and, most importantly, an increased number of restrooms for women – three to each men's room.

ADDRESS West 35th Street and South Shields Avenue
STRUCTURAL ENGINEERS Thornton-Tomasetti, Inc.
COST $135.47 million
SIZE 990,000 square feet (92,000 square metres)
RTT Sox/35th on Red Line
BUS 24, 35, 39
ACCESS check game schedule

Near South Side and Bridgeport

Hellmuth, Obata & Kassabaum, Inc. 1991

Hellmuth, Obata & Kassabaum, Inc. 1991

Hyde Park

John Crerar Library 250

Kersten Physics Teaching Center 252

John Crerar Library

Inaugurated in 1892, the University of Chicago's Neo-Gothic master plan was designed by Henry Ives Cobb. Academic buildings congregated around the ancient collegiate quadrangle were built to medieval proportions and decorated with gargoyles, corbels, and lancet windows. When in 1978 the University decided to consolidate its science and medicine reference collection with that of the John Crerar Library they published stringent guidelines. Neo-Gothic influence had to be acknowledged while fitting in with more recent eclectic additions on the site.

The new library completes the eighth quadrangle on campus. Four storeys high, 300 feet long and 100 feet wide, the reinforced concrete structure is finished in buff Indiana limestone. A few Gothic references are apparent: the choice of materials, fenestrations, and the freestanding arch calling attention to the off-centre main entrance. The windows diminish in size with each level; a glazed curtain wall on the first floor, a sunscreen cantilevered over the smaller second floor openings and on the top level the windows have become slits.

ADDRESS 5730 South Ellis Avenue at East 57th Street
ASSOCIATE ARCHITECTS Loebl, Schlossman & Hackl
STRUCTURAL ENGINEERS LeMessurier Consultants, Inc.
COST approx. $13 million
SIZE 60,000 square feet (14,900 square metres)
RTT for safety reasons it is not advisable to take the L in this area; it is also not a good idea to walk in the surrounding areas off the campus
BUS 4, 6, 55
METRA ELECTRIC 55th/56th/57th Street Station
ROAD Lake Shore Drive south exit at 51st, 53rd, 57th Street
ACCESS Monday–Saturday 09.00–17.00

Hyde Park

Hugh Stubbins Associates 1985

Hugh Stubbins Associates 1985

Kersten Physics Teaching Center

The strongest lasting impression of this narrow, three-storey science facility is its clever circulation system. Designed around a gabled corridor forming an energetic entrance atrium, it continues as a long, narrow hanging spine that becomes the fundamental meeting place within the building. Controlling the waterfall of stairs leading to various levels, this backbone terminates (on the second level) as a pedestrian bridge across 57th Street connecting to the Research Institute. On the third floor the corridor ends as a gridded wall looking onto the student lounge. Organised around this central backbone are the offices, 13 laboratories, lecture halls and classrooms that comprise the buildings programme. A lecture hall is on the ground floor and there is a rooftop observatory.

The entire hallway is attached to a completely glazed exterior wall and topped by a triangular running skylight exaggerating the verticality of the building while simultaneously opening it up to the quadrangle it completes. This south-west wall is adjacent to the main west elevation, a series of glass-walled setbacks forming three levels of open sky terraces and an outdoor scientific gallery. For a serious scientific centre it is pleasantly accessible. In keeping with the neo-Gothic campus, the street façade is formal Indiana limestone with proportions and scale reflecting the surrounding structures.

ADDRESS 5720 South Ellis Avenue
ASSOCIATE ARCHITECT Harold H Hellman/University Architect
COST $6 million
SIZE 57,200 square feet (5300 square metres)
BUS 4, 6, 55, 59
ROAD Lake Shore Drive, south exit at 57th Street
ACCESS open

Hyde Park

Holabird & Root 1985

Holabird & Root 1985

Suburbs South-West

Glendale Heights Post Office 256

Oakbrook Terrace Tower 260

McDonald's Corporation Lodge and Training Center 262

Speigel Corporate Headquarters 264

Illinois State Toll Highway Authority 266

Frederick T Owens Village Center 268

Glendale Heights Post Office

Visibility from the highway was a primary concern in the design of this suburban post office. The only retail operation in an industrial park, the architects planned the façade so it would be readable while cruising past in an automobile. Red, white, and blue, this patriotic building intentionally resembles the Stars & Stripes.

Amongst all this brilliant colour, red and buff brick is still discernible, an attempt at relating to the language of the surrounding utilitarian warehouses. Three-quarters of the front façade is royal blue glazed brick stuck below a horizontal tier of red and white striped wall with angular undulations (the wall pointedly folds in and out). This has the desired effect of making the building resemble a flag billowing in the wind. The two-tone striations wrap all the way around the large shed structure. Golden triangular skylights sit on the roof and are then repeated as foils for the roof drainage system. The blue façade is sprinkled with a symmetrical series of small square windows, allowing daylight in but cleverly preventing a view out to the unpicturesque front parking lot. This bright cheery façade embodies the user-friendly ambience prevalent throughout the scheme.

The simple plan consists of two programmatic parts: a large workroom-warehouse for sorting and processing mail, and a smaller customer area inserted into the front of the warehouse. There are two adjacent main entrances, one directly to the private mailboxes and another to the service counter. Using economical and hard-wearing materials, the dynamic interior continues the flag motif. A larger-than-life Postal Eagle flies across the industrial vinyl mat in the vestibule. Wide waves of colour spotted with stars ripple along the linoleum floor. Even the florescent fixtures are arranged in a funky, flag-waving fashion as stars in a blue background, and in the private mailbox area as white strip lighting against a red ceiling

Ross Barney & Jankowski, Inc. 1989

meant to symbolise stripes. The lockboxes are unusually arranged in three individual islands, across from the red granite waist-high tabletops used for last-minute envelope addressing. Although the imagery is obvious it works so well because it has been executed in a delightful, jovial manner.

There are many conceptual and stylistic similarities between this public facility and the elementary school recently completed by Ross Barney & Jankowski (Cesar Chavez Elementary School, see page 232). For instance: the recognisable programmatic use of colour combined with ordinary materials such as brick and steel, the use of Le Corbusier-inspired 'windows to the heavens', and the creation of architectonic spaces with angular shapes and overlapping planes.

It is wonderful that civic buildings can be made so amiable and energetic. Going to the post office need not be a dull, sterile experience!

ADDRESS Brandon Drive at Bloomingdale Road
STRUCTURAL ENGINEERS Martin/Martin, Inc.
CLIENT United States Postal Service
SIZE 24,000 square feet (2200 square metres)
COST $2 million
ROAD 290 Expressway west, take a right turn to western suburbs, exit Route 64 west to Bloomingdale Road; after approximately 9 miles turn left onto Brandon Drive
ACCESS public

Suburbs South-West

Ross Barney & Jankowski, Inc. 1989

Ross Barney & Jankowski, Inc. 1989

Oakbrook Terrace Tower

An urban phenomenon has been transplanted into suburbia. The tallest building in the suburbs, visible from every approach, this skyscraper is located at a major highway intersection, 25 miles west of the city. Thirty-one storeys and 418 feet high, it towers over the neighbouring commercial and residential buildings. Since the 1970s businesses have been migrating to the city's outskirts at a rapidly increasing pace, usually taking the shape of low industrial parks or sprawling campuses. Exurbia is now the nation's largest area of construction and growth. The addition of underground parking facilities at the Oakbrook Terrace Tower is an indication of the rising land values in this region.

The architects have succeeded in their aim: to construct a singular object with a distinct skyline identity. A blue-green and grey glass-faced octagon, the tower is beautifully detailed. Unusually understated for Helmut Jahn, this edifice is not too shiny or glossy. Fret glass spandrels set in an orthogonal grid are patterned with small dots against a grey background, giving the appearance of a metal mesh. An inverted v is the decorative motif, appearing at several different scales. The roof is pointed and the main entrance echoes this configuration. The form was generated by the play of the vertical and horizontal patterns joining with the building's four diagonal facesg. The ceremonial v is engraved in white marble in the five-storey lobby and the motif recurs throughout the interior.

ADDRESS 1 Tower Lane
STRUCTURAL ENGINEERS Cohen Barreto Marchertas, Inc.
SIZE 714,000 square feet (66,300 square metres)
ROAD 290 west to Roosevelt Road, west to 83; south to first stop light; right on Spring Road to Tower Lane
ACCESS public lobby

Murphy/Jahn 1986

Murphy/Jahn 1986

McDonald's Corporation Lodge and Training Center

Nicknamed Hamburger University, this was built as an exemplary corporate training campus. Two large low buildings are placed in an 81 acre site. The Training Center and Lodge are constructed with friendly materials – wood, brick and Wisconsin lannin stone – in a recognisable Prairie School pot-pourri mingling Frank Lloyd Wright with hints of Mies van der Rohe in the meticulous detailing. The Training Center is organised around clusters of classrooms and offices circling a two-storey, skylit atrium, the centrepiece of a large galleria (decorated with wonderful McDonald's memorabilia) designed to encourage socialising and ideas exchange. An auditorium, seminar/conference rooms, and laboratories are available. The 3000 students who pass through annually live in the 154-room Lodge, planned with the Hyatt Corporation who run the facility. Relaxingly luxurious (with a definite institutional undertone), the Lodge contains both recreational and relaxational spaces designed to continue the social and edifying goals of the training week.

The Lodge has been designed around a 150-year-old Ohio Buckeye tree. The oak forest setting includes a McNature Trail. A partially covered concrete bridge connects the two buildings, affording a windy path over Lake Fred, where fake ducks bob up and down on the calming waters.

ADDRESS 2715 Jorie Boulevard, Oak Brook
SIZE 330,000 square feet (30,660 square metres)
STRUCTURAL ENGINEERS Chris P Stefanos Associates
ROAD 290 west, to 188 west, exit at Route 83 south, turn right on 31st Street, turn left (east) on Jorie Boulevard
ACCESS none

Suburbs South-West

Lohan Associates 1984, 1990

Lohan Associates 1984, 1990

Speigel Corporate Headquarters

This prepossessing building stands at the intersection of two major highways accessible directly off an exit ramp. Headquarters of catalogue-merchandising company Speigal, a dichotomous exterior powerfully expresses the disparate aspects of the site horizontally, one side being adjacent to the freeway and the rear looking out over the Hidden Lake Forest Preserve.

The road façade is a formal rectilinear grid alternating bands of precast concrete and light grey granite panels with an aluminium and green glass curtain wall, exposing every other level of the structural steel system. It is topped by a microwave communications tower adding height (visible from a speeding car) to the 14-storey building.

The other side of the building, attached by a narrow sandwich filling layer, undulates and gently curves in homage to the informal forms found in nature. Hanging over a man-made retention pond, this beautiful serpentine curtain wall has the same green-tinted glass alternating with bands of ceramic-coated glass spandrels. A low circular building jutting out over the pond houses a two-storey cafeteria. This space-age projection allows employees to be surrounded by nature, avoiding the usual suburban sea of cars.

ADDRESS 3500 Lacey Road, Downers Grove
CLIENT Hamilton Partners, Inc.
COST $59 million
SIZE 660,000 square feet (61,000 square metres)
ROAD 290 West to I-88 West, North on 355 to Butterfield Road, exit West to Wood Creek Drive
ACCESS none

Skidmore, Owings & Merrill, Inc. 1992

Skidmore, Owings & Merrill, Inc. 1992

Illinois State Toll Highway Authority

On a grassy meadow smack next door to the highway, the new midrise ISTHA building overlooks its main concern. But the building faces away from the tollway to its west which is invisible from the interior, and as it is organised around an internal central courtyard it seems to be ignoring the roadway as well. According to the architects the façade is covered with images evocative of cars. Not very convincing, curved precast concrete columns decorated with circular blobs of concrete (tollbooth coins perhaps) look vaguely like automobile bumpers and the blue/green tinted fenestrations are farfetched resemblances of headlight fixtures.

The interior, infinitely more interesting than the exterior, is divided by a cylindrical atrium wedged in between two parallel rectangular structures that meet at the ends in service cores. The fracture is the entrance leading into a two-storey atrium with a floating terrazo staircase visible straight ahead. Mechanical references are more apparent here with exposed steel soffitts supporting the ribbed skylights and interior columns resembling engine parts. Industrial-style walkway bridges connect private conference spaces and allow views of the greenery flourishing on the ground floor.

Mostly occupied by administrative offices, the facility also has a secret area where the tolls from across Northern Illinois are counted.

ADDRESS 1 Authority Drive, Downers Grove
STRUCTURAL ENGINEERS Martin/Martin
CLIENT Illinois State Toll Highway Authority
COST $25.5 million
SIZE 185,000 square feet (17,000 square metres)
ROAD take 290 west towards 88, west to 355 south, exit Ogden Avenue
ACCESS none

Lohan Associates 1991

Lohan Associates 1991

Frederick T Owens Village Center

Opposite a sprawling shopping mall that is (scarily enough) the actual hub of the town, three buildings orthogonally ring a man-made retention lake. The complex includes a village hall with government offices and classrooms, a civic meeting centre with gallery space as well as a banqueting hall, a recreation building and an outdoor amphitheatre that projects over the lake. A theatre is planned to complete the quartet. To create visual coherence internal functions have been visibly expressed by external form: circular pavilions indicate meeting halls and columned galleries stand for lobbies.

The spire-topped clock tower of the three-storey symmetrical village hall is the centrepiece of the complex, intended as a new point of reference for the village. A semi-covered curving walkway over the water connects the buildings.

ADDRESS 14700 South Ravinia Avenue, Orland Park
CLIENT Village of Orland Park
SIZE 87,400 square feet (8100 square metres)
COST $11.5 million
ROAD take I-55, exit LaGrange Road south, right on 145th, left on Ravinia
ACCESS public

Perkins & Will 1989

Perkins & Will 1989

Suburbs North

Ameritech Center **272**

Sears Merchandise Group Headquarters **274**

Cooper Lighting Showroom **276**

American Academy of Pediatrics Headquarters **278**

Bradford Exchange **280**

Municipal Fueling Facility **282**

House in Wilmette **284**

Private Residence **286**

North Shore Congregation Israel Synagogue Addition **288**

Private Family Residence **292**

Ameritech Center

Grandiose in scale and formal in style, Ameritech has created its own self-sufficient universe, a small internal city, in the middle of suburban Hoffman Estates. This entirely non-smoking environment houses 2500 employees. Aside from offices, conference space, and a library, the facilities include a sports club, wellness centre and an eating emporium. In the lower depths of the building there is a secret laboratory that simulates and creates new communications systems.

The basic symmetrical plan of the building consists of two crosses joined by a central spine. The main artery off the drive actually cuts right underneath the middle of the building and leads directly to parking. The entry to the immense, grandiose lobby is on the second floor, although it feels like ground level. Security throughout the building is reminiscent of that at an international airport.

Once allowed past the vast glass doors at the back of the lobby, you have arrived at Main Street, the organisational element of the building which functions much like a typical high street. Two identical four-storey atriums in each wing are connected by a tiered network of suspended high-tech walkways that traverse the entire building, cutting directly through workspaces. It is incredibly disorienting. Take a map, experienced tour guide, and hiking boots.

ADDRESS 2000 West Ameritech Center Drive, Hoffman Estates
STRUCTURAL ENGINEERS Chris P Stefanos Associates
SIZE 1,300,000 square feet (121,000 square metres)
COST $304 million
ROAD I-90 west, north on Roselle Road, left on Central: Ameritech is off Central
ACCESS none

Lohan Associates 1991

Lohan Associates 1991

Sears Merchandise Group Headquarters

Significant as a social phenomenon, this is the relocation site for 6000 employees who used to occupy offices in the 1450-foot-tall Sears Tower. Now they occupy a suburban campus consisting of low-rise buildings. Motivated not only by financial incentives, apparently the skyscraper premises were destructive of corporate culture and found alienating by the people working there. The company chose to join McDonalds, Kraft, Spiegal, Motorola and many others in moving to the 'burbs.

A typical, uniformly blue-glass-clad complex, this is a rather nondescript set-up. Well designed and well built, several four- to six-storey buildings are connected by a central atrium originally called 'Main Street'. The banal design houses the average number of facilities in an attempt to be the usual all-inclusive environment.

For many reasons (tourists passing through, sheer size and impersonality) one can understand that the Sears Tower was a difficult place to work, but how can the anonymity and the lack of neighbourhood, specialness and surrounding amenities in this typical homogenous little world be the solution?

ADDRESS Higgins Road, Hoffman Estates
CLIENT Sears Roebuck & Company
STRUCTURAL ENGINEERS Cohen Barreto Marchertas, Inc.
SIZE 1,900,000 square feet (176,500 square metres)
ROAD I-90/94 north-west, I-90 to Hoffman Estates; exit Route 90 north to Route 72 and turn left onto Higgins Road
ACCESS none

Perkins & Will 1992

Suburbs North

Perkins & Will 1992

Cooper Lighting Showroom

Remarkable for its architecturally interesting contents rather than the structure itself, this is an extraordinary product showroom. An information and education centre organised as an interactive museum with hands-on experiments, the facility, known professionally as The Source, has accommodated over 14,000 visitors since opening.

A dramatic glass and steel staircase leads to the introductory room filled with glass lit displays and TV screens. Demonstrations of all major light sources are given in the fundamentals room, a circular space filled with the most intriguing props. A series of well-designed spaces follows, each devoted to a particular aspect of lighting, organised around three principles: technology, effect and performance. A row of example settings, residential, commercial and office, are divided by partitions yet connected by a linear series of columns and are used to demonstrate varying lighting solutions, for example, how warmer coloured light creates a friendlier atmosphere.

After this each space is devoted to one particular type of product in all its possible forms. The power of repetition and conglomeration is apparent in the sheer fascination of seeing all these fixtures in one place. In the overhead lighting room the ceiling resembles a piece of Swiss cheese, allowing designers not only to study effects but to compare mountings.

The cohesive design of the programme/spaces brings home the spatial power of lighting in a logical straightforward fashion.

ADDRESS 400 Busse Road, Elk Grove Village
SIZE 20,000 square feet (1900 square metres)
ROAD 290 to 83 north, exit at Oakton, turn left onto Busse Road
ACCESS by appointment

Suburbs North

Booth Hansen & Associates 1991

Booth Hansen & Associates 1991

American Academy of Pediatrics Headquarters

Dignified and serious, this hybrid combination of classical and vaguely postmodern imagery surrounded by fields and a landscaped lawn creates a peaceful, sedate vista. Visible from the highway, particularly when illuminated at night, the structure stands out from its unattractive neighbours. Structurally a steel frame clad with a two-tone skin of banded brick and limestone, it is refreshing to see a contemporary corporate building in the suburbs without a predominantly glass façade.

The entranceway is at mid level, cutting through the sloping site, leading axially through the lobby and ending in the large atrium that overlooks a man-made lake.

A large conference room faces the lake on the ground level; offices and meeting rooms occupy the other two levels. Wood, terrazo floors and muted primary shades continue throughout the calm interior. Plants abound both inside and outside in the landscaped gardens.

Two fabulous skylights break through the roof over the entrance lobby and the atrium, adding to the dramatic night image.

ADDRESS 141 Northwest Point Boulevard, Elk Grove Village
ROAD Kennedy Expressway to I-90 to Elmhurst Road to Oakden to 83/ Busse Road, right onto Handmeyer leads into Arlington Heights Road
ACCESS none

Hammond, Beeby & Babka 1990

Suburbs North

Hammond, Beeby & Babka 1990

Bradford Exchange

A scheme done in three stages, the final phase being designed by Thomas Hickey & Associates. Rich with avant-garde ideas and hilarious in their hodge podge, bizarre execution, this building (housed in a renovated warehouse and an adjacent ex-Chrysler dealership) is like a project by a wild architectural student gone mad. The building's completely mis-matched façades clash shamelessly on this suburban commercial strip. Exterior walls (with differing heights) alternate between glass and mirror with asymmetrical patterns and a near-naked trellised rear wall.

The interior is a fantasy of misguided exotic ideas made all the more eccentric by the building's programme. The headquarters of the world's largest traders of collector plates, there is actually a small trading floor where you can follow the prices of Rockwell's Golden Moments or the ever-popular Scarlett O'Hara plates. A half disassembled museum next to the trading floor used to be so popular collectors were bussed in.

From the main entrance it is possible to glimpse the weirdness ahead. Three types of gardens unfold through the length of the building. Each one has a theme; either bamboo or orchids surround the wooden path bisecting the waterway that runs the length of the office space. Funky, suspended frosted glass and cable bridges swing precariously above the miniature forest. Above these bridges is the most extraordinary addition, silicone-coated glass-fibre tensile structures that overlap and are held up by tent poles and cables, concealing the industrial ceiling of the building.

ADDRESS 9333 North Milwaukee Avenue, Niles
STRUCTURAL ENGINEERS Getty, White, and Mason
SIZE 175,000 square feet (16,000 square metres)
ROAD Kennedy to Edens North to Dempster West to Milwaukee Avenue
ACCESS none

Weese Hickey Weese 1992

Weese Hickey Weese 1992

Municipal Fueling Facility

An 8-foot-high brick wall links all the programme fundamentals for this Public Works service centre. Enclosing the entire 1 acre corner site, the wall works its way around the perimeter, adapting to the various functional, aesthetic, and landscaping requirements. Alternating between serving as a building wall, a lower screen wall and a support system for the cantilevered secondary roof, the structure even curves to accommodate an oak before mutating into a circular bathroom/storage building.

The middle stage of a three-phase civic project, the gas station is placed at the end of the entire scheme. The top end consists of a building housing administrative offices and a truck repair garage completed in 1984; to date the middle is unfinished.

Basically a freestanding brick and concrete structure, the pumping island is covered by an elongated elliptical steel canopy that appears to float but is supported by six sets of paired narrow steel columns. The smaller, rectilinear cover below it points towards the bathroom/storage space, providing a covered walkway to the corner cylinder. The pedestrian canopy rests on three steel supports and a glass brick wall. The glass blocks are repeated as a circular ribbon around the corner bathroom/storage space and are illuminated at night.

ADDRESS 1333 Shermer Avenue, Glenview
STRUCTURAL ENGINEERS Don Belford Associates
COST $1 million
ROAD I-94 north to Lake Avenue; west over bridge, 4 miles, at intersection of Shermer and Lake turn right
METRA ELECTRIC Milwaukee District North Line train to Glenview; bus 210 WB to Shermer
ACCESS none

Lubotsky Metter Worthington & Law 1988

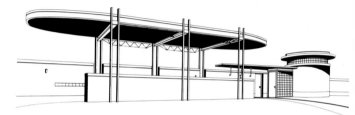

Lubotsky Metter Worthington & Law 1988

House in Wilmette

Wilmette is one of the older, more established residential communities in Greater Chicago, boasting large, solid homes built mainly between the latter half of the 1880s and 1930s. On this quiet, pretty residential street sits the perfect colonial two-kids-and-a-dog home. This delicate small house is traditional suburbia at its best. Modern in its simplicity but historical in its vocabulary, the plain façade and elegant porch are contextually sensitive, blending in perfectly with the surrounding larger homes. Set at the front edge of the site, the grey stucco structure is encircled by a wide wooden porch with fragile columns supporting an entablature. These columns wane significantly towards the top, visually lengthening the height of the porch. The reinvented typical white porch railing has spindles, three-quarters of an inch square, enhancing the dainty effect without seeming too precious.

The interior is organised vertically owing to the restrictive plot size (50 x 170 feet). Three storeys high, it contains two bedrooms, two bathrooms, a sunroom and a dining room that continue with the same vocabulary and materials as the exterior. Great effort was put into good craftsmanship and the interior includes lots of hand-crafted wood detailing.

The only thing missing from this cinematic dream house is the white picket fence.

ADDRESS 821 Forest Avenue, Wilmette
SIZE 2600 square feet (240 square metres)
STRUCTURAL ENGINEERS Gullaksen Getty & White
ROAD I-94 to 41, exit at Wilmette Avenue to Forest Avenue
ACCESS none

Suburbs North

Hammond, Beeby & Babka 1986

Hammond, Beeby & Babka 1986

Private Residence

Treating each function as a separate entity, the plan for this one-bedroom house with guest rooms, swimming pool and cabana resembles that of a village. Originating from a request of the clients that the house be based around an elongated egg, each room has become a spatial unit in its own right, rotating off each other and the original ellipse. Each room becomes a separate volume, with individual colour, form, materials and rooftop. Symbolically and literally, the trace of the original ellipse goes through the house, leaving an imprint through rug, wood floor and tile.

Two decaying obelisks mark the paved plaza entranceway. According to Tigerman, these symbolise the evacuation of the eternal sought-after original space, a metaphysical Garden of Eden. The square cloakroom, cylindrical library, and telephone kiosk are all placed on the internal brick street as separate components. Kitchen, dining space, living room, media room and bedrooms are self-contained spaces on the outskirts of the settlement. The round dining area with signature Tigerman columns and a wonderful high ceiling lends grandeur to the scheme. There is an intriguing, playful juxtaposition of angles and curves as one moves through the house.

This multilayered project follows an intellectual process of testing of what Tigerman describes as 'the potential of activation in architecture as a vehicle to overcome the stasis common to building'.

ADDRESS 1940 Park West Avenue, Highland Park
STRUCTURAL ENGINEERS Beer Gorski & Graff
SIZE 6500 square feet (600 square metres)
ROAD I-94 to 41, exit on Central Avenue, turn left onto St John's Avenue, right onto Park West Avenue
ACCESS none

Tigerman McCurry 1988–1990

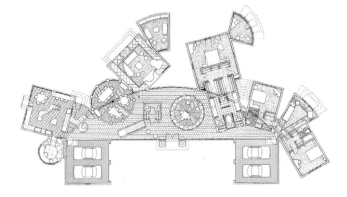

Tigerman McCurry 1988–1990

North Shore Congregation Israel Synagogue Addition

In 1964 a spectacular synagogue designed by Minoru Yamasaki, a vast white free-flowing concrete structure obviously inspired by nature, was erected on this bluff facing Lake Michigan. An unusual interior structural system supports a quirky, petal-like roof that is very 1960s; from the outside one imagines luxurious beanbag pews inside. Seating 1100 congregants (in a rather formal fashion – not beanbags at all), the sanctuary proved too vast for everyday intimate services. Hence the addition, completed in 1984, designed with a very different vocabulary.

With an historicist masonry (sandstone-coloured brick) façade in a cylindrical form with a simplified Palladian portico stuck on, the new building is the complete antithesis of Yamasaki's modern structure. This diversity adds richness, as an attempt at repeating or copying such an idiosyncratic building would have been disastrous.

Based on the layering of space, the new, much smaller (300 seats) addition is a 40-foot-square cube placed within a series of outer circles. Visually symbolic, much of the design process involved the participation of the Rabbi, allowing the incorporation of traditional meaning into the layout. Judaic symbols such as the Star of David formed the basis for details such as the large chandelier in the sanctuary. Disparate religious and social functions are expressed with different forms: the sanctuary is circular and the social hall is a rectangle which contains a noteworthy, lovely series of colourful paintings by the Israeli artist Heinz Seelig.

The modulation of light was an important issue, and the outer circulation ring is punctuated by both large circular windows quite low down and small square cut-outs around the outer rim. A 6-foot circular skylight in the sanctuary allows natural light to pour in over the elegant oak space

Hammond, Beeby & Babka 1984

Hammond, Beeby & Babka 1984

inspired by the vernacular synagogues of Eastern Europe. A perfunctory balcony overlooking the sanctuary calls to mind traditional Orthodox synagogues. The blend of Ashkenazi and Sephardic influences (the two major geographical branches of Judaism) lend a diversity expressive of the architects' desire to show the heterogeneity of the Jewish community in North America. An eminently suitable building.

Suburbs North

ADDRESS 1185 Sheridan Road, Glencoe
ROAD Kennedy north, turn right onto Lake Hook Road, which turns into Sheridan Road
ACCESS call before you go

Hammond, Beeby & Babka 1984

Hammond, Beeby & Babka 1984

Private Family Residence

Situated on a scenic 3 acre plot, a wooded ravine overlooking Lake Michigan, is this dramatic, luxurious home. The clients had specific requirements: their preference was for Modernism, the house had to have large entertaining spaces affording views of the Lake and be a showcase for their spectacular contemporary art collection. The clients interviewed around 20 architects before deciding on Arquitectonica.

The structure is a sprawling one-storey zigzag placed at the top of the site with three lake fronts. A paved courtyard is partially enclosed by the garage wing creating a private enclave in this residential neighbourhood. Clad in a mosaic of mostly pink granite that has been randomly flamed and honed, with a black base and a bluestone terrace, the exterior is an irregular meeting of various angles and planes. The stacked roof is tilted and raised and culminates by cantilevering out past the master bedroom. Assymetrically geometrical windows have been arbitrarily placed, either framing a special view or breaking the rhythm of the façade.

The interior, which carries the black granite exterior base inside as a border, is a series of stunning spaces including an indoor pool and excercise room. The random windows create a sculptural, jazzy ambience inside and the unexpected marble partitions surprise and delight. The living room carpet designed as a giant yellow legal pad (the owner is an attorney) adds a whimsical touch, consistent with the playful atmosphere throughout.

ADDRESS 81 Lakewood Drive, Glencoe
SIZE 7800 square feet (725 square metres)
ROAD I-94 right onto 41, exit Tower Road, follow Sheridan to Lakewood Drive
ACCESS none

Arquitectonica International 1987

Gurnee and Zion

The Power House 296
Illinois Bell Telephone Company, Remote Switching Unit 300

The Power House

This is an interactive museum geared towards teaching the history and uses of energy. The linear building is a simple 336-foot aluminium and steel rectangle with a gabled roof suggestive of local vernacular church architecture. A symbolic temple to energy, the building is elevated on a concrete platform slightly above its parking lot habitat. Liturgical references abound, inspired by both the institution's sacred treatment of energy and the pre-existing religious names of the site boundaries.

Tigerman has written about some of the external forces that formed the building: 'The building's basilica-like form evolves naturally as it is sited at the eastern end of Shiloh Boulevard (the termination of an east–west axis that bisects the Biblically conceived town of Zion ... Additionally, the location of the Zion station is 13-degrees east-south-east from Shiloh Park, putting it into line with Jerusalem, helping to valorise any liturgical connection with the Biblical origins of Zion, which is compounded by each of the four exhibition zones rotating thirteen degrees each)'. This use of the 13-degree angle is apparent in a vaguely deconstructivist increment to the building. Located 200 yards north of the Zion nuclear generating plant, the design responds to it through disjunction. Two emergency fire exits disguised as concrete buttresses and their light steel treillage which also function as brackets for the exhibition hall spear the Power House at 13-degree angles.

Based on a horizontal tripartite plan, the first section conceptually represents a whole that is then deconstructed in the middle area and attempts to be rebuilt unsuccessfully in the final part of the building. This is achieved through the conventional hiding of construction elements in the first section, exaggerating and exposing ductwork, conduits and other structural elements in the midsection (also intended as a symbolic energising or demystifying of the building) and then not fully returning to

Tigerman McCurry 1992

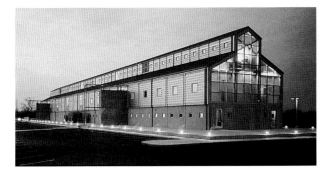

Tigerman McCurry 1992

complete screening of these essentials in the theatre and public rooms at the end of the museum.

This space has then been divided and redivided into eight 42-foot squares which then gain complexity by being diagonally rotated and finally once again orthogonally reconstructed in the same formation as at the entrance.

ADDRESS Shiloh Boulevard, Zion
CLIENT Commonwealth Edison Company
STRUCTURAL ENGINEERS Beer Gorski & Graff
ROAD 294 north to 173 east to Sheridan Road, turn east onto Shiloh, then follow to the lakefront
ACCESS open to the public

Tigerman McCurry 1992

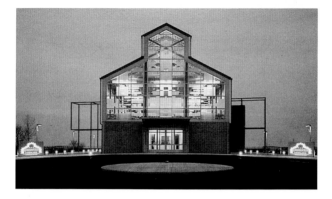

Tigerman McCurry 1992

Illinois Bell Telephone Company, Remote Switching Unit

Slanted white metal pipes and large boulders stand guard over this small brick enclosure. A rectangular box with an off-centre triangular roof balanced on top, the building contains computerised telephone equipment. Programmatically, other than sheltering the apparatus from the weather, this building must do nothing more than properly ventilate the methane gas emitted by telephone cables. An unmanned satellite station, it bears no distinguishing logo or sign.

Although repairmen are the only visitors to this industrial unit, it is seen daily by thousands of shoppers trooping towards the adjacent discount shopping centre. The switching unit is prominently located at the boundary between a large mall and the surrounding horse farms.

The project became a vehicle for exploring the architectural possibilities of representing the idea of machine versus nature. Seven graduated rocks march symbolically across the pavement and lawn towards the building in direct alignment with the northerly pointing roof. This is purely gestural as the boulders serve no function, and sets the contemplative tone of the scheme. Brick, a universal example of technology successfully combined with nature, was chosen as the primary material. Graduated in colour, the shell of the building is intended to appear as though it is rising up out of the ground.

ADDRESS Hunt Club Road at Grand Avenue, Gurnee
CLIENT Illinois Bell Telephone Co., now Ameritech
COST $770,000
STRUCTURAL ENGINEERS Teng and Associates
ACCESS none

Gurnee and Zion

Ross Barney & Jankowski, Inc. 1991

Ross Barney & Jankowski, Inc. 1991

Index

A Epstein & Sons 18, 130, 162
   Associates Center 128
Abatangelo & Hason 50
Abell, John 46
Agam, Yaacov 128
Ahmanson Commercial
   Development 170
Alfred Benesch & Co. 20, 194
Alfred Shaw & Associates 56
Altgeld Court 50
American Academy of Pediatrics
   Headquarters 278
American Furniture Mart 88
American Medical Association
   Headquarters 78
Ameritech 272, 300
Ameritech Center 272
Amoco Building 136
Ando, Tadao 158
Arad, Ron 108
Arquitectonica International
   Private Family Residence
   (Glencoe) 292
Art Institute of Chicago 158
Associates Center 6, 128
AT&T Corporate Center, USG
   Building 188
Athletic Club, Illinois Center 134
Aumiller Youngquist p.c. 44
Austin Company, The 90

Back of the Yards 232
Banana Republic 7, 114
Barnett Apartment 106
Barney, Carol Ross 232
Beeby, Thomas 30
Beer Gorski & Graff 42, 68, 70, 76,
   122, 286, 298
Bertrand Goldberg Associates, Inc.
   River City 220
Bess, Philip 246
Bloomer, Kent 162
Bloomingdale's Building 104
BMT Offices 36
Board of Trade Building 162
Bofill, Ricardo 140
Boogies Diner 112
Booth Hansen & Associates
   Cooper Lighting Showroom 276
   Helene Curtis Corporate
     Headquarters 180
   House of Light 54
   North Pier 88
   Terra Museum of American Art
     122
Bradford Exchange 280
Brown, Roger 170
Buck Company 80
Builders' Building 182
Burgee, John 176
Burnham & Root 176

Burnham Park Harbor Station 228
Burnham, Daniel H 102
Byrne, Jane 220

C F Murphy & Associates 14, 102
Cairo 46
Canal Center 218
Capitanini Family, The 150
Capone's Chicago 74
Caro, Anthony 176
Casa della Luce 54
Casserly, Joseph 30
CBM Engineers, Inc. 136
CBW Engineers, Inc. 134
Cesar Chavez Elementary School 6, 232, 258
Cesar Pelli & Associates 181 West Madison Street 184
Chamberlain, John 138
Charles E Pease Associates 114
Chemical Plaza 178
Chiasso 186
Chicago Architecture Foundation 10
Chicago Athenaeum 80
Chicago Board of Trade 166, 168, 206
Chicago Board Options Exchange 168

Chicago City Day School Addition 28
Chicago Federal Center 152
Chicago Historical Society 58
Chicago Historical Society Addition 56
Chicago Mercantile Exchange 194
Chicago Park District 236
    Burnham Park Harbor Station 228
    Harrison Park Cultural and Recreational Center 236
Chicago Park District Marine Department 228
Chicago Place 7, 116
Chicago Public Library, Conrad Sulzer Regional Branch 30
Chicago Public Schools 234
Chicago Title & Trust Center 142, 200
Chicago White Sox 244
Chinatown Square 242
Chris P Stefanos Associates 54, 116, 120, 124, 210, 262, 272
City Commons 50
City of Chicago Department of Aviation 24
City of Chicago, Department of Public Works, Bureau of Architecture

O'Hare Rapid Transport Station 20

City Place 7, 116

Cityfront Center 88, 96, 98

Cityfront Plaza 96

Clybourn Lofts 50

Cobb, Henry Ives 250

Cohen Barreto Marchertas, Inc. 80, 138, 140, 154, 156, 176, 178, 184, 216, 260, 274

Collins Tuttle & Company 128, 130

Commonwealth Edison Company 298

Commonwealth Edison Substation 76

Cone Kalb Wonderlick 158

Conrad Associates 132

Conrad Sulzer Regional Library 32

Consoer Townsend & Associates 24

Cooper Lighting Showroom 276

Cooper, Eckstut Associates 96

Corbero, Xavier 140

Crate & Barrel 7, 124

Crow Island School 28

Cutrone, Ronnie 106

Dan Shannon Associates 210

David Ekstrom 174

de la Paz, Neraldo 108

de Luigi, Ludovico 166

DeStefano & Partners 140

Don Belford Associates 282

Downers Grove 264, 266

Dubuffet, Jean 144

Eccentric, The 74

Eckenhoff Saunders Architects Canal Center 218

Eckstorm, Christian 88

Ed Debevic's 74

Edward Durrell Stone 136

Elk Grove Village 276, 278

Elkus Manfredi Architects Limited Sony Gallery 118

Embassy Club 50

Engel, Robert W 114

Environdyne Engineers, Inc. 14

Escada Plaza 7

Eva Maddox Associates T W Best Newsstand 208

Exchange Bridge 168

Fidinam (USA), Inc. 178

Fifield Realty Corporation 116

Financial Place Partnership 166

500 West Monroe 188

Florian Twoflat 38

Florian, Paul 40

Florian-Wierzbowski
  Chiasso 186
  Florian Twoflat 38
  Oilily 110
Four Seasons Hotel 104
Frankenstein, Kurt 108
Frederick F Phillips & Associates
  Mohawk Street House 42
Frederick T Owens Village Center
  268
Fry, Gary 18
Fujikawa, Johnson & Associates
  134
  Chicago Mercantile Exchange
    194
  Ralph H Metcalfe Federal Center
    152
Fulton House Condominium 84

General Service Administration 152
Getty, White, and Mason 280
Glencoe 290, 292
Glendale Heights Post Office 256
Glenview 282
Gold Coast 7
Goldberg, Bertrand 7, 220
Graham, Anderson, Probst &
  White 56, 182, 208, 224
Graham, Bruce 94
Grais, A Ronald 132

Greyhound Bus Terminal 216
Greyhound Lines 216
Gross, Julie
  Harrison Park Cultural and
    Recreational Center 236
Gullaksen Getty & White 60, 284
Gurnee 300

Hallberg, L Gustav 180
'Hamburger University' 262
Hamilton Partners, Inc. 264
Hammond, Beeby & Babka 30
  American Academy of Pediatrics
    Headquarters 278
  Chicago Public Library, Conrad
    Sulzer Regional Branch 30
  Daniel F and Ada I Rice Building
    156
  Harold Washington Library 160
  House in Wilmette 284
  North Shore Congregation Israel
    Synagogue Addition 288
Hard Rock Café 74, 76
Harold Washington Library 6, 30,
  160
Harrison Park Cultural and
  Recreational Center 236
Harry Weese & Associates
  Chinatown Square 242
  Fulton House Condominium 84

River Cottages 82
Hartshorne Plunkard, Limited 7
    Barnett Apartment 106
    Peter Elliott Productions 214
Harwood K Smith & Partners 192
Hayden, Michael 18
Heard & Associates 24
Helene Curtis Corporate
    Headquarters 180
Hellman, Harold H 252
Hellmuth, Obata & Kassabaum,
    Inc.
    Comiskey Park 244
Hidden Lake Forest Preserve 264
Highland Park 286
Himmel Bonner Architects
    Boogies Diner 112
    Playboy Enterprises Corporate
        Headquarters 62
Hoffman Estates 272, 274
Holabird & Roche 172, 178
Holabird & Root 56, 174, 178
    Chicago Board of Trade 172
    Chicago Historical Society
        Addition 56
    Holabird & Root Offices 172
    Kersten Physics Teaching Center
        252
    Northwestern University Law
        School Addition 92

Palmolive Building 172
    Soldier Field 172
Holabird & Root Offices 172
Hood, Raymond 98
Horn, Gerald 56
Hotel Nikko 208
House in Wilmette 284
House of Light (Casa della Luce) 54
House with a Bay 68
Hugh Stubbins Associates
    John Crerar Library 250
Hunt, Richard 62
Hyatt Hotel 116

Illinois Bell Telephone Company,
    Remote Switching Unit 300
Illinois Center 96, 134
Illinois State Toll Highway
    Authority 266
Italian Village 148

Jahn, Helmut 14, 136, 146, 170,
    206
Japanese Screen Gallery 158
JMB Urban Realty 104, 194
John Burgee Architects
    190 South La Salle Street 176
John Crerar Library 250
John G Shedd Oceanarium 224
John Hancock Tower 8, 94, 106

Johnson, Philip 176
Jordan Mozer & Associates
    Cairo 46
    Scoozi! 44
    Vivere 148
Jordan, Michael 120, 134

Kamin, Blair 142
Kaskey, Raymond 162
Kenzo Tange Associates
    American Medical Association
      Headquarters 78
Kersten Physics Teaching Center
    252
Kevin Roche-John Dinkeloo &
    Associates
    Leo Burnett Company
      Headquarters 138
Khan, Fazlur R 94
Klaff, Hersch M 132
Knight Architects Engineers
    Planners, Inc 158
Kohn Pedersen Fox
    Chicago Title & Trust Center
      142, 200
    900 North Michigan Avenue
      102, 200
    311 South Wacker Drive 192,
      200
    333 West Wacker Drive 196

225 West Wacker Drive 200
Kolbjorn Saether & Associates 62
Kraft, William 18
Krueck and Olsen
    Steel & Glass House 64
    Victorian Townhouse Extended
      60
Kurokawa, Kisho
    Athletic Club, Illinois Center 134

Lake Fred 262
Larrabee Commons 50
Latoza, Bill
    Burnham Park Harbor Station
      228
LeMessurier Consultants, Inc. 250
Leo Burnett Company
    Headquarters 138
Lester B Knight & Associates 146
Lettuce Entertain You Enterprises
    44
Lev Zetlin Associates 18
Lincoln Park 7, 56
Lincoln Property Company 192
Linpro Company, The 142
Loebl Schlossman & Hackl 250
    City Place 116
    Two Prudential Plaza 136
Loebl, Schlossman, Dart & Hackl
    Water Tower Place 102

Lohan Associates
   Ameritech Center 272
   Illinois State Toll Highway
      Authority 266
   John G Shedd Oceanarium 224
   McDonald's Corporation Lodge
      and Training Center 262
Lubotsky Metter Worthington &
   Law
   Municipal Fueling Facility 282
Luminaire 48

Mackintosh, Charles Rennie 116
Maddox, Eva 208
Magnificent Mile 102, 120
Marina City 220
Martin/Lam, Inc. 170, 234
Martin/Martin 266
Masonic Temple 176
Matta-Clark, Gordon 78
Mayeri, Beverly 106
McClurg Building 172
McCormick Place North 240
McCormick Place On-the-Lake
   240, 242
McDonald's 74
McDonald's Corporation Lodge
   and Training Center 262
McHugh Levin 210
MCL Construction Corporation 50

Melman, Rich 44
Merchandise Mart 88, 198, 208
Metcalfe, Ralph 152
Metropolitan Structures 194
Mexican Fine Arts Museum 236
Midwest Stock Exchange 168
Mies van der Rohe, Ludwig 8, 116,
   134, 152, 262
Miglin-Beitler 184
Miller-Klutznick-Davis-Gray and
   Company 80
Mirò, Joan 106
Mitsui & Co. 170
Mohawk Street House 42
Mondrian, Piet 110
Moriyama & Teshima Architects
   Chemical Plaza 178
Morton International Building
   204
Mozer, Jordan 44, 46, 148
Municipal Fueling Facility 282
Murphy/Jahn
   Northwestern Atrium Center
      206
   O'Hare Rapid Transit Station 20
   Oakbrook Terrace Tower 260
   Savings of America Tower 170
   Thompson Center 144
   United Terminal One Complex
      14

Naess & Murphy 14
   Prudential Plaza 136
Nagle, Hartray & Associates 70
   Greyhound Bus Terminal 216
   House with a Bay 68
   Oprah Winfrey Harpo Studios 214
   Schiller Street Town Houses 70
Nasir-Kassamau Luminaire 48
NBC Tower 96
Neo 46
Nike, Inc. 120
Niles 280
900 North Michigan Avenue 110, 7, 102, 106, 108, 200
North Pier 88
North Shore Congregation Israel Synagogue Addition 288
North Side 7
Northern Trust Company Operations Center 218
Northwestern Atrium Center 206
Northwestern Terminal Building 208
Northwestern University Law School Addition 92

O'Hare International Airport 14
O'Hare International Terminal 22
O'Hare Rapid Transit Station 20

Oak Brook 262
Oakbrook Terrace Tower 8, 260
Oilily 110
Old Colony Building 172
Old Town 7
One Financial Place 166, 168
One Financial Place Partnership 168
One North Franklin 188
181 West Madison Street 184
190 South La Salle Street 176
Onterie Center 94
Oprah Winfrey Harpo Studios 214
Orix Real Estate Equities, Inc 204
Orland Park 268
Otis Building 178

Paine Webber Tower 184
Palmer Group Limited, The 202
Pappageorge Haymes
   Altgeld Court 50
   BMT Offices 36
   City Commons 50
   Clybourn Lofts 50
   Embassy Club 50
   Larrabee Commons 50
   Luminaire 48
Pelli, Cesar 184
Perkins & Will 104, 136, 198, 202
   Frederick T Owens Village

Chicago: a guide to recent architecture

Chicago: a guide to recent architecture

Center 268
Morton International Building 204
O'Hare International Terminal 22
Sears Merchandise Group Headquarters 274
Peter Elliott Productions 7, 214
Philip Johnson Architects 190 South La Salle Street 176
Phillips, Frederick 42
Planet Hollywood 74
Playboy Enterprises Corporate Headquarters 62
Power House, The 296
Presidential Towers 210
Private Family Residence, Glencoe 292
Private Residence, Highland Park 286
Prudential Plaza 136
PSM International Corporation 94
Pugh Warehouse 88
Pugh, James 88

R R Donnelley Building 140
Ralph H Metcalfe Federal Center 152
Ricardo Bofill Taller d'Arquitectura R R Donnelley Building 140

Rittweger & Tokay 226
River City 7, 220
River Cottages 82
Robert L Miller Associates 28
Rogers, James Gamble 92
Rookery building 176
Root, John W 176
Ross Barney & Jankowski, Inc.
Cesar Chavez Elementary School 232
Glendale Heights Post Office 256
Illinois Bell Telephone Company, Remote Switching Unit 300

Saarinenn, Eero and Eliel 28
Sabrina 46
Savings of America Tower 170
Schal Associates 14
Schiller Street Town Houses 70
Schlegman, Sheldon 128
Scoozi! 44, 46
Sears Merchandise Group Headquarters 274
Sears Roebuck & Company 274
Sears Tower 8, 94, 274
Self Park Garage 132
Seymour Lepp & Associates 84, 242
Shaw & Associates, Inc. 80, 176, 184

Shingu, Osamu 134
Siegal, Irene 32
Skidmore, Owings & Merrill, Inc.
  AT&T Corporate Center, USG
    Building 188
  Chicago Board Options
    Exchange 168
  500 West Monroe 188
  McCormick Place North 240
  NBC Tower 96
  One Financial Place 166
  One North Franklin 188
  Onterie Center 94
  Speigal Corporate Headquarters
    264
  303 Madison Street 186
  303 West Madison 188
  225 West Washington Street 188
  222 North La Salle Street
    Addition 182
Smith, Adrian 188
Solomon Cordwell Buenz &
  Associates
  Crate & Barrel 124
  Presidential Towers 210
Sony Corporation of America 118
Sony Gallery 118, 120
Source, The 276
Speigel Corporate Headquarters
  264

State of Illinois Capital
  Development Board 146
State of Illinois Center, The 144
Stearn-Joglekar, Limited 108, 214
Steel & Glass House 64
Stein & Co. 190
Stein & Company Federal Center,
  Inc. 154
Stella, Frank 154
Stern, Robert A M 114
  Banana Republic 114
Stone Container Building 128
Streets
  Adams 156
  Archer Avenue 242
  Authority Drive 266
  Bloomingdale Road 258
  Brandon Drive 258
  Busse Road 276
  Cermak Road 242
  East Adams 158
  East Chicago Avenue 92
  East Delaware 108
  East Delaware Place 104
  East Erie 94, 120, 122, 124
  East 57th 250
  East Huron 116
  East Illinois 90, 98
  East Lake 132, 136
  East Oak 112

Streets (continued)
East Onterie 94
East 23rd 240
East Walton 104
18th 242
Forest Avenue 284
Grand Avenue 80, 300
Greenview 50
Higgins Road 274
Hunt Club Road 300
Jorie Boulevard 262
Lacey Road 264
Lakewood Drive 292
Madison 186
Michigan Avenue 102, 156
North Canal 84, 206
North Clark 142, 146
North Cleveland Street 40
North Clinton 210
North Dearborn 60, 74, 76, 138, 208
North Desplaines 210
North Lake Shore Drive 62
North LaSalle 146, 170, 182
North Lincoln Avenue 32
North Michigan Avenue 102, 104, 110, 114, 116, 118, 120, 122, 124, 130
North Milwaukee Avenue 280
North Mohawk 42

Streets (continued)
North Orchard 68, 70
North Orleans 36, 54, 208
North Riverside Plaza 204
North Rush 112
North State 80
North Stetson Avenue 134, 136
North Wells 46, 58, 180, 208
Northwest Point Boulevard 278
Park West Avenue 286
Polk 218, 222
Schiller 70
Sheridan Road 290
Shermer Avenue 282
Shiloh Boulevard 296, 298
Solidarity Drive 226
South Canal 218
South Clark 150
South Dearborn 150
South Desplaines 216
South Ellis Avenue 250, 252
South Franklin 190
South La Salle 176
South Lake Shore Drive 226
South LaSalle 166, 178
South Marshfield Avenue 234
South Michigan Avenue 158
South Ravinia Avenue 268
South Shields Avenue 246
South State 162

Streets (continued)
South Wacker Drive 192, 194
South Wells 222
South Wood Street 236
Southport 50
Taylor 218
Tower Lane 260
Van Buren 162
Wells 184
Wentworth Avenue 242
West 35th 246
West Adams 174
West Ameritech Center Drive
272
West Congress 162
West Harrison 216
West Hawthorne Place 28
West Huron 44
West Jackson Boulevard 154
West Lake 146
West Madison 184, 206, 208,
210
West Monroe 150, 190, 210
West Ontario 74, 76
West Randolph 146
West Superior 48
West Van Buren 168
West Wacker Drive 138, 140,
196, 198, 200, 202
West Washington Boulevard 214

Wrightwood 50
Stubbins Associates, The
John Crerar Library 250

T W Best Newsstand 208
Tadao Ando Architect & Associates
Japanese Screen Gallery 158
Tange, Kenzo 78
Teng and Associates 300
Terra Museum of American Art
122
Terra, Daniel 122
Terzian, Rouben 36
Thomas Hickey & Associates 280
Thompson Center 6, 144
Thompson, Governor James R 144
Thompson, III, Gordon
Niketown 120
311 South Wacker Drive 192
333 West Wacker Drive 196
311 South Wacker Drive 200
333 West Wacker Drive 6
303 Madison Street 186
303 West Madison 188
Tigerman Fugman McCurry
Hard Rock Café 74
Self Park Garage 132
Tigerman McCurry
Commonwealth Edison
Substation 76

Power House, The 296
Private Residence (Highland Park) 286
Tigerman, Stanley 286
Tishman Speyer Properties 98, 182
Tribune Tower 96, 98
Two Prudential Plaza 136
225 West Wacker Drive 200
225 West Washington Street 188
222 North La Salle Street Addition 182

United Airlines Terminal One Complex 14
United States General Services Administration 154
University of Chicago 250
Urban Investment & Development Company 198
USG Building 188

Victorian Townhouse Extended 60
Vivere 46, 148
VMS Realty Partners 116

Warhol, Andy 106
Water Tower Place 102
Weese Hickey Weese Bradford Exchange 280
Weese Langley Weese Chicago City Day School Addition 28
Weese, Harry 82, 84
Weidlinger Associates, Inc. 118
Wells Engineering 24
Wesselman, Tom 62
Wilmette 284
Winfrey, Oprah 74
Wright, Frank Lloyd 116, 122, 262

Yamasaki, Minoru 288

Zion 298

Photographic
acknowledgements

FRONT COVER Steve Hall,
    Hedrich-Blessing
SPINE courtesy Bertrand Goldberg
    Associates, Inc
p 15 Timothy Hursley
p 17 James R. Steinkamp,
    © Steinkamp/Ballogg Chg.
p 19 Timothy Hursley
p 21 James R. Steinkamp,
    © Steinkamp/Ballogg Chg.
pp 23, 25 Nick Merrick,
    Hedrich-Blessing
p 29 Scott McDonald,
    Hedrich-Blessing
p 31 Hedrich-Blessing, courtesy
    Murphy/Jahn
p 33 Timothy Hursley
pp 39, 41 © Wayne Cable,
    Cable Studios
p 45 James R. Steinkamp,
    © Steinkamp/Ballogg Chg.
p 47 Dan Bakke, courtesy Jordan
    Mozer & Associates, Ltd
pp 49–51 George Pappageorge
p 55 Paul Warchol
p 57 © George Lambros
    Photography
p 59 James R. Steinkamp,
    © Steinkamp/Ballogg Chg.
p 63 Nick Merrick,

Hedrich-Blessing
pp 65–67 Bill Hedrich,
    Hedrich-Blessing
p 69 Mark L. Ballogg,
    © Steinkamp/Ballogg Chg.
p 75 Howard N. Kaplan, © HNK
    Architectural Photography, Inc.
p 77 Van Inwegan Photography,
    Chicago
pp 79, 81 Tillis & Tillis Inc.,
    courtesy Kenzo Tange Associates
p 85 Marco Lorenzetti, Hedrich-
    Blessing
pp 89, 91 © Wayne Cable, Cable
    Studios
p 93 Timothy Hursley
p 95 Gregory Murphey
pp 97, 99 © George Lambros
    Photography
pp 103, 105 Marco Lorenzetti,
    Hedrich-Blessing
pp 107, 109 Sean M. Kinzie,
    courtesy Hartshorne &
    Plunkard, Ltd
p 111 © Wayne Cable,
    Cable Studios
p 113 © Scott Frances/Esto
p 115 Timothy Hursley
p 117 © George Lambros
    Photography

p 119 Hedrich-Blessing, courtesy Elkus Manfredi Architects Ltd

p 121 courtesy Nike, Inc.

pp 129, 131 courtesy A. Epstein & Sons

p 133 Barbara Karant, Karant + Associates, Inc.

p 135 Gregory Murphey

p 137 Scott McDonald, Hedrich-Blessing

p 139 courtesy Kevin Roche John Dinkeloo & Associates

p 141 Mark L. Ballogg, © Steinkamp/Ballogg Chg.

p 143 Barbara Karant, Karant + Associates, Inc.

pp 145, 147 James R. Steinkamp, © Steinkamp/Ballogg Chg.

pp 149–151 David Clifton

pp 153, 155 courtesy Fujikawa Johnson & Associates, Inc.

p 157 Hedrich-Blessing, courtesy Hammond, Beeby & Babka

p 161 Timothy Hursley

p 163 Judith Bromley

pp 166, 167 Jon Miller, Hedrich–Blessing

p 169 Gregory Murphey

p 171 James R. Steinkamp, © Steinkamp/Ballogg Chg.

p 175 David Clifton

p 181 Nick Merrick, Hedrich-Blessing

p 183 Merrick & McDonald, Hedrich–Blessing

p 187 © Wayne Cable, Cable Studios

p 189 Nick Merrick, Hedrich-Blessing

p 191 Hedrich-Blessing, courtesy Skidmore, Owings & Merrill, Inc.

p 193 © George Lambros Photography

p 195 David Clifton

p 197 Barbara Karant, Karant + Associates, Inc

p 199 Gregory Murphey

pp 201, 203 ©Wayne Cable, Cable Studios

p 205 Nick Merrick, Hedrich-Blessing

p 207 Timothy Hursley

p 211 John Apolinski, courtesy Solomon Cordwell Buenz & Associates

pp 214, 215 Sean M. Kinzie

p 219 © George Lambros Photography

p 221 David Belle

Chicago: a guide to recent architecture

Susanna Sirefman

Chicago

Chicago has been at the forefront of architectural progress for more than a century. This book documents the city's recent architecture, starting with the new O'Hare Airport terminal, taking in Playboy Enterprise's headquarters in the Old Town, the giant office towers of the Loop, Helmut Jahn's enormous and controversial Thompson Center, and ending with the houses and municipal facilities of the suburbs.

Exactly 100 buildings, all completed within the last ten years and including the work of such well-known firms as Skidmore, Owings & Merrill, Holabird & Root and Tigerman McCurry, are described and illustrated, with full location and access details.

Susanna Sirefman trained at the Architectural Association in London. She has worked as an architect in London and taught at the University of North London. Now living in her native New York City, she has published numerous articles on contemporar~~~ ~~~~~~~~~ican architecture and has been a guest teacher at Parsons Scho~~~ ~~~~~~~~, Cooper Union, Columbia University and The School of ~~~ ~~~~~~~~~ute of Chicago.

ISBN 1-874056-81-1

9 781874 056812

ISBN 1 874056 81 1

COVER PHOT~
FRONT Ce~~~ ~~~ementary
School
BACK River v~~~

£8.00

● ● ● ellipsis KÖNE**M**ANN

PGF425468